HISTORICAL DICTIONARY

The historical dictionaries present essential information on a broad range of subjects, including American and world history, art, business, cities, countries, cultures, customs, film, global conflicts, international relations, literature, music, philosophy, religion, sports, and theater. Written by experts, all contain highly informative introductory essays of the topic and detailed chronologies that, in some cases, cover vast historical time periods but still manage to heavily feature more recent events.

Brief A–Z entries describe the main people, events, politics, social issues, institutions, and policies that make the topic unique, and entries are cross-referenced for ease of browsing. Extensive bibliographies are divided into several general subject areas, providing excellent access points for students, researchers, and anyone wanting to know more. Additionally, maps, photographs, and appendixes of supplemental information aid high school and college students doing term papers or introductory research projects. In short, the historical dictionaries are the perfect starting point for anyone looking to research in these fields.

HISTORICAL DICTIONARIES OF RELIGIONS, PHILOSOPHIES, AND MOVEMENTS

Jon Woronoff, Series Editor

Orthodox Church, by Michael Prokurat, Alexander Golitzin, and Michael D. Peterson, 1996
Civil Rights Movement, by Ralph E. Luker, 1997
Catholicism, by William J. Collinge, 1997
North American Environmentalism, by Edward R. Wells and Alan M. Schwartz, 1997
Taoism, by Julian F. Pas in cooperation with Man Kam Leung, 1998
Gay Liberation Movement, by Ronald J. Hunt, 1999
Islamic Fundamentalist Movements in the Arab World, Iran, and Turkey, by Ahmad S. Moussalli, 1999
Cooperative Movement, by Jack Shaffer, 1999
Kierkegaard's Philosophy, by Julia Watkin, 2001
Slavery and Abolition, by Martin A. Klein, 2002
Prophets in Islam and Judaism, by Scott B. Noegel and Brannon M. Wheeler, 2002
Lesbian Liberation Movement: Still the Rage, by JoAnne Myers, 2003
Descartes and Cartesian Philosophy, by Roger Ariew, Dennis Des Chene, Douglas M. Jesseph, Tad M. Schmaltz, and Theo Verbeek, 2003
Witchcraft, by Michael D. Bailey, 2003
Unitarian Universalism, by Mark W. Harris, 2004
New Age Movements, by Michael York, 2004
Organized Labor, Second Edition, by James C. Docherty, 2004
Utopianism, by James M. Morris and Andrea L. Kross, 2004
Feminism, Second Edition, by Janet K. Boles and Diane Long Hoeveler, 2004
Jainism, by Kristi L. Wiley, 2004
Wittgenstein's Philosophy, by Duncan Richter, 2004
Schopenhauer's Philosophy, by David E. Cartwright, 2005
Seventh-day Adventists, by Gary Land, 2005
Methodism, Second Edition, by Charles Yrigoyen Jr. and Susan E. Warrick, 2005
Sufism, by John Renard, 2005
Sikhism, Second Edition, by W. H. McLeod, 2005
Kant and Kantianism, by Helmut Holzhey and Vilem Mudroch, 2005
Olympic Movement, Third Edition, by Bill Mallon with Ian Buchanan, 2006
Anglicanism, by Colin Buchanan, 2006
Welfare State, Second Edition, by Bent Greve, 2006
Feminist Philosophy, by Catherine Villanueva Gardner, 2006
Logic, by Harry J. Gensler, 2006
Leibniz's Philosophy, by Stuart Brown and Nicholas J. Fox, 2006

Non-Aligned Movement and Third World, by Guy Arnold, 2006
Salvation Army, by Major John G. Merritt, 2006
Judaism, Second Edition, by Norman Solomon, 2006
Epistemology, by Ralph Baergen, 2006
Bahá'í Faith, Second Edition, by Hugh C. Adamson, 2006
Aesthetics, by Dabney Townsend, 2006
Socialism, Second Edition, by Peter Lamb and James C. Docherty, 2007
Marxism, by David M. Walker and Daniel Gray, 2007
Nietzscheanism, Second Edition, by Carol Diethe, 2007
Medieval Philosophy and Theology, by Stephen F. Brown and Juan Carlos Flores, 2007
Shamanism, by Graham Harvey and Robert Wallis, 2007
Ancient Greek Philosophy, by Anthony Preus, 2007
Puritans, by Charles Pastoor and Galen K. Johnson, 2007
Green Movement, Second Edition, by Miranda Schreurs and Elim Papadakis, 2007
Husserl's Philosophy, by John J. Drummond, 2008
Existentialism, by Stephen Michelman, 2008
Zionism, Second Edition, by Rafael Medoff and Chaim I. Waxman, 2008
Coptic Church, by Gawdat Gabra, 2008
Jehovah's Witnesses, by George D. Chryssides, 2008
Hume's Philosophy, by Kenneth R. Merrill, 2008
Shakers, by Stephen J. Paterwic, 2008
Native American Movements, by Todd Leahy and Raymond Wilson, 2008
Mormonism, Third Edition, by Davis Bitton and Thomas G. Alexander, 2008
Hegelian Philosophy, Second Edition, by John W. Burbidge, 2008
Ethics, by Harry J. Gensler and Earl W. Spurgin, 2008
Environmentalism, by Peter Dauvergne, 2009
Bertrand Russell's Philosophy, by Rosalind Carey and John Ongley, 2009
Baptists, Second Edition, by William H. Brackney, 2009
Islam, Second Edition, by Ludwig W. Adamec, 2009
Homosexuality, by Brent L. Pickett, 2009
Buddhism, by Carl Olson, 2009
Holiness Movement, Second Edition, edited by William Kostlevy, 2009
Reformed Churches, Second Edition, by Robert Benedetto and Donald K. McKim, 2010
The Reformation and Counter-Reformation, by Michael Mullett, 2010
Heidegger's Philosophy, Second Edition, by Frank Schalow and Alfred Denker, 2010
Jesus, by Daniel J. Harrington, S.J., 2010
Metaphysics, by Gary Rosenkrantz and Joshua Hoffman, 2011
Shinto, Second Edition, by Stuart D. B. Picken, 2011
The Friends (Quakers), Second Edition, by Margery Post Abbott, Mary Ellen Chijioke, Pink Dandelion, and John William Oliver Jr., 2011
Hinduism, New Edition, by Jeffery D. Long, 2011

Calvinism, by Stuart D. B. Picken, 2012
Hobbes's Philosophy, by Juhana Lemetti, 2012
Historical Dictionary of the Chinese Communist Party, by Lawrence R. Sullivan, 2012
New Religious Movements, Second Edition, by George D. Chryssides, 2012
Catholicism, Second Edition, by William J. Collinge, 2012
Radical Christianity, William H. Brackney, 2012
Organized Labor, Third Edition, by James C. Docherty and Sjaak van der Velden, 2012
Islamic Fundamentalism, by Mathieu Guidère, 2012
Witchcraft, Second Edition, by Jonathan Durrant and Michael D. Bailey, 2013
Lesbian and Gay Liberation Movements, by JoAnne Myers, 2013
Nietzscheanism, Third Edition, by Carol Diethe, 2014
Human Rights, by Jacques Fomerand, 2014
Welfare State, Third Edition, by Bent Greve, 2014
Wittgenstein's Philosophy, Second Edition, by Duncan Richter, 2014

Historical Dictionary of Wittgenstein's Philosophy

Second Edition

Duncan Richter

ROWMAN & LITTLEFIELD
Lanham • Boulder • New York • Toronto • Plymouth, UK

Published by Rowman & Littlefield
4501 Forbes Boulevard, Suite 200, Lanham, Maryland 20706
http://www.rowman.com

10 Thornbury Road, Plymouth PL6 7PP, United Kingdom

British Library Cataloguing in Publication Information Available

Library of Congress Cataloging-in-Publication Data

Richter, Duncan.
Historical dictionary of Wittgenstein's philosophy / Duncan Richter. — Second Edition.
pages cm. — (Historical dictionaries of religions, philosophies, and movements)
Includes bibliographical references.
ISBN 978-1-4422-3308-9 (cloth : alk. paper) — ISBN 978-1-4422-3309-6 (ebook)
1. Wittgenstein, Ludwig, 1889–1951—Dictionaries. I. Title.
B3376.W564R47 2014
192—dc23
2013045345

The paper used in this publication meets the minimum requirements of American National Standard for Information Sciences Permanence of Paper for Printed Library Materials, ANSI/NISO Z39.48-1992.

Printed in the United States of America

In memory of my mother

Contents

Editor's Foreword

Critics appear to agree about two things regarding Ludwig Wittgenstein: he was definitely one of if not the most significant philosophers of the 20th century, and he turned much of what preceded him upside down and strongly influenced much of what followed. Alas, he is also exceptionally difficult to understand, so much so that even Wittgenstein specialists have been arguing over his philosophy for decades. What better subject, then, for a historical dictionary. This book includes straightforward aspects of the man's life and career, people he knew and worked with, and places he visited. It also addresses his written works, especially the *Tractatus Logico-Philosophicus* and *Philosophical Investigations*. Finally, it tackles the many philosophical issues he investigated, both basic concepts and overriding ideas. This information makes up the dictionary section, a very useful support for those who want to know more about Ludwig Josef Johann Wittgenstein and his school of thought. But the *Historical Dictionary of Wittgenstein's Philosophy* contains more than that, and this second edition includes even more than the first. There is a useful chronology to trace the major events in Wittgenstein's life. An introduction provides an overview of his education, career, and thought. And the bibliography references his writing and that of others, including Wittgensteinians of all stripes, some of whom are included in the dictionary.

This second edition, like the first, was written by Duncan Richter. He was born in England and educated at the University of Oxford and University College of Swansea, in Wales, both of which are associated with Wittgenstein studies. He received his doctorate from the University of Virginia. Dr. Richter was taught by eminent Wittgensteinians, has mixed with many others in his career, and is now teaching at the Virginia Military Institute, where he is professor of philosophy. He has lectured on Wittgenstein, written numerous papers and reviews, attended a large number of conferences, and has published *Wittgenstein at His Word* (2004). Both Dr. Richter and this book, therefore, are good starting points for those who want to know more about the preeminent philosopher of the 20th century.

Jon Woronoff
Series Editor

Preface

This dictionary is intended to be of use to anyone interested in the life and work of Ludwig Wittgenstein. Anyone interested in his work will surely have to read the work itself at some point, but that work is rather notorious for being difficult to understand. It might not be wise to try to make sense of it without help. In the case of his early work, the *Tractatus Logico-Philosophicus*, the difficulty comes from three sources. The book is written very densely, with minimal explanation of what each claim means and how it connects with those around it. Secondly, the book is highly technical, including some symbols that are likely to baffle even seasoned philosophers. Thirdly, the book includes some puzzling claims, such as the famous idea that it is like a ladder that one throws away once one has climbed up it. Even someone who has been reading the book with apparent success might be confused at that point. Is the reader supposed to discard what sense she thought she had made of the text thus far? The experts are still debating this issue. Wittgenstein's later work, such as the *Philosophical Investigations*, is less obviously forbidding, lacking most of the technical terms and symbols. It is still often hard to tell what is going on in that work, however. Even if one understands what he is saying, understanding why he is saying it, what he is driving at, is another matter. (I say more about this below when I discuss the controversy surrounding matters of Wittgenstein interpretation.) Some guidebook to his work is potentially a very useful, even indispensable, tool for those coming to Wittgenstein for the first (or second, or third) time, therefore.

In this new edition of the dictionary I have made changes that I wanted to make ever since the first edition came out, updated information where relevant, and, above all, expanded the content of the book, primarily by adding new entries and improving old entries with additional information and clarification. Most of the entries in the dictionary relate to Wittgenstein's philosophy, but biographical information is included, as is information about people who have worked on Wittgenstein's ideas after his death, including some contemporary scholars. It was not my initial plan to include such people, but it came to seem almost unavoidable for reasons that I hope will be clear from what follows.

As far as possible I have tried not to be controversial in writing this dictionary. I quickly realized, however, that writing such a reference guide to Wittgenstein's philosophy is itself controversial. The sort of thing that one would expect to find in a book of this kind is handy summaries of Wittgenstein's main ideas. That implies that he had ideas that can be summarized, doctrines or theses that can be put just as well (or almost as well) in words other than those he chose to use. This idea, though, is a controversial one. Some people believe that Wittgenstein's work is like poetry in the sense that it cannot be paraphrased without great loss. This is not to say that it *is* poetry, although Wittgenstein was a great writer. But he was very concerned with the ways in which he did philosophy and *any* attempt to "say the same thing" as he did but in a different way is bound to strike some people as doomed. Such people might point, for instance, to proposition 6.54 of the *Tractatus Logico-Philosophicus*, in which Wittgenstein says that all his propositions are nonsense. What he means by this is hotly debated, and I address this controversy in the dictionary (under "NONSENSE"), but a noncontroversial dictionary entry on anything in the *Tractatus* cannot just assume that there *is* anything in the *Tractatus* other than sheer nonsense. Similarly, §133 of the *Philosophical Investigations* says that what Wittgenstein is doing in that book is demonstrating a method by examples. Any claim that he is doing more than this, advancing theories for instance, is therefore controversial. This is especially so since §109 explicitly says that "we may not advance any kind of theory." What can be said noncontroversially then about what are generally thought of as Wittgenstein's theories of truth, mind, and meaning?

Some readers might expect that there would be no controversy here since Wittgenstein is quite explicit: what he says in the *Tractatus* is nonsense and the *Investigations* contains no theories. Such a view though is not at all the mainstream one among Wittgenstein scholars. (It would also make writing a reference guide to Wittgenstein's philosophy rather difficult.) Whether it should be the mainstream view is itself of course controversial, but there is good reason why it is not. The *Tractatus* does not at all seem to be a torrent of nonsense, and the *Investigations* does seem to offer theories, and to support these with arguments that have seemed sound to some very competent philosophers. It is, I have heard it said, simply obvious that the *Investigations* contains arguments, and if it does then why not call their conclusions theories?

What I have done therefore is to try to paraphrase what Wittgenstein seems to be saying, but such paraphrases need a caveat. Not only would other people offer different paraphrases (of course, and I have indicated what some of these are) but some people would insist that what Wittgenstein *seems* to be saying is not (or is rarely) what he really means. It would be tedious at the end of every entry relating to the *Tractatus* to add that some people think the matter discussed in the entry is all nonsense, but sometimes this has seemed worth mentioning. It should be borne in mind for all such entries, however. Similarly, if I seem to claim that Wittgenstein offers any arguments or has any theories in his later work, it should be remembered both that some people have different readings of these arguments and that others will insist that the real work in Wittgenstein's later philosophy is done not by the force of argument but by the strength of appeal to the reader's own sense of grammar. How different these things are in the end I am not sure, but one seems more impersonal or objective while the other is interpersonal or intersubjective, the writer claiming no more authority than the reader and appealing to nothing beyond their mutual authority as competent users of the language. It is inevitable that summaries such as those found in this dictionary should tend to sound like accounts of theories and arguments. I have tried to minimize this appearance, while inviting the reader to consider a variety of interpretations and, of course, to consult other sources, especially Wittgenstein's own texts.

Another, related, controversy surrounds the question of how many Wittgensteins there are. Typically his work is divided into early and late periods (those of the *Tractatus* and the *Investigations*, respectively), but some insert a middle period (the time of such works as the *Blue Book*) and others want to add a last period after the others (consisting perhaps exclusively of *On Certainty*). I have not, though, provided two, three, or four entries on each subject. Where appropriate I have pointed out differences and similarities between the different periods of Wittgenstein's career. The major ones all seem to me to be between the early and the late.

Of course I cannot expect to avoid controversy by any of these means, especially since my personal sympathies lie with some minority views. We all have our biases. This is another reason to read Wittgenstein's work itself, however forbidding it may appear. This book can only be an introductory guide. I have attempted to make it as clear a guide as possible both to Wittgenstein's life and work, and to the scholarly reception of that work. I let the reader judge how useful it is.

Acknowledgments

I have many people to thank for what is good and none to blame (except myself) for what is bad in this book. I should first thank Jon Woronoff for inviting me to engage in what has been a great exercise in re-reading and trying to articulate clearly thoughts that I have, in some cases, never had to write out before now. These thoughts have been shaped mostly by Wittgenstein himself of course, but my reading of Wittgenstein has been inspired and influenced by a series of teachers. My first philosophy teachers, Edmund Prestwich and Geoff Willis, were not Wittgensteinians but did inspire in me a love of the subject. I was really introduced to Wittgenstein's work by my friend Jane Davies, who studied his work formally with Stephen Mulhall. As a graduate student at Swansea I learned from Rush Rhees, my supervisor D. Z. Phillips, and my friend Catherine Gardner. I was also introduced there to the work of Cora Diamond, who was later my dissertation adviser at the University of Virginia. Since then, in developing the understanding that was reflected in the first edition of this book, I benefited from discussions with Bill Brenner, Lars Hertzberg, Tim Kjeldsen, Stuart Mirsky, Guenter Trendler, Kirby Urner, and T. P. Uschanov. That was almost a decade ago. In the intervening time I have continued to learn from some of the people I named above and from some new people, notably the members of the Virginia Wittgenstein Workshop started by James C. Klagge; from commenters on my blog (http://languagegoesonholiday.blogspot.com/), especially Reshef Agam-Segal, Philip Cartwright, Joshua Kortbein, and Matthew Pianalto; and from my students at the Virginia Military Institute. I am grateful to them all.

Some of these names are well known to Wittgenstein scholars and indicate where my sympathies lie in the scholarly debates described in the rest of this book. So these acknowledgments are also a kind of confession.

Reader's Note

Some of the entries in the dictionary are significantly longer than others. Usually these will also be the easiest for the beginner to understand, because they generally explain the issues in question (as they relate to Wittgenstein) from the ground up, as it were. To avoid repetition, other entries assume more knowledge or understanding of the area in question. It will be useful therefore for the reader to follow cross-references, which are indicated by **bold type** or given in the *See* or *See also*.

Acronyms and Abbreviations

Anscombe	G. E. M. Anscombe. An Introduction to Wittgenstein's Tractatus. Philadelphia: University of Pennsylvania Press, 1971.
Bartley	William Warren Bartley. *Wittgenstein*. London: Cresset, 1986.
Beaney	Michael Beaney, ed. *The Frege Reader*. Oxford: Blackwell Publishers, 1997.
Bearn	Gordon C. F. Bearn. Waking to Wonder: Wittgenstein's Existential Investigations. Albany: State University of New York Press, 1997.
Black	Max Black. Companion to Wittgenstein's Tractatus. Ithaca, NY: Cornell University Press, 1964.
Bouwsma	O. K. Bouwsma. *Wittgenstein: Conversations 1949–1951*. IN: Hackett, 1986.
CV	Ludwig Wittgenstein. *Culture and Value.* Trans. Peter Winch. Ed. G. H. von Wright in collaboration with Heikki Nyman. Oxford: Blackwell, 1980.
Frascolla	Pasquale Frascolla. Understanding Wittgenstein's Tractatus. New York: Routledge, 2007.
Friedlander	Eli Friedlander. Signs of Sense: Reading Wittgenstein's Tractatus. Cambridge, MA: Harvard University Press, 2001.
Hacker	P. M. S. Hacker. Insight and Illusion: Themes in the Philosophy of Wittgenstein. Bristol, UK: Thoemmes Press, 1997.
Hintikka	Jaakko Hintikka. On Wittgenstein. Belmont, CA: Wadsworth, 2000.
Janik	Allan Janik. Assembling Reminders: Studies in the Genesis of Wittgenstein's Concept of Philosophy. Stockholm: Santérus Academic Press Sweden, 2006.
Kripke	Saul A. Kripke. *Wittgenstein on Rules and Private Language: An Elementary Exposition*. Cambridge, MA: Harvard University Press, 1982.

LC	Ludwig Wittgenstein. *Lectures and Conversations on Aesthetics, Psychology and Religious Belief.* Compiled from notes taken by Yorick Smythies, Rush Rhees and James Taylor. Ed. Cyril Barrett. Oxford: Basil Blackwell, 1966.
Letters to Ogden	Ludwig Wittgenstein. Letters to C. K. Ogden. Ed. G. H. von Wright. Oxford: Blackwell, 1973.
McGuinness	B. F. McGuinness. "The So-Called Realism of the Tractatus," in Perspectives on the Philosophy of Wittgenstein. Ed. I. Block, pp. 60–73. Cambridge: MIT Press, 1981.
McManus	Denis McManus. *The Enchantment of Words: Wittgenstein's* Tractatus Logico-Philosophicus. Oxford: Oxford University Press, 2006.
Monk	Ray Monk. *Ludwig Wittgenstein: The Duty of Genius*. New York: Free Press Maxwell Macmillan International, 1990.
Nordmann	Alfred Nordmann. Wittgenstein's Tractatus: An Introduction. Cambridge: Cambridge University Press, 2005.
Ostrow	Matthew B. Ostrow. *Wittgenstein's Tractatus: A Dialectical Interpretation*. Cambridge: Cambridge University Press, 2002.
PG	Ludwig Wittgenstein. *Philosophical Grammar*. Trans. Anthony Kenny. Ed. Rush Rhees. Oxford: Blackwell, 1974.
PI	Ludwig Wittgenstein. *Philosophical Investigations*. The German text, with an English translation by G. E. M. Anscombe, P. M. S. Hacker, and Joachim Schulte. Revised 4th edition by P. M. S. Hacker and Joachim Schulte. Oxford: Wiley-Blackwell, 2009.
PO	Ludwig Wittgenstein. *Philosophical Occasions 1912–1951*. Eds. James Klagge and Alfred Nordmann. IN: Hackett, 1993.
PPO	Ludwig Wittgenstein. *Ludwig Wittgenstein: Public and Private Occasions*. Eds. James C. Klagge and Alfred Nordmann. Lanham, MD: Rowman & Littlefield, 2003.
Rhees	Rush Rhees. *Without Answers.* New York: Schocken Books, 1969.

RPP	Ludwig Wittgenstein. *Remarks on the Philosophy of Psychology*. Volumes I and II. Trans. G. E. M. Anscombe. Ed. Anscombe and G. H. von Wright. Oxford: Blackwell, 1980.
Schulte	Joachim Schulte. *Wittgenstein: An Introduction.* Trans. William H. Brenner and John F. Holley. Albany: State University of New York Press, 1992.
Stenius	Erik Stenius. *Wittgenstein's Tractatus: A Critical Exposition of Its Main Lines of Thought*. Ithaca, NY: Cornell University Press, 1964.
Tractatus	Ludwig Wittgenstein. *Tractatus Logico-Philosophicus*. Trans. D. F. Pears and B. F. McGuinness. London: Routledge & Kegan Paul, 1961. (I have amended the translation in some quotations.)
White	Roger M. White. *Wittgenstein's Tractatus Logico-Philosophicus*. London: Continuum, 2006.
WLC	Ludwig Wittgenstein. *Wittgenstein's Lectures, Cambridge 1930–1932*. From the notes of J. King and D. Lee. Ed. Desmond Lee. Oxford: Blackwell, 1980.

Chronology

1808 The King of Westphalia, Jérôme-Napoléon Bonaparte, decrees that Jewish people must take a family name. Ludwig Wittgenstein's great-grandfather, Moses Meier, thus becomes Moses Meier-Wittgenstein, Wittgenstein being the name of the county in which he works as a steward for the Prince of Seyn-Wittgenstein.

1838–39 Moses Meier-Wittgenstein changes his name to Hermann Christian Wittgenstein. He also marries Franziska ("Fanny") Figdor in a Lutheran church, the two of them having converted to Christianity.

1847 8 April: Karl Ludwig Wittgenstein (Ludwig Wittgenstein's father) is born to Hermann and Fanny in Gohlis, near Leipzig.

1850 14 March: Leopoldine ("Poldi") Kalmus (Ludwig Wittgenstein's mother) is born into a Jewish family in Vienna. Her father is a successful businessman.

1872 Through family connections and a shared interest in music, Karl Ludwig Wittgenstein and Leopoldine Kalmus come to know one another.

1874 14 February: Karl and Leopoldine marry in Vienna.

1876 Karl Wittgenstein becomes managing director of a steel-rolling mill in Teplitz, in the Sudetenland.

1878 Karl is elected to the mill's managing board and becomes its main shareholder. His business interests continue to grow after this.

1889 26 April: Ludwig Josef Johann Wittgenstein is born in Vienna, the youngest child of one of the wealthiest families in Europe. He is baptized as a Catholic and educated at home until he is 14 years old.

1898 Karl Wittgenstein resigns from all the various offices he holds and uses his fortune to buy real estate and stocks and shares in Switzerland, the Netherlands, and the United States.

1903 Ludwig goes to school in Linz in Upper Austria (Hitler attended the same school 1904–1905). While there he loses religious faith and reads works by Arthur Schopenhauer, Otto Weininger, and Ludwig Boltzmann.

1906 23 October: Begins studies in mechanical engineering at the Technische Hochschule in Berlin. While there, inspired by the diaries of Gottfried Keller, he starts to write down his philosophical reflections in dated notebook entries.

1908 Spring: Goes to Manchester, England, to conduct research in aeronautics. Experiments with kites at the Kite Flying Upper Atmosphere Station, near Glossop in Derbyshire. **Fall:** Becomes a research student at the University of Manchester, studying aeronautics. Develops an interest first in the mathematical part of engineering, then pure mathematics, and then the philosophy of mathematics. Reads Bertrand Russell's The Principles of Mathematics and Gottlob Frege's *Grundgesetze der Arithmetik.*

1911 Summer: Draws up plans for a book on philosophy. **Fall:** Visits Gottlob Frege in Jena, Germany, who advises him to study with Russell at Cambridge. **18 October:** Introduces himself to Russell at Trinity College, Cambridge.

1912 January: Impresses Russell with a manuscript he has written over the vacation. **1 February:** Admitted as a member of Trinity College. Attends G. E. Moore's lectures. Meets and befriends David Pinsent. **November:** Admitted to the Apostles but soon resigns.

1913 20 January: Father dies. Receives a very large inheritance. **6 March:** Reviews The Science of Logic by P. Coffey for the *Cambridge Review.* **September:** Goes to Norway with Pinsent and works on logic, especially Russell's theory of types. Gives "Notes on Logic," his first philosophical writing, to Russell. **8 October:** Moves to Norway.

1914 1 April: Begins to dictate notes on logic to Moore, who is visiting him in Norway. Moore's failure to persuade Cambridge University to accept this work, entitled *Logik*, as a BA thesis enrages Wittgenstein. **June:** Returns to Austria for the first part of the summer. Gives 100,000 crowns to artists in need. **28 July:** Austria declares war on Serbia. **7 August:** Joins army, despite being exempt from service because of a double hernia. Serves on a ship on the Vistula River and in a repair depot in Krakow. Reads Leo Tolstoy's *Gospel in Brief*, Ralph Waldo Emerson's *Essays*, and the collected works of Friedrich Nietzsche. Continues to write philosophical notes, later published as *Notebooks, 1914–1916*. By the end of the year brother Paul, a pianist, has lost his right arm and been taken prisoner by the Russians.

1916 March: Posted to the Russian Front (after many requests for a transfer). Reads Fyodor Dostoevsky's *The Brothers Karamazov*. Continues philosophical work, which results in the *Tractatus Logico-Philosophicus*. **1 September:** Promoted to rank of corporal.

1918 1 February: Promoted to rank of lieutenant. **3 March:** Transferred to the Italian Front. **8 May:** Pinsent dies in an accident. **June:** Cited for bravery and recommended for the Gold Medal for Valor (instead was awarded the Band of the Military Service Medal with Swords). **Summer:** Finishes *Tractatus* while on leave at his uncle Paul's house in Hallein, near Salzburg. **October or November:** Kurt Wittgenstein commits suicide. **3 November:** Taken prisoner in Italy. Reads Immanuel Kant's *Critique of Pure Reason.*

1919 January: Transferred to Cassino. Decides to become an elementary school teacher after the war. **21 August:** Released from prisoner-of-war camp. **September:** Gives what is left of his inheritance to his sisters Helene and Hermine, and his brother Paul. Enrolls in college for elementary school teachers in Vienna. Moves out of the family home. Contemplates suicide. Struggles to find a publisher for the *Tractatus.*

1920 August: Works as a gardener at the Klosterneuburg monastery outside Vienna. **September:** Starts first elementary school teaching job in Trattenbach, a village in Lower Austria. His high expectations, ear-boxing, and hair-pulling do not go down well with students or parents.

1921 *Logisch-philosophische Abhandlung* published in German only, including many errors, by Wilhelm Ostwald in the series *Annalen der Naturphilosophie* (Annals of Natural Philosophy).

1922 A parallel German-English text of his book, now called *Tractatus Logico-Philosophicus*, is published. **September:** Starts teaching at a secondary school in the village of Hassbach. **November:** Moves to Puchberg to teach at an elementary school.

1923 Frank Ramsey reviews Tractatus. **September:** Ramsey visits him in Puchberg. Makes some changes to *Tractatus* that are included in later editions.

1924 September: Leaves Puchberg to teach in another village, Otterthal. Produces *Wörterbuch für Volksschulen* (a spelling dictionary for elementary school children).

1925 August: Visits England, seeing John Maynard Keynes in Lewes, William Eccles in Manchester, and W. E. Johnson and Ramsey in Cambridge.

1926 The *Wörterbuch* published. **April:** Strikes sickly 11-year-old Josef Haidbauer two or three times, causing the boy to collapse; is subsequently accused of using undue force but acquitted of misconduct. Quits teaching. Starts work as a gardener with monks in Hütteldorf, outside Vienna. **Sum-**

mer: Helps Paul Engelmann build a house for Gretl on Kundmanngasse in Vienna. Falls in love with Marguerite Respinger. Their relationship lasts until 1931.

1927 February: Meets Moritz Schlick. **Summer:** Meets with some of the Vienna Circle, including Rudolf Carnap, Herbert Feigl, and Friedrich Waismann, on Monday evenings. Reads Keynes's *A Short View of Russia*, which presents Soviet Marxism not as an economic theory (in which terms Keynes rejected it as erroneous and unworkable) but as an exciting new religion.

1928 March: Attends a lecture by L. E. J. Brouwer in Vienna on "Mathematics, Science, and Language." Seems to be stimulated to return to philosophical work.

1929 January: Returns to England to work with Ramsey in Cambridge. Meets Piero Sraffa and Maurice Drury. Renews friendship with G. E. Moore. **18 June:** Awarded Ph.D. with the *Tractatus* counting as his thesis. **July:** "Some Remarks on Logical Form" published. Meets Gilbert Ryle. **17 November:** Gives a lecture on ethics to a Cambridge society called "The Heretics."

1930 Starts work on a collaboration with Waismann. Ramsey dies. Gives some lectures in which he talks of philosophy as an attempt at getting rid of "puzzles of language." Writes what has since been published as *Philosophical Remarks*. **Summer:** Dictates list of "Theses" to Waismann in Vienna. **December:** Given five-year fellowship at Trinity College, Cambridge.

1931 Writes the first of the remarks later included in *Philosophical Investigations.* Starts to work on Sir James Frazer's *The Golden Bough.* Writes seemingly anti-Semitic remarks in his notebooks. **Summer:** Goes to Norway, relationship with Respinger cools.

1932 August: Attacks Carnap for stealing his ideas. Dictates "the Big Typescript." Meets Francis Skinner.

1933–34 Dictates the *Blue Book*, in which he introduces the notions of language-games and family resemblances.

1934 Considers moving to Russia with Skinner.

1934–35 Dictates the *Brown Book.*

1935 September: Goes to Russia (without Skinner, who is ill). Is offered work teaching philosophy, but not the kind of manual labor he and Skinner want. Returns to England. Begins lectures on "Sense Data and Private Experience." Meets Rush Rhees. Begins final year of fellowship at Trinity.

1936 June: Moritz Schlick is murdered. Abandons collaboration on a book with Waismann. **August:** Returns to Norway (without Skinner). Starts Philosophical Investigations, completing, roughly, §§1–188. Writes a confession. **November:** Writes to friends to whom he intended to confess his sins insisting that he see them over Christmas. **December:** Goes to Vienna and confesses to several friends and family members.

1937 January: Visits Cambridge and confesses to several more friends. Returns to Norway. Work begins to go badly. Leaves Norway to spend the summer with his family, and then with Skinner. **10 August:** Back to Norway. **September:** Skinner visits him for two weeks. Writes Part I of the *Remarks on the Foundations of Mathematics*. **December:** Returns to Austria.

1938 8 February: Moves into Drury's old apartment in Dublin. **12 March:** Austria becomes part of Nazi Germany. **April:** Teaches again at Cambridge, where he lives with Skinner. Meets Norman Malcolm. Lectures on aesthetics and religious belief.

1939 11 February: Becomes professor of philosophy at Cambridge, succeeding G. E. Moore. At lectures he argues with Alan Turing. **14 April:** Becomes a British citizen.

1940 February: Malcolm returns to the United States.

1941 September: Starts work as a dispensary porter at Guy's Hospital in London. Works on *Remarks on the Foundations of Mathematics*, parts 4–7. **11 October:** Skinner dies.

1942 Summer: Visits Rhees in Swansea, partly to recover from an operation to remove a gallstone. Discusses Sigmund Freud.

1943 Spends some more time in Swansea with Rhees, again talks about Freud. **29 April:** Moves to Newcastle-upon-Tyne to work with Reeve and Grant on wound shock.

1944 16 February: Returns to Cambridge to lecture and write. **March:** Goes to Swansea to work on *Philosophical Investigations*. Becomes more interested in the philosophy of psychology than in the philosophy of mathematics. **October:** Returns to Cambridge.

1945 Begins final version of Part I of *Philosophical Investigations*. **7 May:** Germany surrenders.

1946 Finishes Part I of *Philosophical Investigations*. Falls in love with Ben Richards. **May:** Sraffa decides to stop having conversations with Wittgenstein. **26 October:** Argues with Karl Popper at the Moral Science Club.

1947 Writes Volume I of *Remarks on the Philosophy of Psychology*. Decides to give up lecturing. **August:** Moves to Ireland.

1948 Writes Volume II of *Remarks on the Philosophy of Psychology* and *Last Writings on the Philosophy of Psychology*. Georg von Wright becomes professor of philosophy at Cambridge.

1949 Reads various history books. Talks with Drury about religion. Dictates "Philosophy of Psychology—A Fragment" (formerly known as Part II of *Philosophical Investigations*). **July:** Goes to United States to visit Norman Malcolm at Cornell University. **October:** Returns to England and works on *On Certainty*. **25 November:** Diagnosed with cancer of the prostate. **24 December:** Goes to Vienna.

1950 January: Reads Goethe's *Farbenlehre* and writes Part II of *Remarks on Colour*. Continues work on *On Certainty*. **23 March:** Returns to England. Writes Part III of *Remarks on Colour*. **25 April:** Moves into G. E. M. Anscombe's house in Oxford. **Summer:** Writes §§65–299 of *On Certainty*. **October:** Visits Norway with Richards.

1951 Goes to die in Dr. Bevan's home in Cambridge. Writes §§300–676 of *On Certainty* and Part I of *Remarks on Colour*. **29 April:** Dies. His last words, to Mrs. Bevan, are: "Tell them I've had a wonderful life." He is buried in St. Giles's Church, Cambridge.

1953 *Philosophical Investigations* is published.

1956 *Remarks on the Foundations of Mathematics* is published.

1958 *The Blue and Brown Books* is published.

1964 *Philosophical Remarks* is published.

1967 *Zettel* is published.

1969 *Philosophical Grammar* and *On Certainty* is published.

1970 Anscombe becomes professor of philosophy at Cambridge.

1977 *Culture and Value* is published.

2000 Publication of *Wittgenstein's Nachlass: The Bergen Electronic Edition*. This includes all Wittgenstein's writings on CD-ROM.

2009 Publication of fourth edition of *Philosophical Investigations*, with Anscombe's translation improved by P. M. S. Hacker and Joachim Schulte.

Introduction

Ludwig Wittgenstein was the most influential, and arguably the greatest, philosopher of the 20th century. This fact about his influence is not only a matter of how much he influenced people but also of how many people he influenced. His early work was taken up by some of the pioneers of analytical philosophy. His later work helped spawn another movement within analytic philosophy, that of ordinary language philosophy (sometimes called Oxford philosophy). He is also considered by some to be a key postmodern thinker, and an interest in his work is a distinguishing feature of many post-analytical philosophers who seek to bridge the gap between analytical and so-called continental philosophy. All this means that Wittgenstein is an important philosopher to understand, but it also means that we need to pay careful attention to which Wittgenstein we are talking about (early or late, for instance) and whose interpretation (positivist or postmodern, say) we have in mind. The dictionary that follows contains entries on Wittgenstein's major works and on some of his most important interpreters. The purpose of this introduction is to provide an overview of this complex terrain.

WITTGENSTEIN'S LIFE

Ludwig Josef Johann Wittgenstein was born on 26 April 1889 in Vienna, Austria. His father was an immensely wealthy industrialist who tried to push all his sons into industry despite their strong artistic leanings (which made them more like their very musical mother than their businessman father). Wittgenstein was the youngest of eight children, five boys and three girls. The Wittgenstein brothers tended toward the arts, homosexuality, and suicide. Three of them are believed to have killed themselves. Whether this was because of clinical depression, career plans thwarted by an overbearing father (or lack of talent), the pressure of being gay in an unsympathetic society, or something else, we do not know. But Wittgenstein himself had a deep love of literature and music, seems to have been either bisexual or gay (despite his relationship with Marguerite Respinger), and was tempted to kill himself. He was a deep and intense man with a taste for extremes of either seriousness or childish silliness. The half-baked, half-thought-out, half-serious was not for him.

He was not easy to be friends with and seems to have doubted, at least at times, whether sexuality was compatible with morality, and whether love was compatible with his work as a philosopher. Nevertheless, he attracted deep devotion in some people and has had an appeal to philosophers even after his death that is sometimes considered to owe more to personal charisma and literary style than philosophical worth. Whether there is any merit in this idea must be judged by looking at his work in philosophy. Before turning to this work, though, it is worth considering the life and times of Wittgenstein the man.

His career was varied. Having studied engineering in Berlin, Germany, and Manchester, England, he became increasingly attracted to philosophy and moved to Cambridge in order to study there with Bertrand Russell. This interest in philosophy had begun when he was a schoolboy in Austria (he seems always to have read widely) but appears to have become more serious when his work in engineering led him to study first mathematics and then the foundations of mathematics, on which Gottlob Frege and Bertrand Russell were doing important work at the time. It was Frege who, in 1911, suggested that Wittgenstein try to work with Russell. He was admitted to Trinity College, Cambridge, the following year.

World War I then interrupted his studies. While Russell went to prison rather than violate his pacifist principles, Wittgenstein ignored his medical exemption from military service and actively sought a frontline position in the Austrian army. During the war he was promoted to the rank of lieutenant, decorated for bravery, and finally taken prisoner in Italy in October 1918. In World War II, in contrast, he did medical work in England (as a hospital porter and helping with medical research) and worked on the *Philosophical Investigations*. He also did important work during the first war, writing the *Tractatus Logico-Philosophicus*, the only philosophical book he would publish during his lifetime. After his release from the Italian prisoner-of-war camp, he gave all his inheritance away, mostly to members of his family, and became first a schoolteacher, then a gardener, and then an architect, designing a house for his sister Gretl with Paul Engelmann. His interest in philosophy seems to have been revived by meetings with the Vienna Circle (a group of philosophers who highly admired the *Tractatus*) and by a lecture given by the mathematician L. E. J. Brouwer. In 1929 Wittgenstein returned to Cambridge, where he became a Fellow of Trinity College and taught philosophy on and off for most of the rest of his life.

He was always somewhat ambivalent about the academic life, however. Often he would get away from Cambridge to work in more isolated, rural places, from the populous but less cosmopolitan Swansea in Wales to his lonely Norwegian cottage, accessible only by boat. He even planned for a while in the 1930s to move to the Soviet Union with his friend Francis Skinner. These plans came to nothing, though, when Wittgenstein saw first-hand what life under the corrupt and bureaucratic regime was like and was offered only academic positions there, not the manual work that he wanted. His friends and the intellectual stimulation they offered kept bringing him back to Cambridge, but eventually he quit his post as professor of philosophy there in 1947, being replaced by his student Georg von Wright. Only a few years after this, in 1951, he died of cancer, leaving his *Philosophical Investigations* unfinished.

WITTGENSTEIN'S EARLY WORK

Wittgenstein's interest in philosophy seems to have begun when he read the work of Arthur Schopenhauer as a teenager. He did not study the subject formally though until led to it by his interest in mathematics. This route brought him not to the dramatic fusion of post-Kantian idealism and Asian religion offered by Schopenhauer but to the drier study of logic and the foundations of mathematics studied by Gottlob Frege and Bertrand Russell. Both Frege and Russell had an enormous influence on Wittgenstein, and the ideas he got from them about sense and meaning enabled him to return critically to Schopenhauer's idealism and, indeed, to all the major problems of philosophy.

Wittgenstein's first book was the *Tractatus Logico-Philosophicus*. In it he claimed to have found the solution to all philosophical problems on all essential points. He also said that he had shown how little was achieved when this is done. So the book simultaneously makes claims very grand and very modest. It has been regarded as the greatest ever work in philosophy and as complete nonsense (even by some of its biggest admirers!). It is, in short, a hard book to read or to make sense of. The preface of the book says that the problems of philosophy are posed as a result of misunderstanding the logic of our language. The apparent implication is that these problems ought not to be posed. Yet the same preface says that its author has found the solution to those problems, implying that he has found them worth posing and even answering. We might think that the solution referred to is not in fact an answer as such but instead simply the 'solution' of not posing the problems in the first place, perhaps as a result of coming to see why it is a mistake to pose them. Then we are likely to wonder why that would be a mistake. Are the problems in question unreal or simply ineffable, impossible to express in words? Either way, we are likely to be disconcerted by Wittgenstein's claim to have solved the problems of philosophy by expressing thoughts whose truth is unassailable and definitive. How could unreal problems be solved at all? How could the expression of unassailable truths touch on the ineffable? These questions remain unanswered (at least to the satisfaction of all) to this day. Standard readings of the *Tractatus* focus on the truths that are taken to be expressed in the book rather than on any wilier rhetorical strategy that Wittgenstein might have been employing in order to hint at the ineffable or to undermine the whole project of philosophy.

The most important of these truths are the picture theory of meaning and the doctrine of logical atomism. These theories are intimately connected. The picture theory tells us that language pictures reality. It might not do so in an obvious way, but when properly analyzed it will be revealed to do so quite clearly. Thus for instance the sentence "Passengers are requested not to board the train while it is in motion" (when announced at a railway station) is not a simple statement of fact but is in fact a polite form of command not to board the train when it is moving. And a command, according to some analyses, is itself a statement of the speaker's desires, or an implicit kind of threat. Ultimately, Wittgenstein suggests, all sentences must turn out to be statements about the world. The sample sentence just discussed might not be a description of a request that someone or other is said to have made, but it will be a description of something (the fact that those who board moving trains are subject to punishment, say). Or else it will be meaningless.

What then if a sentence describes a situation that does not exist? Will its meaning be nonexistent too? The picture theory says no. The meaning of a sentence is the state of affairs that obtains if the sentence is true. For a sentence to be meaningful all that is required is that this state of affairs be possible. (For a sentence to be true, the state of affairs must be actual. It must in fact be the case.) That means that the objects to which the elements of the sentence refer (whatever these turn out to be after a full analysis has been made) must be capable of combining in just the way indicated by the sentence. And this is a matter of the combinatorial possibilities of these objects.

Logical atomism is the theory that the ultimate constituents of the world are such objects, whatever it might be to which the ultimate constituents of fully logically analyzed sentences correspond. Notoriously, Wittgenstein never offered such an analysis nor said what these objects might be. Likely candidates seem to be sense data, such as points of color in one's visual field or notes heard in a tune. Since a sound cannot be red, for instance, sentences seeming to refer to "red noises" must be meaningless (or else in need of further analysis). Hence metaphysical possibility corresponds with linguistic possibility, the possibility of meaning or sense. What can be, what can exist, can be described in language, and what cannot be described cannot be. Logic is the mirror or map that shows this correspondence.

So language pictures possible states of affairs. Anything that looks like language but that does not picture a possible state of affairs is in fact nonsense. The category of nonsense thus defined turns out to be rather large and interesting. Imperatives that are not threats or statements of desire (or other psychological states) seem to belong to it. So do judgments of aesthetic quality and claims about the transcendent. Indeed, strictly speaking, so do statements about logic and the metaphysical conditions for the possibility of meaning. How strictly Wittgenstein thought we ought to speak is a matter of considerable debate. He does offer a possible solution to this dilemma, though, distinguishing between sentences that lack sense (i.e., that do not represent a possible state of affairs) and those that are mere nonsense. Typically, the *Tractatus* is thought to condemn the ethical, the aesthetic, the religious, and (in that kind of sense) the metaphysical to the category of nonsense, while the more respectable metaphysics and philosophical logic that largely constitute the *Tractatus* are taken to be merely senseless in a fairly harmless, technical way. They may indeed say nothing, strictly speaking, but they show important truths about reality, or important features of reality. This distinction between saying and showing is another important idea found in the *Tractatus*.

The picture theory and Wittgenstein's logical atomism then can be seen as two sides of the same coin. It is a coin that has attracted many people, but to sacrifice ethics, aesthetics, and religion for it might seem too much to ask. This is especially so when we consider Wittgenstein's almost all-consuming concern with these aspects of life. Is he guilty of raw, scientistic positivism, rejecting all that smacks of the humanities (or even of humanity)? Or is this the ultimate asceticism, denying himself and others the high cultural values that he loves so much? Or is Wittgenstein in fact a mystic, pointing the way to an ineffable spirituality? The dust has not yet settled on these debates.

Perhaps the one generating the most heat today concerns the idea, first put forward by Cora Diamond, that the point of the *Tractatus* is not any of these things. Diamond argues for a resolutely or austerely strict speaking about sense and nonsense in the *Tractatus*. If she is right, then most of the *Tractatus* itself is sheer nonsense, including the parts that put forward the picture theory and logical atomism. This might be hard to believe, and it is widely disputed, but if it is right then Wittgenstein's first book would turn out to be a kind of joke (albeit one with a serious purpose) at the expense of both positivists and mystics. If it is such a joke, then we can finally understand Wittgenstein's claim in the preface that the book would achieve its purpose if it gave pleasure (not insight or enlightenment) to one person who read it and understood it.

THE LATER WITTGENSTEIN

Although the *Tractatus* is still highly regarded as a classic of early analytic philosophy, Wittgenstein himself became dissatisfied with it and most philosophers today consider it to be at least flawed. (In some ways, oddly, it is those who read it as utter nonsense who have the most respect for the book's integrity and value: for showing the complete worthlessness of what it purports to endorse.) Taking himself to have solved all the main problems of philosophy, Wittgenstein gave up philosophy after the First World War. Instead he became a schoolteacher, an architect, and a gardener. When he eventually returned to philosophy he wrote, rewrote, and re-edited notes that never seemed to satisfy him fully. The most important of these, in an almost finished form, were published in 1953, two years after his death, as *Philosophical Investigations*.

The *Investigations* starts with a consideration of something very reminiscent of the picture theory of language. As early as §23 there is an explicit reference to "the author of the *Tractatus Logico-Philosophicus*." (This, I suppose, may or may not be Wittgenstein himself, if that book can be read as being like one of Søren Kierkegaard's pseudonymous works, intended to expose its own views as erroneous.) The main ideas that the *Investigations* (whose preface says that its goal is to bring light, not pleasure) sets out to combat are these: that words all or essentially stand for objects; that these objects are the meanings of the words; and that this naming of objects is the essence of all language.

These ideas can all be found in a passage from the *Confessions* of St. Augustine with which Wittgenstein begins the *Investigations*. The passage is quoted in Latin, meaning that readers have to translate it (or simply rely on the translation provided), and translation is an issue that the content of the passage brings up. Augustine describes how he thinks he learned language as a boy, but the account he gives reads as if he already knew one language and then simply had to translate this into the language of his elders, essentially learning nothing but a new vocabulary. Wittgenstein goes on to describe a couple of situations in which words do function something like this: someone buys apples with a set of written instructions that are then followed rather mechanically by the shopkeeper, and two builders use a language consisting only of names for building materials.

Each of these "language-games" is strikingly unlike normal uses of language and still does not really fit the Augustinian/Tractarian picture of how language is supposed to work. What look like names of objects in fact function as commands, so that the shopping list "five red apples" means (to the shopkeeper) something like count to five, look up "red" on the color chart, open the drawer marked "apples," and then remove a quantity of the contents corresponding to the number counted and the color identified on the chart. Even in the seemingly robotic or zombie world of Wittgenstein's builders, who do nothing but build and say nothing but the names of building components, the connection between words and actions is quite clear and unbreakable. This is something that seems to be completely lacking from the picture theory of language. To picture an object is not to call for it on a construction site or to ask for it in a shop. Wittgenstein emphasizes the variety of language-games that are found in real life, bringing out even more ways in which we use words for purposes other than simply naming or referring to objects.

We might be surprised to find a lover of Fyodor Dostoevsky and Kierkegaard championing the rather utilitarian and pragmatist idea that the meaning of a word is the work it does in the language (so that nonsense is what happens when language takes a vacation). However, it is this idea that leads us to see that language does not function in only one way, essentially naming and describing. It is more like an organism than a machine. And once we see the variety of ways in which words work we might give up as uselessly simplistic the crude slogans of utilitarianism and pragmatism. (The more sophisticated ideas associated with those theories might be harder to overcome, but they also might not be things we should want to overcome.) The good and the true might be defined by a pragmatist as whatever works, but what is meant by the word "works" in such a claim? If we understand it simplistically then we will be a long way from Wittgenstein, but if we have a rich enough idea of what work is, or can be, then we will be much closer. And certainly some pragmatists do see a similarity between their ideas and Wittgenstein's.

Besides this, it is important to note that Wittgenstein did not define all meaning as use, as is sometimes thought. Attending to the variety of ways in which language works might help to free us from the tendency to think of all questions or problems as being of the same type, and therefore soluble by the same kind of means (scientific ones, say). In this way Wittgenstein's philosophical work on language can be seen as a kind of attack on scientism (and certain versions of utilitarianism and pragmatism). So, although questions of meaning are not reducible to questions of ethics, they are importantly related to them. This connection seems to have been what drove Wittgenstein, early and late, to focus his attention on what might seem to be merely technical questions of logic and language. Of course, as an honest scientist, mathematician, and then logician, he would hardly have ignored problems in logic just because they did not fit his prejudices. But, while his philosophical work cannot be judged by ethical standards, its connection with Wittgenstein's own ethical, spiritual, and cultural concerns is noteworthy, and is one important connection between the early and the late Wittgenstein.

MEANS AND ENDS

The approach to philosophy taken in the *Tractatus* (at least ostensibly) is *a priori*. The main question motivating what Wittgenstein says there seems to be "How is meaning possible?" How can marks on paper or sounds made with the mouth be *about* something? The picture theory says that meaning is produced by a kind of mirroring. A thought or sentence has the same logical form as the state of affairs that it represents, and such representation is the essence of language. The form of all propositions is: this is how things are. Ultimately this representation involves the most basic linguistic units standing for (or meaning) the most basic things in the world (objects). This talk of what is most basic should be qualified, though, by pointing out that objects are necessarily related to possible states of affairs and meaning is only possible in propositions. Objects carry, as it were, inside themselves, all their possibilities for combining with other objects in states of affairs, and a word has no meaning outside the context of a proposition. So says the *Tractatus*.

The *Investigations* has a more *a posteriori* flavor to it. Here Wittgenstein looks at actual and imaginary uses of language to see how sense is (and is not) made. Language can be seen to be more variable and dynamic than the picture theory conceives. This is not linguistic anthropology, however. It is not genuinely *a posteriori*. Instead, Wittgenstein's approach is dialectical. This is to say not only that the *Investigations* often reads like a dialogue, with some parts surrounded by quotation marks, for instance. The dialectical nature of the book is, we might say, deeper than that. For, like the *Tractatus*, it contains little overt argument. The reader seems to be expected to agree with Wittgenstein's views without being convinced in the way that most philosophers try to convince their audience that they are right.

Because of this, most people who have read Wittgenstein's works have taken them to rely on implicit arguments. After all, the *Tractatus* is clearly very compressed, treating ideas as connected without explaining the connections. Wittgenstein even accused Rudolf Carnap of plagiarism when he put forward ideas that Wittgenstein considered to be implicit in the *Tractatus*. Similarly, the preface to the *Investigations* tells us that Wittgenstein did not want to "spare other people the trouble of thinking" (p. viii). A natural inference is that the reader is expected to fill in the gaps in order to reconstruct the arguments on which Wittgenstein relies. Unfortunately, though hardly surprisingly, there has been considerable disagreement about what these arguments are.

As far as the *Tractatus* goes, this might not matter very much if Diamond and her followers are right. The implicit arguments would all be nonsense anyway, and the most important thing would be that the reader came to see this. Other students of the *Tractatus* have concluded that Wittgenstein meant, but simply failed, to provide a coherent account of his thoughts in that book. Few people take the later work to be incoherent though, either intentionally or otherwise.

The standard view, as I have indicated, is that works such as *Philosophical Investigations* do rely on arguments to make their points. There is disagreement about what these arguments are, especially those regarding "private language" (see below) and rule-following, but that there are arguments of some kind is generally taken to be obvious. Certainly Wittgenstein is trying to change minds by rational means, so he is offering arguments at least in this loose sense. On the other hand, he makes various methodological claims that seem to fit rather badly with the idea that he is giving arguments in defense of theses (such as the impossibility of a private language). For instance, in §109 he says that "we may not advance any kind of theory," and §128 strongly implies that advancing theses is not what he is about. Without theories or theses there might be no need for arguments.

So what else could Wittgenstein be up to? There are basically two alternative ideas about this. One is that he is offering a kind of therapy intended to remove certain mental puzzles. Philosophical methods are like different therapies, according to §133, and Wittgenstein makes several similar remarks elsewhere in the book, comparing his philosophical work with the therapeutic work of a psychoanalyst. The other purpose attributed to the later Wittgenstein is clarity. Throughout his career he claimed to value clear thinking and clear writing. The motto of the *Tractatus* says that "whatever is not mere rumbling and roaring . . . can be said in three words." In §5 of the *Investigations* Wittgenstein talks about dispersing fog so that we can see clearly how words function. An express desire for clarity is evident elsewhere in the book, occurring about as often as metaphors of therapy. And Wittgenstein is known to have valued clarity not merely for instrumental reasons but for its own sake. In the end the question of whether Wittgenstein offers arguments in defense of theses is perhaps only a semantic one. He says what he says. The important question is what the point of it all is. It was not, I think, to advance theses or theories in a quasi-scientific way. Nor do I think we need to choose once and for all between the goals of therapy and clarity. Those who need philosophical 'therapy,' as Wittgenstein saw it, are precisely those whose vision or thinking is not clear. So we need not think in terms of a dichotomy here (although some do, and this is not the place for me to take sides on that issue).

RULES AND PRIVATE LANGUAGE

The obvious question that now arises is what kind of clarity Wittgenstein has in mind, or what kind of confusion it is that he means to overcome. The best way to answer such questions is to look at some examples. I have already mentioned the idea of a private language, so let me start with that.

Modern philosophy is in large part a response to the programs set forth by René Descartes and John Locke, both of whom wanted philosophy to be importantly related to science. Descartes wanted to provide a philosophical foundation on which science and mathematics could build. Locke wanted philosophy itself to be based on the empirical approach of scientists and to provide a kind of janitorial or bulldozing service to science, clearing the conceptual ground to make way for the construction of the edifice of human knowledge. Both Descartes and Locke started with an investigation into ideas, making their nature and function both central and foundational to modern philosophy. Both treat ideas as a kind of private property, objects only contingently related to the "external world" (that is, everything outside one's own mind). Since ideas have a sense, this way of thinking implies that sense, too, either is or at least can be private, having an independent existence inside one's own mind.

Wittgenstein tackles this idea in two ways. First of all he takes up the issue of rule-following. Whatever has sense or meaning can be thought of as a feature of some language (be it English, German, American Sign Language, semaphore, or "body language"). Making sense within any given language depends on following certain rules, which Wittgenstein calls grammar. These rules are flexible, allowing a certain amount of innovation, and need not be known at all consciously by those who follow them. Still, they are important. Not just any combination of English words will make a comprehensible sentence. So rules are an important feature of language, and hence of sense or meaning.

Now, we might ask, what is a rule? It need not be spoken or written, or even consciously noticed. And it need not be absolutely strict or cover every conceivable situation. Still, it must (if it is to be a rule) rule some things in and others out. Rules involve (or perhaps are) standards of correctness and incorrectness. One important interpretation of Wittgenstein's remarks on rule-following is that such standards require other people to be able to make corrections in one's behavior, so that solo rule-following is only conceivable if we imagine the existence of others who could (at least hypothetically) step in and enforce the standard. So there cannot be a language, or any other rule-governed practice, known only by one person. Meaning is necessarily social.

Another interpretation has it that there need not actually be others who know the rule in question but that it must be possible that there *could be* such people. In other words, we do not need to imagine others who could enforce the rule, but any rule that can be followed by one person must be capable of being followed, in principle, by others. Its standard cannot be something essentially private, such as an object that exists in, and is knowable by, only one person's mind.

Other Wittgensteinians maintain that Wittgenstein says and implies nothing about what can or cannot be done but simply draws our attention to what we ourselves would or would not count as rule-following. Most of these people too would say that our paradigms of rule-following are all social practices, and that the very idea of an essentially private rule is incoherent, cannot in fact be imagined.

What Wittgenstein himself calls a "private language" is precisely this strongly private kind of language, one in which the words refer to sensations had (as far as it is possible to tell) only by the person whose language it is. These sensations are declared to have no characteristic physical manifestation, making it impossible for anyone else to tell when they are occurring or to have any ability to use the words that refer to them. If we think of these sensations as objects, Wittgenstein suggests, then we cannot conceive of a language that refers to them. Because genuine reference involves meaning, meaning involves rules, rules involve standards of correctness, and a completely subjective standard is no standard at all.

Imagine I have a sensation such as those just described, and I decide to call it *S*. A few days later I have the same sensation again and write down *S* in my diary. If *S* means anything, then there are rules for its correct use, criteria that determine whether what I am calling *S* now is the same as what I experienced before when I named my sensation *S*. But what criteria might these be in this case? The original sensation is no longer with me. If I try to conjure it from my memory, how will I know I have retrieved the right thing? It would have to be the same as the sensation I am experiencing now, but what are the criteria of sameness for *S*? All I have is a feeling, a phenomenon, what we might call a seeming. So the only 'definition' I can have of *S* is "seems like *S*" or words to that effect. Or perhaps we should even say: seems like what I think I remember *S* having been like. This is pure subjectivity, yet it is my standard. The problem is not that I cannot tell whether I have followed my original rule. The problem is that my rule tells me nothing about what I am to call *S* and what I am not to call *S*. It is in fact no rule at all, and *S* has no meaning. So a thoroughly private language might *seem* to be conceivable but in reality is not.

The exact relation between Wittgenstein's remarks on rule-following and those on private language proper is controversial, as is the correct exegesis of his remarks on *S*, but what I have written here should give a rough idea at least of the kind of issue that interested Wittgenstein in the *Investigations*. The upshot is that huge amounts of modern philosophy from Descartes to the present day presuppose, implicitly or (especially since Wittgenstein) explicitly, the reality of something that, Wittgensteinians hold, is not even conceivable. This is the kind of confusion he sought to expose and to undo.

Perhaps more important to Wittgenstein than attacking specific confusions, though, was demonstrating ways in which people might try to banish their own philosophical muddles. Philosophy, Wittgenstein once wrote, is really a working on oneself. He also wrote that the same puzzles are likely to arise again and again, because we are misled by the grammar of our language (that is, the superficial appearance of that grammar belies the reality that appears upon more careful inspection). So, confusions cannot be killed once and for all. Instead, we need to find a way to fight them again and again. Methods for doing this are what the *Investigations* tries to teach. Wittgenstein's followers have gone on to apply them to a range of issues relating to religion, ethics, politics, aesthetics, literature, and law, as well as the subjects about which he wrote most: language, logic, psychology, and mathematics. Doing so has gone somewhat out of fashion, but whether Wittgenstein's techniques are effective, and whether they can be used by anyone but him, must be decided by each puzzled philosopher who tries them.

The question of technique is interesting in relation to all of Wittgenstein's work. Biographical information about him might lead one to expect him to oppose the rather scientistic idea that there must be a technique for solving every kind of problem. This hardly seems very spiritual or romantic. Yet the *Tractatus* implies that every problem for which there is no solution-technique is a pseudo-problem. The *Investigations* seems much the same, taking pretty much for granted the idea that philosophical problems are pseudo-problems and offering techniques for removing the feeling that they are real. It is implausible that this is meant ironically, but there is no reason to suppose that Wittgenstein would consider all *apparently* philosophical problems to be spurious. They could, I think, be disguised spiritual, religious, or ethical problems. In which case Wittgenstein, like science, offers no solutions at all. Removing such disguises might be an important part of the clarity that he aims to offer. What to do with it is up to us.

WITTGENSTEIN'S INFLUENCE

Wittgenstein's influence on philosophy was immediate. Since he studied with Russell, one of the foremost philosophers of the 20th century, any new ideas he had went straight to the top (unless they went over Russell's head, as Wittgenstein sometimes seems to have thought they did). Thus Russell presented his lectures on logical atomism, while Wittgenstein was at war, as presenting his student's ideas, and was deterred from serious work in philosophy for a while after being stung by Wittgenstein's criticisms. The various members of the Vienna Circle were also influenced greatly by the *Tractatus*, even if they did not share Wittgenstein's ethical outlook, and he rejected their verificationism. Before the Second World War Wittgenstein was clearly the most influential philosopher in the English-speaking world, although of course he too was influenced by Frege and Russell, and those he influenced, such as Rudolf Carnap, had important ideas that were original with them.

This was the great era of analytic philosophy, the movement that sought to further our understanding of the world by analyzing and clarifying our concepts (and leaving the discovery of facts about the world to science). Since 1945, philosophy, and Wittgenstein's place in it, has become harder to describe. In a word, the reason for this is science. If we accept Immanuel Kant's distinction between synthetic judgments (about the world) and analytic judgments (about concepts), then science deals with the former, and philosophy deals with the latter, according to classical analytic philosophy. The two can work together to tell us everything there is to know, but they are distinct areas, or modes, of inquiry.

One problem with this picture is that it presents all knowledge as being either scientific or conceptual. It is hard to make room within the picture for knowledge of, say, the transcendent, the beautiful, or the good. It is hard to make room also for the in-principle unknowable. So metaphysical, ethical, and religious talk starts to look like nonsense. This is part of the appeal of the picture for some hardheaded, scientifically minded people. The early Wittgenstein often seems to be such a person, although his *Tractatus* has also been interpreted mystically. Certainly his agreement with the Vienna Circle was less than wholehearted. So, it is not clear to what extent Wittgenstein himself ever accepted the somewhat scientistic worldview that his own work fueled, and his later work clearly reacts against it. Early analytic philosophy presents itself as a kind of sidekick of science, a helpful friend, but it is open to question whether Wittgenstein ever meant to provide this kind of useful service rather than something more mystical or more subversive of the general trend of Western culture. His relations with Russell and Carnap, at least, were very strained at times.

Other philosophers argued that analytic philosophy was a mistake or a waste of time. Karl Popper famously and vigorously objected to Wittgenstein's claim that there are no genuine philosophical problems, only pseudo-problems that philosophers should dissolve. Popper wanted philosophy to be much more constructive than that, as science is. The charge that linguistic philosophy is barren (that is, both boring and pointless) has been a common one ever since. More influentially, Willard van Orman Quine has argued against the analytic-synthetic distinction, thus opening up the world of empirical fact to philosophers. Work in the philosophy of mind is now mixing together with work in psychology and artificial intelligence, while work in the philosophy of language is similarly mingling with work in linguistics. The flavor of philosophy in the analytic tradition is now much more empirical, much more scientific, than it was during Wittgenstein's life. Perhaps this would not have happened if more concepts had been satisfactorily analyzed by the earlier analytic philosophers, or perhaps it was inevitable given the scientistic currents that Wittgenstein, as well as Kierkegaard and Dostoevsky, discerned and opposed.

For a decade or two after World War Two Wittgenstein's main influence shifted from Cambridge to Oxford. This was the heyday of so-called ordinary language philosophy, associated primarily with Gilbert Ryle and J. L. Austin. Their style of philosophy, however, passed out of fashion, partly because their theories seemed implausible to many philosophers, and partly because what they were trying to achieve was no longer what was wanted. They made no claim to be relevant in the way that science can be and, some would say, paid the price. Ryle's influence lives on in the work of his student Daniel Dennett, as Austin's does in John Searle, but neither Dennett nor Searle is either primarily or orthodoxly Wittgensteinian in method or beliefs. Stanley Cavell, another of Austin's students, is much closer to Wittgenstein, but still a unique voice.

Such is the way of academic influence. Anyone who merely parroted Wittgenstein's views would be unlikely to publish much or gain a good reputation. Those in positions of influence must be at least somewhat original. And so Wittgenstein's influence has inevitably dwindled over the years. His own approach to philosophical problems has proved very hard to apply satisfactorily, and more promising, more scientific methods have become preferred instead. Philosophers such as Hilary Putnam and John McDowell, who bring Wittgensteinian insights to mainstream debates, have found a receptive audience, but the general view seems to be that Wittgenstein was little more than an important figure in the history of the analytic tradition, a tradition that has since largely moved on from conceptual analysis as such.

On the other hand, where that tradition should go now is somewhat in question. Many philosophers prefer to get on with trying to solve problems as best they can without worrying too much about history, methodology, or the state of the discipline. Others believe in working still more closely with the sciences. Still others believe in greater cooperation with the other main philosophical tradition to emerge from the last century, so-called continental philosophy. These 'post-analytic' philosophers and their continental counterparts often regard Wittgenstein as a figure of central importance. So if the dust ever settles on philosophy's current methodological restlessness, it could turn out that Wittgenstein will emerge to be regarded as either a hero or as a fool. Which interpretation of Wittgenstein that would be, of course, also remains to be seen.

A

AESTHETICS AND ART. Wittgenstein was born into a sophisticated and cultured family, so it is not surprising that he had a lifelong love of the arts. Johannes Brahms and other composers often visited the Wittgenstein family's house in Vienna, and Wittgenstein's ability to whistle musical pieces accurately and even beautifully was well known. He also practiced sculpture and architecture, sculpting the head of a young woman (possibly Marguerite Respinger) and designing a house for his sister Gretl with Paul Engelmann.

Despite all this, aesthetics does not feature very prominently as a subject in Wittgenstein's philosophical work. The same goes though for **ethics** and **religion**, about which he felt very strongly, so the absence of much direct tackling of the subject does not imply a lack of interest in it on Wittgenstein's part. In proposition 6.421 of the ***Tractatus Logico-Philosophicus*** he wrote: "Ethics and aesthetics are one and the same." The implication might seem to be that both are matters of style, of doing things in a certain way, that is, beautifully or simply well. His previous two sentences, though, **say** that ethics cannot be put into words and that ethics is transcendental. So there is reason to doubt that Wittgenstein would say that ethics is a matter of style (or of anything else that can be put into words). Ethics and aesthetics might be the same, in his view, simply because they *are* transcendental or beyond words. One interpretation of the *Tractatus* is that it means to point the reader toward ineffable **truths** of great **value**. These might be regarded as being beautiful and/or good.

Alternatively, it is at least possible that Wittgenstein took ethics and aesthetics to have in common the fact that both concern judgments of value or importance. They are concerned with what is important or with how one looks at things (which, proposition 5.5423 implies, amounts to the same thing, since focusing on one **aspect** of something rather than another is just focusing on one set of **facts** rather than another). To say that one *should* attend to this more than that (to saving lives more than to saving money, to Beethoven more than to the Beatles) in any absolute sense (that is, in any sense that is not reducible to means-end reasoning about hypothetical or contingent ends, to **psychology**) is **nonsense**. The absolute is beyond **lan-**

guage, or, in other words, in language there is no absolute. Another interpretation, though, has it that Wittgenstein meant the reader to discard as mere nonsense any supposedly ineffable truths. Aesthetic matters were clearly important to Wittgenstein the man, but what his philosophical judgment of them was in his early work is still a matter of some controversy.

In the summer of 1938 he gave a series of lectures in **Cambridge** on the subject of aesthetics. In these lectures he describes the subject as "very big and entirely misunderstood" (see LC p. 1). Characteristically, he focuses not on how one identifies what is beautiful but on how one is taught and then goes on to use words such as 'fine' and 'beautiful.' He notes that people who express themselves well rarely use such words at all. The real issue in aesthetics, he suggests, is appreciation, and it is impossible to describe what this consists in. It is part of a whole way of living. People who have learned to think and feel a certain kind of way will regard some things as right and others as wrong. These jeans are too tight, that dress too matronly, these curtains too short, that painting too kitschy, and so on. This might seem to imply a kind of cultural **relativism** about aesthetic standards, but Wittgenstein does not explicitly commit himself to such a view and seems more concerned to make apparent the superficiality of some Europeans' enjoyment of 'charming' African art.

Throughout the lectures Wittgenstein opposes the desire to reduce aesthetics to something else, such as the **science** of the production of psychological feelings of a certain kind. An aesthetic judgment is not one that can be found to be true or false by scientific means. Understanding a work of art's effect on us is not typically a matter of identifying some causal mechanism by which it produces a certain effect. It is much more a matter of coming to appreciate what is so good about the work of art. In some cases, though, Wittgenstein says that appreciation is not the issue. Certain masterpieces do not simply get everything just right. Instead of following the rules perfectly, he seems to be suggesting, they break the rules or create new ones. These are the works that we consider tremendous.

It is notable also that Wittgenstein considers a wide range of examples in these lectures, including a variety of very specific cases of judgments about fashion, painting, food, **music**, architecture, and **poetry**.

AGREEMENT. In Wittgenstein's later work he emphasizes the importance of agreement in **language**. Following **rules** together involves agreeing on what counts as the same thing, whether this thing be the application of the rule (for instance, both this and that are instances of adding two) or an object to which a rule is applied (this **color** is the same as that, so one should use the same word to describe both). Examples as explicit as these prompt thoughts of situations in which disagreement is readily imaginable. Agreement in these cases is what Wittgenstein calls agreement in opinion. Students of arithmetic might, for instance, agree that when someone goes from -5 to -3, from -3 to -1, and then from -1 to 1 she is doing the same thing (adding two) in each case, despite the potentially confusing difference in notation for negative and positive integers. One can imagine them agreeing because one can imagine them disagreeing. (In cases where disagreement is inconceivable, it is hard to make sense of the idea of agreement.) But what Wittgenstein tries to draw out is the fact that the kind of thinking or discussion that might be provoked by, or resolve, such a disagreement itself involves a kind of agreement or harmony in the language that is used. Disagreement is not mere incomprehension. And no disagreement (or agreement, for that matter) would ever be noticed if there were not countless things on which people agree without ever noticing this **fact**.

Some commentators would say that Wittgenstein points out that agreement in **form of life** is necessary, a prerequisite, for the existence of a shared language. ***Philosophical Investigations*** §242 implies that agreement in judgments is a precondition for language to be a means of communication. Others would say instead that, as Wittgenstein puts it in §241, agreement in language *is* agreement in form of life. Perhaps a distinction should be made between agreement in judgments (which Wittgenstein seems to think is a necessary precondition for language) and agreement in form of life (which is not). ***Zettel*** §351, though, says that our concept of color would not exist without agreement in judgment about the colors of things and explicitly *contrasts* this with the idea that such agreement is a necessary precondition, something without which we *could not* have our concept of color. So both agreement in judgment *and* agreement in form of life here seem to be presented as being **internally related** to agreement in language (that is, to what it means to have the same language).

AMBROSE, ALICE (1906–2001). An American student of Wittgenstein's who later taught at Smith College. She was part of the group of students to whom he dictated the ***Blue Book*** and of the pair (the other being **Francis Skinner**) to whom he dictated the ***Brown Book***. He broke with her when she refused to give in to his insistence that she not publish an article called "Finitism in **Mathematics**" in the journal *Mind* putting forth what she took to be Wittgenstein's ideas on the subject. This kind of secondhand dissemination of his ideas prompted Wittgenstein eventually to prepare his ***Philosophical Investigations*** for publication, to set the record straight about what his thoughts really were.

ANALYSIS. Wittgenstein was one of the pioneers of the idea that the work of **philosophy** is or should be a kind of analysis. Along with **Gottlob Frege**, **Bertrand Russell**, and **G. E. Moore**, he is one of the most important early analytic philosophers. Roughly speaking, the guiding idea of this movement is that **Immanuel Kant** was wrong to think that there could be such a thing as synthetic *a priori* knowledge. Synthetic knowledge is knowledge about **the world**, involving a synthesis or combination of different **concepts**. For instance, the fact (if it is a fact) that bachelors eat a lot of pizza combines the concepts bachelors and pizza. In contrast, analytic **truths** are about concepts (not the world) and do not involve referring to anything not already contained in, or presupposed by, the concept in question. For instance, that bachelors are male is a fact about the concept bachelor, or about what the word 'bachelor' means, not about nature itself. Kant believed that philosophers could discover truths about the world, synthetic truths, purely by *a priori* means, that is, just by thinking, without any empirical research. He argued that the truths of **mathematics** and some of physics are of this kind (for instance, the fact that a straight line is the shortest distance between two points, since the concept of straightness seems to imply nothing about length). Philosophers, according to Kant, might try to discover truths about **metaphysics**, the ultimate nature of reality, in the same kind of way.

Analytic philosophers disagree. They believe that synthetic truths can be discovered only by *a posteriori* means, by actually looking at how the world is, in other words, by **science**. Philosophers, who are not scientists, must content themselves with discovering analytic truths. These might be truths about concepts, as Kant conceived of analytic truths, or about the true **logical form** of **propositions**, which is more what Russell had in mind. This kind of work might seem dull, but at least, as these philosophers see it, it is honest, whereas pretending that metaphysics is possible is either fraudulent or **confused**. Besides which, some concepts can be quite interesting, and it is these that have typically occupied philosophers. These are concepts such as **free will**, God, and the **mind**. A purported science such as **psychology** would seem to need to know just what the concept of mind really is (what the word 'mind' really means) before it can properly begin. So analytic philosophy promises to help science. This distinction between philosophy and science has been questioned by **W. v. O. Quine**, but it was insisted on by Wittgenstein. (Which is not to say that there is no connection at all between philosophy and science, in Wittgenstein's view.)

The ***Tractatus Logico-Philosophicus*** (in proposition 4.221, for instance) says that all complex propositions can be analyzed into **elementary propositions**. In this way one can see more clearly what they mean. The only propositions that mean anything are those that make claims about **states of affairs**. Analysis, Wittgenstein suggests, can show which propositions are genuine and which are merely pseudo-propositions (perhaps of metaphysics), seeming to make sense only when unanalyzed.

This idea that there is something hidden that philosophical work can uncover is attacked in the ***Philosophical Investigations*** (see especially §§60–64). There Wittgenstein suggests that there is not only one correct way to see the world, or only one ultimately correct description of it. The proper work of philosophy might, at least in part, be called analysis, but it is a matter of making clear (or seeing clearly) what is already in plain view, not a matter of discovering or unearthing anything that might come as a surprise. This later kind of analysis requires a good grasp of **grammar**, of how to use language correctly, but not technical expertise in **logic**.

ANSCOMBE, GERTRUDE ELIZABETH MARGARET (1919–2001). A student and friend of Wittgenstein's, known for smoking cigars, wearing a monocle, and staunchly defending superficially implausible ideas. Her unfashionable views on **ethics** reflected her strong **Christian** faith, and her often counterintuitive philosophical work was strongly influenced by Wittgenstein. That said, the originality of her mind is undeniable.

With her husband **Peter Geach**, she had seven children and wrote *Three Philosophers* (1961), about **Aristotle**, St. Thomas Aquinas, and **Gottlob Frege**. From 1970 to 1986 Anscombe was the professor of philosophy at **Cambridge University**, a post held previously by her mentor Wittgenstein.

Anscombe's interests ranged widely, but her main impact has been through her work in three areas: on the philosophy of action, on ethics, and on Wittgenstein. She was one of his three original literary executors (the others were **Rush Rhees** and **G. H. von Wright**), translated some of his best work, including the ***Philosophical Investigations***, into English, and wrote one of the best-known books on his ***Tractatus Logico-Philosophicus*** as well as numerous papers on various aspects of Wittgenstein's work.

She almost single-handedly reinvented the philosophy of action as a field of inquiry in her book *Intention* (1957), which explores action and related concepts in a Wittgensteinian style with noticeable Aristotelian influence. Like Wittgenstein's, her work resists summary, but its aim is to expose the sources of the philosophical **confusion** that typically occurs in thinking about action, reasons, intention, our knowledge of our **minds**, and so on. In particular, Anscombe shows that knowledge need not always be passive. One's knowledge of what one intends to do is not derived from introspection, for instance, or any other kind of observation.

Anscombe argued in her 1958 paper "Modern Moral Philosophy" that this kind of work in the **philosophy** of **psychology** is just the kind of work that needs to be done in order for moral philosophy to be productive. This is the paper that started the contemporary interest in virtue ethics. In it she argued that (1) moral philosophy should stop being done, at least for the time being; (2) seemingly essential moral concepts, such as moral obligation and the moral sense of 'ought,' are incoherent; and (3) all modern moral philosophy is worthless, being either confused (see thesis 2) or corrupt (see below). Thesis 3 is true, she says, because decent modern ethics depends on the concepts rejected in thesis 2.

Anscombe's second claim can be traced back to Wittgenstein, **Arthur Schopenhauer**, and **Fyodor Dostoevsky**, but it was she who developed it and most successfully argued for its relevance to moral philosophy. The idea is that ethicists spend their time wondering what is permissible or forbidden in various circumstances without, it seems, having anyone in mind who might do the permitting or forbidding. God used to fill this position, but if he does not exist, or is not methodologically acceptable, then nothing can be either permitted or forbidden. Nor is it clear how it could be 'obligatory' or even 'right' or 'wrong.' Anscombe suggests that most modern moral philosophy incoherently tries both to rely on theism (for the concepts it uses) and to reject it (for methodological reasons of assuming as little as possible, or else from simple atheism). The rest is corrupt. The charge of corruption applies most obviously and most importantly to consequentialism (a term she invented), which countenances even the most unthinkable evil (and thus makes it thinkable, she suggests) so long as the consequences are sufficiently beneficial. (The best-known form of consequentialism is **utilitarianism**, although Anscombe coined the term 'consequentialism' in order to distinguish it from old-fashioned utilitarianism. Apparently she saw an important difference, obscure to others, between utilitarianism before Henry Sidgwick and after.) So, in her view, all modern moral philosophy should be abandoned.

Instead, Anscombe suggests philosophers look to the ancient moral philosophy of Aristotle, who concerned himself primarily with questions of virtue and vice, that is, of character. However, Aristotle's own theory was also found wanting by Anscombe, who criticized his notion of *eudaimonia*, or flourishing, as hopelessly vague. Before Aristotelian moral philosophy can be revived, she argued, an explanation of the relation between acts and character traits is needed, as well as an explanation of exactly what makes for a good character. *Intention* had been a step in this direction, but Anscombe clearly did not think that it was all that needed to be done. Until the project described in "Modern Moral Philosophy" is complete, her advice, if she was not being purely ironical, was to stop doing moral philosophy altogether.

As a devout theist, Anscombe herself saw no reason to shut up about moral matters. She became a Roman Catholic in the last 1930s and publicly opposed unjust wars (including **World War II**, as she saw it), the use of the **atomic bomb** against Hiroshima and Nagasaki, contraception, **homosexuality**, and pacifism (which, she argued, is not only wrong but also encourages the in-for-a-penny attitude that anything goes in war).

ANTHROPOLOGY. Wittgenstein's interest in, and relevance to, the study of anthropology is varied. Most obviously relevant are his ***Remarks on Frazer's*** **Golden Bough**, but his interest in **forms of life** and **relativism** could also apply to anthropology. He also took great interest in fictional anthropology, inventing practices and tribes (such as those of the **builders** and **woodsellers**, for instance) in order to illuminate existing practices and **concepts** by way of contrast. Part of the point of such examples is to show that philosophers sometimes misdescribe the way that we use our words. If a **theory** is suspect in this way, one might see how wrong it is by imagining a people that really did behave as the theory describes our behavior and then seeing how different this is from what we actually do. Another part of the point is to show the range and diversity of possible **language-games** and forms of life. If we think that our concepts are somehow necessary or right, then it might help to imagine people who do things differently or live in a world with different facts of nature. Then, perhaps, we will see that our practices and concepts are more contingent than we had realized.

See also APPLES, FIVE RED (EXAMPLE OF); MYTHOLOGY.

ANTIREALISM. *See* REALISM AND ANTIREALISM.

ANTI-SEMITISM. Wittgenstein was raised as a **Christian**, but he counted as a Jew by Nazi standards, and so anti-Semitism posed a grave threat to his family (he was safely in England during the Nazi period). Nevertheless, Wittgenstein himself has been accused of anti-Semitism because of remarks of his about **Jewish** character that are not always flattering. Of course, he has in mind himself as much as, if not more than, anyone else when he makes these remarks, so it is possible that they should be taken as self-deprecatory in character rather than anti-Semitic. For instance, in ***Culture and Value*** he refers to Jews having an "intellectualistic" character. He writes that "the Jew is a desert region, but underneath its thin layer of rock lies the molten lava of spirit and intellect" (p. 13e). Less positively he suggests that "genius" (the quotation marks are his) in Jews is found only in holy men, and that even the greatest Jewish thinkers are merely talented (p. 18e). Here he refers specifically to himself as an example. The parenthetical qualification, though, is worth noting in the sentence from later in the same passage: "It might be said (rightly or wrongly) that the Jewish mind does not have the power to produce even the tiniest flower or blade of grass."

Certainly Wittgenstein sometimes thought in terms of such ethnic groups as Jews, and his attitude toward Jews was somewhat ambivalent, but there is no evidence that he thought of any other group as superior (or inferior), and there is some reason to believe that his ambivalent remarks about Jews were motivated as much by modesty as by any anti-Semitism that he might have picked up from the culture that produced and admired the likes of **Otto Weininger** (not to mention **Adolf Hitler**). Late in his life, **O. K. Bouwsma** reports (on 28 August 1950), Wittgenstein "thought this notion of patterns—Jews—Englishmen—Germans—as quite natural as an account of thought, but not as an account of real thinking" (Bouwsma p. 56). He links this kind of stereotyping with **Plato's** search for **essences**, something that Wittgenstein considered understandable but misguided.

APOSTLES (CAMBRIDGE GROUP). Also known as the **Cambridge** Conversazione Society, and simply the Society, the Apostles was a select group of open-minded, irreverent intellectuals that began in 1820. Wittgenstein was elected as a member in November 1912 but resigned soon afterward. Prominent members included **Bertrand Russell**, **G. E. Moore**, **John Maynard Keynes**, and Lytton Strachey. From such an elite group, resignation was almost unheard of (it had happened only once before), but Wittgenstein found discussions with the Apostles fruitless, and he personally disliked some other members of the society.

APPLES, FIVE RED (EXAMPLE OF). ***Philosophical Investigations*** §1 invites the reader to imagine a use of **language** that might fit the picture that Wittgenstein finds in his opening quotation from **St. Augustine**. In the example, Wittgenstein sends someone out to buy five red apples with the words "five red apples" written on a piece of paper. In response, the shopkeeper finds a drawer marked "apples" and opens it, looks up red on a **color** chart, and counts out five apples from the drawer that match his color sample. This bizarre scene, the reader is led to understand, is how things would be if Augustine's picture were really right. Wittgenstein says that we *do* operate with words in this "and similar ways," but this is clearly not a normal way to buy and sell apples. It is more like the way a mute, child, or foreigner might shop for hardware. The example seems designed to show, to get the reader to see for himself, that language use is much more varied than the Augustinian picture suggests.

Other themes introduced in this section are the relation between the **meaning** of a word and its use (Wittgenstein contrasts meaning with use here), the question of how **rule-following** can work (how the shopkeeper knows what to do with the 'instructions' "five" and "red"), and the apparent fact that **explanations** must come to an end at some point, that one cannot just go on asking "But why is *that*?" each time one is given a reason for something. (Someone could make those sounds until she was blue in the face, but there would come a point at which she was no longer asking a question.)

ARBITRARINESS OF GRAMMAR. Rush Rhees once described ***Philosophical Investigations*** Part II (now known as "**Philosophy of Psychology—A Fragment**") §xii as the single most useful statement for understanding the whole book. In this remark Wittgenstein says that "if anyone believes that certain **concepts** are absolutely the correct ones, and that having different ones would mean not realizing something that we realize—then let him imagine certain very general facts of nature to be different from what we are used to, and the formation of concepts different from the usual ones will become intelligible to him."

It is not obvious, though, how best to interpret this statement. It would be understandable if someone were to read it as saying that no concepts are absolutely the correct ones, so that it is at least somewhat arbitrary which concepts people use. In the following paragraph, however, Wittgenstein suggests that people do not have any choice about the concepts they have. When a man has a specific objective, such as carving a piece of wood into a certain shape, any cut he makes is right as long as it achieves the right result. The same is not true with **language** or **mathematics** though. The **rules** of mathematics are not justified by this kind of practical usefulness (at least not entirely). They have a kind of independence.

In ***Philosophical Grammar*** Wittgenstein makes it plain that he thinks people should not, but tend to, confuse rules with empirical propositions. For instance, he compares the assertion that carbon and oxygen yield carbonic acid with the assertion that a double **negation** yields an affirmation. Here it looks as though a property of negation is being described, when in fact what is happening is simply that a rule is being stated, according to Wittgenstein. So it is important to beware of any treatment of such rules that makes it sound as though there is something that exists, some property of the universe, which the rule or procedure simply reflects or encapsulates. The rules of negation could, after all, treat a double negation as a doubly strong negation, not an affirmation at all. Such an alternative rule, were anyone to decide to use it, would not be wrong in the way that an alternative chemistry (adopted on a whim, not with good scientific reason) would be.

It does not follow that there can be no possible justification of rules of **grammar**, but there are some kinds of justification that cannot be found. For instance, language is not justified as a means to some end, say communication. It cannot be said that language is necessary for communication because the concepts *language* and *communication* are **internally related** in the sense that the concept of language is already contained in, or implied by, the concept of communication.

One kind of justification for the language people use is the fact that some procedures, rules, and concepts are natural to them. It is not arbitrary that people follow rules that they find useful or relatively easy to follow. While partially removing one kind of arbitrariness, however, this does nothing to provide something by which to guide procedures and check results. What suits human **psychology** is not necessarily what is best or correct. For this one might look to the "very general facts of nature" that Wittgenstein talks about. Some of these are facts of nature in a straightforward sense, like the fact that more things in the world are red than just the tips of certain leaves in autumn (see ***Remarks on the Philosophy of Psychology*** *Volume I* §47) and the fact that cheese does not regularly expand or shrink to any dramatic degree (see *Philosophical Investigations* §142). Facts like these show that the standard use of the concept red and the practice of weighing dairy products in some sense fit the way **the world** is.

The 'justification' of rules of grammar, like the justification of concepts, is entirely different from that of sentences. A given proposition in mathematics may be justified by reference to other principles and axioms within mathematics, but the whole of mathematics cannot be justified in this way. Likewise a grammatical rule may be justified by its practical usefulness and its naturalness to a particular people (or species). A particular rule might be changed if it ceased to be useful or natural in this sense. But the whole of grammar cannot be changed in this way. Particular rules and principles can be changed; the whole language or grammar cannot be. Nor can grammar as a whole be justified. Justification occurs only within a system or **language-game**. The system or language itself cannot be justified from the inside, and there is no such thing as getting outside to judge it. If one were outside language, one could neither speak nor think, let alone judge. So it makes no sense to condemn grammar as arbitrary, nor to defend it as non-arbitrary.

For the later Wittgenstein, grammar is arbitrary in the sense that there is no determinate or absolute **logic** of the world against which to measure the logic of language. (In the earlier ***Tractatus Logico-Philosophicus***, in contrast, logic does seem to be part of the world, in particular of the **objects** that make up the **facts** that constitute the world. As he writes there in proposition 2.0123, "If I know the object then I also know all the possibilities of its occurrence in states of affairs.") However, it is not arbitrary in the way that some kinds of **pragmatism** and **relativism** suggest. Grammar has a certain autonomy in the sense that rules for the correct use of words are not (cannot be) true or false, since they are normative rather than positive. This is not to say, however, that the concepts of **truth** and falsity are arbitrary or that any grammar is just as good (in every sense) as any other.

Within a language some (probably pragmatic) justification of this concept or that rule can be given. But if human psychology changed (to be more like Wittgenstein's imaginary **wood-sellers** perhaps), or if general facts of nature changed, then such justification might no longer work. So what justification one can give is contingent. Grammar itself, though, a whole language, cannot be justified at all without (at best) obvious circularity or (at worst) complete meaninglessness, since the concept (and the practice) of justification is part of that very language. This fact is sometimes referred to by talk about the autonomy (or arbitrariness) of grammar, but such talk can give the impression that the non-autonomy of grammar is conceivable, which, on Wittgenstein's view, it seems not to be.

ARCHITECTURE. Wittgenstein's interest in architecture was both directly practical and more theoretical. With **Paul Engelmann**, he designed a house for his sister **Gretl**, but he also reflected on the nature of architecture in his notebooks and in his lectures on **aesthetics**. In ***Culture and Value*** Wittgenstein says that "Working in philosophy—like work in architecture in many respects—is really more a working on oneself" (p. 16e). Work in architecture is also like work in **philosophy**, which Wittgenstein conceives of as **grammatical** investigation, because architecture is like **language**. Wittgenstein writes: "Remember the impression one gets from good architecture, that it expresses a thought. It makes one want to respond with a gesture" (*Culture and Value*, p. 22e). If good architecture expresses a thought, then it is not so much *like* language, rather it *is* part of language. But Wittgenstein says this only of *good* architecture (which he elsewhere simply calls architecture, as opposed to mere building for a purpose), and that such architecture only gives the *impression* that it expresses a thought, it does not necessarily actually do so. Still, he does seem to have believed that the best architecture is part of language, not as words are, but in the way that a gesture is.

Because, *pace* some of his interpreters on the subject of **rule-following**, he did not believe himself to be committed to following what was ordinarily asserted by the community of language-users in which he found himself, Wittgenstein was able to be idiosyncratic with regard to matters of taste. He brought a critical eye to his own Modernist attempt at architecture: "the house I built for Gretl is the product of a decidedly sensitive ear and *good* manners, an expression of great *understanding* (of a culture, etc.). But *primordial* life, wild life striving to erupt into the open—that is lacking. And so you could say it isn't *healthy* (**Kierkegaard**)" (*Culture and Value*, p. 38e). In the terms he uses in his lectures on aesthetics, we might say that Wittgenstein believed himself to have demonstrated appreciation for good architecture but not achieved anything tremendous. The style of the building is similar to that of work by **Adolf Loos**.

ARGUMENT. Either a series of assertions logically supporting a conclusion or an independent variable (part of a **function**). Argument in the former sense is often taken to be crucial to **philosophy**, being one of the main characteristics marking the difference between mere opinion (as in "my philosophy is . . .") and real philosophy. There is widespread agreement that it is hard to make out exactly what the arguments are in Wittgenstein's later work, however, and some scholars maintain that he does not offer any. After all, he suggests that philosophy is about describing uses of **language** rather than putting forward theses. See ***Philosophical Investigations*** §109 and §128. Descriptions do not seem to stand in need of supporting arguments.

Whether there are arguments in Wittgenstein's work depends partly on what one counts as an argument. In both his early and late work he certainly appears to have been trying to change his readers' minds by rational means. **Logic** features heavily in the ***Tractatus Logico-Philosophicus***, both as the topic being addressed and as the apparent means to get from one proposition to another, although Wittgenstein leaves the reader a lot of work to do in making connections. In his later work he provides descriptive reminders of how we use words and invitations to imagine various alternatives. This is not argument in the usual sense, but some scholars believe that his ideas could be translated into standard argument form. Others believe that the absence of argument is a distinctive and important feature of Wittgenstein's approach to philosophy.

The other notion of argument (an independent variable) is relevant in the *Tractatus* because of the influence of **Gottlob Frege**.

ARISTOTLE (384–322 BC). Plato's best student, and the founder of the academic study of **logic**. Aristotle's syllogistic logic dominated the field for millennia and was not significantly improved upon until the time of **Gottlob Frege**. Aristotle's logic differs from Frege's in that it does not use a **concept-script**, and it is designed to deal with predicates rather than propositions. Thus it can be used to understand **arguments** of the form: "All men are mortal; Socrates is a man; therefore, Socrates is mortal." However, it cannot handle arguments in which the place of an object such as Socrates is taken by a **proposition**. Or rather, it can only handle such arguments by treating propositions as if they were objects, which simplification is sometimes undesirable.

In **ethics**, Aristotle's emphasis on character, rather than the kind of almost formulaic principles one finds in the ethics of **Immanuel Kant** or **utilitarianism**, is regarded as somewhat Wittgensteinian by some commentators. The recent interest in Aristotelian virtue ethics owes much to **G. E. M. Anscombe** and others influenced by Wittgenstein.

ART. *See* AESTHETICS AND ART.

ASPECT-SEEING. Wittgenstein discusses seeing aspects, or seeing something as something, in several places, but the most famous such discussion concerns Joseph Jastrow's duck-rabbit picture, which can be seen as a duck's head and as a rabbit's. Seeing it as a rabbit's head, Wittgenstein suggests, is a sort of cross between seeing and **thinking**. What one sees when one sees it as a rabbit's head is just the same as what someone who sees it as a duck's head sees. There is not some other **object**, in the head, say, that one 'really' sees. The object of perception is public and ambiguous. Yet one can see it, think of it, unambiguously as either a rabbit or a duck. This unambiguous taking in one way and not another does not require some inherently unambiguous object. Wittgenstein's thinking here seems to go against his claim in proposition 5.5423 of the ***Tractatus Logico-Philosophicus*** that seeing one aspect of a figure and then another is really a matter of seeing two different **facts**. This no doubt is part of the point of the discussion of the duck-rabbit.

Another point concerns what he calls aspect-blindness. Wittgenstein imagines someone who sees things, but cannot see them *as* something else. A two-dimensional drawing of a cube, for instance, would never seem to such a person to stand out from the page. For other people it sometimes does and sometimes does not. In the ***Philosophical Investigations*** ("**Philosophy of Psychology—A Fragment**" xi §261), Wittgenstein says: "The importance of this concept lies in the connection between the concepts of seeing an aspect and of experiencing the meaning of a word." His point seems to be that someone missing this kind of experience would indeed be missing something but would still be able to use the word, just as an aspect-blind person could still make use of geometrical drawings. So no subjective experience is so necessary to a word as to be the **meaning** of the word. (One might say that the meaning of '**pain**' is a certain kind of subjective feeling, but one can know the meaning of 'pain' without feeling pain, by reading a dictionary for instance.)

An aspect-blind person can use two-dimensional drawings of three-dimensional objects in certain ways but would not react to them as others do. She would probably not, for instance, enjoy the illusions of M. C. Escher. Similarly, a meaning-blind person would probably have little taste for **poetry** and would presumably not **understand** words used in a **secondary sense**. It might also be hard for such people to see the **family resemblances** that inform the use of some words, making it hard also for them to follow the **rules** that other people take to quite readily. They would perhaps be like the imaginary **lion** that can speak.

See also PHYSIOGNOMY.

ATOMIC BOMB. Once when **Bertrand Russell** was going to a meeting of the World Organization for Peace and Freedom (or some such thing), Wittgenstein exclaimed that he would prefer "by far" a society for war and slavery (see Schulte p. 23). His distaste for self-righteousness is the most likely motive for this comment, but Wittgenstein also seems to have been against opposition to war or weapons of mass destruction motivated by fear. For instance, there is a passage in ***Culture and Value*** (on pp. 48e–49e, from

1946) in which he calls fear of the atomic bomb "hysterical." This hysteria "almost suggests" that there is something good about the bomb. All that this could be though, he adds, is that it holds out the prospect of the destruction of "our disgusting soapy water **science**." The passage leaves it ambiguous whether he imagines this destruction as being by means of bombs or by way of the effect of such inventions on public attitudes toward science. He is also ambivalent about whether such destruction would be beneficial in the long run, since what came after it might be even worse than the *status quo*. He ends on an unambiguous note: "The people now making speeches against producing the bomb are undoubtedly the *scum* of the intellectuals." Russell was a public opponent of the bomb.

ATOMISM, LOGICAL. *See* LOGICAL ATOMISM.

AUGUSTINE OF HIPPO, ST. (354–430). Wittgenstein was a great admirer of St. Augustine and especially his *Confessions*. The ***Philosophical Investigations*** begins with a quotation from the *Confessions* that expresses, in Wittgenstein's opinion, a particular view of language. This view, often called the Augustinian picture even though some Augustine scholars deny that he held it, is then the target of attack for much of the rest of Wittgenstein's book. This 'Augustinian' picture of language can also be found in Wittgenstein's earlier ***Tractatus Logico-Philosophicus***. The key elements of the picture are that words stand for **objects**, that these objects are the **meanings** of the words, and that this kind of representation is the **essence** of human language. Against this, Wittgenstein tries to show in the *Investigations* that words do not all necessarily stand for any kind of object (in the **mind** or head or anywhere else), that the meaning of a word is not necessarily an object but is very often its use in the language, and that there need not be any such thing as the essence of language.

AVOWAL. Wittgenstein observes that if I tell you that I am in **pain**, then it seems that I cannot be mistaken. I might be lying, and I might mis-speak, but otherwise it seems that what I say must be correct. In this way, at least, some sincere **first-person** avowals appear to be necessarily true, grammatically indisputable. That is, it makes no sense to doubt them. In this way they are different from reports or descriptions. If I report that I have cut myself shaving or describe my chin as bleeding, then I might be wrong. Perhaps I am shaving in a crowded room and seeing someone else's face in the mirror. It is not similarly conceivable that I might mistake someone else's pain for my own, or mistake pleasure for pain.

Nor are avowals just like prelinguistic reactions to, or expressions of, sensations such as pain and emotions such as grief. "I am sad" has a meaning and grammar in a way that crying does not, even though one might learn to replace actual crying with linguistic utterances such as "I am sad," giving the sentence the same role in one's life as crying **behavior** previously had. In ***Philosophical Investigations*** §244, Wittgenstein gives the example of a verbal expression such as "I'm in pain" replacing the pain-behavior of a child, such as crying. "That hurts" might play a similarly expressive role in our language, and should therefore not be mistaken for a description of anything. Wittgenstein explores the similarities and differences between descriptive reports, natural expressions, and learned verbal expressions.

B

BAKER, GORDON PARK (1938–2002). An American philosopher who spent most of his career at Oxford University, noted for his scholarly work on Wittgenstein. Most of this was done in close collaboration with **Peter Hacker**, but from around 1990 onward the two wrote more independently as a result of disagreements about how to interpret Wittgenstein's work. The main difference was over **theories**, Hacker maintaining that Wittgenstein did advance philosophical theories (and good ones) in his later writings, despite his claims to the contrary. Baker came to take Wittgenstein more at his word on this issue. He also worked on philosophers related to Wittgenstein, such as **Bertrand Russell**, **Friedrich Waismann**, and **René Descartes**. Alone and in collaboration with others, he wrote numerous books and articles, including *Wittgenstein, Frege and the Vienna Circle* (1988). With P. M. S. Hacker he wrote the four-volume *Analytical Commentary on the Philosophical Investigations* (1980–1996) and *Scepticism, Rules and Language* (1984), which contains their response to **Saul Kripke's** interpretation of Wittgenstein on **rule-following**.

BARTLEY, WILLIAM WARREN (1934–1990). The author of a notorious book called *Wittgenstein* that covers the period 1919–1929 and suggests that the Austrian **School Reform Movement** influenced Wittgenstein's later philosophy. The book's notoriety stems from its claim that Wittgenstein was not just gay but promiscuously so with "rough young men" in the Prater, a large park in **Vienna** (see Bartley p. 24). This claim has been denounced strongly, but not refuted, by several friends and students of Wittgenstein's. Ray Monk, Wittgenstein's biographer, notes that Bartley has not revealed the source of the information he uses to support his claim and suggests that Wittgenstein is much more likely to have looked at, and perhaps fantasized about, the young men in question than to have actually had sex, or even conversation, with them. Monk presents Wittgenstein as valuing love highly, but being uncomfortable about sex, whether homosexual or heterosexual.

BEETLE IN THE BOX (ANALOGY OF). The beetle occurs in §293 of the ***Philosophical Investigations***, in which Wittgenstein imagines that everyone has a box and calls its content a "beetle," even if the contents keep changing or the box is empty. Each box might contain something quite different, but there is no knowing because no one can look in another's box and each knows what a "beetle" is only by looking in his or her own box. It follows, Wittgenstein suggests, that the thing in the box would then have no place in these people's **language**. It just would not matter to their use of the word "beetle" what, if anything, each person's "beetle" was. The point of the example relates to the **private language argument** and Wittgenstein's thoughts about the **inner** and **mind** more generally.

If one thinks of sensations (**pains**, for instance) as private objects, knowable only by the owner of each particular sensation, then what these objects are, their nature, is irrelevant to the shared use of sensation language. That is not to say that such objects do not exist. *Philosophical Investigations* §304 rejects the model of object and designation for understanding the **grammar** of sensation language. Hence a sensation "is not a Something, but not a Nothing either!" The whole language of things is misleading, and therefore misplaced, here. It is possible that Wittgenstein got the idea of the beetle in part from his reading of *The Brothers Karamazov* by **Fyodor Dostoevsky**.

BEHAVIOR AND BEHAVIORISM. Wittgenstein emphasized the importance of the use of words in **language**. Words relating to **psychology**, he suggested, need **criteria** for their correct application, and these criteria must be public, observable. ***Philosophical Investigations*** §580 reads: "An 'inner process' stands in need of outward criteria." These criteria are generally taken to be behavioral, and so Wittgenstein has been thought of by some as a behaviorist. He implies in the *Philosophical Investigations* that this is not correct, but of course he could be wrong about the nature of his own views (not so much with regard to what they are but to what they amount to or imply). It is also important to consider the various meanings of 'behaviorism.' One (**metaphysical**) kind denies that there is anything to human psychology but (potentially) publicly observable behavior. Another (methodological) kind holds merely that it is *useful* for psychologists to concern themselves only with what can be publicly observed. A third (logical) kind, inspired by Wittgenstein, holds that the **meanings** of psychological terms can be reduced to actual or potential kinds of observable behavior.

It is the metaphysical kind of behaviorism that Wittgenstein most explicitly rejects, at least as an interpretation of what he says about mental processes. The methodological kind seems rather alien to his interests as a philosopher. The third kind is close to what Wittgenstein says, but his remarks are open to a variety of interpretations. The logical behaviorist interpretation is consistent with much that he wrote, but not really with his methodological claims about advancing no theses and saying only what everyone admits. Scholarly orthodoxy tends to discount these remarks, but the view that Wittgenstein was any kind of behaviorist is still a minority one.

His interest in behavior is clearly (from the remark quoted above) related to his interest in the '**inner**' and in criteria. Behavior, according to Wittgenstein, provides the outer criteria of which concepts relating to the inner stand in need. Such criteria are not *evidence* (inductive or analogical) of another's mental state, as philosophers have tended to think. Only as a sick **joke** would one say that someone's screaming was *evidence* that the hot coals beneath her feet were causing her **pain**. Nor though are outer, behavioral criteria so **internally related** to inner states and processes that a man so screaming *must* be in pain. It could turn out that he is screaming for some other reason, that the coals are not really hot, and so on. That is to say, such criteria are defeasible. If thinking this amounts to a kind of behaviorism, then perhaps Wittgenstein is a behaviorist after all, but not of the simple logical kind defined above.

BELIEF. Wittgenstein might say that belief is what we mean when we use the word 'belief.' One can come to a philosophical understanding of belief, then, by attending to use of the word 'belief,' and this use is in connection with outward **criteria**. So the meaning of 'belief' is not something inevitably hidden away in the **minds** of others or something in one's own mind that is utterly subjective and permanently beyond the comprehension of others. Rather it is something one can read off, really remind oneself of (assuming one already knows the meanings of the words in the language), from people's (including one's own) **behavior** with the word 'belief' and its cognates. This is not to deny that there is a difference between behaving some way because of a belief and behaving that way for some other reason, such as deception or acting. But Wittgenstein stresses the connection between belief and behavior, so much so that some have read him as being a behaviorist about belief and other **psychological** states.

BERLIN. Wittgenstein spent two years at the Technische Hochschule (School of Technology) in Charlottenburg, Berlin, matriculating on 23 October 1906 and graduating on 5 May 1908. He studied mechanical engineering there and lived with the Jolles family, Dr. Stanislaus Jolles being one of his professors. Wittgenstein corresponded with the family during **World War I** but felt increasingly out of sympathy with them as the war made him more serious and less tolerant of the well-meaning pleasantries that their letters offered.

THE BIG TYPESCRIPT. Written in 1933, typescript (TS) 213 has become known as "the Big Typescript" and is often referred to in the scholarly literature. The work is 768 pages long, divided into chapters and sections. It is the source of the remarks published as ***Philosophical Grammar***, which consists of parts of a revised version of the first two-thirds of the Big Typescript and the final, unrevised, third. One chapter not included is about the nature of **philosophy**. This is Wittgenstein's longest and perhaps clearest account of what he takes philosophy to be. It has since been published in ***Philosophical Occasions 1912–1951***, edited by James Klagge and Alfred Nordmann. In 2005 the entire thing, *The Big Typescript: TS 213*, was published by Wiley-Blackwell.

BIPOLARITY. In ***Tractatus Logico-Philosophicus*** 2.21 Wittgenstein says that a **picture** is either true or false, correct or incorrect, in agreement with reality or not in agreement with it. **P. M. S. Hacker** has called the idea that every proposition must be capable of being either true or false the "bipolarity principle." If it is capable of neither agreeing with nor disagreeing with reality, then it says nothing at all about it, and is, apparently, **nonsense**. Denis McManus (p. 59) has objected to Hacker's view on the grounds that it would rule out the possibility of propositions that are necessarily true or necessarily false having sense. A necessarily true sentence is not capable of disagreeing with reality, after all, and so is not bipolar in the relevant way. McManus is also troubled by the fact that, according to Hacker, the bipolarity principle is based on nothing more than intuition.

See also BROUWER, LUITZEN EGBERTUS JAN (1881–1966).

BLACK, MAX (1909–1988). An Azerbaijani-born American mathematician-turned-philosopher influenced by Wittgenstein. He is best known for his work in the **philosophy** of **mathematics**, **logic**, and **language**. After an English education, he emigrated to the **United States** in 1940 and taught at Cornell University. His main works include *The Nature of Mathematics* (1933), *Language and Philosophy* (1949), *The Importance of Language* (1962), *A Companion to Wittgenstein's Tractatus* (1964), *The Prevalence of Humbug* (1983), and translations of works by **Rudolf Carnap** and (with **Peter Geach**) by **Gottlob Frege**.

BLUE AND BROWN BOOKS. This single volume contains the *Blue Book* and the *Brown Book*, both preliminary studies for the ***Philosophical Investigations***, which Wittgenstein dictated in English to his students. The names given to these works come from the wrappers in which they were bound and were not given to them by Wittgenstein. The *Blue Book* consists of notes dictated to **Francis Skinner**, Louis Goodstein, H. S. M. "Donald" Coxeter,

Margaret Masterman, and **Alice Ambrose** in the academic year 1933–1934 at **Cambridge University**. The idea, Wittgenstein said, was to give his students something to take away in their hands even if they took nothing from his lectures into their brains. The *Brown Book* was dictated only to Skinner and Ambrose in 1934–1935. It is longer and more like a draft of a publishable work than the previous year's notes. When Wittgenstein abandoned revising it he began work on what is now the *Philosophical Investigations*.

BOLTZMANN, LUDWIG (1844–1906). A professor of physics at the University of **Vienna**, and a neo-**Kantian** philosopher. Boltzmann developed statistical mechanics, using probability to calculate the behavior of systems containing large **numbers** of atoms. He also pioneered the use of coordinates in a multidimensional space (three axes for space, one for temperature, one for pressure, and so on) to specify the exact physical state of a system. Wittgenstein acknowledged a debt to Boltzmann, and his influence can be seen in remarks such as proposition 3.411 of the ***Tractatus Logico-Philosophicus***: "In geometry and logic alike a place is a possibility: something can exist in it." Boltzmann contrasted **philosophy** with **science**, the former resolving **confusion** and the latter picturing reality. He was criticized by the **logical positivists** and committed **suicide** in the year that Wittgenstein left school, putting an end to Wittgenstein's thoughts of studying with him.

BOUWSMA, OETS KOLK (1898–1978). An American philosopher who was dissuaded from his early **Hegelianism** by **G. E. Moore** and later taught at Cornell University, Smith College, the University of Nebraska, and the University of Texas. He was at Cornell when Wittgenstein visited in 1949. Despite the whimsical style of some of his philosophical work, Bouwsma's seriousness about philosophy seems to have impressed Wittgenstein. The two had numerous conversations with each other and Bouwsma's recollections of these have been published, edited by J. L. Craft and Ronald E. Hustwit. These recollections provide a picture of Wittgenstein comparable to that provided by **Norman Malcolm's** memoir, and the book has been called "The best thing written on [Wittgenstein] I know," by Wittgenstein's nephew, Thomas Stonborough. It is a useful source of information about Wittgenstein's views on **ethics** and **religion** as well as of anecdotes about his time in the **United States**.

BRENNER, DER. *See* FICKER, LUDWIG VON (1880–1967).

BROUWER, LUITZEN EGBERTUS JAN (1881–1966). A Dutch mathematician with interests in the foundations of **mathematics**, **philosophy** more generally, and **mysticism**. Brouwer held the post of extraordinary professor of set theory, function theory, and axiomatics at the University of Amsterdam from 1912 until 1951. He is best known for his work in topology and, above all, in developing the doctrine of mathematical intuitionism. Intuitionism in mathematics rejects both **Platonism** and **David Hilbert's** formalism in favor of the **Kantian** idea that mathematics is founded on the pure intuition of time (roughly: thinking in terms of one thing after another, or serially). Since it is mental activity that makes **propositions** true or false on this view, Brouwer rejects the ancient logical law of excluded middle, which states that every proposition is either true or false (one cannot *become* one or the other from a state of having been neither). He views **logic** as the study of patterns in the linguistic expression of mathematical thinking and thus rejects **logicism**, which holds logic to be the basis of mathematics. His major papers are included in two volumes of *Collected Works*, published in 1975 and 1976.

BROWN BOOK. *See BLUE AND BROWN BOOKS.*

BUDDHISM. Despite being not only one of the major religions of the world but also a major philosophical tradition, Buddhism was more or less ignored by Western philosophers until **Arthur Schopenhauer** related it and Hinduism to his own quasi-**Kantian** ideas. The best-known ideas of Buddhism are that life in this world is fundamentally unsatisfactory or imperfect; that our dissatisfaction is caused by worldly attachments and desires; that such attachment can be overcome; and that the way to overcome it is to follow the noble path between self-indulgence and self-denial, doing everything the right way in every aspect of one's being. The end result is nirvana, which is the divine extinction of worldly attachments (hence, from a worldly perspective, complete extinction).

Since Wittgenstein read Schopenhauer at a young age, it is possible that he was influenced by Buddhist beliefs, which are generally interpreted by Western philosophers as advocating detachment from things of this world and, like Schopenhauer, emphasizing the suffering within it. It is also possible that Wittgenstein came to a similar view on his own. In fact, though, his personal beliefs seem to have been closer to **Christianity**. Nonetheless, the alleged **mysticism** and **quietism** of the ***Tractatus Logico-Philosophicus*** have repeatedly been compared with ideas from, especially, Zen Buddhism.

See also KODER DIARIES.

BUILDERS (EXAMPLE OF). Wittgenstein introduces his famous example of the builders in §2 of the ***Philosophical Investigations***. Unlike the previous example with **apples**, it is presented explicitly as an exercise in imagining a situation to which **Augustine's picture** of **language** would seem to apply.

There is a builder, A, and an assistant, B. Their language consists only of four words: "block," "pillar," "slab," and "beam." When A calls out a word, B brings the appropriate stone. The reader is asked to think of this as a complete "primitive language." According to §6, we can imagine a whole tribe having this as its entire language, with children being brought up to use the words as A and B do, calling them out when such-and-such a stone is needed or bringing one in response to a call by another. This is then used by §7 as an example of what Wittgenstein means by the term "**language-games**."

Rush Rhees has argued that this is not a real language. The people seem too much like automata, their 'language' being unusable for conversation, asking questions, or anything one might recognize as real **thought**. Thus the example raises questions about what counts as real language, about, one might say, the **essence** of language. It also invites the reader to think of **understanding** in connection with **behavior** (an assistant who brings a slab when a builder calls "slab" seems to understand the **meaning** of the word "slab") and to relate thoughts about language with thoughts about how one learns language and how a society or culture uses language. It is possible that the point of the example is precisely to issue an invitation to such thought.

C

CALCULATING. *See* MATHEMATICS; RULE-FOLLOWING; THOUGHT/THINKING.

CALCULUS MODEL OF LANGUAGE. The appeal of **thinking** of **language** as a kind of calculus was important to Wittgenstein. **Gottlob Frege's** application of **mathematical** concepts, such as function and **argument**, to **logic** suggested an interpretation of language as having the precision and clarity of mathematical calculi. This ideal can be seen in the early ***Tractatus Logico-Philosophicus*** where, for instance, Wittgenstein suggests in proposition 4.04 that the word 'mathematical' can (at least in some cases) be a substitute for the word 'logical.'

In the ***Philosophical Grammar***, written during Wittgenstein's middle period, language is said to be a calculus (p. 193). That is to say, a language is described as a system with a fixed set of **rules**, the kind of thing that a computer deals with. This idea is rejected in the ***Philosophical Investigations***. There the variety of uses of language, some like a calculus and some not, is emphasized.

CAMBRIDGE UNIVERSITY. Wittgenstein first went to Cambridge on the advice of **Gottlob Frege** to visit **Bertrand Russell**. He arrived unannounced on 18 October 1911 and was admitted as a member of Trinity College on 1 February 1912. There he met **G. E. Moore** and **David Pinsent**, and worked closely with Russell. In 1913 he left to live alone in **Norway** and later fought in **World War I**. He returned to Cambridge in 1929 and received his Ph.D., submitting the ***Tractatus Logico-Philosophicus*** as his thesis. The following year he became a Fellow of Trinity College and taught there until 1935 before moving to Norway again. He returned to Cambridge in 1938 and succeeded Moore in the chair of **philosophy** in the following year. After **World War II** he taught again at Cambridge until 1947. He often expressed distaste for the intellectual atmosphere of the place, disliking the conversation even of the intellectually elite **Apostles**, and seemed to prefer remote, rural places in Norway, **Ireland**, and Wales.

CANTOR, GEORG (1845–1918). An important mathematician. Born in Russia but dying as a German citizen, Cantor developed modern set theory. He is thus a key figure in the recent history of both **mathematics** and **logic**. Wittgenstein was highly critical of his work, referring to it (along with the work of Karl Weierstrass and Richard Dedekind) as "a cancerous growth" on the body of mathematics (see Monk p. 439). In Wittgenstein's view, Cantor had proved nothing but instead had introduced a new way of talking and thinking about, for instance, infinity. Such **grammatical** innovation is not necessarily bad, as Wittgenstein saw things, but was in Cantor's case producing only **confusion**. A new way of speaking that seems to be much more than this is likely only to do harm, according to Wittgenstein.

CARNAP, RUDOLF (1891–1970). One of the most important philosophers of the early 20th century. Of all the **logical positivists** and members of the **Vienna Circle**, Carnap was one of the least in sympathy with Wittgenstein's ideas. He studied physics and **mathematics** at Freiburg and Jena (where he studied with **Gottlob Frege**) and went to **Vienna** in 1926 at the invitation of **Moritz Schlick**. In 1935 he moved to Chicago. He founded the journal *Erkenntnis* with Hans Reichenbach, and is perhaps best known for his 1928 book *Der logische Aufbau der Welt* (The Logical Structure of the World) in which he defines scientific concepts in terms of immediate sensory experience, as **empiricists** had long believed ought to be possible.

CARTESIAN. *See* DESCARTES, RENÉ (1596–1650).

CAUSAL NEXUS. In **proposition** 5.1361 of the ***Tractatus Logico-Philosophicus***, Wittgenstein claims that **superstition** is belief in the causal nexus. This last sentence would be more literally rendered as "Belief in the causal nexus is *superstition*," but despite Wittgenstein's italics this remains ambiguous, whereas he has told us unambiguously what the sentence means: "I didn't mean to say that the belief in the causal nexus was one amongst superstitions but rather that superstition is nothing else than the belief in the causal nexus" (*Letters to Ogden*, p. 31).

Some commentators take Wittgenstein to be denying that there is any necessity in the relation between the type of events we identify as causes and those we identify as effects. **David Hume** famously noted that we experience the events we call causes and those we call effects, and we experience a pattern of the latter following the former, but we do not, he believed, ever experience the inevitability or necessity of this correlation. Wittgenstein might then have been going a step further and calling belief in such necessity superstition, rather than simply an interesting and automatic feature of the way the human mind functions, as Hume seems to have regarded it.

Arthur Schopenhauer refers to the causal nexus in *On the Fourfold Root of the Principle of Sufficient Reason* (trans. E. F. J. Payne, Open Court, 1974). He writes: "it is most important for us clearly to recognize first and foremost that the law of causality relates solely and exclusively to *changes* of material states, and to nothing else whatever. Consequently, it must not be introduced when *these* are not mentioned. Thus the law of causality is the regulator of the *changes* undergone in time by objects of external *experience*; but all these are material. Every change can take place only through another having preceded it, which is determined according to a rule, but by which it then takes place as having been necessarily brought about. This necessity is the causal nexus" (pp. 55–56, italics in the original translation).

It might also be worth comparing the following passage from **Friedrich Nietzsche**'s *Beyond Good and Evil* "On the Prejudices of Philosophers" §21: "It is *we* alone who have devised cause, sequence, for-each-other, relativity, constraint, number, law, freedom, motive, and purpose; and when we project and mix this symbol world into things as if it existed 'in itself,' we act once more as we have always acted—*mythologically*" (p. 219 Everyman, 1992, *Basic Writings of Nietzsche*, edited by W. Kaufmann).

Pasquale Frascolla interprets Wittgenstein's remark about belief in the causal nexus as a rejection of some of Schopenhauer's views. For instance, Schopenhauer's idea that motivation is causality seen from the inside, and that the relation cause-effect can be assimilated to the relation premise-consequence (see Frascolla p. 133). Allan Janik, however, sees Wittgenstein as making a basically Schopenhauerian point against **Bertrand Russell** (see Janik p. 86). In the passage quoted above Schopenhauer makes the point that the law of causality applies to nothing but changes of material states. It is a mistake, therefore, (according to his view) to look for or talk about the cause of material states themselves, or the cause of experiences of material states except insofar as such experiences consist in changes of material states. Yet in *The Problems of Philosophy* Russell argued that our sense data are caused by physical objects. Russell himself admitted that this argument was weak, and Schopenhauer would have rejected it utterly. His reason for doing so is that the concept of causation applies only to the objects of our experience, not to that experience itself. It seems clear, though, that Schopenhauer does not reject belief in the causal nexus, whereas Wittgenstein does.

See also CAUSATION.

CAUSATION. Wittgenstein did not deny that events have causes, but he was wary of going too far with belief in causation. In proposition 5.1361 of the ***Tractatus Logico-Philosophicus*** he writes: "The belief in the **causal nexus** is **superstition**." There might be causation, but there is no reason to believe that all events are part of some interconnected web. Indeed, if one thinks of a cause as a necessary connection between two events (that the cause necessitates the effect), then Wittgenstein would seem to deny causation altogether. As he sees it in the *Tractatus*, the only **necessity** is logical, not causal.

In his later work ("Cause and Effect: Intuitive Awareness" written in 1937 and published in ***Philosophical Occasions 1912–1951*** pp. 373–377) Wittgenstein denies that there must be some difference in two seemingly identical seeds if they produce different kinds of plant, leaving open the apparent possibility that some things might 'just happen.' He also underlines the differences between reasons and causes: reasons justify while causes merely explain; we know our reasons for acting, whereas we might not know the causes of our actions; and any chain of reasons always comes to an end, which need not be true of chains of cause and effect. To insist that every event must have a cause is not necessarily illegitimate (*pace* his earlier pronouncement about superstition) but is to insist on a conception of **the world** that cannot be proved either logically or scientifically, however useful this conception might be to **scientists**, mechanics, and others. This view, and its relevance to the philosophy of **mind**, is summarized in ***Zettel*** §608.

CAVELL, STANLEY (1926–). An American philosopher who studied with J. L. Austin at Oxford and later taught at Harvard University. Cavell is best known for his work on Wittgenstein, Ralph Waldo Emerson, Henry David Thoreau, **Martin Heidegger**, **Friedrich Nietzsche**, William Shakespeare, film, and **Freudian** psychoanalysis. His work characteristically brings together two or more of these subjects for careful reading and mutual elucidation. Cavell's reading of Wittgenstein's work as primarily therapeutic (aimed at removing **confusion**, not advancing **theories**) has significantly influenced the "American" interpretation of his work. His rather Emersonian view of such therapy, though, is not always thought to square well with Wittgenstein's claim that clarity itself had **value** for him and that this (rather than anything more obviously moral or spiritual) was the goal of his philosophical work. Nevertheless, Cavell's reading of texts is so unusually careful that his interpretation of Wittgenstein cannot very well be ignored. He is the author of numerous books, most notably *Must We Mean What We Say?* (1969), *The Claim of Reason* (1979), *This New Yet Unapproachable America* (1989), and his autobiography *Little Did I Know: Excerpts from Memory* (2010).

CERTAINTY. Wittgenstein's last writings were on the subject of certainty. He wrote in response to **G. E. Moore's** attack on **skepticism** about the external world. Moore had held up one hand, said "Here is one hand," then held up his other hand and said, "and here is another." His point was that things outside the **mind** really do exist, everyone knows they do, and that no grounds for skepticism could be strong enough to undermine this commonsense knowledge.

Wittgenstein did not defend skepticism, but questioned Moore's claim to *know* that he had two hands. Such 'knowledge' is not something that one is ever taught, or finds out, or proves. Actually, it is the kind of thing one teaches young children, but not in the way that other knowledge is taught. One is likely to smile and say *of course* (most, anatomically paradigmatic) people have two hands. **Truth** of this kind, as Wittgenstein presents it, is more like a background against which one comes to know other things. Some philosophers think of it as providing a **foundation** for knowledge. Wittgenstein compares this background to the bed of a river. This riverbed provides the support, the context, in which claims to know various things have **meaning**. The bed itself is not something one can know or doubt. In normal circumstances no sane person doubts how many hands she has. But unusual circumstances can occur, and what was part of the riverbed can shift and become part of the river. One might, for instance, wake up dazed after a terrible accident and **wonder** whether one's hands, which one could not feel, were still there.

This is quite different, though, from **René Descartes's** pretended doubt as to whether he has a body. Such radical doubt is really not doubt at all, from Wittgenstein's point of view. It is merely hypothetical or, one might say, philosophical. And so it cannot be dispelled by a proof that the body exists, as Moore tried to do. All such 'proof' effectively urges the skeptic not to be so silly, when in fact he was being not silly but abstractly theoretical. Wittgenstein's view seems to be that the skeptic will take Moore simply to have missed the point, which, in a sense, he has, even though there is an important sense in which he is right. Moore misses the point of skepticism in the sense that the truths of which he wants to remind his audience are held to be in doubt by the skeptic, so Moore begs the question. On the other hand, he is right that skepticism is incompatible with things that philosophical skeptics in fact hold so surely that to call them 'beliefs' can seem too tentative. This, arguably, shows the way in which philosophical skepticism fails to be meant seriously.

Recently some scholars have found in these ideas an additional stage in Wittgenstein's development as a philosopher beyond that of the ***Philosophical Investigations***. This "third Wittgenstein" no longer eschews theories and **arguments**, rather he develops a new argument against skepticism. This argument is foundational. According to it, language requires a certain **form of life**, which in turn requires living beings and the physical environment necessary to sustain them. Any doubt can only be expressed in **language**, and therefore presupposes or implies the existence of these requirements. They are the foundation of all our knowledge. To doubt their existence is to imply in language that the very requirements for language might be absent. This can only be a mistake.

Critics of this view suggest that if parts of the allegedly foundational riverbed can become part of the river itself, then the foundation metaphor is not really apt. The planet Earth is not logically necessary for human language, and the human form of life itself might change. So if our form of life and the environment needed to keep it going are foundational, then the foundation in question is far from stable. Nor does anyone claim that Wittgenstein's foundationalism, if there is such a thing, is like that of other foundationalists in treating the indubitability of certain experiences or the truth of certain propositions as foundational. Instead, what Wittgenstein is supposed to regard as foundational is a certain form (or forms) of life, or the physical environment needed for such a form of life. This difference from paradigmatic foundationalists is another reason not to apply that label (i.e., 'foundationalist') to Wittgenstein. Finally, while expressions of doubt might indeed require language, language itself consists in such things as expressions of doubt. Without any doubting our very form of life might no longer be recognizable as such. If that is the case, then it seems potentially misleading to call our language or our form of life a necessary precondition, or foundation, for expressions of doubt. Such expressions seem to be parts of it more than distinct entities built upon it. For these reasons the idea of a third, foundationalist Wittgenstein is rejected by many scholars.

CHRISTIANITY. Wittgenstein was raised and buried as a Christian, but throughout most of his adult life he denied that he was religious, and his friends worried that they might be making the wrong decision in burying him with Catholic rites. He claimed to see every problem from a religious point of view but said that he did not have faith and could call no one Lord. Certainly he admired such Christian thinkers as **St. Augustine**, **Søren Kierkegaard**, and **Leo Tolstoy**, and they influenced his thinking, but he did not regard their religion as any kind of **theory** or doctrine with which he might agree. The kind of **religion** that struck Wittgenstein as most genuine and attractive is the kind that goes to the core of one's being and colors every action and reaction. He expressed admiration for Mormonism, for instance, in a sense for the very reason that leads others to reject it: he regarded it as requiring strong faith and an ability not to ask certain awkward questions. He was aware of lacking any such deep-rooted belief himself, and did not seem particularly to want it, although he admired those who had it, on condition that their faith was genuine. In some of his diaries, notably the so-called **Koder diaries**, he reveals himself to have wrestled with Christianity, drawn to it like a moth to a candle and yet unable to accept it. Several of his students, such as Yorick Smythies and **G. E. M. Anscombe**, converted to Catholicism.

COLOR. In proposition 6.3751 of the ***Tractatus Logico-Philosophicus*** Wittgenstein writes: "the simultaneous presence of two colours at the same place in the visual field is impossible, in fact logically impossible, since it is ruled out by the logical structure of colour." In his later work, especially the ***Remarks on Colour***, he returned to the question of the **logic** or **grammar** of color. Certain truths about color, including necessary **truths** or those whose falsity is unthinkable, might seem to be physical in nature, contradicting Wittgenstein's claim that all true **necessity** is logical. Or these truths might seem to belong to a sphere somewhere between **science** and **logic**, as they had to **Johann Wolfgang von Goethe**, whose work on the subject Wittgenstein studied. What is unthinkable, as Wittgenstein sees it, is unsayable, and that is defined by grammar, the **rules** of **language**. So even visual phenomena are in a sense subject to the rules of language, almost like a **Kantian** limit on possible experience. Or rather, what might seem to be limits to the experiences one can possibly have are in fact rules of language. For instance, nothing can be both red and green all over because it would violate grammar to call anything red and green all over, *not* because this is physically impossible. That is not to say that language somehow limits possible experience. Rather, one cannot know whether it is physically impossible unless one knows what "red and green all over" **means**, but in fact these words, taken together like this, have no meaning.

CONANT, JAMES FERGUSON (1958–). An American philosopher who has similar views to those of **Cora Diamond**. Conant and Diamond are noted for their 'resolute' reading of the ***Tractatus Logico-Philosophicus***, according to which, when Wittgenstein refers to propositions of **metaphysics**, **ethics**, and **aesthetics** as either nonsensical ('*unsinnig*') or meaningless ('*bedeutungslos*'), he really means that they are **nonsense**. Since Wittgenstein says in *Tractatus* proposition 6.54 that his own **propositions** are nonsensical and must be overcome, Conant and Diamond argue that the entire book is an attempt to get the reader to see that its apparent content (the **picture theory** of **meaning**, **logical atomism**, and so on) is really quite meaningless, that the book really has no content. Thus rather than there being two Wittgensteins (the early author of the *Tractatus* and the later critic of the *Tractatus*), there is really only one, since 'both' reject the illusory pseudo-doctrines contained in the *Tractatus*. This is not to say that Conant and Diamond recognize no differences at all between the *Tractatus* and the ***Philosophical Investigations***, but they certainly see much more continuity in Wittgenstein's work than do most commentators.

This "new," "American," "austere," or "resolute" reading of Wittgenstein is rejected by most Wittgenstein scholars. **P. M. S. Hacker** stands out as their most vocal (and able) critic. In his view there is strong evidence external to the text of the *Tractatus* (such as reports of conversations with Wittgenstein by various friends and students, and things Wittgenstein wrote later) that Wittgenstein really did believe in at least some of the doctrines that the *Tractatus* seems to defend. Hacker also believes that these doctrines (and those he finds in the later work too) are true and important, and so should not be dismissed as mere nonsense. This debate is ongoing.

Conant also works on American **philosophy**, **Gottlob Frege**, **Søren Kierkegaard**, and **Friedrich Nietzsche**. He has edited several books and written numerous articles. Since 1999 he has been a professor of philosophy at the University of Chicago, having previously taught at the University of Pittsburgh.

CONCEPTS. Concepts are to words what propositions are to sentences. That is to say, the same concept might be referred to by different words in different languages, or even within the same language. Saying what a given concept is without using any particular **language**, though, cannot be done. So a conceptual investigation of the kind undertaken by Wittgenstein in his later works can have the appearance of a rather parochial investigation of ordinary language. On the other hand, any denial that a conceptual investigation is a linguistic investigation is likely to suggest that concepts exist somehow beyond language in something like a Platonic realm. Given a choice between these horns, Wittgenstein would surely reject the Platonic option. However, his interest in language was not that of an anthropologist. Wittgenstein's kind of grammatical investigation would not be helped by studying a handbook of English (or German) **grammar**. His view was that the basic problem of **philosophy** is **confusion** about concepts. This arises not because there is anything wrong with these concepts but because people are easily misled by the grammar of their language. When one sees clearly, the confusion, the temptation to bad **metaphysics**, will (if Wittgenstein is right) disappear.

CONCEPT-SCRIPT. It was **Gottlob Frege** who first invented a concept-script (*Begriffsschrift*) or system of logical notation in order to make clear the **logic** of **thoughts** and their relations to one another. A concept-script should have the clarity of **mathematics**, something seemingly missing from the **confusion** of natural languages. For instance, in English the word 'is' has a variety of uses. It can be used to express identity ("The third planet from the sun is Earth"), or to say that something exists ("God is"), or as the copula (in sentences such as "This book is green"). A good concept-script should remove this kind of ambiguity, using different signs whenever appropriate and making the role of each sign clear. Logical constants, for instance, should not look (in use or form) like signs for **propositions** or names of objects. In the

Tractatus Logico-Philosophicus Wittgenstein modified the conceptual notations of Frege and **Bertrand Russell** to suit his purposes. In his later work rarely any use of a concept-script is made.

CONFESSION. The idea of confession relates to Wittgenstein in two important ways. Most obviously, he made a point of confessing what he thought of as his main sins to several of his friends, often to their embarrassment. One such friend was Rowland Hutt. Hutt was a close friend of **Francis Skinner** who got to know Wittgenstein in 1934. Wittgenstein confessed his sins to him in 1937 (loudly, in a Lyons tea shop). Among the sins were that Wittgenstein had once had to overcome initial fear before carrying bombs over a stream on a wobbly plank, that he had once reacted to the news of the death of an acquaintance as if he had not heard it before, and that, contrary to what most people would have thought, he had had sexual relations with at least one woman in his life.

Secondly, since he begins the ***Philosophical Investigations*** with a quotation from **Augustine's** *Confessions*, several commentators have wondered about the connection between this work and Wittgenstein's own. Some of the voices to be heard in the *Philosophical Investigations* have been identified as voices of temptation, of things Wittgenstein himself is tempted to say, which must then be struggled against (the temptation must be confessed and overcome). Some of these temptations can be traced back to the ***Tractatus Logico-Philosophicus***, so at least some of the ideas criticized in the *Investigations* seem to have been held at one point by Wittgenstein himself, although there is disagreement about whether these ideas are advocated or merely exposed in the *Tractatus*.

CONFUSION. Throughout his career Wittgenstein saw the work of **philosophy** as being a battle against confusion. ***Tractatus Logico-Philosophicus*** proposition 3.324 says that the whole of philosophy is filled with fundamental confusions. Proposition 3.325 adds that the way to avoid this problem is to use a well-designed **concept-script**. Since Wittgenstein did not believe in laws of **logical inference**, there would seem to be little for **logic** or philosophy to do except to develop just such a means of displaying **thoughts** clearly.

In his later work he had a similar aim but used different means. The ***Philosophical Investigations***, for instance, makes no use of a concept-script but instead tries to demonstrate the logic of (natural) **language** (or to demonstrate a method for so doing). In both his early and his late work, the primary goal seems to be clarity or the dispelling of confusion.

Many commentators find more (or less) than clarity in Wittgenstein's work, however. Instead, or as well, they find **metaphysical** or logical theories and theses, especially in the *Tractatus*. Whether Wittgenstein ever advanced any theses at all is a controversial matter, since he claimed not to do so (this is fairly explicit in *Investigations* §109 and §128, and arguably implicit in *Tractatus* 6.54), yet the vast majority of philosophers who have studied his work have identified at least some theses in it, whether they approve of them or not.

CONSCIOUSNESS. Consciousness, and its relation to the brain, can seem to be one of the most mysterious things there is. This sense of mystery is precisely the kind of thing that sets off Wittgenstein's philosophical suspicions. In §412 of the ***Philosophical Investigations*** he talks of a feeling of giddiness similar to that one can get when thinking about **Georg Cantor's** set theory.

To be conscious is something like being awake, so it is possible to think of consciousness as a feature of life, but it is no more an object than 'awakeness' (or **pain**) is. So it is not a mysterious **object**. Nor would Wittgenstein accept that it is a mysterious phenomenon, since phenomena are what appear to consciousness. People are conscious of this and that phenomenon, and thus able to know that they are conscious (as when a boxer is able to count the number of fingers held before him). But consciousness itself is not one of these phenomena. Wittgenstein also seems to equate being conscious with having a **mind**. One knows who is conscious the same way one knows who has a mind, not by any psychic seeing within others (or indeed oneself) but by living with others in a certain way, reacting to them, and learning to treat them in the ways one reacts to and treats **human beings**.

CONSERVATISM. Wittgenstein's later philosophical method has been accused of being biased by an inherent conservatism, linked to its use of **ordinary language**. If what is ordinarily (or perhaps traditionally) said and thought is normative for philosophers, then new ideas will fare badly. Wittgenstein himself was somewhat conservative in his taste and values (although not politically), but most commentators agree that his descriptive method serves the interest of clarity, not conservatism of any kind. Wittgenstein's philosophical interest was in **logic** or what makes sense, and it is by no means true that only old-fashioned ideas make sense. What might seem to be radical new ideas could in fact be quite meaningless, but so too might old ways of speaking cease to make sense (such as claims about witchcraft, perhaps). Neither the old nor the new has a monopoly on sense. So Wittgenstein's interest in sense supports neither an innovative nor a conservative agenda.

CONTEXT PRINCIPLE. The context principle is derived from **Gottlob Frege** (see his *Foundations of Arithmetic* Introduction, §60, §62, and §106), who argued that a word has **meaning** only in the context of a **proposition** or sentence. Thus the word "cow," for instance, spoken or written on its own, says nothing, whereas "The cow is in the field" tells us something (true or false) about the world. So for Frege the basic unit of semantics is the proposition. Wittgenstein seems to have adopted this idea wholesale and stuck to it throughout his career (but this claim is controversial). In the ***Tractatus Logico-Philosophicus*** proposition 3.2 he refers to the elements of a propositional **sign** (he calls these **names**) and says that their meanings are the **objects** for which they stand. This might seem to make names more semantically fundamental than propositions, but it is only *in a proposition* that a name represents an object (3.22). "Cow" could be an abbreviated proposition of course, as in the exchange "What's that?" "Cow." The real meaning of this answer, though, would be something like, "That is a cow," something that is obviously a sentence and not just a word.

In a piece of real **nonsense**, though, such as "Cow yellows religiously," the context principle says that "Cow" is not a meaningful word at all. If the sentence is in code or some slang, then "Cow" might mean something, but there is no knowing what, or even whether it is a noun or some other part of speech, unless one knows that it is in code, say, and knows what this code is. Assuming that the 'sentence' really is nonsense, then "Cow" here is *not* the meaningful word with which we are familiar. If it were, then "Cow yellows religiously" would contain three meaningful words whose meaning somehow added up to nothing. As Wittgenstein puts it in ***Philosophical Investigations*** §500, its sense would be senseless. But, he says there, that is not how it is.

Reading this view back into the *Tractatus* is controversial because most scholars read the book as trying to show what, according to the **picture theory**, we cannot **say**. It does this, the **argument** goes, by using meaningful words in senseless sentences. If there cannot be any such use of words, then this argument appears to be in trouble. So it is dangerous to claim that the author of the *Tractatus* would have agreed with *Investigations* §500, but certainly he held some form of the context principle.

In *Investigations* §43 Wittgenstein says that the meaning of a word is often its use in the **language**. So for this sense of 'meaning' something like the context principle still applies, although the context is now explicitly the whole language, whereas before it had been merely a whole sentence (although perhaps the concept of sentence or proposition implies that of language). In §49 Wittgenstein says that naming a thing does nothing by itself, since only in the **language-game** does a thing have a name at all. He adds that this is what Frege meant by his context principle.

The context of sentences, as well as of words, was important to the later Wittgenstein. **O. K. Bouwsma** reports that **Max Black** once argued that in some circumstances a sentence such as "I am here" or "I exist" would serve no purpose but that, even then, if one were asked whether it was true or false, one would say that it was true. To this, Bouwsma says, Wittgenstein responded, "No! No! Of course not, etc. Context determines use" (Bouwsma pp. 14–15). Presumably Wittgenstein would consider this kind of context-free 'use' of a sentence to be **nonsense**, despite the fact that philosophers such as Black and **G. E. Moore** have wanted to think of them as true and even, in Moore's case, important (for combating **skepticism**). If context determines use and use is meaning, then without a context there can be no meaning. This might sound like a **theory** of meaning, but it could be taken as a kind of **analytic** truth that clarifies the meaning of 'context.' It should also be remembered that *Investigations* §43 does not say that 'meaning' always means use. Indeed, it explicitly denies this. So Wittgenstein does not hold a "use theory of meaning" (at least in any straightforward sense).

CONTINUITY IN WITTGENSTEIN'S WORK. Wittgenstein is generally considered to have changed his thinking considerably over his philosophical career. His early work culminated in the ***Tractatus Logico-Philosophicus*** with its **mysticism** and **picture theory** of **language**, according to this view. Then there came a transitional middle period when he first returned to philosophical work after realizing that he had not solved all the problems of **philosophy**. This period led to his mature, later period, which gave us the ***Philosophical Investigations*** and ***On Certainty***.

There certainly are marked changes in Wittgenstein's work over time. Two central discontinuities are these: whereas the *Tractatus Logico-Philosophicus* is concerned with the general form of the **proposition**, the general nature of **metaphysics**, and so on, in his later work Wittgenstein is very critical of "the craving for **generality**," and in the *Tractatus* Wittgenstein speaks of the central problems of philosophy, whereas the later work treats no problems as central. Another obvious difference is in Wittgenstein's style. The *Tractatus Logico-Philosophicus* is a carefully constructed set of short propositions. The *Philosophical Investigations*, though also consisting of numbered sections, is longer, less clearly organized, and more rambling, at least in appearance. This reflects Wittgenstein's rejection of the idea that there are just a few central problems in philosophy, and his insistence on paying attention to particular cases, going over the rough ground.

On the other hand, the *Tractatus* itself says that its propositions are **nonsense** and thus, in a sense (not easy to understand), rejects itself. The fact that the later work also criticizes the *Tractatus Logico-Philosophicus* is not, therefore, proof of discontinuity in Wittgenstein's work. The main change may have been one of method and style. In the later work problems are investigated one at a time, although many overlap. There is not a full-frontal assault on *the* problem or problems of philosophy. Otherwise, the *Tractatus Logico-Philosophicus* and the *Philosophical Investigations* can be read as attacking much the same problems, just in different ways. This is a topic of considerable controversy, however, especially between **Cora Diamond** and **James Conant**, on the one hand, and fairly orthodox Wittgensteinians, such as **P. M. S. Hacker**, on the other.

CONTRADICTION. In the ***Tractatus Logico-Philosophicus*** Wittgenstein treats contradictions as complements of **tautologies**. Like tautologies, they are without sense, **saying** nothing. Unlike tautologies, which are unconditionally **true**, they are false in all conditions. A **proposition** that is false for all truth-possibilities is a contradiction. "Contradiction is the outer limit of propositions," according to *Tractatus Logico-Philosophicus* 5.143.

In ***Philosophical Investigations*** §125 Wittgenstein writes that *the* philosophical problem is the status of a contradiction in civil life. So contradictions do have special importance for **philosophy**, but are not in themselves necessarily problematic. A contradiction might be perfectly in order (in a game or work of **art**, perhaps). It is contradictions that do harm, that generate **confusion**, that we either do not notice or else refuse to give up, that are the problem. *See also* BIPOLARITY.

CONVENTIONALISM. The view, sometimes attributed to Wittgenstein, that logical **necessity** depends on, or just is, linguistic convention. ***Philosophical Investigations*** §355 says that all **language** is founded on convention. Similarly ***Tractatus Logico-Philosophicus*** 4.002 says that the **understanding** of everyday language depends on tacit conventions. We might infer that Wittgenstein believes that language, including all the **rules** of **grammar** (and hence **logic**), depends on mere human, contingent convention or **agreement**. Alternatively, we might regard such a reading as both inherently implausible (since it seems to make necessity contingent) and blatantly contrary to Wittgenstein's express purpose of mere elucidation. *Tractatus* 4.002 by no means constitutes explicit conventionalism, but *Investigations* §355 is harder to read any other way. It is worth noting, though, that what Wittgenstein means by 'convention' might not be what is ordinarily thought of in connection with this term (just as he uses the idea of agreement in novel ways) and that *Investigations* §372 seems to hold up conventionalism as an example of philosophical thinking gone wrong. He links it there with the apparent **arbitrariness of grammar**.

CRAVING FOR GENERALITY. In the ***Blue Book*** Wittgenstein suggests that it is better to study particular cases, especially relatively simple ones, and to build up thereby a picture of complicated forms of language rather than to try to give general answers to general questions such as, "What are signs?" For example, we might consider a use of signs such as that made by people buying and selling **apples**. We resist this approach, he says, because of what he calls both "the contemptuous attitude towards the particular case" and the "craving for **generality**." This craving comes from four tendencies: a) the tendency to look for something in common shared by all things that fall under the same name (instead of recognizing that they might be united only by a **family resemblance**), b) the tendency to think that if we understand a general term then this means that we have a general image in our minds, like one of **Francis Galton's** composite photographs, c) the tendency to confuse mental states such as toothaches with states of mental mechanisms, and d) our preoccupation with the method of **science**.

CRITERIA. Wittgenstein observes that words are used in accordance with **rules** and that therefore there are certain standards of correctness for a word's use. Since our **language** is shared and one learns it from others, these standards are public, even when one is using words that might seem to refer to an entirely private sphere (**'the inner'**). When someone describes her **pains** or hopes she must do so in accordance with public criteria if others are to **understand** her (and if she is to talk about what others mean when they say 'pain' or 'hope').

Wittgenstein distinguishes between symptoms of such things as pain and defining criteria. Symptoms are contingently related phenomena, as bleeding is related non-necessarily to pain, whereas criteria are necessarily related. For instance, if a substance is found to consist of H_2O molecules, then this is more than a mere symptom of its being water. Being composed of such molecules might be said to be the **essence** of water. In the ***Blue Book***, though, Wittgenstein warns that one should not, as philosophers tend to do, expect everything to have an essence or, in other words, for the distinction between symptoms and criteria to be sharp always in practice. The rules of language need not be strict for it to work perfectly well. Thus criteria in some cases might be necessary and sufficient conditions, in others they might be merely necessary conditions, and in still others they might be necessarily good, but still defeasible, evidence. For instance, if a substance is found to consist of H_2O molecules, then it just is (necessarily) water. If a man is a father, then he must (necessarily) have children (but having children is not *sufficient* to make one a father: women have children too). Or if someone is screaming on the floor, there is (necessarily, definitively) good reason to believe she is in pain, but she could be pretending. Consisting of H_2O molecules, having children, and screaming on the floor in these examples might all be considered criteria. Which of these examples is best, or whether any more than one of them is really an example of what Wittgenstein means by 'criteria,' is a matter of scholarly dispute. The last example seems closest to what Wittgenstein says on the subject, but he was open to different uses of words.

CULTURE AND VALUE. Edited by **G. H. von Wright** in collaboration with Heikki Nyman, these notes date from between 1914 and 1951, when Wittgenstein died. Originally published in German as *Vermischte Bemerkungen* (Miscellaneous Remarks), the book contains Wittgenstein's thoughts on a variety of subjects implied by the English title, including **religion** and the **arts**. It is much easier to read than his philosophical work but still relevant to it, providing some sense of what motivated him and including a number of thoughts about **philosophy** itself. A new translation of the book by Alois Pichler was published in 1994, which includes a **poem** thought to have been written by Wittgenstein.

D

DARWIN, CHARLES (1809–1882). Wittgenstein was not convinced by Darwin's **theory** of evolution. It was too simple, too reductionistic, for his taste. He also insisted that the evidence for it was too thin and that people believed it because they felt that somehow it *must* be right, largely because of its simplicity. It should be noted that Wittgenstein was no creationist, either, and that more evidence has been found in favor of evolution since his death in 1951. The main source for his views on evolution is a remark he makes in his lectures on **aesthetics** (see LC pp. 26–27) in which he is interested in the **psychology** of **belief** in theories that strike people as *obviously* right. Although the subject of the lectures is aesthetics, he is at this point in the midst of a discussion of **Sigmund Freud** and how his theories can be so persuasive. Theories like Freud's and Darwin's, Wittgenstein suggests, are not necessarily false but are much more readily accepted than is warranted by what evidence there is in their favor.

DEATH. In the ***Tractatus Logico-Philosophicus*** propositions 6.431–6.4312 Wittgenstein briefly discusses death and its relation to the life of the **self** or **soul**. He describes death here not as an event in the lives of those who are left behind but from the subjective point of view. In this sense, he says, death is not something that any subject experiences (although dying might be). Rather, it is the termination of such experiences. One no more experiences death than one sees the edge of one's visual field.

Wittgenstein's own death came on 29 April 1951, caused by prostate cancer. He was treated by Dr. Edward Bevan and moved into Dr. and Mrs. Bevan's home, "Storeys End," for the last few months of his life. There he wrote much of ***On Certainty***. It was to Joan Bevan, who had told him that some of his friends were coming to see him, that Wittgenstein said his last words: "Tell them I've had a **wonderful** life."

DEFINITION. Many **analytic** philosophers look not so much for a dictionary definition of a word as for the **essence** of a **concept**. **Bertrand Russell** maintained that dictionaries offer descriptions of **meanings** rather than meanings themselves, since the meaning of 'red,' for instance, is a certain kind of **object** or sense-datum, not a collection of words such as one finds in a dictionary definition. The goal of defining a word is related, however, to that of analyzing a concept, since a definition is something like a description of essence. This is philosophy in the tradition of **Socrates** and **Plato**. At least in his later work, Wittgenstein set himself against this tradition. He did not deny that essences can be found but challenged the assumption that there must be an essence corresponding to every concept, and he worked to subvert this **picture** of **language** and **the world**.

See also OSTENSIVE DEFINITION.

DESCARTES, RENÉ (1596–1650). A French philosopher and mathematician, generally regarded as the father of modern **philosophy**. In his *Meditations on First Philosophy* Descartes attempted to start philosophy afresh, assuming no knowledge and accepting only what he could prove to himself to be true beyond doubt. From such an epistemologically secure **foundation**, he claimed to prove that the **mind** is distinct from, and better known than, the body, and that God exists. The Cartesian picture of the mind and its contents as constituting a special kind of object is one of Wittgenstein's main targets, especially in his later work. Wittgenstein also rejects the idea that the existence of God is a kind of hypothesis that might be proved or disproved (he has a different conception of what **religion** is about) and the attempt to provide the kind of epistemological foundation that Descartes sought.

DESCRIPTION. Early (in the ***Notes on Logic***) and late (***Philosophical Investigations*** §109) Wittgenstein maintained that philosophers should provide descriptions, not deductions or **logical inferences**. This goes hand in hand with his goal of clarification or, put another way, the battle against **confusion**. ***Tractatus Logico-Philosophicus*** proposition 6.53 says that the only strictly correct method in **philosophy** would be to state only **propositions** of natural **science**, in other words, descriptions of **the world**. This method, Wittgenstein acknowledges, would not be satisfactory, however. Instead, the *Tractatus* sets out to elucidate the **logic** of our **language**. This is more a kind of perspicuous presentation than a description.

Something similar though, but without the use of a **concept-script**, is what Wittgenstein does in the *Investigations*, and there he does call it description. The description he says that he offers there is of "the workings of our language" (§109) so as to make us recognize their logic or **grammar**. This is not a scientific or **anthropological** description of the phenomenon (or phenomena) of language then. The purpose of the 'description' comes from the particular philosophical problems with which one is dealing. The goal is not a complete account of all grammar but a clearer view of those areas that cause trouble. And it is clear to any reader of the *Investigations* that what Wittgenstein offers as descriptions, for instance in the cases of the **builders** and the person buying **apples**, are not straightforward accounts of everyday uses of language.

DETERMINACY OF SENSE. In the ***Tractatus Logico-Philosophicus*** proposition 3.24 Wittgenstein writes that when an element of a **proposition** signifies a complex, some combination of simple **objects**, there is a vagueness, an indeterminacy, of the proposition's sense. The suggestion appears to be that there cannot be any indeterminacy in **the world**: its components must be arranged in some particular way or other. (**Arthur Schopenhauer** uses a similar idea as a premise in his **argument** against **free will**.) If this is so, and if **language** mirrors the world in **pictures**, then it too must contain at most apparent indeterminacy. A proposition containing vagueness, then, must stand in need of further analysis. Wittgenstein does not explain why this should be so, but he may have simply taken the idea over from **Gottlob Frege**. White suggests that it is helpful to read *Tractatus* 3.24 in connection with pp. 59–71 of the ***Notebooks 1914–1916***.

In Wittgenstein's later work he seems to be more accepting of the idea of vagueness, or indeterminacy, in language. The very idea of determinacy can itself be regarded as vague, having only a relative or context-dependent **meaning**. In some contexts or for some purposes two pints is a precise measure, but for others it might be hopelessly vague.

DIAMOND, CORA ANN (1937–). An American philosopher who studied under **G. E. M. Anscombe** and later taught at the University of Virginia. Diamond is a noted ethicist, and studies **Gottlob Frege** as well as Wittgenstein. Within the field of Wittgenstein studies she is best known, as is her philosophical ally **James Conant**, for espousing the "resolute" or "austere" reading of what Wittgenstein means by his various references to **nonsense** (using the German words '*Unsinn*,' '*sinnlos*,' and '*bedeutungslos*' and their cognates) in the ***Tractatus Logico-Philosophicus***. Thus Diamond is a key figure among the so-called new or American Wittgensteinians.

Diamond's view is that Wittgenstein really meant that the **ladder** of his propositions should be thrown away (as he puts it in proposition 6.54) because they are not only without sense in a somewhat technical way but because they are genuinely nonsensical. Thus, in her view, Wittgenstein did not put forward one set of **theories** in the *Tractatus* and then attack them in the ***Philosophical Investigations*** (perhaps to replace them with another, as is generally believed). Rather, the *Tractatus* itself undermines the very theories it appears to be advocating. This reading is controversial, and has been attacked most notably by **P. M. S. Hacker** in his contribution to *The New Wittgenstein* (edited by Alice Crary and Rupert Read, 2000) and elsewhere since.

Diamond has also written influential papers on the relation between theory, **argument**, literature and ethics, and in defense of animals. Many of her best papers are collected in her book *The Realistic Spirit* (1991), and she is the editor of *Wittgenstein's Lectures on the Foundations of Mathematics* (1976).

DISCIPLES. Throughout his life Wittgenstein attracted and was attracted to various people, usually men and usually at least slightly younger than himself, who are often referred to as "disciples" of his. These were certainly close friends, but given the controversy surrounding claims about Wittgenstein's **sexuality**, there is little agreement or clarity about whether any of them was more than this. Those who knew Wittgenstein best have tended to insist that he was ascetic. The philosophical biographer Ray Monk also points to evidence that the objects of Wittgenstein's affection were sometimes quite unaware of the strength of his feelings for them. The clearest case of a disciple who was also a lover is **Francis Skinner**, with whom Wittgenstein wrote in his diary that he "lay" several times (see Monk p. 376).

The first of all these disciples seems to have been Arvid Sjögren. There is no evidence of this having been a sexual relationship at all. Sjögren's father was the director of a steelworks belonging to the Wittgenstein group, and the two families were on friendly terms. In November 1919, Wittgenstein moved in with the Sjögrens at their house in **Vienna's** Thirteenth District. Under Wittgenstein's influence, their middle son, Arvid, decided to train as a mechanic rather than attend a university. He later visited Wittgenstein when he was teaching in **Trattenbach** and traveled to Yugoslavia in order to get false passports for Hermine and Helene **Wittgenstein**.

DOSTOEVSKY, FYODOR MIKHAILOVICH (1821–1881). A great **Russian** novelist, journalist, and short-story writer. Dostoevsky's novels combine autobiography with **philosophy**, his characters taking different positions with regard to such issues as **free will**, **religion**, politics, and **ethics**. During his imprisonment in Siberia for being a socialist, Dostoevsky became a monarchist and a devout Russian Orthodox **Christian**. He was one of Wittgenstein's favorite authors. Wittgenstein read *The Brothers Karamazov* so often that he knew large parts of it by heart, and it was one of the very few possessions that he took with him to the front in 1916. He was particularly impressed by the saintly and wise character Father Zosima, who through years of experience of listening to and advising people had gained almost supernatural psychological insight. The example of Zosima shows how it is possible to be a good Christian despite the powerful case against it presented by Ivan Karamazov. It is Ivan who believes that if God does not exist, then nothing is forbidden, a thought later developed by Wittgenstein's student **G. E. M. Anscombe**, who attacked all godless, modern ethical theories as empty or corrupt. In the same novel (in chapter 11 of Book Three), Dmitri Karamazov is described as hitting his chest as if his dishonor were an object in a bag hanging round his neck, which perhaps helped inspire Wittgenstein's idea of the **beetle in the box**.

DREAMS. In ***Remarks on the Philosophy of Psychology*** *Volume I* §935 Wittgenstein asks rather rhetorically whether the verb 'to dream' has a present tense (see ***Zettel*** §399). One could never learn how to use this tense correctly, or perhaps, rather, one could never learn that one were not using it correctly. No one can correct a sleeper. Instead, the verb is used almost exclusively in the past tense and learned from people who must take one's word for it that one dreamed what one says one dreamed (although of course sometimes lies can be detected and then one might be corrected). The point is that, as with the **beetle in the box**, there is no **object** against which to check one's own memory of a dream or someone else's report of her dream. In this sense dreams are not like films, which do exist as public objects. A dream, Wittgenstein might say, is not a something but not a nothing either (as he says of other **inner** 'objects' such as **pains**). This claim would be based not on an investigation of dreams but on how one learns to use the word 'dream' and what counts as a meaningful use of it.

DRURY, MAURICE O'CONNOR (1907–1976). A student at **Cambridge** who met Wittgenstein in 1929 and followed his advice first to leave theological college, then to study medicine, and then to specialize in psychiatry. He is the author of *The Danger of Words* (essays on **philosophy** and psychiatry) and a valuable memoir of conversations with Wittgenstein. He and Wittgenstein remained friends until the latter's death.

DUCK-RABBIT (ANALOGY OF). *See* ASPECT-SEEING.

DUMMETT, MICHAEL ANTHONY EARDLEY (1925–2011). A leading British antirealist philosopher and **Gottlob Frege** scholar. Dummett took the Wittgensteinian view that **understanding** the **meaning** of a sentence must be something like an ability or tendency to behave in certain kinds of ways. It is not a purely **inner**, private state or process but must instead have publicly observable **criteria**. Thus the understanding of **truth**, of what it would mean for a sentence to be true or false, is **internally related** to the capacity for such **behavior**. The concept of truth cannot refer to something wholly independent of human beings. Therefore, truth cannot be wholly independent of human beings.

It is easy to see how such antirealism seems to fit Wittgenstein's views on **language** and behavior, but there is some reason to doubt that he would have accepted either **realism** or its opposite. His characteristic response to similar philosophical debates was to reject both horns of the apparent dilemma as resting on a common misconception or **confusion**.

Dummett was the Wykeham Professor of Logic at Oxford from 1979 until his retirement in 1992. He was knighted in 1999. He wrote numerous books, including *Frege: Philosophy of Language* (1973), *Truth and Other Enigmas* (1978), *The Interpretation of Frege's Philosophy* (1981), *Frege and Other Philosophers* (1991), *Frege: Philosophy of Mathematics* (1991), *The Logical Basis of Metaphysics* (1991), *Origins of Analytical Philosophy* (1993), and *The Seas of Language* (1993).

E

ELEMENTARY PROPOSITIONS. Elementary **propositions** are introduced in the ***Tractatus Logico-Philosophicus*** as the simplest propositions there can be, asserting the existence of atomic **facts**. Elementary propositions are combinations of the **names** of absolutely simple **objects**. Since these names only have **meaning** within a proposition, it is these elementary propositions that are the basic units of **language**. Thus all meaning depends on them. According to proposition 5 of the *Tractatus Logico-Philosophicus*, all propositions are **truth-functions** of elementary propositions, with elementary propositions being truth-functions of themselves. Thus all **truth**, in this sense, depends on elementary propositions. No elementary proposition can contradict or be inferred from any other. Every statement of fact is thus independent of every other, just as every individual **state of affairs** is independent of every other. These, then, the *Tractatus* asks us to believe, are the basic units of reality, truth, and meaning. Unfortunately, Wittgenstein tells us little more than this. He gives no examples, for instance, of such units.

Later, in the ***Philosophical Grammar***, he says that "Here there is a red rose" is an example of a sentence that fits the *Tractatus*'s account of an elementary proposition. But from this one *can* infer something, for instance that "here there is not a green rose." So it fits the account only in one way, namely of being a proposition that does not contain a truth-function and that is not defined by an expression that contains one. The *Philosophical Grammar* rejects what the *Tractatus* says as being the result of unclear thinking. Apparently Wittgenstein had thought that **logical analysis** ought to be able to break complex propositions down into simple components that, being quite simple, should be logically independent of one another. But, he came to think, that there is something wrong with this idea is shown by the fact that one cannot say what it means. Wittgenstein was never able to give any examples of the objects to which he refers or of their names, which are supposed to make up elementary propositions. Thus he could give no examples of the elementary propositions into which all other propositions are meant to be analyzable. Later, in the ***Philosophical Investigations*** (§126 for instance), he said that there is nothing hidden in our propositions that something called 'logical analysis' might bring out.

ELUCIDATION. ***Tractatus Logico-Philosophicus*** proposition 3.263 says that the **meanings** of primitive **signs** can be explained through elucidations, and that these elucidations, which are **propositions** containing the signs in question, can only be understood by someone already familiar with the meaning of the signs. This does not sound very helpful. It is echoed in proposition 6.54, which tells us that Wittgenstein's propositions elucidate in the following way: whoever understands him ultimately perceives his propositions as nonsensical. It also calls to mind the first sentence of the foreword, in which Wittgenstein suggests that his book might be understood only by someone who has already had similar thoughts of her own.

White (p. 61) suggests that '*Erläuterungen*' be translated as "illustrative examples" rather than "elucidations." To teach someone the meaning of a name we must use the name in sample sentences, since merely pointing to the object does not define how the name is to be applied. "We must then leave it to chance whether the other catches on to the meanings of those sentences, which is something that can only be done by grasping the meaning of the name."

G. E. M. Anscombe (p. 26) suggests that this passage, along with 3.261, provides the best evidence for thinking that the elementary propositions of the *Tractatus* are simple observation statements, such as "This is a red patch." Names and only names are primitive signs. Logical signs, as Wittgenstein indicates elsewhere, are not primitive signs. But what elucidates a name need not be an elementary proposition (see Anscombe p. 27). And from 6.3751 it follows directly that "This is a red patch" cannot be an elementary proposition. Anscombe concludes that elementary propositions are not simple observation statements, and that this explains why Wittgenstein did not refer to observation in connection with them. What they are he cannot say, but they must exist. See, for instance, 5.5562, in which he suggests that we know on logical grounds that there must be elementary propositions. In 4.221 he does more than suggest this, asserting that it is obvious that analyzing propositions must lead us to elementary propositions.

EMPIRICISM. An approach to **philosophy** that can be traced back to **Aristotle** but that is especially associated with British philosophy, particularly during the time of **John Locke** and **David Hume**. The basic empiricist idea is that knowledge should be (or just is) based on experience rather than reason, as rationalists such as **René Descartes** have it. This is not a rejection of reason, but a decision about the starting point for philosophical inquiry. Reason is treated by empiricists as a useful tool, but not by itself a means to discover interesting **truths** *a priori*.

Empiricism can seem to be a commonsensical approach to philosophy, but philosophical analyses of experience often lead to **skeptical** doubts about how one can know anything but one's own subjective experience, and hence to **solipsism**. Wittgenstein's mentor **Bertrand Russell** was a philosopher in the empiricist tradition.

ENGELMANN, PAUL (1891–1965). An **architect** who studied with **Adolf Loos**. It was Loos who introduced Wittgenstein to Engelmann in 1916. He had been invalided out of the army a few days after joining it in 1915 and later became a pacifist. During the rest of **World War I** he helped **Karl Kraus** produce his satirical journal ***Die Fackel***. Later Engelmann and Wittgenstein became architectural partners and together designed a house for Wittgenstein's sister **Gretl** in 1925–1926.

Engelmann writes interestingly about Wittgenstein in his *Letters from Wittgenstein with a Memoir*, especially regarding questions of **value**. For instance, he shared Wittgenstein's admiration for the **poem** "Graf Eberhard's Weissdorn" ("Count Eberhard's Hawthorn") by Ludwig Uhland. Wittgenstein wrote to Engelmann that this poem shows something without trying to **say** it and thus achieves its purpose in the only possible way, a magnificent way. In the poem Uhland tells of a man who lives in patient harmony with a tree, perhaps in the spirit in which **Martin Heidegger** wanted people to live with nature. Any such summary or commentary though is likely to try to say what, according to Wittgenstein, could only be shown and thus miss what he would consider to be the whole point. A somewhat similar image, linking human life and struggle with nature (indeed with plant life) frames **Leo Tolstoy's** novella *Hadji Murad*, which Wittgenstein admired greatly.

ESSENCE AND ESSENTIALISM. Essence can be understood in terms of necessary and sufficient conditions. A necessary condition is a condition that something, call it *x*, must meet in order to be a thing of a certain kind, say, a shark. Being a fish is a necessary condition for being a shark (since all sharks are fish). But if *x* is a fish, it might not be shark, so being a fish is not a *sufficient* condition for being a shark. Being a great white, on the other hand, is a sufficient condition for being a shark (all great whites are sharks) but not a necessary one (since not all sharks are great whites). If we know the necessary and sufficient conditions for being a shark, then we know the essence of sharks. Any other feature that a shark might have, the exact contents of its stomach, say, would be merely 'accidental' (irrelevant to its being a shark).

Since **Socrates**, philosophers have tried to identify the necessary and sufficient conditions or essences of **truth**, justice, knowledge, the **soul**, and the like. Wittgenstein described his work as being, in a way, the opposite. He tried to show not so much what all things that go by the same **name** have in common but rather how they differ. He is thus generally regarded as an anti-essentialist, denying that there are any essences. His notion of **family resemblances** is relevant as an alternative to the traditional idea of essences.

Not everyone reads Wittgenstein this way, however. He does not explicitly deny that there are essences, and his best-known remark on the subject, "*Essence* is expressed by grammar" (***Philosophical Investigations*** §371), can be interpreted as implying that there *is* such a thing as essence. Presumably essence so conceived would not be of the **Platonic** kind, but Wittgenstein does not say. He could conceive of essence as belonging to **concepts** and thus being **logical** rather than **metaphysical**. Or he could, as some people think, be a linguistic **idealist**, which would blur the distinction between the conceptual/logical and the metaphysical.

ETHICS. Wittgenstein did not write or lecture much on ethics. He advanced no theory such as **utilitarianism**. Indeed, when he did once **lecture on ethics** (in 1929), he said that "the tendency of all men who ever tried to write or talk Ethics or **Religion** was to run against the boundaries of **language**," that is to talk or write **nonsense** (PO p. 44). In his conversations with **O. K. Bouwsma** he suggests that there is no point in philosophers trying to teach ethics: they will either preach, which is not their business, or else they will produce trivial or distorted **theories** (talk nonsense, in other words).

As a man, though, Wittgenstein was constantly concerned with ethics. He wanted desperately to be decent, indeed perfect, and was pained by the feeling that this was impossible for him. His main vices, he seems to have felt, were vanity (especially in connection with his intellect), laziness, cowardice (although he was decorated for bravery in **World War I**), and dishonesty (which was apparently the main subject of his well-known **confession** to his friends and family). Others have condemned him, when they have, more for his rudeness, which perhaps Wittgenstein would have put down to their bourgeois values and failure to understand why it was so important for him to behave as he did. Examples of such rudeness would include dominating discussions and being painfully blunt when criticizing his friends. He did not believe in condemning or praising anyone for their nature (which suggests that it is a mistake to think that he was tormented about his **homosexuality**, especially since his sexuality seems to have been rather ambiguous and minimal).

In both his philosophical work and in his personal life, Wittgenstein's thinking on ethics is tied up with his thoughts on religion. He had a lifelong interest in religion and claimed to see every problem from a religious point of view, although he never committed himself to any formal religion. His various remarks on ethics also suggest a particular point of view, and Wittgenstein often spoke of ethics and religion together. This point of view or attitude can be seen in the four main themes that run through his writings on ethics and religion: goodness, **value** or **meaning** are not to be found in **the world**; living the right way involves acceptance of, or **agreement** with, the world, or life, or God's **will**, or fate; one who lives this way will see the world as a miracle; and there is no answer to the problem of life, rather the solution is the disappearance of the problem.

In 1929 Wittgenstein gave a lecture on ethics to a student organization at **Cambridge** called the **Heretics Society**. In this lecture he identifies ethics with **aesthetics** as well as religion, suggesting that all three have to do with experiences that we feel are supremely important. He gives three examples of the kind of feelings he has in mind. The least surprising of these, which is often overlooked, is the feeling of guilt. Certain kinds of action make us feel bad when we do them, but rather than try to get rid of these bad feelings, as we would with a headache, we value the feelings as intimately related to something important, namely ethics. The rational thing would seem to be to try to take some kind of moral aspirin, which no doubt some people do in one way or another, but that is not what we think of as the right thing to do.

Another example that Wittgenstein gives is the feeling of **wonder** at the very existence of the world. Being able to sense, whether what we sense is pleasurable or painful, seems good to us, perhaps most obviously when we think about being able to see. Of course, sight is useful, but even if it did you no good at all, it is something you would probably still want very much to have. This comes out in Shakespeare's play *King Lear*, which Wittgenstein wanted to quote in the motto to a book he planned to write, and which also contains the idea that life is a miracle to be treasured, no matter how badly things might go. This wonder at the existence of the world, at being able to see, or sense, or be conscious, or alive, at the fact that there is something rather than nothing, is often said to be the beginning of philosophy. For some philosophers it has been the end too, the goal of their work being to bring this feeling back into a world whose increasing rationality seems to them to be stifling it.

The other feeling that Wittgenstein talks about is the feeling of being absolutely safe. This might relate to belief in immortality. **Socrates** famously said while he was awaiting execution that a good person cannot be harmed. Perhaps he felt absolutely safe. No *real* harm could come to him, he seems to have believed, even if he was made to drink poison until he died. Belief in life after **death** is very familiar, of course, but we all know that when you are dead you are dead. So what can "life after death" mean? Well, what can it mean to think that it is ever good to feel bad? What can it mean to value a life in which you lose everything you ever had and loved, to love life despite its very worst contents?

Rather than try to explain the meaning of such feelings, or the sentences that we produce when we try to express them, Wittgenstein rejects the idea of reconciling value with sense. All rational talk of value can only ever be in terms of what will satisfy our various preferences most efficiently, he believes. So talk of real value, the kind of value that actually has value, can only be nonsense. Wittgenstein accepts this, encourages others to accept it too, without trying to wriggle out of it by pretending that nonsense can make sense after all or contain profound truths. If we are to avoid hypocrisy, sentimentality, bad taste, and wishful thinking, then we must accept that we cannot express the feelings that give our lives a sense of meaning or value. We should make no attempt to do so. This does not mean, though, that we should have different feelings (how could we?) or live as someone would who had no such feelings (why should we?).

Certainly Wittgenstein worried about being morally good, and he had great respect for sincere religious conviction. This, combined with his remark about nonsense quoted above, gives support to the view that Wittgenstein believed in **mystical truths** that somehow cannot be expressed meaningfully but that are of the utmost importance. It is hard to conceive, though, what these 'truths' might be. An alternative view is that Wittgenstein believed that there is really nothing to say about ethics. This would explain why he wrote less and less about ethics as his life wore on. His "accept and endure" attitude, as **Cora Diamond** calls it, and belief in going "the bloody hard way" are evident in all his work, especially after the ***Tractatus Logico-Philosophicus*** (see Rhees pp. 169–172). Wittgenstein wants his reader not to think (too much) but to look at the **language-games** (any practices that involve language) that give rise to philosophical (personal, existential, or spiritual) problems. His approach to such problems is painstaking, thorough, open-eyed, and receptive. He seems to have believed that this was the way to approach any problem in life, or perhaps the world itself.

There is little that one can say about such an attitude short of recommending it though, as Wittgenstein sees things. In a world of contingency one cannot prove that a particular attitude is the correct one to take. If this suggests **relativism**, it should be remembered that it too is just one more attitude or point of view and one without the rich tradition and accumulated wisdom, philosophical reasoning, and personal experience of, say, orthodox **Christianity** or **Judaism**. Indeed, crude relativism, the universal judgment that one cannot make universal judgments, is self-contradictory. Whether Wittgenstein's views suggest a more sophisticated form of relativism is another matter, but the spirit of relativism seems far from Wittgenstein's **conservatism** and absolute intolerance of his own moral shortcomings. Compare the tolerance that motivates relativism with Wittgenstein's assertion to **Bertrand Russell** that he would prefer "by far" an organization dedicated to war and slavery to one dedicated to peace and freedom (see Schulte p. 23). This assertion should not be taken literally: Wittgenstein was not a warmonger and even recommended letting oneself be massacred rather than taking part in hand-to-hand combat. It was apparently the complacency, and perhaps the self-righteousness, of Russell's liberal cause to which Wittgenstein objected so strongly.

Wittgensteinian ethics is a highly controversial field, however. Paul Johnston and **D. Z. Phillips** read him as a kind of neo-**Kantian**, believing in absolute right and wrong. Others, influenced perhaps by **G. E. M. Anscombe** and Wittgenstein's considerations of **rule-following**, interpret him as being closer to **Aristotle**. **Stanley Cavell's** Wittgensteinian values are different again.

The best sources for Wittgenstein's personal ethics are Ray Monk's biography, **Bouwsma's** recollections, and ***Ludwig Wittgenstein: Public and Private Occasions***. The best sources for his more philosophical thoughts on ethics are the ***Notebooks 1914–1916***, the *Tractatus*, the lecture on ethics (in ***Philosophical Occasions***), and ***Culture and Value***.

See also REALISM AND ANTIREALISM.

EXPLANATION. In ***Philosophical Investigations*** Wittgenstein says that what is needed is not an explanation, although that is what philosophers think they need, but a **description** in order to solve problems in philosophy (or to dissolve or remove them). Explanations belong to **science**, not to **logic**, he suggests. One knows what **negation**, say, is if one knows how to use the **concept** of negation. And philosophers do know this already. They might feel the need for an explanation, but in fact what they need is a reminder of how the word is used. Wittgenstein attributed the inspiration for this approach to **Heinrich Hertz** and repeatedly emphasized its importance (for instance, see p. 379 and p. 399 of PPO). In **philosophy**, according to the later Wittgenstein, there are no mysteries waiting to be uncovered, as the ***Tractatus Logico-Philosophicus*** might imply. There is instead only a false sense of mystery (that is to say, **confusion**) waiting to be dispelled.

EXTERNAL PROPERTIES. In 2.01231 of the ***Tractatus Logico-Philosophicus*** Wittgenstein distinguishes between the internal and external properties of **objects**. In **proposition** 4.123 he writes: "A property is internal if it is unthinkable that its object should not possess it." According to **G. E. M. Anscombe**, "The only 'external properties' his [i.e., Wittgenstein's] simple objects can have, of course, are those of actually occurring in certain facts" (p. 111).

Marie McGinn (p. 152) says that Wittgenstein's point, as she sees it, is that if two objects are really simple, then the difference between them cannot be given by definitions. "Red" and "blue" refer to exactly the same kind of thing, namely **colors**. Of course different things are red than are blue, but these are external differences between red and blue. Apart from these, the only difference between them is that they are different colors.

F

FACE, IDEA OF. *See* PHYSIOGNOMY.

***FACKEL DIE* (JOURNAL).** *Die Fackel* (The Torch) was an influential magazine published every two weeks by **Karl Kraus** in Vienna. It ran from 1899 to 1936, satirizing what Kraus took to be shoddy uses of **language**, reflecting shoddy thinking. 'Shoddy' here means sloppy and/or wicked, or (perhaps better) wicked out of sloppiness, thoughtless. Wittgenstein liked the journal so much that he had it sent to him even while he was in Norway.

It was an article in *Die Fackel* about **Ludwig von Ficker** that brought Ficker to Wittgenstein's attention. When he was getting rid of his inherited fortune, Wittgenstein gave 100,000 crowns to Ficker to distribute among Austrian artists in need, 10,000 of which were to go to Ficker's own journal *Die Brenner* (The Burner).

FACTS. ***Tractatus Logico-Philosophicus*** proposition 1.1 says that "**The world** is the totality of facts." Black (p. 27) says that this distinction is "the outstanding innovation of Wittgenstein's ontology," distinguishing him from all the most famous philosophers from **Aristotle** to the early **Bertrand Russell**. The universe is implicitly not a thing, not something that can be referred to by a name. Black takes Wittgenstein's references to "the world" to mean the universe, explaining that this use is more common in German than it is in English.

A fact is defined in the *Tractatus* as the existence of a **state of affairs** or combination of **objects**. The world is not simply the totality of objects that exist, since these objects exist in particular relations with each other, just as a room is not identical merely with the contents of the room (even if the walls, floor, and ceiling are included in the contents). Those contents must always be in some arrangement, even if it is a messy heap. This 'must' is not the kind that goes with an 'or else . . .' but the must of logical **necessity**. It is unthinkable for objects to exist in no relation whatsoever to each other, whether this relation be spatial, temporal, or some other, such as the 'darker than/lighter than' relations of **colors**.

So the basic unit or atom of Wittgenstein's ontology here is the fact or state of affairs (not the object), just as the basic unit of **meaning** according to the *Tractatus* is the sentence or **proposition** (not the word). Even if only one object existed, the possibility of there being others with which it might combine in some state of affairs would still exist. And it is possibility that concerns **logic**, and logic that concerns Wittgenstein. (A concern with what, from all the possibilities, is in fact the case is scientific.) Every object has within it its possibilities for combining with others, and there is no object that lacks such possibility (see proposition 2.0121). Objects are independent of each other in the sense that they can combine with various other objects in all possible states of affairs, but they are in a sense dependent on states of affairs, since they must always be in one or another.

Facts or existing states of affairs (propositions 1.1 and 2.04 imply that they are the very same thing, the world being said to be all of each of them) are also independent of one another (see 2.061) but must exist in **logical space**. (So too, therefore, must the objects that make them up, which is why these objects must always relate to each other in some way.) The dimensions of logical space Wittgenstein calls the forms of objects (see 2.0251). This space is the realm of all possible states of affairs, both the real and the merely conceivable. **Science** discovers which possibilities are the case, while logic charts the realm of possibility. This is closely related to the realm of meaningful propositions (or just propositions since no genuine proposition is **nonsense**), the latter picturing the former.

According to the **picture theory** a **thought** is a picture of a fact (see 3), and a proposition is a perceptible expression of such a picture (see 3.1). 2.141 says though that a picture *is* a fact. So a thought is both a fact and a picture of a fact. Proposition 3.12 says that a propositional **sign** ('*Satzzeichen*') is the sign with which we express a thought. Proposition 3.14 says that a propositional sign is a fact too. Such a sign need not consist of words but could, for instance, be an arrangement of furniture (see 3.1431). Someone might leave a book on a chair as a sign to another to leave her book on her chair. Or a book on a chair might mean "Flee, the police are on to us." Clearly any such arrangement of objects is itself a state of affairs as well as the representation of a state of affairs (wanting another to flee, say).

One might **wonder** how one fact *means* another. It does so by picturing, Wittgenstein says, which is done by sharing the **logical form** (or pictorial form or logico-pictorial form) of what is pictured (see 2.18, 2.181, and 2.2). Such form is shared, for instance, by a piece of music, the notation with which that music is written down, and a recording, in any medium, of that piece of music (see 4.014). A proposition (truly or falsely) declares or asserts its **truth** (but cannot show itself to be true) and shows its sense, how things are if it is true (but cannot ***say*** what this is) according to 4.022. That is, a proposition is a picture or model of reality (see 4.010), a kind of claim about how things are. The facts determine whether any such claim is true or false, but the picture remains what it is nonetheless. Its sense, or content, remains the same (see 4.061).

One might further wonder how this can be true, given that an arrangement of furniture can be a propositional sign. When, one might ask, is a book on a chair just a book on a chair? **Norman Malcolm** suggests a possible answer to this question with his interpretation of Wittgenstein's remarks on the **method of projection**. In Malcolm's view a mental act gives meaning to a proposition. So a book on a chair that is not intended by anyone to have a meaning has no meaning. This interpretation is not without its own problems, however. Another possible answer is suggested by propositions 3.326–3.328, which link the meaning of symbols with their use or employment. (3.32–3.322 make clear that what signs we use is arbitrary and that it is symbols that really matter when it comes to meaning.) If this controversial answer is correct, then Wittgenstein's early views on meaning were remarkably close to his later thoughts on the subject.

Facts of logic might be thought to belong to a different class from facts about the world. They can be inferred from one another, for instance, and so are not independent of each other. However, since propositions of logic do not depict states of affairs, they in fact say nothing at all, according to Wittgenstein (see 5.43). They might show **logical form**, but they are not propositions in the full sense. The truths of **mathematics** and logic are not verified by checking them against reality. In this sense they are what Wittgenstein later called **grammatical** propositions.

Gottlob Frege has a notion of fact that is worth bearing in mind here. "A fact is a thought that is true" (Beaney, p. 342). Thoughts are imperceptible. We may see the sun rise, but we do not in the same sense see *that* the sun rises. That the sun is rising, is a thought. The sentence "The sun is rising" expresses this thought. Thoughts are not external, perceptible objects, but neither are they **private**, subjective, individual, psychological ideas. "A third realm must be recognized," Frege says (see p. 337).

Frege asked Wittgenstein how "The world is the totality of facts" differs from "The world is everything that is the case." Wittgenstein's reply was: "The meaning of these two sentences are one and the same but not the conceptions (*Vorstellungen*) that *I* associated with them when I wrote them down." (This is in a letter quoted in Nordmann p. 124, note 70.)

Ostrow (p. 23) quotes Wittgenstein later saying to Desmond Lee that the opening of the *Tractatus* says: "The world does not consist of a catalogue of things and facts about them (like a catalogue of a show). . . . What the world is is given by description and not by a list of objects" (WLC p. 119). At 4.1272 Wittgenstein calls the concept of an object a pseudo-concept.

In his *Notebooks* Wittgenstein wrote that "Properties and relations are objects too" (16/6/1915). And, as Ostrow notes (p. 49), in 1930–1931 Wittgenstein is reported to have said that, "'Objects' also include relations: a proposition is not two things connected by a relation. 'Thing' and 'relation' are on the same level. The objects hang as it were in a chain" (WLC p. 120). Frascolla says (p. 79) that the point about the chain is that there are no such things as "relations" that relate or connect things/objects. The work that might be thought to be done by something called "relations" is (already) done by what Wittgenstein calls "objects."

FAMILY RESEMBLANCE. In §67 of the ***Philosophical Investigations*** Wittgenstein introduces the important concept of family resemblance. He suggests that there need not be any one thing held in common by all things that go by the same **name** in virtue of which we apply that name to them. He gives the examples of **language** and games. Some games involve balls, others do not. Some involve boards, others do not. Some are played just for fun, others are not. And so on. They might have some features in common, such as having **rules** perhaps or involving animate beings in some way, but these features are shared by things that are not games. There need be, in other words, no necessary and sufficient conditions that define exactly what is and what is not a game. Instead, people call things games that strike them as being relevantly similar to some, but not necessarily all, members of the family of games.

The notion of family resemblance can be seen to replace the concept of **essence**, but Wittgenstein does not say that all concepts are family resemblance concepts. The clearest example of a philosopher who would be expected to disagree is **Plato**, who seems to have believed that all games, for instance, must have something in common, namely their resemblance of, or participation in, the Form of the Game. Wittgenstein introduces the idea of **language-games** not to deny that such Forms exist, but to loosen the grip of the idea that some such things *must* exist.

FICKER, LUDWIG VON (1880–1967). The editor of a **Krausian** journal called *Die Brenner* (The Burner) published in Innsbruck. Wittgenstein tried to persuade Ficker to publish the ***Tractatus Logico-Philosophicus*** in *Die Brenner*, telling him that the important part of the book was all that was not written in it, that the book avoided all gassing (*das Schwefeln*), and that it drew limits to the sphere of the **ethical** in the only rigorous way possible, from the inside. Ficker declined to publish it himself, fearing the financial implications and, possibly, not understanding the book. He did try to help Wittgenstein find a publisher, however.

In 1914 Wittgenstein donated 10,000 crowns to Ficker for the journal and asked him to distribute another 90,000 to Austrian artists in need. The beneficiaries included **Rainer Maria Rilke**, Georg Trakl, and Carl Dallago (20,000 crowns each); Karl Hauer and **Oskar Kokoschka** (5,000 each); Else Lasker-Schüler (4,000); **Adolf Loos**, Theodor Haecker, Theodor Däubler, Ludwig Erik Tesar, Richard Weiss, and Franz Kranewitter (2,000 each); and Hermann Wagner, Josef Oberkofler, Karl Heinrich, and Hugo Neugebauer (1,000 each).

FIDEISM. Followers of Wittgenstein, such as D. Z. Phillips, have been accused, most notably by Kai Nielsen, of a kind of fideism, that is, the belief that **religion** is immune from criticism on grounds of irrationality. This is either because it is a distinct **language-game** with its own **rules** or because faith is really a matter of certain forms of **behavior** and feeling that lie beyond the reach of rational critique. It might be irrational to believe in a being for whose existence there is insufficient evidence, but it cannot be irrational to kneel on Sundays (assuming one wants to do so) or to sing various songs. If religion is a matter of behaving in ways like this, rather than of holding various beliefs, then it seems to be immune to a popular kind of criticism. Wittgenstein liked to emphasize the nonrational aspects of religion, such as practices, rituals, vestments, attitudes, and so on. If religion is nonrational, then it seems that it cannot be either irrational, as some of its critics would like to say, or rational, as some of its defenders would insist that it is.

Wittgenstein would probably agree that **philosophy** as such cannot criticize religion, but this does not mean that there is anything wrong with individuals' doing so. As with **ethics**, philosophy does not, as he sees it, have the power to tell us what to believe or to do, but neither does it tell us not to reject this or that ethical theory or religious belief. Claims about the rationality (or otherwise) of religion in general would seem to go against Wittgenstein's explicit methodology. When he writes about philosophy, he says that it should offer **descriptions**, not **explanations** or, he seems to mean, judgments (at least not controversial ones). Not surprisingly, then, judgments about the rationality of religious **belief** are not to be found in his writings (except, arguably, implicitly). What he tries to do is to describe uses of **language** relating to religion. Any judgments would then be left to individuals, just as is whether to believe or not. Whether Wittgenstein succeeds in adhering to his methodological principles is another, and controversial, matter. Those who read him as saying that all religion is an expression of emotion, so that ritual is a nonrational acting out of feeling in the way that kissing a photograph is a nonrational expression of love, seem to commit Wittgenstein to a false conception of religious belief and to overlook nonexpressivist moments in his remarks on religion and ritual. Those who seek to attack the expressivist reading by pointing to his reference to **superstition** in connection with some beliefs seem to commit Wittgenstein to methodological hypocrisy. The debate about how best to read the relevant remarks is ongoing.

THE FIRST-PERSON SINGULAR. ***Philosophical Investigations*** §410 says that the word 'I' is no more the name of a person than 'here' is the name of a place. This might be taken as a denial of the **Cartesian** idea that 'I' refers to one's **mind** or **soul**, the nonphysical part of the human person. Wittgenstein does not deny that here is a place, though. Nor, similarly, does he deny the truth of "I am a person," or the correctness of the Cartesian theory of what a person is. He is instead remarking on the **grammar** of the first-person singular pronoun, its role in the lives of those who use it. This role is not that of the kind of objective designation used in physics or other **sciences**.

According to §404, when one says "I am in **pain**" one no more names somebody than one does when one groans with pain. It is not as if one matches up (even with great ease) the pain with the particular person who has it. There are no other candidates for the position of pain-possessor, in the way that there might be for wound-possessor if one is in a tangle with others and sees that someone's leg is bleeding. This connects with Wittgenstein's discussion of the **visual room** in §398. The space of imagination cannot (does not) contain the person that imagines, or any other real person, and it is not within the three-dimensional space that this person occupies either. So the person does not contain it. One cannot say it is mine as if one owns it in the way that one owns other things. Such '**inner**' phenomena occupy their own worlds, that is to say, they have their own grammar. Of course a person's pains and imaginings are no one else's. But they are not objects that could be traded with others, say, or that have any size or shape. The 'I' implicit in talk of "my pains" is not one human being among others. It is more like the **self**-described in ***Tractatus Logico-Philosophicus*** 5.641. It is not part of the world, something to which one could point, say. And, at least the later Wittgenstein would say, this is not because it is a very special kind of **object** but because it is no kind of object at all. 'I' here is not used to designate a person (or anything else). This does not mean that the word is never used in that way, but in first-person psychological **avowals** ("I am in pain," "I believe in God," and so on) it typically is not. Another useful source for Wittgenstein's thoughts on the first-person singular is ***The Blue and Brown Books*** (pp. 61–70).

FORM OF LIFE. The notion of a form of life (*Lebensform*) is one of the most famous in the ***Philosophical Investigations*** even though the term is used rarely in that book (or anywhere by Wittgenstein) and is never very clearly defined. Wittgenstein introduces the term in §19 where he connects it with his discussion of the **builders**. When we imagine a **language**, he says, we are imagining a form of life. So if a **language-game** such as theirs cannot be conceived as being a form of life, an entire linguistic way of life, then perhaps it is not really imaginable or possible after all. Wittgenstein himself makes the connection between forms of life and language-games in §23 where he says that the term "language-game" is designed to bring out the fact that *speaking* a language is part of a form of life or activity.

Without sharing certain attitudes toward the things around them, sharing a sense of relevance and responding in similar ways, communication between one person and another would be impossible. It is important, for instance, that nearly all people agree nearly all the time on what **colors** things are. Such **agreement** is part of the concept of color, Wittgenstein suggests (see ***Zettel*** §351). Regularity of the use of such concepts and agreement in their application are part of language, not a logically **necessary** precondition of it. One cannot separate the life in which there is such agreement from the concept of color itself. To imagine a different form or way of life is to imagine a different language with different **concepts**, different **rules**, and a different **logic** (compare *Philosophical Investigations* §19 and §241).

There are two other significant references to form of life in ***Philosophy of Psychology—A Fragment***. The first is on p. 183 (that is, section i) where Wittgenstein says that "the manifestations of hope are modifications of this complicated form of life." He means that only something, or someone, who lives as people do will ever hope, and "living as people do" here means having mastered the use of a language. A baby might want her mother, but it is absurd to think that she would think, "Would that my mother were here!" or any such thing. Hoping that her mother will come counts for Wittgenstein as something of this sort. The examples that he gives here involve animals, not human infants, but the point is the same. A dog can rage, fear, believe, and so on, but not hope. That is to say, it is inconceivable that a dog might hope. This is not because of what we know about dog psychology but because the concept of hope does not apply to dogs. To say that "My dog is hoping for a bone next week" is, Wittgenstein implies, to stop making sense. Such a comment is, intentionally or not, a **joke**. The language might change so that this kind of sentence became meaningful, but right now (when Wittgenstein is writing at any rate, according to him) it is not.

This is perhaps what he means when he writes in *Philosophy of Psychology—A Fragment* §345 that the given, that which must simply be accepted, is forms of life. These data, like **logical space** in the ***Tractatus Logico-Philosophicus***, seem to determine what can and what cannot meaningfully be said. In other words, one "must" accept forms of life in a logical sense. One has no choice about it, any more than one can choose whether or not to use words when speaking or writing. It seems not to be a pragmatic claim (that if one tries to change one's form of life one will very probably fail) and even less to be an **ethical** or **conservative** one (that changing one's form of life is *bad*).

Some commentators regret that such an important concept gets so little explanation from Wittgenstein. Some treat forms of life as synonymous with language-games. Others think of them as something like cultures. Others still treat them as biological life-forms, or at least something of the sort, so that all human beings share a form of life. If they are cultures and are fundamental to logic or making sense, then a kind of cultural **relativism** might seem to follow. One culture might be unable to judge another simply because it could not understand it. If forms of life are life-forms, then perhaps one could talk of species-relativism. Human beings could understand other cultures but not, for instance, **lions**. Alternatively, if the relevant form of life is that of biological (living, or perhaps embodied) rationality, then no kind of relativism is suggested. The fact is that Wittgenstein does not say enough to settle any dispute about this.

FORM OF REPRESENTATION. Proposition 2.15 of the ***Tractatus Logico-Philosophicus*** says that the structure of a **picture** is the way its various elements relate to one another, and introduces the term "form of representation" (*Form der Abbildung*), which has also been translated as 'pictorial form' and 'form of depiction.' The idea is clarified in 2.151, which says that "form of representation" refers to the possibility that things are related to each other in the same way that the elements in the picture are related to each other. This form of representation must be shared by reality and the picture, even if the picture is false, in order for the picture to be able to picture reality at all (see 2.17). In ***Philosophical Grammar*** (pp. 162–163) Wittgenstein writes: "what I said really boils down to this: that every projection must have something in common with what is projected no matter what is the **method of projection**. But that only means that I am here extending the concept of 'having in common' and making it equivalent to the general concept of projection."

According to propositions 2.181 and 2.182, a picture is called a logical picture when its form of representation is **logical form**, and therefore every picture is a logical picture, although some might also be pictures of other kinds (spatial, for instance). That is to say, every picture must be logical, must be in logical order, in order to be a picture rather than an arbitrary mess. Propositions 2.22 and 2.221 add that it is by its form of representation that a picture presents its sense.

Ostrow (p. 39) says of standard interpretations: "Wittgenstein's answer to the question of how the picture—and hence language—can always be about the world is thus supposedly to be: they share a form." And yet: "the strategy of taking recourse in talk of an isomorphism is empty; it amounts to no more than the claim that depicting the world is possible because the world has the possibility of being depicted."

FORMAL CONCEPTS. Discussed in the ***Tractatus Logico-Philosophicus*** propositions 4.126–4.1274, these are concepts signified by words such as "**object**," "number," "**fact**," and "function." Wittgenstein also refers to them as pseudo-concepts. In a clear **concept-script** such concepts should be expressed by the use of variable names such *x* and *y*, he says. Thus instead of "There is an object," one should write something like "There is some *x* such that . . ." To understand how it could be nonsense to talk about objects and **numbers**, some knowledge of what the *Tractatus* says about **meaning** is necessary.

What **propositions** have in common with the reality that they **picture**, Wittgenstein says, is **logical form**. This common form is something that is shown but cannot itself be pictured (one cannot '**say**' it). A picture (or proposition) cannot explain picturing, just as an instruction manual on instruction manuals is not the answer for someone who does not understand how to use instruction manuals in the first place. Similarly, the formal properties of a concept must be shown and cannot be said. That a number is a number will be apparent from its role in the system. It does no good at all, tells nobody anything, if one tries to say that 1, 2, 3, and the rest are numbers. The attempted proposition "One is a number" is, in fact, mere **nonsense** (see proposition 4.1272). This might be easier to see with some other examples. For instance, the sentence "2 + 2 = 4 is a fact" says no more than the sentence "2 + 2 = 4." The addition of the words "is a fact" only appears to provide extra information. The same goes for the sentences "This is a table and a table is an object" and "This is a table." Such useless 'additions' as "and a table is an object" seem to be saying something and yet are really not. Thus they are nonsensical (*unsinnig*). Words such as 'object' and 'fact' do not stand for any *thing*. Rather, they refer to the role that things play, the kind of **logical space** that they occupy. Tables are in three-dimensional or 'object space,' numbers are in what we might call 'arithmetical space,' and so on. This might sound **metaphysical** or even **Platonic**, but we should remember that Wittgenstein's concern is with **logic**. It does not matter for him what these spaces (or their ontological status) might be. What matters is the role in **language** of such words as 'table,' 'three,' and so on. Since these roles are different, the notation used in logic should reflect this difference. Whatever symbols are used to represent concepts of different kinds should be clearly different, not in shape but in function, in their use within the system. There will then be no need for any potentially confusing terms that might appear to be names of objects but are in fact designations of different roles for symbols within the notation. All that is needed are the different roles themselves, not names for them.

FORMALISM. In the **philosophy** of **mathematics**, the **theory** that mathematics is merely a formal game. Mathematics is viewed by formalists as nothing but the manipulation of certain symbols in accordance with certain **rules**. The symbols do not stand for **Platonic** (or any other) entities, and the results of mathematical operations therefore tell us nothing about **the world** (*pace* **Immanuel Kant**). Wittgenstein rejected this view, pointing out, for instance, that mathematics is used in engineering and that such usefulness is part of the reason why mathematicians use the particular rules they do. Mathematical **truths** might be a kind of grammatical proposition or rule, rather than something like empirical truths, according to Wittgenstein, but **grammar** is not completely **arbitrary**.

FOUNDATIONALISM. The theory in epistemology that knowledge rests on some foundation of absolute **certainty**. A paradigmatic foundationalist is **René Descartes**, who sought an Archimedean point on which to build the structure of all human knowledge, be it scientific, mathematical, or philosophical. This point was his famous *cogito ergo sum*, "I think therefore I am" (or, arguably, the certainty of God's existence). From here Descartes goes on to try to prove that reason and the senses are reliable guides to **truth** and thus that what people claim to know is, at least for the most part, really true. Other popular candidates for such foundational certainty in the Western philosophical tradition are truths of **mathematics**, such as 1 + 1 = 2, and facts about one's 'immediate,' **inner** experience, such as "I (seem to) see red" or "This is **pain**."

Wittgenstein's conception of **philosophy** seems to make it ill-suited to provide any such foundation for **science**, and he is generally read as opposing all of Descartes's best-known ideas (that the **mind** is a nonphysical object, that the existence of God can be proved using logical **argument**, and that foundationalism is true). If mathematical truths are more **rules** of **language-games** than discoveries about the world, and if private experience is only comprehensible in terms of a public **language**, then the solitary Cartesian ego looks very badly placed to be certain of anything. This is one reason why the **private language argument** is so important.

However, some scholars consider Wittgenstein's ***On Certainty*** to offer a new kind of foundationalism, in which our knowledge depends on a foundation of certainty ('beliefs' the doubting of which makes no sense). The kind of certainty in question is the kind one has that the earth is very old or that one cannot jump to the moon. This certainty itself might be thought to have its own foundation in **agreement** in judgment or **form of life**. In turn, this form of life can be thought of as depending on the earth itself, the air that all human beings breathe, and so on. Such **theories** are regarded as unacceptably **metaphysical** by most Wittgenstein scholars, however. The idea of form of life is certainly important in Wittgenstein's later philosophy, but it is doubtful that it should be considered a *foundation* of anything. If language and form of life are inextricably linked, or **internally related**, then one surely cannot be a foundation for the other.

FOURACRE, ROY. *See* GUY'S HOSPITAL.

FRAZER, JAMES GEORGE (1854–1941). A British **anthropologist** and author of *The Golden Bough*, among other works, a multi-volume study of magic and **religion** (the first edition was 2, the third 12 volumes long, all published between 1890 and 1915). Frazer believed in a kind of evolutionary progress from magic to religion to **science** as each culture gained a better **understanding** of the world around it. He treated magical and religious beliefs as hypotheses that are now known to be false.

Wittgenstein disagreed. In 1931 he wrote a set of remarks in response to volume one, which **M. O'C. Drury** read aloud to him. In 1936 Wittgenstein made further notes on the book, based on an abbreviated, one-volume version of it. These two sets of notes can be found in ***Philosophical Occasions***. In these remarks Wittgenstein criticizes Frazer's understanding of the nature of magic and religion. Magic and religion need not be seen as failed attempts at, or steps on the road toward, science, according to Wittgenstein. Instead, they can be understood on their own terms, having different subject matters, so to speak. Indeed, even magic (as in witch-doctors, not conjuring tricks) is fairly comprehensible to the minds of modern people. Vestiges of ancient rites and beliefs live on in **language**, in words such as 'spirit' and 'glamour' (which originally meant a spell), and in various seasonal practices (of the kind often opposed by fundamentalist Christians). Anyone who can shudder with horror at the thought of human sacrifice, Wittgenstein suggests, can understand the power that such practices have been felt to have. To presume or insist that they must have had some **utilitarian** goal is unjustified. One might say, and some Wittgensteinians do, that magic and science are different **language-games**.

This kind of claim, though, sounds too much like **relativism** for some people's comfort. Wittgenstein has been accused of **fideism**, of holding religion, and even magic, to be immune from criticism with regard to its rationality. This does not seem to have been Wittgenstein's intent. Rather, his purpose seems to be to show that Frazer is wrong to assume that his understanding of ancient and foreign practices *must* be right. Whether he went beyond this intention is controversial. Wittgenstein is often interpreted as claiming that all ritual **behavior** is expressive of emotion, not instrumental in intent at all. This would be a rather implausible claim, though, and Wittgenstein never makes it except, arguably, implicitly.

FREE WILL. The belief that the human **will** is somehow free is often opposed to determinism, the belief that every event has a cause. Wittgenstein opposed both **scientism** and the **religious** doctrine of predetermination, regarding the latter as acceptable only when understood as something like a cry of despair, not as a **theory** (see ***Culture and Value*** p. 30). This suggests that he might have been opposed to determinism. However, ***Tractatus Logico-Philosophicus*** proposition 6.32 says that the law of causality is the form of a law, which has been taken by some people to imply a kind of **necessity** in the scientific belief in cause and effect. All scientific laws, according to this view, must relate somehow to **causation**. This idea is akin to **Immanuel Kant's** idea that the human mind cannot but experience the world as one of events, each caused by another. Propositions 6.321–6.344, however, talk instead of the *possibility* of scientific laws having the form of causal laws. This suggests that the link between causation and scientific laws is contingent, not necessary. And the reference to form suggests that Wittgenstein is getting at something logical, not something empirical, in these remarks.

According to the *Tractatus*, what is formal cannot in fact be said. Hence, proposition 6.36 implies, there is no law of causality. *If there were*, then it would be along the lines of: there are laws of nature. This, however, Wittgenstein tells us, must be shown, as one cannot say it. **Saying** "there are laws of nature" is like saying "there are **facts**," something that merely appears to be informative. One might wonder at this point whether he means that determinism is an ineffable **truth** or sheer **nonsense**. A kind of answer to this question is suggested earlier in the *Tractatus*.

Wittgenstein rejects determinism in proposition 5.1361 and affirms the freedom of the will in proposition 5.1362. One could only know what someone was going to do in the future, he says there, if causality (which he does not deny exists except universally or as a nexus) had the same kind of necessity as **logic**, which it does not. So all future events and actions are contingent, and one cannot *know* what is going to happen. Proposition 5.1362 seems to define the freedom of the will as such ignorance or uncertainty, implying perhaps that there is no such object as "the will" that could be either free or unfree. Indeed, if any attempt to express a law of universal causality is bound to result in nonsense, then so too is the denial of such a 'law.' So the whole concept of free will is thrown in doubt by the *Tractatus*. So is the idea of determinism. Proposition 6.362 says that what the law of causality is intended to rule out cannot be described at all, so the law rules out nothing, contradicts only nonsense. The contradiction of nonsense is itself nonsense, serving no purpose at all.

Wittgenstein's later work on this subject is less dogmatic. This work consists primarily of a pair of lectures (probably given in 1939), notes from which are published in ***Philosophical Occasions***. His goal here might have been mere clarity, but it could also have been to show that belief in freedom of the will is not an offense against **grammar** or science. It is, as he sees it, a moral position. To regard people (including oneself) as having free will is to hold them responsible for what they do. To deny free will (in anything more than words) would then be not to hold people responsible, which would seem to mean completely abandoning **ethics** as it is ordinarily understood.

It seems possible to many philosophers that we could have free will even if determinism were true. Wittgenstein does not deny this. For instance, one might try to look at human actions in two ways, one scientific and deterministic, the other moral. This kind of Kantian approach might be made Wittgensteinian by talking about **language-games** of science and of ethics. Wittgenstein himself does not do this, but his attempt to clarify what it makes sense to say in this area leaves that option open (as it should all coherent options).

See also CAUSAL NEXUS; CAUSATION.

FREGE, GOTTLOB (1848–1925). An important mathematician and philosopher, and the greatest logician since **Aristotle**. Frege taught at the University of Jena from 1874 to 1918. In 1879, he published the *Begriffsschrift* ("**Concept-script**") in which, starting from a set of "primitive principles" and using only specified rules of **logical inference**, he derived all the laws of **logic**. This was the first time that the propositional calculus had been formulated systematically. Frege was the first also to develop a method for dealing in formal logic with **arguments** involving more than one quantification (such as "Everybody knows something"). Perhaps his greatest contribution to logic was to introduce various mathematical elements into formal logic, including quantification, **functions**, arguments (in the mathematical sense of something substituted for a variable in a function), and the value of a function. In logic this value, according to Frege, is always either "the True" or "the False," hence the notion of truth-value.

His overriding interest was in **logicism**, the **theory** that most of **mathematics** could be shown to be a branch of logic. This contrasts with the views of **Immanuel Kant** (who held mathematical **truths** to be instances of synthetic *a priori* knowledge, dependent on the workings of the **mind**) and **John Stuart Mill** (who argued that mathematical truths are **empirical** generalizations, that 2 + 2 = 4, for instance, is something known from experience). Against these influential theses, Frege tried to show in his *Grundlagen der Arithmetik* (The Foundations of Arithmetic 1884) that the truths of arithmetic are **analytic**. A fundamental part of this demonstration involved showing that **numbers** could be defined in terms of the purely logical concept of classes. Thus, for instance, all reference in arithmetic to the number two could, in principle, be replaced by reference to the class of pairs.

Despite all his achievements and lasting contributions to philosophy and logic, Frege's logicist program was derailed by **Bertrand Russell** and **Kurt Gödel**. Russell discovered that Frege's version of set theory was internally inconsistent, implying the paradoxical notion of a class of classes that are not members of themselves. (To see the paradox one needs simply to ask: Is this class a member of itself?) Gödel later proved that no axiomatization of arithmetic can be both complete and consistent. Wittgenstein too criticized Frege's work, but Frege's influence on Wittgenstein was enormous. Some measure of this can be seen in the preface to the ***Tractatus Logico-Philosophicus***, where Wittgenstein says that he is "indebted to Frege's great works and to the writings of my friend Mr Bertrand Russell for much of the stimulation of my thoughts" (p. 3). For some insight into whether Frege or Russell had the greater influence one can consider whether one would rather be recognized for his or her great works or for simply being a friend.

As a young man Wittgenstein was a Schopenhauerian idealist, until he encountered the works of Russell and Frege. **Schopenhauer's** work is notable for its commitment to **ethics**, but there is, arguably, a certain sloppiness to it that might be regarded as unethical. His rejection of **solipsism**, for instance, is based more on common sense and wishful thinking than rational argument. Frege is rather different. According to Joan Weiner: "What Frege has to offer us is a model of philosophical virtue. Almost everyone who has grappled with Frege's writings has been moved by Frege's intellectual honesty" (Joan Weiner *Frege in Perspective* Cornell University Press, 1990, p. 12).

Another virtue of Frege's is intellectual humility. Schopenhauer's concerns might be summarized as life, the universe, and everything, but Frege was much less ambitious. His philosophical starting point was the unglamorous but undoubtedly challenging work of trying to get at the foundations of arithmetic. Common sense and wishful thinking might lead many of us to think that there is no need to inquire into the precise nature or basis of mathematics, but Frege was not satisfied with this lack of rigor and attempted to demonstrate that arithmetic could be reduced to logic. This project resulted in some failure, which Frege faced up to, but also to the greatest advance in logic since Aristotle. Frege developed a way of representing propositions and arguments that has ever since provided the basis for symbolic logic, on which, among other things, computer programming is based.

In his book *The Foundations of Arithmetic* (trans. J. L. Austin, Northwestern University Press, 1980), Frege says (p. x) that he has followed "three fundamental principles":

always to separate sharply the psychological from the logical, the subjective from the objective;
never to ask for the meaning of a word in isolation, but only in the context of a proposition;
never to lose sight of the distinction between concept and object.

These principles are thought to have influenced Wittgenstein considerably.

He first met Frege in 1911, and the two corresponded at least until 1920. Wittgenstein studied Frege's *Grundgesetze der Arithmetik* (Basic Laws of Arithmetic) during his first year in **Manchester** (1908–1909) and requested a copy of the same book in 1919 when he was a prisoner of war. He is known to have read other works of Frege's too, such as his 1918 essay "Thought" (which attacks idealism) and the 1892 "Sense and Reference," which has become Frege's best-known work.

According to Frege, words with a sense may lack a reference, e.g., "the least rapidly convergent series" (Beaney p. 153) or "the only living boy in New York." There is no such series or boy to refer to, but we know this precisely because we understand the sense of these words. We might say that these words *have* a meaning (what Frege calls sense) even though there *is* nothing that they mean (what he calls reference). The internal images evoked by words vary from person to person, and might differ even with the same person and the same word from one time to another. Sense, though, belongs to humanity's "common store of thoughts," which it transmits from one generation to another (Beaney p. 154). The reference of a word or phrase is more objective still: it is the object itself, which the relevant **sign** designates.

Psychology is concerned with the origins of our ideas, their subjective nature, and physiological underpinnings. Logic (and mathematics) is concerned with none of this, only with concepts and ideas themselves, and with truth. "A proposition may be thought, and again it may be true; let us never confuse these two things," Frege writes (*The Foundations of Arithmetic*, p. vi). The distinction between subjective ideas (something like mental pictures, sensible and different for each person) and objective concepts (shared and in principle non-sensible) "stands or falls with that between psychology and logic" (*The Foundations of Arithmetic* §27.) Both sense (because it is shared) and reference belong to the latter category, though reference does so more obviously.

The distinction between sense and reference cannot strictly be defined according to Frege. But it is real, and we can grasp it by thinking of the difference between direct and indirect speech, or between nonfiction and fiction. Reference is ultimately all that matters for logic and **science**, all that matters to those concerned with truth (sense matters here too, but not quite as ultimately). It is a matter of objects, not ideas. These objects are particulars. They are public. They are determinate or definite. They are such things as

Julius Caesar, the number one, and the True. (Controversially, Frege argues that what true sentences refer to is "the True." In the true sentence "My cat is unusually long," the words "My cat" refer to my cat, but, Frege believes, the sentence as a whole must also refer to something. According to him, its reference is that which is true: "the True.") Objects are, in short, whatever we refer to in **language**.

Against empiricists, Frege argues that the sense of a word is not a mental image. He shows that mental images are irrelevant to everything except, perhaps, the tone of certain words. Even there, though, it might be doubted that there are different images associated with the words 'but' and 'and,' or 'dead' and deceased,' to use one of Michael Dummett's examples (*Frege: Philosophy of Language* Harvard University Press, 1973, p. 85). Many words have no mental image associated with them. When an image is associated with a word, it might vary from person to person. And if we know the image, we still need to know what to do with it. "No image can portray the role of the word in the sentence" (Dummett, p. 158). This is why it is a mistake to consider the meaning of a word in isolation. We should always, Frege argues, take into account its place in the context of a sentence. So, we separate the psychological from the logical because the former is **private** and therefore irrelevant to shared efforts to discover truth.

Despite Wittgenstein's admiration for his work, Frege comes in for criticism at several points in the *Tractatus*. Proposition 3.143 objects to his having called a **proposition** or sentence a complex **name** (for either "the True" or "the False"). Proposition 4.1272 argues that **formal concepts** should be represented by variables rather than functions or classes as Frege and Russell believed. Proposition 5.132 criticizes Frege's reliance on laws of logical inference. Proposition 5.4 denies that there are any logical **objects** for which **logical constants** stand, as Frege had thought. If there were, then one might have to choose between Frege's and Russell's ideas about which signs in logic are genuinely primitive (most basic), but they are in fact interchangeable and interdefinable, as proposition 5.42 points out.

Nevertheless, it is quite clear that without "the great works of Frege" the *Tractatus* would not have existed. Frege was one of the first philosophers to take the "linguistic turn," attempting to make sense of (or get clear about) talk about numbers, for instance, in order to understand what numbers are. He invented the **context principle**. And he opposed **psychologism**, roughly the idea that logic is a branch of **psychology**. Logic is normative, concerned with how one ought to think, not positive or open to empirical study. In a similar vein, Frege opposed the idea that thoughts are subjective in any sense relevant to philosophy. The thought "I wandered lonely as a cloud" is just like the proposition or sentence expressed by those words. Any subjective feelings or associations that one might have with it are irrelevant for **philosophy** or logic. This emphasis on the importance of language, emphasis on context, and opposition to psychologism had an enormous impact on Wittgenstein throughout his career, and on philosophy generally for most of the 20th and 21st centuries.

FREUD, SIGMUND (1856–1939). The great Austrian inventor of psychoanalysis and one of the most influential thinkers of the 20th century. Freud got his medical training at the University of **Vienna** and specialized in neurology. His research was at first carried out in collaboration with Joseph Breuer, to whom Wittgenstein credited some of Freud's ideas, but he went on to work independently. This work included the development of the concepts of the unconscious, of infantile sexuality, and of repression. He also, like **Plato**, proposed a tripartite account of the **mind**, consisting of the id, the ego, and the super-ego. His idea that dreams and even slips of the tongue ("Freudian slips") have implicit significance was also original. This new way of conceiving of the mind was intended to help in the treatment of people with psychological problems. Indeed, Freud hoped to help even whole societies or cultures. Great things have been claimed for psychoanalysis, but its practitioners have moved on in various directions since Freud's day, and its status as a **science** is contested. Nevertheless, some of Freud's ideas are now widely accepted. For instance, his claims that much of our mental life is not conscious, that we have powerful sexual and aggressive instincts, and that mental illness lies on a continuum with normal mental life.

Wittgenstein once described himself as a **disciple** of Freud's, but expressed great **skepticism** about his **thinking** in a series of conversations on **psychology** that he had with **Rush Rhees**. Wittgenstein admired Freud's originality and considered at least some of his innovative ideas to be useful. What he seems to have questioned, as others have, was the grounds Freud claimed to have for his **beliefs**, and his tendency to generalize excessively. For instance, Freud put forward the idea that all dreams are wish-fulfillments, yet some seem clearly not to be, and this is not the kind of proposition that can ever be proved. To see some dreams as evidence of suppressed desires might be insightful, but to hold that all dreams are like this is to insist on an unjustified and untestable hypothesis. Freud in fact was not a scientific psychologist by today's standards, nor even much of a philosopher if philosophers are judged by the quality (the logical validity, for instance) of their arguments. Instead, Freud offered a new way of thinking, as **Georg Cantor** had done in **mathematics**. The important difference, as Wittgenstein saw it, was that Cantor's ideas led only to **confusion**, whereas Freud's could be much more productive.

FUNCTION. In mathematics, a relation between inputs and outputs such that each input has exactly one output. Roughly speaking, a function is a **rule** that specifies the output to be associated with each input. The input is called the "**argument**," and the output is the "value" of the function. In ***Tractatus Logico-Philosophicus*** 3.318 Wittgenstein says that, like **Gottlob Frege** and **Bertrand Russell**, he regards a **proposition** as a function of the expressions contained in it. At 3.333 Wittgenstein adds that a function cannot be its own argument because a functional sign contains the prototype of its own argument, but it cannot contain itself. This sounds obscure, but if we think of the rule 'multiply by two' then it is clear enough that this function cannot be multiplied by two. The idea makes no sense. If it ever looks as though a function could be its own argument, then we need to remind ourselves of the relevant **grammar**, the **logical syntax**, or the **sign/symbol** distinction.

G

GALTON, FRANCIS (1822–1911). A British meteorologist, psychologist, and eugenicist, knighted in 1909. Of all his many interests and achievements, the one most relevant to Wittgenstein is Galton's invention of composite portraiture. This involves superimposing multiple photographs to produce an image of a general type. For instance, if photographs of the faces of Korean people are superimposed in this way, then a picture of a generic Korean face will emerge. With his friend Moritz Nahr, Wittgenstein produced a composite photograph from pictures of himself and his three sisters, bringing out their **family resemblance**. His **lecture on ethics** makes explicit reference to Galton at the beginning, when Wittgenstein defines the subject matter of the lecture by giving a list of "more or less synonymous expressions" in order to reveal the characteristic features of what he means by **ethics**. Galton's name comes up again in the ***Blue Book*** when Wittgenstein diagnoses four sources of "our **craving for generality**." One of these, he says, is the tendency to think that someone who has understood a general term such as 'leaf' has thereby come into possession of a mental image of no particular leaf but of leaves in general. Such an image, he implies, would be something like a Galtonian composite photograph.

GEACH, PETER THOMAS (1916–2013). A British philosopher who married Wittgenstein's student **G. E. M. Anscombe**. Geach himself studied with Wittgenstein and became a noted philosopher and logician in his own right, working on mental acts, the **philosophy** of **religion**, and **ethics**, as well as translating and writing on some of the works of **Gottlob Frege**. He was known as the father of "analytical Thomism," a philosophical movement combining elements of Wittgensteinian **analytical** philosophy with the Catholic philosophy of St. Thomas Aquinas. His published works include *Mental Acts* (1967), *God and the Soul* (1969), and *The Virtues* (1977).

GENERAL PROPOSITIONAL FORM. *Tractatus Logico-Philosophicus* proposition 4.0031 credits **Bertrand Russell** with having shown that the true **logical form** of a **proposition** is not always apparent. All propositions, though, according to the *Tractatus*, have a general form in common. Proposition 4.53 tells us that "The general propositional form is a variable." Proposition 6 says that this form is the same as the general form of a **truth-function**. Proposition 4.5 says that it is: "This is how things stand." Propositions 5.471 and 5.4711 tell us that the general propositional form is the **essence** of a proposition, that this is the essence of all **description** (or at least that giving the former means giving the latter), and that this is (or gives) the essence of **the world**. The implication is that to say "This is how things stand" somehow gives us the essence of the world. Perhaps this takes us back to the very first proposition in the book, which says that the world is everything that is the case.

GENERALITY. Proposition 3.24 of the ***Tractatus Logico-Philosophicus*** says that the notation for generality contains a prototype. Proposition 4.0411 considers various possible ways of expressing generality in logical notation and rejects each one of them on the grounds that it lacks the necessary mathematical **multiplicity**. This refers back to 4.04, which tells us that a **proposition** must contain just as many things to differentiate as there are in the state of things that the proposition represents. In 5.1311 he suggests that no **sign** for generality is necessary, because the symbol "(x).fx" already contains generality. That is, in this context *x* already implies that whatever x is, it is true that fx. And generality is implicit in that 'whatever.' We do not need to add any notation to specify that there is generality here. Indeed, 4.0411 implies that it is impossible to do so.

Tractatus 5.522 says that two things are peculiar about the symbolism of generality. The first is that it points to a **logical prototype**. The second is that it emphasizes **logical constants**. In 5.4 Wittgenstein denies that logical constants exist in the sense used by **Gottlob Frege** and **Bertrand Russell**. They, according to 5.521, introduced generality in connection with the **logical sum** or **logical product**. **G. E. M. Anscombe** (pp. 141–143) says that Frege and Russell did not at all explicitly do what Wittgenstein says here. The relevant Frege paper is "Function and Concept," and Russell offers similar explanations of generality in his work (White [p. 94] says that Wittgenstein's target here seems mainly to be what Russell says in *Principia Mathematica*). Frege explains his sign for generality in terms of what it means, and specifically in terms of when it means what he calls "the true." Wittgenstein believes that the truth of a general proposition is the truth of a logical product. Hence his claim here about what he takes to be implicit in Frege and Russell. Universal propositions ("For all x, . . ."), he thinks, each say that some logical product is true, and particular propositions ("For some x, . . .") each say that some logical sum is true.

See also CRAVING FOR GENERALITY.

GÖDEL, KURT (1906–1978). A mathematician and logician born in Austria who moved to the **United States** in 1940, having worked at the University of **Vienna** for the previous decade. He argued that **mathematics** is essentially incomplete, and so that any formal system containing arithmetic must contain statements that count as true within that system but that cannot be proved to be so. This undermined the **logicist** project of **Gottlob Frege** and **Bertrand Russell** to show that pure mathematics could be deduced from a set of logical axioms.

GOETHE, JOHANN WOLFGANG VON (1749–1832). A great German **poet** and dramatist much admired by Wittgenstein (and by **Friedrich Nietzsche**). Wittgenstein studied Goethe's **theory** of **color** (*Farbenlehre*) primarily, he said, because it stimulated him to think, despite its being "partly boring and repelling" (see Monk p. 561). Goethe's **mind** was original and attracted to original, nonacademic ways of thinking. He also, perhaps like Wittgenstein, sought a kind of morally serious alternative to **religion**. As well as his work on color, Wittgenstein studied Goethe's book on plants (*Die Metamorphose der Pflanze*), in which Goethe, some would say confusedly, tries to study plant life in a systematic way without resorting to mechanistic explanations.

His aim was to provide an **overview** of plant life, making clear what plants could logically exist, that is, the limits and nature of the class of things that are called plants. There is an explicit comparison of this method with the correct approach to **philosophy** in **Friedrich Waismann's** book ***Logik, Sprache, Philosophie*** on which Wittgenstein collaborated. Wittgenstein said that the phrase "Im Anfang war die Tat" (In the beginning was the deed) from Goethe's *Faust* might serve as a motto for his later philosophical work.

GRAMMAR. Wittgenstein refers often to grammar, especially in his later work, in a way that might be confusing. He does not appear to mean 'grammar' in quite the usual sense, since this has little obvious connection with philosophy. However, if he means 'grammar' in some technical sense, then one might **wonder** both why he is resorting to the kind of technical language that he generally avoids in the later work and what precisely he means by this term. What he seems to have in mind is the **rules** for the correct use of words in a **language**, not particularly in the narrow or superficial sense generally intended when people refer to grammar but also, and especially, in a more fundamental or advanced sense. For instance, it might be regarded as part of grammar that a noun refers to a person, place, or thing. But the word 'God' does not refer to a person in the usual sense of that word, nor to a thing on a level with any other thing. Nor does 'justice' refer to a thing in the way that 'milk' does. Failure to appreciate the sophistication of the rules that govern the use of words such as 'God' and 'justice' can lead to philosophical error, either to overhasty rejections of belief in God or justice (etc.) or to superstitious or otherwise crude forms of belief in them.

It is probably helpful to understand Wittgenstein's later use of the idea of grammar in relation to his earlier thinking. ***Tractatus Logico-Philosophicus*** proposition 3.325 says that in order to avoid the fundamental confusions with which **philosophy** is filled it is necessary to use a sign-language (**concept-script**) that is governed by logical grammar or syntax. In his later work Wittgenstein treated natural languages as having something like such a grammar, as being inherently logical. **Confusion** arises, he held, when philosophers fail to adhere to the rules of their own language. Careful attention to grammar then can cure people of philosophical confusion. So the concept of grammar somewhat replaces that of **logic**, which is a more technical idea than the later Wittgenstein wanted and might imply that language is in fact a kind of **calculus**. The notion of grammar, in contrast, is less linked with **mathematics** and more obviously connected with **human beings** and, perhaps, **forms of life**.

See also ARBITRARINESS OF GRAMMAR; *PHILOSOPHICAL GRAMMAR*.

GRETL. *See* THE WITTGENSTEIN FAMILY.

GUY'S HOSPITAL. In 1941, wanting to contribute to the war effort, Wittgenstein began working at Guy's in London as a dispensary porter. While there he lived with the medical staff at Nuffield House. Soon after going there he became a pharmacy technician, making Lassar's ointment. During this time he wrote what are now Parts IV, V, VI, and VII of the ***Remarks on the Foundations of Mathematics***.

He left Guy's in 1943 to work with a Dr. R. T. Grant. Grant had worked at Guy's on "wound shock." He suggested that the term "shock" was not useful since too many various cases were diagnosed in this way, making it impossible to assess the value of different treatments. Because of this, it is hard to say precisely what wound shock is, but it has more to do with loss of blood than "shell shock" or post-traumatic stress disorder. Wittgenstein discussed the issue with Grant and worked as a laboratory assistant for him from 29 April 1943, after Grant's unit moved from London to Newcastle-upon-Tyne. He left the unit on 16 February 1944, by which time Dr. E. G. Bywaters had taken over from Grant. Together with Dr. Basil Reeve, Grant produced a report entitled "Observations on the General Effects of Injury in Man," which persuaded researchers to abandon several projects based on what they now thought of as misguided ideas about shock.

While he was at Guy's, Wittgenstein met Roy Fouracre, who was working in the dispensary. They became good friends and stayed in touch for the rest of Wittgenstein's life. Wittgenstein seems to have valued Fouracre's straightforward decency and sense of humor.

H

HACKER, PETER MICHAEL STEPHAN (1939–). A British philosopher and influential Wittgenstein scholar. Hacker interprets Wittgenstein as offering genuine **arguments** in defense of theses such as the impossibility of a **private language**. This seems to go against Wittgenstein's own claims about his methodology (he claimed merely to **describe language**, not to argue, and implied that he would propose no theses in his **philosophy**). Nevertheless, it is a very natural way, and indeed the orthodox way, to read Wittgenstein's work. Probably the least orthodox of Hacker's ideas about Wittgenstein is his conviction that there is no logical impossibility of a language developed and used by only one person. This would not be a private language in Wittgenstein's sense, merely a case of solitary **rule-following**.

Hacker's influence on Wittgenstein scholarship stems from both the quality and the quantity of his publications, which include line-by-line analyses of the ***Philosophical Investigations***, as well as the quality of his former students. He has vigorously opposed controversial new interpretations of Wittgenstein by **Saul Kripke**, **Cora Diamond**, and **James Conant**.

Hacker is a Fellow of St. John's College, Oxford. Among other works he is the author of *Insight and Illusion* (1972), *Appearance and Reality* (1987), and *Wittgenstein's Place in Twentieth-Century Analytic Philosophy* (1996). He has also written a number of books with **G. P. Baker**: *Language, Sense and Nonsense* (1984) and *Scepticism, Rules and Language* (1984), as well as the four-volume *Analytical Commentary on the Philosophical Investigations* (1980–1996).

HAIDBAUER CASE. While working as a schoolteacher (which he did in the years 1920–1926), Wittgenstein used corporal punishment on many of his students. One of these was Josef Haidbauer, whom Wittgenstein struck in April 1926. Haidbauer was a sickly 11-year-old who died three years later of leukemia. When Wittgenstein hit him on the head, the boy collapsed. Wittgenstein dismissed the class and took Haidbauer to the principal's office, where he waited for a doctor. Wittgenstein left the village that night and handed in his resignation. He was later cleared of misconduct.

HARDY, GODFREY HAROLD (1877–1947). A brilliant British mathematician and one of the examiners (the other being **Bertrand Russell**) of the work later published as ***Philosophical Remarks***, which won Wittgenstein a five-year fellowship at Trinity College, **Cambridge**, in 1930. Wittgenstein was highly critical of Hardy's philosophy as expressed in his paper "**Mathematical Proof**" (published in the journal *Mind* in 1929) and as revealed in his textbook *Pure Mathematics*. Hardy's **philosophy** of **mathematics** was not so much wrong, in Wittgenstein's view, as muddled, cloudy, and likely to **confuse** students.

HAYEK, FRIEDRICH AUGUST VON (1899–1992). An economist, libertarian political philosopher, and a distant cousin of Wittgenstein's who in 1953 wrote an unfinished biography of Wittgenstein for private circulation. Copies of this biography are owned by Boston University and McMaster University in Canada.

HEGEL, GEORG WILHELM FRIEDRICH (1770–1831). A German philosopher whose work was savagely denounced by **Arthur Schopenhauer**, whom Wittgenstein admired. However, Wittgenstein expressed qualified approval of Hegel's method in **philosophy**. He described the Hegelian dialectical method, which involves surveying different views on an issue, as "very sound" (see WLC p. 74). However, he also warned that it should stick to trying to find out where ambiguities in **language** lie, rather than attempting to forge a new, complex synthesis. Wittgenstein's pronouncement that Hegel's method is sound is surprising given Hegel's tendencies toward obscurity and precisely the kind of grand **metaphysical theory** that Wittgenstein seems consistently to oppose. It should be borne in mind, though, that Wittgenstein was commenting here on C. D. Broad's characterization of Hegel's method, not on this method as actually used by Hegel. Wittgenstein, in fact, described his own method as contrary to Hegel's in practice. Hegel, he said, seemed to want to find similarity in apparent difference, whereas Wittgenstein said that he wanted to do just the opposite.

HEIDEGGER, MARTIN (1889–1976). An anti-**Cartesian** German philosopher and one of Wittgenstein's rivals for the title of greatest philosopher of the 20th century. Heidegger's great work was *Sein und Zeit* (Being and Time), which tries to bring ontology, the study of being, back to center stage in **philosophy** and is considered one of the classic works of existentialist philosophy. In his later work Heidegger was more interested in the **arts** (especially **poetry**), although, as with Wittgenstein, the question of how much he changed his mind, or, on the contrary, of how much **continuity** there is in his work, is disputed.

Heidegger's approach to philosophy is, at least superficially, quite different from Wittgenstein's. Heidegger's prose, for instance, is notoriously obscure, and his **metaphysics** is often held up as a paradigm of the kind of **nonsense** that Wittgenstein and other **analytic** philosophers have set out to expose. Wittgenstein himself, though, was relatively sympathetic about Heidegger in the few remarks he is known to have made about him in conversation with **Friedrich Waismann**. He did regard Heidegger as talking nonsense, as all philosophers do according to Wittgenstein, but it was, he said, understandable why he should write as he did. This is very muted praise, of course, but much less than the mocking rejection with which Heidegger's work has often met.

THE HERETICS. The Heretics Society was a **Cambridge University** group along the lines of the **Apostles** but more interested in **science**. It was to them that Wittgenstein delivered his **lecture on ethics** on 17 November 1929, having been invited to do so by **C. K. Ogden**.

HERTZ, HEINRICH RUDOLF (1857–1894). A great German physicist listed by Wittgenstein in 1931 as an influence on his thinking (see ***Culture and Value*** p. 19). Wittgenstein says in this note that he thinks only reproductively (an alleged characteristic of **Jewish** thinkers) and that he has taken over ways of thinking from **Ludwig Boltzmann**, Hertz, **Arthur Schopenhauer**, **Gottlob Frege**, **Bertrand Russell**, **Karl Kraus**, **Adolf Loos**, **Otto Weininger**, **Oswald Spengler**, and **Piero Sraffa**.

As a teenager Wittgenstein read Hertz's *Principles of Mechanics* in which it is proposed that when one is puzzled by a **concept** such as 'force' in **Newtonian** physics, the thing to do is to restate Newtonian physics without using 'force' as a basic concept. Wittgenstein wanted to take a similar approach to philosophical puzzlement generally, removing illegitimate questions without answering them directly. ***Philosophical Grammar*** §89 (p. 421) quotes Hertz as follows: "The whole task of **philosophy** is to give such a form to our expression that certain disquietudes (or problems) vanish." Theodore Redpath quotes Wittgenstein as saying in 1939 that this "seemed to him to sum up philosophy" (see PPO p. 379).

HILBERT, DAVID (1862–1943). A German formalist mathematician who tried to produce a metamathematics, thereby laying a foundation for arithmetic that could be proved to be consistent. Wittgenstein denied that the 'game' of mathematics could be justified in any such way. The foundation must connect with the rest of the structure, he argued, and then it is part of it, more of the same, not something that had been needed all along but only just supplied. Along with **Georg Cantor** and **G. H. Hardy**, Hilbert was the kind of mathematician that Wittgenstein liked to criticize in his lectures.

HINGE PROPOSITIONS. In ***On Certainty*** §341 Wittgenstein writes that "the questions that we raise and our doubts depend upon the fact that some **propositions** are exempt from doubt, are as it were like hinges on which those turn." Such propositions have become known as hinge propositions. They are thought of as propositions or sentences that both are not and ought not to be doubted. After all, if they are doubted, then they are not exempt from doubt, and if our questioning and doubting depend on these propositions' not being doubted then it would seem that we ought not to doubt them. One question that then arises is which propositions exactly these are. Another is whether any such propositions exist at all. Wittgenstein might have been wrong, after all, especially since *On Certainty* consists of notes that he was working on shortly before he died. It is not a finished work.

See also FOUNDATIONALISM; SKEPTICISM.

HITLER, ADOLF (1889–1945). The German dictator attended the same school as Wittgenstein, the *K. u. k. Realschule* in Linz, during the year 1904–1905. Hitler attended the school from 1900–1904 and was only a few days older than Wittgenstein, but they overlapped for just one year because Hitler was behind the average by a year and Wittgenstein was ahead, also by a year. After this year Hitler had to leave because of his bad record. It has been speculated that Hitler took a disliking to Wittgenstein and that this was the beginning of his **anti-Semitism**, but there is no proof that they had anything to do with each other. There were few **Jewish** children at the school, and Hitler's descriptions of one of them do seem to match Wittgenstein (Hitler mentions stammering, for instance), but such evidence is no more than suggestive at best. Certainly the idea that a reaction against Wittgenstein in particular led to Hitler's lifelong hatred of Jews is far-fetched.

HOMOSEXUALITY. *See* SEXUALITY.

HUMAN BEING. Against the philosophical tendency to think in terms of **René Descartes's** "thinking things" and **John Locke's** "persons," the later Wittgenstein insists on the use of ordinary (non**metaphysical**) **language** and the ordinary (non-theorized) life in which human beings belong. Thus psychological and moral concepts come from and belong to a certain kind of life, one in which people act and react toward each other in certain kinds of ways. (If this seems vague, Wittgenstein might say, that is because there is too much to say about human life to fit it all into a few words or, perhaps, one philosophical **theory**.) The 'each other' here is human beings, not hypothesized metaphysical entities, even if one thinks of others as having **souls**. To think of people as having souls, Wittgenstein suggests, is not to hold some theory or opinion but to regard and treat others in a certain kind of way. As far as **psychology** goes, **inner** processes stand in need of outward **criteria**, and these are closely linked with the human body. One can ascribe psychological states to animals and even to inanimate objects, but only by a kind of analogy. The **concepts** one employs when talking and **thinking** about such states belong to a particular **form of life**.

HUME, DAVID (1711–1776). One of the greatest British **empiricist** philosophers. Hume was a noted skeptic, arguing against such philosophers as **René Descartes** that it is in fact impossible to know very much for certain and that **human beings** are much less rational, and more creatures of habit and instinct, than some people might like to believe. He rejected Descartes's idea of the **self** as nonphysical **soul**, instead arguing that the self is a bundle of changing perceptions (ideas and impressions). This idea has been compared to the **Buddhist** doctrine of no-self.

Hume is also known for his ideas about **causation** and **induction**. He argued, somewhat against his empiricist principles, that the idea of causation does not come from sensory perception, since it implies or includes the idea of **necessity**, and this is something that the senses can never detect. In a somewhat similar way he argued that inductive reasoning, reasoning from known, particular facts, to general conclusions about all relevantly similar cases, is not rational. The senses can know nothing about unobserved or unexperienced phenomena (in the future or distant in space, for instance) and *a priori* reasoning tells one nothing about matters of empirical fact. So, Hume argued, inductive reasoning cannot be justified even as being probably true. This is not to say that it is *irrational*, however. Reason is simply silent, according to Hume, about the future and about unobserved phenomena. This **skepticism** about induction has been likened to Wittgenstein's later views on **rule-following**.

On the whole Wittgenstein seems to have shared Hume's anti-Cartesianism but not his skepticism. He expressed disdain for Hume's work but could have been influenced nonetheless by way of Hume's influence on **Immanuel Kant** and **Bertrand Russell**.

HUTT, ROWLAND. *See* CONFESSION.

I

IDEALISM. The **metaphysical** theory that all reality is ultimately mental, consisting of such entities as **minds**, ideas, and spirits. Wittgenstein's first encounter with such a philosophy came when he read **Arthur Schopenhauer's** *The World as Will and Representation* as a teenager. Schopenhauer defended a form of transcendental idealism, the belief that there is something unreal, merely apparent, about **the world** of sensory experience.

An extreme form of idealism that interested Wittgenstein is **solipsism**, which in the ***Tractatus Logico-Philosophicus*** he said coincides with pure **realism** (its apparent opposite) when its implications are followed through strictly. When the metaphysical **nonsense** is stripped from such **theories**, perhaps Wittgenstein meant, the meaningful content remaining is the same.

In the ***Philosophical Investigations*** he returns to the relation between idealism, solipsism, and realism. In *Philosophical Investigations* §402 he says that one party (presumably the idealists and solipsists) attack normal ways of speaking as if they were attacking metaphysical theses, while the other (presumably the realists) defend these forms of expression as if they were facts that everyone accepts as true. So the two sides are not the same, but they have in common a misunderstanding of the nature of **language**. **Ordinary language** is not metaphysically committed, in Wittgenstein's view. Philosophers who think that metaphysical theories such as idealism are either implied or denied by everyday uses of language are, Wittgenstein appears to believe, trapped in something like the **Augustinian** picture of language, assuming that when people speak they picture reality as being this way rather than that. Of course sometimes people do just this, but other times the **meaning** of words is their use in people's lives, and such use is rarely metaphysical (even implicitly).

IDENTITY, CRITERION OF. When one identifies some object as being the same as some other, Wittgenstein suggests in the ***Philosophical Investigations***, one needs some criterion of identity. Thus if someone says that the bird in this tree is the very one she saw yesterday, she will do so on the basis of some distinguishing features of the bird, or else be merely guessing or lying. Important **psychological** concepts are not like this according to Wittgenstein. If one says, "I am in **pain**," one does not identify the sensation as pain by noting one or more of its properties. Nor does one identify oneself as oneself in any such way, either. The **grammar** of **the first-person singular** pronoun and "pain" is not like the grammar of words that refer to **objects** such as birds and trees. The idea of making a mistake is absurd when it comes to first-person psychological **avowals**, at least in ordinary circumstances. If a man says, "I have a headache" or "I want Smith to win the election," then he might be lying, but he cannot be making a mistake (assuming that he is a competent speaker of English). One is 'infallible' in this way not because it is so easy to identify sensations, and other **inner** states, but because there is no such thing as identifying a sensation in the way that there is such a thing as identifying a bird. There is simply no place in the **language-game** for the notion of making a mistake or checking to make sure that no mistake has been made. This **analysis** of the grammar of psychological language is part of Wittgenstein's diagnosis of what is wrong with philosophical **theories** based on treating psychological phenomena as objects of a peculiar kind. The same could be said of theories that treat sensations as objects of *any* kind.

IDENTITY, LAW OF. Wittgenstein consistently rejected the law of identity, which states that A = A. (Which is not to say that he *denied* that A = A.) In ***Tractatus Logico-Philosophicus*** proposition 5.533 he says that a **sign** for identity, without which the law could not be expressed, is not essential to **logical** notation because identity can be shown by simply using the same sign for the same **object**. In the "**Big Typescript**" he suggests that the law of identity is **nonsense**, rather than something of fundamental importance as has been thought. ***Philosophical Investigations*** §216 says that there is no better example of a useless **proposition** than that "A thing is identical with itself." It tells one nothing, but seems important (as it has to **Gottlob Frege** and Ayn Rand, for instance).

IMAGINATION. It is clear that the imagination is important in Wittgenstein's ***Philosophical Investigations***. The book's first numbered remark begins with a quotation from **Augustine** in which he describes how he learned which objects were referred to by which words. He is surely imagining what he thinks must have happened rather than actually remembering the process, and Wittgenstein comments that Augustine's words present a certain **picture** of human **language**, a picture that, true or false, surely exists in the imagination: a picture is a way of imagining or taking something to be.

Imagination is also important for Wittgenstein's way of doing **philosophy**. Not only does he talk about what Augustine is thinking primarily of (namely, certain kinds of nouns) but he also instructs the reader to use her imagination in certain ways too. Thus we find him telling us in §1, "Now think of the following use of language . . . ," in §2, "Let us imagine a language for which . . . ," and in §4, "Imagine a script in which . . ." In all this Wittgenstein imagines or speculates about what Augustine is imagining or how he is picturing language. Wittgenstein follows this with invitations and commands to imagine different languages and uses of language. How we think about, conceive of, picture, or imagine language working is his primary concern. To attack the Augustinian picture, he manipulates the readers' imagination, loosening the grip of one picture by opening up the mind to other possibilities.

We can imagine not only strange activities, such as uses of language, and objects, such as mythical beasts, but also *that* something or other is the case. For instance, we can imagine that certain words make sense. The law of **identity**, Wittgenstein says in §216, is a useless proposition, and yet the imagination can play with it. Somewhat like the experience of staring at a thing, going cross-eyed, and then staring at it normally again, so that what had appeared as two now appears once again as one thing, one can imagine that one is putting an object into its own shape and seeing that it fits. In each case it is as if a discovery has been made or confirmed: what appeared as two is really one, this thing is this thing. The discovery is less about the object in question and more about our ability to perceive or think about it in different ways though. I do not so much make use of the law of identity in my imagination (as if this were as good a place as any to get things done) as I (merely) imagine that I have found a use for it. The imagination can be misleading as well as liberating.

Another concern of his is with what the imagination is. We might think of it as a kind of internal theatre, in which pictures are displayed and words spoken, but this is only a picture of what imagining is, and a potentially misleading one at that. The imagination is more of a faculty than a place, imagining being something that we do, and it is not always **private** or personal. We can imagine things together, as Wittgenstein invites his reader to do with him at the start of the *Investigations*. The way to decide or see what the imagination is, he says in §370, is to think about or look at how the word 'imagination' is used, not to focus one's attention on one's own imagination or acts of imagining. The imagination is what we talk about when we talk about imagination, so investigating such talk tells us not only about words (as some critics of Wittgenstein have alleged) but about imagination itself. If we try to understand the imagination by looking inward and describing what we 'see,' then we run the risk of investigating too narrowly (perhaps I will think only to imagine objects and not activities or facts, say) or of including too much by imagining that we find what is not really there, perhaps because of some preconceived ideas about the imagination.

INDUCTION. A form of reasoning, sometimes described as going from the particular to the general, which has been famously argued to be nonrational by **David Hume**. Roughly, Hume's claim is that observed cases tell us nothing at all about unobserved cases. The belief that unobserved cases will probably resemble observed cases, especially when there have been many observed cases that all follow the same pattern, is not justified by **logic**. It may be natural for human beings to expect the next swan they see to be white if they have seen many swans and every one has been white so far, but it is now well known that some swans are black. Deductive reasoning from premises about the swans with which we are familiar supports no conclusion about unfamiliar swans. Wittgenstein's view is similar to Hume's.

Induction, Wittgenstein says in ***Tractatus Logico-Philosophicus*** proposition 6.363, is a matter of assuming that the future will follow not only the past but the simplest pattern that can be discerned in past events. This might be how people cannot help thinking, but it has no logical justification. *Tractatus* proposition 6.31 denies that the law of induction can be a logical law, because it has significant content. Logic need not justify **psychology**, so inductive reasoning is not a problem or bad thing, but it is a mistake to think that identifying such a pattern (a "natural law") thoroughly explains nature. **Science** does not so much **explain** as **describe** what happens, as Wittgenstein sees it.

The ***Philosophical Investigations*** (see §§324–325) similarly avoids questions about the justification of induction and, instead, focuses not on psychology but on the use of reasoning about the future in **language-games**. In some, one might regard past experiences as causing someone to be certain that, say, fire will burn her if she touches it. In others, one might appeal to past experience to justify a claim about what will happen if one does this or that. **Causation** and justification are not the same kind of thing, though, so Wittgenstein points out that beliefs of which one is **certain** might not have been reached by any process of reasoning. A terrified man being dragged toward the flames is not thinking that the flames will very probably, based on past experience, burn him. He might not be thinking anything at all. He might just be terrified.

INNER/OUTER. Psychology is often thought to have to do with what is in some sense inside of people or their heads. Of course it is not, though, simply about internal organs or their contents. **René Descartes** expressed quite clearly and influentially the idea that the 'inner' is not really spatial at all but is a different order of substance, consisting of nonspatial, insensible **minds** and ideas, whereas sensibility is the hallmark of the 'outer,' physical, or corporeal, and extension (three-dimensionality) is its **essence**. Hence the famous mind-body problem of how two components with different essences (nonspatial mind and essentially spatial brain/body) could combine interactively to form one **human being**. More recent theories have rejected Descartes's rather spiritual view in favor of reductions of the mental to the physical, in terms of either overt **behavior** or the brain and its activities.

Instead of thinking of the inner and the outer as different (or indeed the same) kinds of stuff, Wittgenstein presented the idea that stuff, in the sense of **objects**, is all outer, whereas the inner is not stuff at all. This is meant not as a **metaphysical theory** but as an observation about the **meaning** of the words used to talk about people's inner lives. One does not, according to Wittgenstein, use words such as '**thought**,' '**dream**,' '**pain**,' and so on, in the way one uses words that designate objects. So it is a mistake to think of thoughts, etc., as objects of a special kind, as Descartes did, or of an ordinary, physical kind, as many contemporary thinkers are inclined to do. Nor should one reject **ordinary language** as false on the grounds that the objects to which it refers do not really exist (as some 'eliminativists' do). It does not refer to objects at all, not even imaginary ones, according to Wittgenstein. This has led some people to think that Wittgenstein is a behaviorist, and indeed the most famous philosophical behaviorist, **Gilbert Ryle**, was inspired by Wittgenstein. It is doubtful that this is a correct interpretation of what Wittgenstein meant, however, and he explicitly denied being a behaviorist.

INTENDING AND MEANING SOMETHING. In ***Philosophical Investigations*** §34 Wittgenstein says that when one gives a definition and intends or means it in a certain way, this intending is not a mental process that accompanies the giving of the definition. That is, there is not one physical process of making certain sounds and then an additional, parallel, psychological process that somehow determines what I mean by those sounds. What I mean is not inaccessible to others in the way that this dual-process **picture** suggests. The circumstances or context are relevant too: What have I just been talking about? What do I go on to talk about or point at, etc.? The relevant context involves not only events immediately surrounding the words spoken. One can only intend to play chess, or have in **mind** chess when one says, "Let's play a game later," in a world or culture in which the game of chess exists (see *Investigations* §337). Similarly, one can only mean something by something in a world or culture in which there is a **language**. And then the language will affect what you can mean by what. In English, "I admire the president" can mean either that I admire the holder of that office, whoever it is, or that I admire the current president. But unless I do some work to establish a new **meaning**, I cannot mean "I hate your shoes" by the words "I admire the president." Imagining that *x* means *y*, or wanting *x* to mean *y*, is not the same thing as *x*'s meaning *y*. Meaning depends on context, and this is not controlled psychically.

Such emphasis on behavior and context might make Wittgenstein sound like a **behaviorist**, but his aim is far more to dispel false ideas than to propose any particular **theory**. In this case the false idea is that if I say "I'm going to walk the dog" and mean Fido rather than Spot, then I must perform or experience some process of meaning, such as having an image of Fido (and perhaps also one of Spot crossed out) float before my mind's eye while I speak. But this just does not happen in every case (so it does not have to happen in order for one to mean Fido), and even if it did, how would the appearance of such an image affect the meaning of my words? Imagine that a picture of Fido occurs to me every time I ask for a cup of coffee. This would not mean that I was really talking about Fido rather than coffee. The same kind of thing might be said about any mental process that accompanied speech. It does not appear to affect, let alone determine, the meaning of what is said.

See also INTENTIONALITY; METHOD OF PROJECTION.

INTENTIONALITY. Intentionality is a concept that can be traced back to the Scholastic **philosophy** of the Middle Ages but which is today associated primarily with the **psychologist** and philosopher Franz Brentano (1838–1917). The concept in question is that of what is taken to be a special feature of **consciousness**, namely that it points to or intends some **object**. Thus if one desires a glass of water, then a glass of water is the intentional object of one's desire. All desire is taken to be intentional in this way. Much the same goes for any psychological state. Each **belief** is about something, each fear is of something, and so on, so that intentionality ('about-ness,' 'of-ness,' 'for-ness') is sometimes regarded as the defining feature of 'the mental' or used simply as another name for consciousness. Brentano's point, though, was that intentionality is not the same thing as consciousness, the bare concept of which does not imply directedness toward an object (although it is hard to imagine someone being conscious without being conscious *of* anything).

A problem seems to arise when one considers that the object in question might not exist. It is possible to think of things, and talk about things, that do not exist. But a thought of something that does not exist, one might think, is a thought of nothing, which is therefore not a thought at all. The **picture theory** of the ***Tractatus Logico-Philosophicus*** suggests that a thought of, for instance, Santa Claus is a picture of **objects** that do exist (red cheeks, black boots, and so on) in an arrangement in which they could, but do not in fact, exist (a jolly old elf).

Wittgenstein's later philosophical work makes clear that he does not think of beliefs and the like as objects of any kind. Rather someone who believes something has a certain attitude toward **the world**, expects certain things, will be surprised by certain others, and so on. He also notes that sensations, feelings, and some moods and emotions lack intentionality, meaning that it is not the defining feature of all mental states.

INTERNAL RELATIONS. An internal relation, according to ***Tractatus Logico-Philosophicus*** proposition 4.014, is a logical pattern held in common. **Language** and **the world** must have such an internal relation if the one is to represent the other. But in another sense internal relations can also exist between two **objects** that are related in a particular kind of way. *Tractatus* 4.123 gives the example of a light and a dark shade of blue. It is unthinkable (and hence in this sense internal) that these very colors should fail to stand in that relation to each other.

An internal relation, though, is not a relation proper, according to **proposition** 4.122. It is not a relation that can be 'said' (or asserted to exist) but one that must instead be shown or made manifest. If someone knows what 'darker' means, then one cannot (**meaningfully**) tell her that *this* shade (pointing, say, to something navy blue) is darker than *that* one (pointing to something sky blue), as proposition 4.123 makes clear. Such a claim not only would not but *certainly* would not, *could* not, tell her anything. It would be a kind of **nonsense** (4.124 uses the word '*unsinnig,*' 'nonsensical'). This is not to say that one cannot meaningfully **say**, "Navy blue is darker than sky blue." That certainly could be informative to someone who did not know, for instance, what shade navy blue is. Indeed one can *say*, "This shade is darker than that one," but what one will be doing by uttering these words, if anything, is partially explaining what 'darker' means. In other words, the real form of one's proposition will be something like: "The word 'darker' is used to refer to relations between colors such as the relation between this color and that one." The sentence "Navy blue is darker than sky blue" will only ever be useful for teaching people the meaning of one or more of its constituent words. It will never inform anyone of anything if they already know these meanings, so as a genuine proposition, a statement of how things stand in the world, it is quite useless, nonsensical. It looks like a meaningful proposition because one can imagine it being used as something other than a (literal or direct) proposition. Wittgenstein also makes this point in the ***Philosophical Investigations*** (in a note by §38), and in ***On Certainty*** he takes great interest in sentences that look like statements of empirical fact but that really play a quite different role in the language (see §§95–101, for instance).

When there is an internal relation between possible **states of affairs**, there is an internal relation between the propositions that represent them (see proposition 4.125). This internal relation would be a **necessary** relation, a matter of **logic**. It cannot itself be represented or expressed by means of a proposition. Hence there are no laws of **logical inference**, simply propositions that follow from one another (because they are internally related).

IRELAND. Wittgenstein first went to Ireland in 1934 when he stayed in Connemara with **Maurice Drury** and **Francis Skinner** for a week's vacation. He also visited Drury in Dublin in 1938. In 1947 he returned for a longer stay, living first in Dublin, at Ross's Hotel, before moving to a farmhouse in Red Cross, County Wicklow, as a guest of Richard and Jenny Kingston. He prized Wicklow for the peace he found there, which enabled him to work on what is now the main text of the ***Philosophical Investigations*** (i.e., Part I of the third edition of the *Investigations*) and Volume I of the ***Remarks on the Philosophy of Psychology***. He also loved the beauty of the countryside and simply being away from **Cambridge**. His health suffered though, both physically and mentally (he complained of indigestion and feared that he might be going mad), so he moved, going to Rosro, the cottage he had earlier vacationed at, on 28 April 1948. There he lived miles from any civilization except a few neighboring cottages. He was looked after by Thomas Mulkerrins, an employee of the Drury family, which owned the cottage. He spent the winter of 1948 in Ross's Hotel. There he wrote ***Last Writings on the Philosophy of Psychology***. In April 1949 he went to his dying sister **Mining** in **Vienna**, before returning to Dublin on 16 May. He left Dublin in June, going first to Cambridge and Uxbridge (to see Ben Richards) and then to the **United States**.

J

JAMES, WILLIAM (1842–1910). An American **psychologist** and **philosopher** known for his defense of **pragmatism**, roughly the identification of **truth** with ideas that have useful consequences. Wittgenstein liked James's *Varieties of Religious Experience*, declaring that it did him good to read it. He told **Maurice Drury** that it was James's being "a real human being" that made him a good philosopher (see Monk p. 478). Even so, in teaching, Wittgenstein used examples from James's *Principles of Psychology* to illustrate the kind of **confused** thinking that Wittgenstein wanted to combat. The ***Philosophical Investigations*** makes contact at numerous points with ideas expressed by James. He is mentioned several times by name, but there are echoes of James's ideas (mostly being rejected as confused) throughout the book and in ***Zettel***. A useful list of these passages, giving references to both James's work and Wittgenstein's, is given in Appendix 2 of *A Wittgenstein Workbook* edited by Christopher Coope, **Peter Geach**, Timothy Potts, and Roger White (1970).

JEWISHNESS. His concern with moral perfection led Wittgenstein at one point to insist on **confessing** to several people various sins, including that of allowing others to underestimate the extent of his "Jewishness." His father Karl **Wittgenstein's** parents were born Jewish but converted to Protestantism and his mother Leopoldine (née Kalmus) was Catholic, but her father was of Jewish descent. Wittgenstein himself was baptized in a Catholic church and was given a Catholic burial, although between baptism and burial he was neither a practicing nor a believing Catholic. Some of Wittgenstein's recorded remarks on Jewishness generally, and in particular relation to himself, have led people to accuse him of **anti-Semitism**.

JOHNSON, WILLIAM ERNEST (1858–1931). A **Cambridge** logician, Fellow of King's College, who tried to teach Wittgenstein when he first went there, but found him an unwilling student, more likely to argue than to listen and learn. In Wittgenstein's defense, it should be noted that Johnson is said to have been an imperfect teacher, failing sometimes to focus on what was most important about an issue. The two became friends, though, sharing a love of **music**, and Wittgenstein donated £200 a year from 1913 onward to help support Johnson's work on **logic**. (Details are sketchy about exactly in which years Johnson received payment. It would have been difficult, certainly, for Wittgenstein to pay him during **World War I**.) Johnson's best-known work is his three-volume *Logic*, published between 1921 and 1924.

JOKES. ***Philosophical Investigations*** §111 says that the depth of **philosophy** is the depth of a **grammatical** joke. This is not to say that philosophy is itself a grammatical joke, but it clearly implies a connection between the two. Their sharing the same depth cannot be a coincidence in Wittgenstein's view. He gives an example of a joke like this in §42, involving his imaginary **builders**. Wittgenstein here imagines a language consisting of **names** for tools that B is to hand to A when the name is given. If the relevant tool is broken B might shake his head, and then the **sign** for that tool still has a place in the **language-game**, a **meaning**, even though the **object** to which it refers is no more. The same might happen, Wittgenstein suggests, if A gives a sign that has never been used to name any tool. This could be "a sort of joke" between A and B, he says.

Jokes are important to Wittgenstein not only as examples but because the humor of some jokes stems from the absurdity of what some philosophical **theories** ask one to **believe**. The theories are not obviously **nonsensical**, but a good joke can bring out what is wrong with them. He once told **Norman Malcolm** that a good philosophical book could be written that would consist entirely of jokes. Some of the work of comedians such as Woody Allen and Stephen Wright might be thought of as belonging to this kind of humor. Consider for instance Woody Allen's joke about cheating on his **metaphysics** exam by looking into another student's **soul**. If **René Descartes** is right about the nature of the **mind**, then something like such cheating ought to be possible. Allen's joke brings out not so much the falsity or impossibility but the absurdity of this idea.

JOLLES FAMILY. *See* BERLIN.

JUDAISM. *See* JEWISHNESS.

K

KANT, IMMANUEL (1724–1804). Generally regarded as one of the greatest philosophers of all time and best known for his *Critique of Pure Reason* (1781) and *Groundwork of the Metaphysic of Morals* (1785). Wittgenstein read the former work while a prisoner of war in 1918. His personal **ethics** have been compared to Kant's deontological view that there are certain things one simply must (or must not) do, regardless of the consequences, for the simple reason that it is one's duty. Kant claimed, though, to offer not a new ethic but a new formula or way of expressing an old view, and there is no evidence that Kant's ethical **theory** influenced Wittgenstein. Kant's epistemology and **metaphysics**, however, do indeed seem to have affected Wittgenstein's thinking.

Kant defended metaphysics (within certain limits), the attempt to discover **truths** about the ultimate nature of reality using nonempirical, rational, *a priori* means. He argued that **the world** of experience is shaped by the **mind** with which it is experienced, and so that one can know in advance of any particular experience what the general form of experience, of the empirical world, will be. He also probed the limits of reason, of what can be understood and what must remain matters of faith.

In a similar way the ***Tractatus Logico-Philosophicus*** draws a line between that of which we can speak and that of which we must be silent, as well as positing a parallel structure in both **logic** and the world. In Wittgenstein's later work, **grammar** might be thought to play a similar role to the "**concepts**" and "forms of intuition" (roughly, mental structures) that Kant describes. If there is a line of influence here, it passes also through **Arthur Schopenhauer**, who developed a Kantian metaphysic of his own and by whose work Wittgenstein was impressed at a young age.

Wittgenstein is not at all straightforwardly Kantian though. Not only does he use different terminology, but following **Gottlob Frege**, he rejects Kant's philosophy of **mathematics** (which treats mathematical truths as features of the phenomenal world, the world of experience, made inevitable by the form of the mind). Given how important mathematics was to Wittgenstein as a subject for philosophy, and given the close connections between what he says about mathematics and, for instance, **rule-following** and the **arbitrariness of grammar**, it seems unwise to exaggerate the similarities between his thinking and Kant's.

KENNY, ANTHONY JOHN PATRICK (1931–). A British philosopher and Wittgenstein scholar. Kenny is a noted authority also on St. Thomas Aquinas, **René Descartes**, **Gottlob Frege**, and the philosophies of **mind** and **religion**. At Oxford University he has served as Pro-Vice-Chancellor, Warden of Rhodes House, and Master of Balliol College. He is the author of many books, including *Wittgenstein* (1973), *The Legacy of Wittgenstein* (1984), *Frege* (1995), and *A Brief History of Western Philosophy* (1998). He is also the editor of *The Wittgenstein Reader* (1994).

KEYNES, JOHN MAYNARD (1883–1946). One of the most influential British economists of the 20th century. His greatest work was *The General Theory of Employment, Interest and Money* published in 1936. This book almost single-handedly created what is now called macroeconomics, and it led governments to begin thinking of themselves as responsible for employment levels. Wittgenstein met Keynes at King's College, **Cambridge**, and they became friends. Keynes was a member of the **Apostles**, helped Wittgenstein arrange various financial matters (such as his support for **W. E. Johnson**), and intervened with the Italians to try to secure Wittgenstein's release from prison at the end of **World War I**.

KIERKEGAARD, SØREN (1813–1855). The greatest ever Danish philosopher, associated with both existentialism and **fideism**. Unusually for a philosopher, he emphasized the importance of the subjective and the nonrational. Many of his works were published under pseudonyms, leaving the reader in some doubt as to whether the views presented are Kierkegaard's own or not. Kierkegaard himself wrote that he wanted people to think for themselves. Wittgenstein admired his work, and it has been suggested by **James Conant** that Wittgenstein used Kierkegaardian indirection in the ***Tractatus Logico-Philosophicus***, putting forward views that he did not hold for the reader to recognize them as **nonsense**.

O. K. Bouwsma reports that Wittgenstein regarded Kierkegaard as very serious (which would usually be a compliment, coming from Wittgenstein), but that he "struck him almost as like a snob, too high, for him, not touching the details of common life" (Bouwsma p. 46, from 11 October 1949). Perhaps one should not rely too much on such secondhand reports of Wittgenstein's views. Wittgenstein says little directly and unambiguously about Kierkegaard, however. In ***Culture and Value*** he agrees with Kierkegaard that faith is a passion, in contrast to **wisdom** (p. 53, from 1946). Elsewhere

Wittgenstein speaks of Kierkegaard's greatness (see PPO p. 219) and purity (PPO p. 213), comparing him favorably in the latter regard even with **Fyodor Dostoevsky**, Wittgenstein's favorite novelist.

KINESTHESIS. Feelings of movement in the body. Wittgenstein raises the question in ***Philosophical Investigations*** §621 whether the kinesthetic sensations one has when raising one's arm are the willing of the act. Presumably the answer is No, but if an intentional act is not one caused by a psychological act of **intending**, then one might expect the intention to be some kind of accompaniment to the arm's rising, just as one might think of **meaning** words in a certain way as a psychological process accompanying the uttering of those words.

In ***Philosophy of Psychology—A Fragment*** Part VIII Wittgenstein discusses the relation between kinesthetic sensations and our knowledge of the movement and position of our body parts. It seems that we can describe where our limbs and digits are in relation to each other, e.g., whether one's legs are crossed, without necessarily having any clear feelings to go by. We can apparently know the position of our limbs in the sense that we can describe it, without deriving this knowledge from any experience or observation. **G. E. M. Anscombe** discusses this non-observational knowledge of the body in her book *Intention*.

THE KING OF THE DARK CHAMBER. *See* TAGORE, RABINDRANATH (1861–1941).

KLIMT, GUSTAV (1862–1918). A well-known Austrian painter who founded the school of painting known as the **Vienna** Sezession. His style was noted for its eroticism. Klimt was commissioned to paint the portrait of Margarete **Wittgenstein** (Ludwig's sister) when she married in 1905. His work was collected by Karl Wittgenstein, who financed Klimt's mural *Philosophie* and the Secession Building, at which works by Klimt were exhibited. His best-known painting is the 1909 work *The Kiss*.

KODER DIARIES. Manuscript 183 of Wittgenstein's *Nachlass* contains diaries given to Rudolf Koder by Wittgenstein's sister **Margarete**. They were written between 1930 and 1932, and between 1936 and 1937, the early part while he was in **Cambridge** and the latter while he was in **Norway**. Having been discovered only in 1993, the diaries have been little commented on, but they provide an interesting mixture of personal and philosophical remarks, many of which have to do with questions of **ethics** and **religion**, especially Wittgenstein's own relation to religious faith, which is troubled.

He describes himself as attracted to Christianity, but seems incapable of real belief. The diaries are published in ***Ludwig Wittgenstein—Public and Private Occasions***.

KÖHLER, WOLFGANG (1887–1967). A psychologist and author of *Gestalt Psychology* (1929), which influenced Wittgenstein significantly. Wittgenstein would sometimes start a lecture by reading from this book and then comment on its philosophical significance. For Köhler, following **Johann Wolfgang von Goethe**, *Gestalt* means not just form or shape, as it does in ordinary German, but a segregated or organized whole. The emphasis in *Gestalt* **psychology** is on the active role of the **mind** in organizing what is perceived into wholes, for instance, not just three dots but a triangle.

Wittgenstein shared Köhler's opposition to **behaviorism** and was interested in many of the same issues, but was dissatisfied with Köhler's treatment of them. In Wittgenstein's view it was a mistake to talk about a *Gestalt* as some kind of private **object** that is perceived. It is, one might say, a way of seeing some object or objects, but not an object itself. This is reminiscent of Wittgenstein's claim in ***Tractatus Logico-Philosophicus*** proposition 5.5423 that when one sees the same figure in two different ways, then what one really sees is two different **facts**. A fact is not an object, though, so even here Wittgenstein is not saying what Köhler did, and Wittgenstein's later views on **aspect-seeing** are expressed in quite different terms.

KOKOSCHKA, OSKAR (1886–1980). A writer and painter associated with **Gustav Klimt** and supported by **Adolf Loos**. Kokoschka left his native Austria for Germany, then, alarmed at what was happening in Germany and Austria, moved to Czechoslovakia in 1934. His work was controversial and denounced by the Nazis. In 1938 he moved to England. His paintings were exhibited at the Secession Building in **Vienna**, financed by Wittgenstein's father Karl. Kokoschka was one of the beneficiaries of Wittgenstein's donation to struggling artists, receiving 5,000 crowns through **Ludwig von Ficker**, who acted as intermediary.

KRAUS, KARL (1874–1936). An Austrian satirist noted for his wit and his ethical commitment to proper use of the German **language**. Misuse of language he thought of not so much as an offense against Germanic culture but as contributing to bad **thinking**, which can result in such disasters as **World War I**. Exactly how sloppy uses of language can cause wars is not clear, but propaganda often relies on simplistic thinking and distortions of the truth, and if propaganda is ever effective, then perhaps the careless use of generalizations, slogans, and stereotypes really is a threat to peace. The antidote proposed by Kraus is very careful attention to the details of what one says in order to ensure that they match the reality being described. He attacked hypocrisy, militarism, and Nazism primarily through his journal ***Die Fackel*** (*The Torch*), which Wittgenstein read and admired. He was also a **poet** and a playwright.

Kraus shared Wittgenstein's view that **aesthetics** is linked with **ethics**. Partly because of such similarities in their ideas, and partly because they both knew **Paul Engelmann** and **Adolf Loos**, Wittgenstein hoped that Kraus would help with the publication of the ***Tractatus Logico-Philosophicus***. It was not to be. Wittgenstein later came to think of Kraus as little more than a brilliant stylist (see, for instance, PPO p. 213).

KRIPKE, SAUL AARON (1940–). An important American logician and philosopher of **language**. Kripke developed a semantics for quantified modal **logic** when he was only 15 years old and was the youngest person ever to be so when, in 1973, he was chosen to give the **John Locke** lectures at Oxford University. He is also the author of *Wittgenstein on Rules and Private Language* (Oxford, 1982), one of the best-known works on Wittgenstein's writings on this important topic.

Kripke is struck by the idea that anything might count as continuing a series or following a **rule** in the same way. It all depends on how the rule or series is interpreted. And any rule for interpretation will itself be subject to a variety of interpretations, and so on. What counts as following a rule correctly, then, is not determined somehow by the rule itself but by what the relevant linguistic community accepts as following the rule. So whether two plus two equals four depends not on some abstract, extra-human rule of addition but on what language-users, and especially the people they regard as experts, accept. **Truth** conditions are replaced by assertability conditions. To put it crudely, what counts is not what is true or right (in some sense independent of the community of language-users), but what one can get away with or get others to accept.

Kripke's **theory** is clear and ingenious, and owes a lot to Wittgenstein, but is doubtful as an interpretation of Wittgenstein. Kripke himself presents the **argument** not as Wittgenstein's, nor as his own, but as "Wittgenstein's argument as it struck Kripke" (Kripke, p. 5). That the argument is not Wittgenstein's is suggested by the fact that it is a theory, and Wittgenstein rejected philosophical theories, and by the fact that the argument relies heavily on the first sentence of ***Philosophical Investigations*** §201: "This was our paradox: no course of action could be determined by a rule, because every course of action can be brought into accord with the rule." For Kripke's theory as a reading of Wittgenstein, it is not good that the very next paragraph begins by noting "That there is a misunderstanding here . . ." Still, it is no easy matter to see just where Wittgenstein does diverge from the hybrid person sometimes referred to as 'Kripkenstein.' The key perhaps lies later in the same paragraph, where Wittgenstein writes that "there is a way of grasping a rule which is *not* an interpretation."

Many scholars, notably **G. P. Baker** and **P. M. S. Hacker**, have gone to great lengths to explain why Kripke is mistaken. Since Kripke is so much easier to understand than Wittgenstein himself, one of the best ways into Wittgenstein's **philosophy** is to study Kripke and his Wittgensteinian critics. At the very least, Kripke introduces his readers well to issues that were of great concern to Wittgenstein and shows their importance. He is the author also of *Naming and Necessity* (1980).

L

LADDER, IMAGE OF. ***Tractatus Logico-Philosophicus*** 6.54 compares the **propositions** of the book to rungs of a ladder that is to be thrown away after one has climbed up it. The ladder image occurs in **Fritz Mauthner's** *Beiträge zu einer Kritik der Sprache* (Stuttgart: Cotta, 1901–1903), volume I, p. 2, and in **Arthur Schopenhauer's** *The World as Will and Representation* volume 2, p. 80. Black (p. 377) also quotes Sextus Empiricus comparing a skeptic who proves the nonexistence of proof to a man who kicks over a ladder after he has used it to climb to a high place.

Compare also CV p. 7: "Anything that I might reach by climbing a ladder does not interest me." This suggests, as do several other remarks, that Wittgenstein came to think that the *Tractatus* was a flawed work.

LANGUAGE. Like many other philosophers of the 20th century, Wittgenstein paid careful attention to language. This is at least partly because he did not think of language as a mere means for communication, as if one could have **thoughts** without language, or have a purely **private language**. Instead, language for Wittgenstein is more like a system of **meaning**, so that any thought must, by definition, be in language (since a meaningless thought is no thought at all: a thought is something like an opinion or a position, something that one can hold, and one cannot be of the opinion that bububu, because, as this line of thought reveals, bububu is not a thought but mere **nonsense**). This is not a **theory** about what language really is but more a kind of implicit methodological stipulation. Wittgenstein is interested in language because he is interested in meaning, in making sense.

His early ***Tractatus Logico-Philosophicus*** famously contains the **picture theory** of meaning, according to which the **essential** function of language is to depict or represent reality. The later ***Philosophical Investigations*** attacks this theory, suggesting that language works in a variety of ways and perhaps has no one essential function or nature. Language in Wittgenstein's later work is closely related to the ideas of **language-games** and **forms of life**. The close connection that Wittgenstein sees between language and **logic** is suggested by his emphasis on **grammar** (the **rules** of language) in his later work. Really this connection is there from the *Tractatus* on though, as Wittgenstein's interest in that book is very clearly in logic and language together.

LANGUAGE-GAMES. Early in the ***Philosophical Investigations*** Wittgenstein introduces the concept of language-games using the examples of someone shopping for **apples** and a pair (later a whole society) of **builders**. The key ideas contained in the concept of language-games seem to be that, like games, uses of **language** are bound by certain **rules (grammar)** and that, also like games, they are human activities. This is a more dynamic conception of language than that implied by the earlier **picture theory**. Since the term language-games is plural, there is also a clear implication that the rules that govern one area of language might not apply in some other, so that before one could tell whether a sentence made sense or not, one would have to identify the region of language to which it belonged. Since Wittgenstein emphasizes the diversity of games and their lack of any common **essence** (instead, he says, they are all called games in virtue of a **family resemblance**), it seems reasonable to infer that language, in his view, likewise has no essence.

Philosophical Investigations §7 gives the following list of things to which the term 'language-game' can be applied: the games by means of which children learn their native language; primitive languages; the ostensive teaching of words, such as the process of naming stones, as adopted by the builders in §6; the process of repeating words after someone, as in a game like ring-a-ring-a-roses; and finally, "the whole, consisting of language and the actions into which it is woven." This last definition is strikingly different from the others (with the possible exception of primitive languages, however exactly they might be defined) and suggests that the idea of a language-game is closely related to that of **form of life**.

LAST WRITINGS ON THE PHILOSOPHY OF PSYCHOLOGY. Edited by **G. H. von Wright** and Heikki Nyman, these remarks date from the last years of Wittgenstein's life. Volume I consists of preliminary studies for ***Philosophy of Psychology—A Fragment*** (formerly known as Part II of the ***Philosophical Investigations***) and consists of transcribed notes from manuscripts 137–138, dating from 22 October 1948 to 20 May 1949. These notes continue on from those published as ***Remarks on the Philosophy of Psychology***, but existing only in manuscript form (unlike the typed and more polished earlier remarks), they are rougher and more repetitive.

Volume II consists of all the notes contained in manuscripts 169–171, parts of manuscript 173, and most of manuscripts 174 and 176. The general theme throughout is the **inner** and the outer, and all the remarks contained here date from the period 1949–1951. This second volume of Wittgenstein's last writings (he was also writing at this time on **color** and **certainty**) contains a wealth of remarks that are quite different from those to be found in the *Investigations*. This is not to say that they represent a new set of ideas, but that they are a rich source of evidence for what Wittgenstein was trying to get at in his later period. In contrast, most of the material in Volume I and in the earlier *Remarks on the Philosophy of Psychology* will seem quite familiar to anyone who has read the *Philosophical Investigations* and ***Zettel***.

LEAVIS, FRANK RAYMOND (1895–1978). A well-known and influential **Cambridge** literary critic, noted for his early praise of D. H. Lawrence, strong sense of the moral value of literature, and opposition to what he saw as cultural decline. Wittgenstein became a friend of his despite disliking his literary criticism, which Wittgenstein encouraged him to give up (probably not entirely seriously).

LECTURE ON ETHICS. An address given by Wittgenstein on 17 November 1929 to the **Heretics** Society of **Cambridge University**. Often overlooked because of its brevity, its appearance outside the canonical ***Tractatus Logico-Philosophicus*** and ***Philosophical Investigations***, and its accessible, seemingly nonrigorous style, this lecture is nonetheless interesting because it is Wittgenstein's most sustained discussion of **ethics**. It is also interesting to see what subject he chose to address when speaking to a nonspecialist audience, and this is the only record we have of such an occasion.

The lecture begins with a kind of definition of its subject matter, but Wittgenstein gives the definition not in terms of a specifiable **essence** but rather in terms of a number of similar expressions (such as the inquiry into what is really important, or most valuable, or the meaning of life) in order to convey a common idea. Wittgenstein compares this kind of definition with the composite photography of **Francis Galton**, who superimposed photographs of different faces in order to produce a kind of average that was not the face of any one individual. This is not the same as, but seems related to, Wittgenstein's later idea of **family resemblance**.

Wittgenstein goes on to relate ethics to a certain kind of experience. Chief among these is the experience of **wonder** at the very existence of the world. The others are feeling absolutely safe, and feeling guilt. These are experiences that Wittgenstein says he has had, and he apparently expects others to have had similar experiences too, but he regards them as impossible to talk about without lapsing into **nonsense**. This is because he considers meaningful **propositions** to **say** something about **the world**. "I wonder at the existence of the world," though, makes no sense, he says, because the world could not possibly not have existed. The world, as the *Tractatus Logico-*

Philosophicus asserts at the beginning, is all that is the case. It would be nonsense to suggest that all that is the case is not the case. So the existence of the world is logically necessary, and no more to be wondered at than that A = A or that 1 + 1 = 2. Similarly, "absolute safety" makes no sense either, because it is always conceivable that one could be harmed in some way, and because part of the (supposed) idea of absolute safety is that one will be safe even if one dies. But this is a contradiction of the very **meaning** of safety. **Socrates's** claim that a good person cannot be harmed is either very obviously false (he was forced to drink poison until he died shortly after making this claim) or else nonsensical (if, as was surely the case, Socrates did not count being killed as a kind of harm). Finally, although Wittgenstein says very little about this example, it makes questionable sense to think of one's actions as bad if they advanced one's self-interest. If I lie to get ahead at work and the tactic succeeds, then it seems I should be happy. Feelings of guilt, which 'say' that this was a bad thing, make no sense in terms of the normal meanings of 'good' and 'bad.' Getting a promotion is a good thing in the normal sense of the word 'good,' not something to feel bad about.

This normal sense of 'good,' Wittgenstein says, is relative to some end that one may or may not have, and it makes uses of 'good' potentially statements of **fact**. Thus if I want to get to Grantchester, then a good road to take is one that goes there. This goodness is relative to my desire to go to that particular place, but it is a straightforward matter of fact that if I do want to go there and this road is the quickest path to take, then this route is a good way for me to go. Ethics, according to Wittgenstein, involves the use of 'good' in a different, absolute sense. This is not relative to what anyone wants and is not convertible to any statement of scientific fact. It is similar to **Immanuel Kant's** idea of a categorical imperative, that is, a necessity that does not depend on anything hypothetical, such as "If you want to get to Grantchester . . ." or "If you want to avoid trouble with the police . . ." A categorical imperative simply tells you what you must do, regardless of such hypotheticals. Lying, for instance, is ruled out. This is not because lying is regarded by Kant as likely to lead to unhappiness, or to prison, or to hell, but simply because lying is wrong. It is bad, in Wittgenstein's terms, in an absolute sense.

But since this sense does not relate to facts about the world, it is not natural but supernatural. And not referring to the world, such uses of language do not make sense. Wittgenstein considers some possible ways that one might try to regard it as making sense but rejects these right away. The very point of ethical statements, he says, is to go beyond the facts, beyond the accidents of desire, beyond the natural world. It belongs to the essence of ethics, therefore, that it cannot be put into words that make sense, even though the experiences these words try to express are real. People really do feel "wonder at the existence of the world" even though "wonder at the existence of the world" makes no sense. Or so Wittgenstein claims. It is possible that he would later have referred to this kind of use of words not as nonsense but as an instance of the use of words in a **secondary sense**.

The lecture on ethics is also a lecture about **religion**. Wittgenstein believes that when people have said that God created the world, and that we are in God's hands, and that God will judge our sins, what they have meant is the same as what is meant by people who talk about wondering at the existence of the world, about being absolutely safe, and about feeling guilt. It is also, he says without explanation, about the most essential part of **aesthetics**.

LEIBNIZ, GOTTFRIED WILHELM (1646–1716). A great German **philosopher** and **mathematician** admired by Wittgenstein. Leibniz belongs to the rationalist school of thought founded by **René Descartes**, and was an important influence on **Immanuel Kant**. In **metaphysics** he defended the view that **the world** is made up of monads. A monad is like a mathematical point in that it has a 'point of view' but no size. It is like a **mind** or **soul** in that it is the kind of **object** that has **consciousness**. Each monad, according to Leibniz, is completely self-contained or "windowless." Thus each is independent of the others, to the extent that none can even perceive another, let alone act on it. Each person's mind is a monad, programmed by God as part of His pre-established harmony to experience an unfolding sequence of events from its own unique point of view but otherwise wholly parallel to the experience of others. Hence two monads, minds, or souls, will see a pane of glass, say, break at the same time, even though neither really perceives anything outside itself, and the glass is merely a representation of a number of invisible monads. Moreover, the rock that breaks the glass is itself a representation of monads, and these monads do not break anything. The true cause of all events is God Himself.

It was Leibniz who first identified the problem of **rule-following** that **Saul Kripke** finds being raised and solved in Wittgenstein's ***Philosophical Investigations***. Leibniz also independently invented calculus at around the same time as did Sir **Isaac Newton**.

LION (EXAMPLE OF). In ***Philosophy of Psychology—A Fragment*** (formerly known as Part II of the ***Philosophical Investigations***) Wittgenstein famously claims that if a lion could talk, we would not be able to **understand** it. He brings up the example of the lion in the context of discussing the idea that we can only know what is outwardly observable with other people, not the **inner**. This remark is not presented as a hypothesis about animal **psychology**, although it has been treated that way, but as an uncontroversial case of a phenomenon taken to be familiar to people who have traveled from one country to another. Even when one knows the **language** of another country, Wittgenstein says, one might not understand the people themselves, and not because one cannot read their **minds**. Presumably he means that their culture or **form of life** is so alien that one cannot find one's feet with them. One would not 'get' or know what to expect from their culture, **jokes**, and so on. Indeed one can, and Wittgenstein did, feel alien in this way even with some people from one's own culture. This sense of being lost is very similar to the feeling one has when dealing with a **philosophical** problem, Wittgenstein suggests.

LITERATURE. Wittgenstein took a great interest in literature, and literary writers have in turn taken an interest in his work. He loved some well-known classics such as **Fyodor Dostoevsky's** *The Brothers Karamazov* and Charles Dickens's *A Christmas Carol*, but he also enjoyed more obscure works, such as Norbert Davis's *Rendezvous with Fear*, a lighthearted detective story. Wittgenstein liked it so much that he thought about writing a fan letter to its author. What he seems to have looked for above all else when reading is wisdom, saying once that there was more wisdom in detective stories than the philosophical articles published in the prestigious journal *Mind*.

Wittgenstein has featured in works of literature in various ways since his death. Perhaps the first instance of this is Iris Murdoch's 1954 novel *Under the Net*, in which the character Dave Gellmann is often thought to be based on Wittgenstein. References to Wittgenstein have been made in numerous other novels, including Thomas Bernhard's *Wittgenstein's Nephew*, Bruce Duffy's *The World as I Found It*, and W. G. Sebald's *Austerlitz*. His influence can also be found in other areas of the **arts** too. Derek Jarman made a film about him (*Wittgenstein*, 1993), the composers Elisabeth Lutyens and Anthony Powers have set his words to music, and poets have been inspired as much as novelists have by his work.

See also POETRY.

LOCKE, JOHN (1632–1704). A major English philosopher, widely regarded as the founding father of British **empiricism**. Locke's theories about the mind and its ideas can be seen as the target for some of Wittgenstein's attacks, especially in the ***Philosophical Investigations***, although Wittgenstein rarely mentions his targets by name, and (or perhaps because) he seems to have in mind not this or that philosopher but a whole tradition or way of thinking in which such people as Locke and **René Descartes** figure prominently but not exclusively. Locke is also known for his political philosophy, which was a major influence on Thomas Jefferson, but this is independent of the ideas of his that Wittgenstein criticizes.

LOGIC. Logic is one of the main traditional branches of **philosophy** since the time of **Aristotle**, and was clearly important to Plato even if he did not recognize it as a specific area of study but thought of it rather as a general means to the **truth**. The formal study of logic, roughly speaking of which kinds of **arguments** are good and which are bad, progressed little after Aristotle until the work of **Gottlob Frege**. Wittgenstein's most obvious contribution was the invention of truth-tables, although there is some dispute as to whether it was Wittgenstein, or indeed any one person, who invented this device. (Credit is also given to Frege, **Bertrand Russell**, Emil Leon Post, Charles Sanders Peirce, and others.) Otherwise, logic has a strange place in Wittgenstein's work. Deductive arguments can be hard to find in his work, more often seeming to be implied than explicitly stated. Some commentators hold that there are no real logical arguments in any of his work, that its nature is rhetorical rather than logical. Yet logic (and/or **grammar**) seems to have been at the very heart of Wittgenstein's conception of philosophy, at least with regard to its subject matter.

This is not to say that there *are* logical arguments in his work. In the ***Tractatus Logico-Philosophicus***, after all, Wittgenstein says that his propositions are **nonsense** (see proposition 6.54). Opinions differ as to how to interpret this remark, but at face **value** it seems to deny that the book contains any real arguments (since a genuinely logical argument would not include any nonsense). Similarly, ***Philosophical Investigations*** §109 says that philosophical work must consist of "**description** alone." Yet a logical argument is not a description. On the other hand, both books seem to be attempts at rational persuasion, and are generally considered to consist of nothing but arguments.

Some of the disagreement about how much logical argument there is in Wittgenstein's work probably depends simply on what one counts as an argument. Clearly Wittgenstein is out to change people's **minds** in honest and nonarbitrary ways. If such efforts fit one's definition of an argument, then there are arguments in his work. The question then arises of why Wittgenstein wrote as he did, not making his arguments more obvious or clear. Views on this vary from those who believe that he really had logically sound arguments in mind but preferred to adopt a more literary or **poetic** style (because of vanity or simply his personal taste) to those who think that the particular views that Wittgenstein attacked or defended did not really matter to him and that his real goal was to "demonstrate a method," as he puts it in *Investigations* §133. This method is not the traditional one of advancing theses supported by logical arguments. Most scholars though have focused on the arguments (good or bad) that they discern in Wittgenstein's work. **P. M. S. Hacker** is an especially erudite and productive exemplar of this approach. **Stanley Cavell** tends toward the opposite approach (Beth Savickey is another example, though less influential).

See also LOGICAL ATOMISM; LOGICAL CATEGORIES; LOGICAL CONSTANTS; LOGICAL FORM; LOGICAL INFERENCE; LOGICAL SPACE; LOGICAL TRUTH; PSYCHOLOGISM.

LOGICAL ANALYSIS. The means by which **Bertrand Russell** hoped, or believed in theory that one ought to be able, to find **logical atoms**. The idea is an important part of the method of early analytic **philosophy**, but perhaps makes work in philosophy sound too much like work in physics. Physical analysis might reveal physical atoms while logical analysis might reveal logical atoms, but the kinds of analysis and atoms in each case are very different. Russell, of course, was aware of this, but Wittgenstein emphasized the difference between **science** and philosophy, and might have been less comfortable with the analogy implicit in talk of logical atoms than Russell was.

See also ANALYSIS.

LOGICAL ATOMISM. The ***Tractatus Logico-Philosophicus*** says that **the world** can be divided into **facts**, that each fact is the existence of a **state of affairs**, and that a state of affairs is a combination of **objects**. These objects must have written into them the possibility of every state of affairs in which they could occur. New possibilities cannot, as it were, arise later. Since in **logic** all is **necessary**, all the possibilities with which logic deals must be there, in the very substance of the world, from the beginning. Thus objects constitute the unalterable form of the world. Since they are the primary, simple components of the world, they are like atoms. Since their forms, the possibilities of their occurring in states of affairs, determine all possibilities, and since logic deals with all possibilities, the **theory** that there are such objects is called logical atomism. This name also helps to distinguish the philosophical research program of **logical analysis** and its metaphysical commitment to atoms of one kind (something like momentary perceptions of **color**, perhaps) from the atomism of physics. It is considered a problem for logical atomism that Wittgenstein could never give an example of the kind of object that would count as a logical atom. The theory was first supported by **Bertrand Russell**, who credited Wittgenstein (then in the Austrian army in **World War I**) in his lectures on the subject. Whether Wittgenstein would have supported Russell's version of the theory then is unknown. It does not appear in Wittgenstein's later work.

LOGICAL CATEGORIES. In the ***Tractatus Logico-Philosophicus*** Wittgenstein says that it is **nonsense** to say that "1 is a number" (see proposition 4.1272). This is because *number* is a logical category to which *1* belongs. Since this is shown (or would be by a good **concept-script**), it cannot be **said**

(see proposition 4.1212). The **meaning** of "1" can be seen by attending to its use in a given system or **language**. Any attempt to state this meaning in a **proposition**, however successful it might seem, can only be a failure therefore. It will be nonsense. This applies not only to **numbers**. No logical category can be predicated of one of its members, according to Wittgenstein.

See also FORMAL CONCEPTS.

LOGICAL CONSTANTS. Logical constants are symbols that play the same kind of role as words such as 'or,' 'and,' 'not,' and so on. In ***Tractatus Logico-Philosophicus*** proposition 4.0312 Wittgenstein writes that his "fundamental thought" is that these symbols do not represent anything. **Bertrand Russell** had thought that **logic** describes reality in its most general form. In his *The Principles of Mathematics* (Cambridge University Press, 1903, p. vii) Russell gives the name "logical constants" to indefinable logical concepts the discussion of which "forms the chief part of philosophical logic" (*ibid.*, p. v). Russell conceives of these constants as entities with which the **mind** can be directly acquainted. In *Theory of Knowledge: The 1913 Manuscript* (Routledge, 1992), Russell argues that it is a kind of experience or immediate knowledge that allows us to understand such words as 'particulars,' 'universals,' 'relations,' and 'predicates' (see *Theory of Knowledge* p. 97). Russell adds that acquaintance with certain logical **objects** must be involved in our understanding words such as 'or,' 'not,' 'all,' and 'some.' He denies that these things are entities, but he still thinks of them as objects of some kind.

Wittgenstein denied this, and insisted that **propositions** of logic say nothing at all. A proposition such as "Either it is raining or it is not raining" is a **tautology**, saying nothing about **the world**. There is not some feature of reality that 'either/or' represents. Rather, this kind of proposition (perhaps not always when used in English but always when used in formal logic) shows (but does not '**say**') a legitimate way of combining **meaningful** propositions, such as "It is raining."

H. O. Mounce's *Wittgenstein's Tractatus: An Introduction* (p. 12) says of Wittgenstein's "fundamental thought" that "logic . . . reflects, on Wittgenstein's view, by showing not by saying. This indeed is the central doctrine of the *Tractatus*. Logic differs from all the other sciences because the other sciences say something about the world whereas logic only shows something." There is no representation, but there is reflection, in other words.

Schroeder (on pp. 85–86 of *Wittgenstein: The Way Out of the Fly Bottle*) suggests that it is not clear why Wittgenstein described this thought as fundamental, given that it is purely negative. It is still important, though, because it disposes of the views of Frege and Russell.

Hintikka (p. 19) gives a possible explanation of why this one, negative idea is so important to Wittgenstein: "The *Tractatus* is nothing more and nothing less than Russell's 1913 theory [as set out in *Theory of Knowledge*] *sans* logical forms as objects of acquaintance." Propositions 4.0312 and 5.4 can be seen as evidence of this. This leaves Wittgenstein with a question as to what holds a proposition together if not logical forms conceived as objects of acquaintance. "Wittgenstein's answer was: A proposition is held together, not by any additional 'tie' or 'glue' but by the forms of its constituents." See 2.03.

Hacker (p. 35) identifies Wittgenstein's target in *Tractatus* 5.4, where he says that there are no logical constants: "Frege argued that truth and falsehood were special logical objects named by sentences. Finally, he treated the logical connectives as names of literal functions, viz. 'not' as the name of the concept of negation (a unary function), the binary connectives as names of relations, and the quantifiers as names of second-level functions." Frege also tried to prove that **numbers** were logical objects.

LOGICAL FORM. Logical form is what the ***Tractatus Logico-Philosophicus*** says must be had in common by reality and any **picture** that is to represent it in any way. This form cannot be represented (*Tractatus* 4.121) by **propositions**, but it is mirrored in them. It is thus a case of what one cannot **say** but must instead show. The commonality thus shown will be an instance of what Wittgenstein calls an **internal relation**.

Ostrow (p. 47), following Burton Dreben, suggests that the point of the notion of logical form is to ease us into the idea that written propositions are pictures of reality, even though they do not appear to be (see 4.011). Otherwise, the concept of pictorial form would seem to have been pointless—Wittgenstein could just have referred to logical form throughout.

LOGICAL INFERENCE. In ***Tractatus Logico-Philosophicus*** propositions 5.11–5.156, Wittgenstein claims that there is no need for any laws of inference to justify inference from one **proposition**, or set of propositions, to another. If *r* follows from *p* and *q*, then it follows from *p* and *q*, not from those propositions in conjunction with anything else. Valid inference depends only on the **internal relations** between the senses of propositions.

LOGICAL POSITIVISM. A set of ideas associated with the **Vienna Circle**. The main idea is that every meaningful **proposition** is either **empirical** or **tautological**. Tautological propositions, which logical positivists, drawing on work by **Bertrand Russell** and Wittgenstein, take to include propositions of **logic** and **mathematics**, say nothing about **the world**. Empirical propositions are those that can be verified empirically. Theological and **metaphysical** propositions, falling into neither category, are dismissed as **nonsense**. Not surprisingly, the **verification principle** is controversial. Wittgenstein insisted that he never held it, although he did emphasize the value of asking how a proposition might be verified in order to **understand** its **meaning** more clearly. The principle is rejected by most philosophers today because it is not itself empirical and seems not to be a tautology, thus apparently failing its own standard of meaningfulness.

LOGICAL PRODUCT. The conjunction of two propositions. In ***Tractatus Logico-Philosophicus*** 4.465 Wittgenstein writes that the logical product of a proposition and a **tautology** says the same thing as the proposition on its own. Thus for instance, "This is a tomato and either it's raining or it's not raining" says the same as "This is a tomato." The addition of a tautology adds nothing to what is said, because tautologies say nothing. In 6.3751 he states that the logical product of two **elementary propositions** can never be a tautology or a contradiction. Otherwise one could add propositions with positive content and get zero content as a result. This can never be.

LOGICAL PROTOTYPE. In ***Tractatus Logico-Philosophicus*** 3.315 Wittgenstein introduces the notion of a logical prototype. He writes there that if we were to convert into variables all **signs** in a **proposition** whose **meaning** depends on an arbitrary agreement, then there will be a class of propositions that are all the values of the resulting variable proposition. This class will not depend on any agreement but only on the nature of the proposition. It will correspond, he says, to a **logical form**, and he refers to this as a logical prototype. In 5.522 he says that its pointing to a logical prototype is one of the things that is peculiar to the symbolism of **generality**.

LOGICAL SPACE. Logical space (*logischer Raum*) is a term used in the ***Tractatus Logico-Philosophicus*** to indicate the range of possibilities. Wittgenstein got the term from **Ludwig Boltzmann**, who thought of the different properties of a physical system as coordinates that together define a 'space' of possible states of the system. Wittgenstein does not define the term and uses it somewhat metaphorically.

LOGICAL SUM. The disjunction of two **propositions**. Thus the logical sum of propositions p and q is $p \vee q$ ("p or q"), meaning that either p or q or both are true.

See also LOGICAL PRODUCT.

LOGICAL SYNTAX. A term introduced in ***Tractatus Logico-Philosophicus*** 3.325. Wittgenstein there identifies it with what he calls logical **grammar**. It is apparently a very important idea, since Wittgenstein presents the use of a **symbolism** that obeys logical syntax as necessary for the avoidance of fundamental **confusions**, of which the whole of **philosophy** is full according to 3.324. The required symbolism will neither use the same **sign** for different symbols nor use signs that signify in different ways without this difference being clearly evident. To understand this, one needs to remember that a sign is what is perceptible of a symbol (see 3.32). Thus in the number 77 we have the same sign twice (namely, *7*) but two different symbols, one for tens and one for units.

In 3.33 Wittgenstein adds that in logical syntax the meaning of a sign must play no role. At least in part this is a criticism of the **theory of types** developed by **Bertrand Russell**. In 3.331 Wittgenstein says that Russell's having to refer to the meanings of signs when putting his rules for signs together shows that he has gone wrong.

In 3.334 Wittgenstein writes that the rules of logical syntax must be self-evident to someone who knows how each sign signifies. One need not know *what* it signifies, because the meaning of the signs is to play no role, but one does need to know *how* it signifies. What signifies in a symbol, according to 3.344, is the common feature of all symbols that are capable of taking its place according to the rules of logical syntax. If we know these **rules** for any sign language, says 6.124, then we know thereby all the **propositions** of **logic**.

LOGICAL TRUTH. Logical truths are **necessary** truths. It is unthinkable that they should be false. This kind of **truth** naturally interests philosophers, especially since **René Descartes** began his famous *Meditations* in search of such a point of **certainty**. In Wittgenstein's day, **Bertrand Russell** argued that these truths are descriptions of the most general features of **the world**. **Gottlob Frege**, on the other hand, held that they were descriptions of relations between logical **objects**. Rejecting both of these views, Wittgenstein's ***Tractatus Logico-Philosophicus*** maintains that logical truths are **tautologies**. This is not to deny that they are important, but their importance cannot be of the kind that many philosophers have taken them to have. For a tautology says nothing at all about the world (although it might **show** something about **logical form**). To know a tautology is not to know an important general truth about the world. It is to know nothing.

LOGICISM. The attempt to **show** (or the **theory** that it could be shown) that some or all of **mathematics** (especially arithmetic) can be reduced to, or is an extension or part of, **logic**. Both **Bertrand Russell** and **Gottlob Frege** preached and practiced logicism, albeit perhaps in different ways. Frege argued that arithmetic is not, *pace* **Immanuel Kant**, a body of synthetic *a priori* knowledge but is, rather, **analytic**. Russell also rejected Kant's view, but regarded logic as synthetic. How much Frege and Russell were in agreement depends on exactly what they meant by 'analytic,' 'synthetic,' and 'logic,' which is not entirely clear.

Wittgenstein opposed logicism, most notably in his ***Remarks on the Foundations of Mathematics***. He was in general opposed to reductions of one thing to another.

LOGIK, SPRACHE, PHILOSOPHIE. **Friedrich Waismann's** book *Logik, Sprache, Philosophie* (Logic, Language, Philosophy) was written with help from Wittgenstein and was originally intended as an introduction to the ideas contained in the ***Tractatus Logico-Philosophicus***. The book changed as Wittgenstein's **thinking** changed, but eventually he stopped helping with it. It was published in 1965, after Waismann's death, as *The Principles of Linguistic Philosophy*.

LOOS, ADOLF (1870–1933). An Austrian **architect** who worked mostly in **Vienna** and is best known for his opposition to ornament. He valued craftsmanship and cultural sensitivity. Wittgenstein was sympathetic, donating money to Loos (2,000 crowns) and other artists. When Wittgenstein designed a house for his sister **Margarete**, he adopted Loos's style, eschewing ornament, and using interlocking split-levels in the lower stories. Although he later denounced Loos's "bogus intellectualism" (in a letter to **Paul Engelmann** dated 2 September 1919), in 1931 Wittgenstein listed Loos as one of the most important influences on his thinking (see ***Culture and Value*** p. 19).

LUDWIG WITTGENSTEIN: PUBLIC AND PRIVATE OCCASIONS. A selection from Wittgenstein's diaries and correspondence together with notes on various lectures and discussions led by Wittgenstein, edited by James C. Klagge and Alfred Nordmann, published in 2003. The diary entries (from 1930–1932 and 1936–1937) are interesting both in terms of what they reveal about Wittgenstein's life and in terms of the personal **religious** belief that they portray. Wittgenstein constantly addresses God and yet seems to repeat a belief that God is absent or nonexistent (see pages 193, 229, and 231). Much of the other material offers alternative explanations of Wittgenstein's thoughts on **meaning** and **rule-following**, confirming, for instance, that he did not identify all meaning with use, as has been thought. Most of this material consists of notes taken by people other than Wittgenstein, so it cannot be relied on too heavily as a guide to his exact thoughts. Much, too, is ambiguous even as reported, but still provides plenty of ammunition for scholarly debates about interpretation, regarding the ***Tractatus Logico-Philosophicus*** and Wittgenstein's thoughts on **Søren Kierkegaard**, for instance.

See also KODER DIARIES.

M

MALCOLM, NORMAN ADRIAN (1911–1990). A friend and student of Wittgenstein's who became a well-known philosopher in his own right, working mostly on the **philosophy** of **mind** and epistemology. Malcolm taught for many years at Cornell University and was one of the main routes through which Wittgenstein's ideas entered the **United States**. His books include *Dreaming* (1959), *Ludwig Wittgenstein: A Memoir* (1962), and *Nothing Is Hidden* (1986).

MANCHESTER. When Wittgenstein was 19 years old, in 1908, he went to Manchester, England,to study aeronautics. He first worked at the Kite Flying Upper Atmosphere Station near Glossop, where he designed and built kites. During this time he lived at the Grouse Inn on the Derbyshire moors. There he met William Eccles, an engineer who became a good friend of Wittgenstein's. It was a letter from Eccles in 1925 that persuaded Wittgenstein to return to England for the first time after **World War I**.

In the fall of 1908 he registered with the Engineering Department of Manchester University as a research student. It was then that he became interested in pure **mathematics** and the **philosophy** of mathematics, especially as discussed by **Bertrand Russell** in *The Principles of Mathematics*. He left Manchester in 1911 to pursue his interest in philosophy, having devised an impractical plan for an aircraft engine (which was later adapted successfully for use in helicopters) and patented a design for propellers.

MARGARETE. *See* THE WITTGENSTEIN FAMILY.

MARXISM. Wittgenstein's **conservatism** with regard to **ethics** and his taste in **music** did not extend to **politics**. Between 1922 and 1937 he was interested in going to the Soviet Union to live and work there, possibly with **Francis Skinner**. After an exploratory trip to **Russia**, Wittgenstein gave up this plan, but for a while he believed that there was something good happening there. He did not believe in the theory of Marxism, but did believe in rejecting material greed and consumerism. He also opposed fascism and sympathized with the left's concerns about unemployment.

MATHEMATICAL PROOF. Wittgenstein insisted that proof in **mathematics** is quite different from other kinds of proof. Mathematics does not deal with reality in the way that engineering does, for instance. To some extent work in engineering is tested quite practically: Does the bridge stand or fall? (Of course if the work is done badly enough the project might not be allowed to advance far enough to test the planned bridge.) Proofs in mathematics, though, depend either on appealing to what is self-evident (as in Euclid's proofs) or on applying existing rules in new ways. In a sense something new is discovered when a new proof is presented, but in another sense something new has been *created*. The connection between the new finding and the pre-existing set of rules or beliefs had never been made before. This might make mathematics sound more arbitrary than it really is, but Wittgenstein's writings on mathematics are not sufficiently finished for any interpretation of them to be quite certain. It is likely that his main concern was to combat **Platonism**, the idea that mathematical proofs are discoveries about a special realm of being.

MATHEMATICS. Despite leaving the subject for **philosophy**, Wittgenstein seems never to have lost his interest in mathematics. What he wrote on the philosophy of this subject reflects what he writes elsewhere about **rule-following** and related issues. Some of the work published as ***Remarks on the Foundations of Mathematics*** was originally intended to be a part two to the ***Philosophical Investigations***. In these works Wittgenstein rejects **Platonism**, the **logicism** of **Bertrand Russell** and **Gottlob Frege**, **empiricist** accounts of mathematical **truth** as derived from experience, and **formalism**.

Instead of logicism and empiricism, Wittgenstein resists reductionism of any kind and presents mathematics as a kind, or region, of **language**, with its own '**grammatical**' rules. Thus what one might think of as mathematical truths are not so much facts as something more like norms. If one puts first two stones and then two more into a bucket and counts five in total, one does not consider revising the belief that $2 + 2 = 4$. Instead, one would assume that the bucket must already have contained a stone, or that one stone had broken in two, or something like this. Truths of this kind, that is to say, have a type of **certainty** about them that makes them unlike empirical **facts**.

See also HARDY, GODFREY HAROLD (1877–1947); MATHEMATICAL PROOF.

MAUTHNER, FRITZ (1849–1923). An Austro-Hungarian writer and philosopher. In ***Tractatus Logico-Philosophicus*** proposition 4.0031 Wittgenstein writes that all **philosophy** is "critique of **language**," but not in Mauthner's sense. Mauthner was skeptical about the ability of language to convey truth because, he thought, it only **pictures** reality, never actually coinciding with nature. For Mauthner, language is conventional and based on metaphor, so it can never really grasp the real world.

MEANING. Wittgenstein's early pronouncements on meaning are found in the **picture theory** of the ***Tractatus Logico-Philosophicus***. According to this **theory**, meaning is a property of sentences or **propositions**, the basic components of which stand for **objects**, which are their meanings. This theory is rejected in Wittgenstein's later work (and, some argue, in the *Tractatus* itself, which refers to its own contents as **nonsense** in proposition 6.54).

The picture theory of meaning holds that propositions are meaningful insofar as they picture **states of affairs** or matters of empirical **fact**. Anything normative, supernatural, or (one might say) metaphysical must, it therefore seems, be nonsense. This has been an influential reading of parts of the *Tractatus*. Unfortunately, this reading leads to serious problems since by its own lights the *Tractatus*'s use of words such as "object," "reality," and "**world**" is illegitimate. These concepts are purely formal or *a priori*. A statement such as "There are objects in the world" does not picture a state of affairs. Rather it is, as it were, presupposed by the notion of a state of affairs. The picture theory therefore apparently denies sense to just the kind of statements of which the *Tractatus* is composed, to the framework supporting the picture theory itself. In this way the *Tractatus* pulls the rug out from under its own feet.

Various responses have been proposed to this problem. One is to distinguish between the senseless (*sinnlos*) propositions of **logic** and nonsensical (*unsinnig*) propositions such as "The good is more identical than the beautiful." On this view senseless propositions can be understood, making their senselessness a rather technical issue. Nonsensical propositions, in contrast, cannot be understood, but what they fail to say can still, at least in some cases, be shown. There might be no showing the good's being more identical than the beautiful, because there is no such thing to show, but ineffable truths about **ethics**, for instance, might be revealed in the world, perhaps through human actions.

Against this interpretation of the *Tractatus* is a view associated primarily with the American philosophers **Cora Diamond** and **James Conant**. They are more resolute or austere about nonsense, rejecting the distinctions between senselessness and nonsense, and between sayable and showable truths. If anything identifiable as a truth can be shown, then it is possible to say what this truth is. Any proposition that genuinely has no sense, though, is mere nonsense. In this way the *Tractatus* itself really does turn out to be nonsensical, and its sentences should be thrown away, just as Wittgenstein says in 6.54. This might be a more consistent reading of the *Tractatus* than the more popular version (whose proponents sometimes think of the *Tractatus* as consisting of internally consistent but mutually incoherent parts), but it comes at a cost. If the sentences that provide the content of the *Tractatus* are really nonsense, then why do at least some of them seem to be true? And how is the book to have any value at all? Which kind of interpretation is to be preferred continues to provide fuel for debate.

The most important statement about meaning in the later work is §43 of ***Philosophical Investigations***, which says that "For a *large* class of cases of the employment of the word 'meaning'—though not for *all*—this word can be explained in this way: the meaning of a word is its use in the language."

The main rival views that Wittgenstein warns against are that the meaning of a word is some object that it **names** and that the meaning of a word is some psychological feeling. In the former case, it would seem that the meaning of a word could be destroyed, stolen, or locked away, but this is nonsense. In the latter, each user of a word could mean something different by it, having a different feeling, and communication would be difficult if not impossible. Wittgenstein famously argues against the idea of a **private language**, although there is disagreement about exactly what he meant by this idea. Rather than an object or a feeling, he suggests that the meaning of a word might be any from a range of things.

Knowing the meaning of a word can involve knowing many things: to what objects the word refers (if any), whether it is slang or not, what part of speech it is, whether it carries overtones, if so what kind they are, and so on. To know all this, or to know enough to get by, is to know the use of the word. And generally knowing the use means knowing the meaning. Philosophical questions about **consciousness**, for example, then should be responded to by looking at the various uses made of the word "consciousness." Scientific investigations into the brain are not directly relevant to this inquiry (although they might be indirectly relevant if scientific discoveries lead people to change their use of such words). The meaning of any word is a matter of what people do with their **language**, not something hidden inside anyone's **mind** or brain. This is not an attack on neuroscience. It is merely distinguishing **philosophy** (which, as Wittgenstein conceives of it, is properly concerned with linguistic or conceptual **analysis**) from **science** (which is concerned with discovering facts).

One exception to the meaning-is-use rule of thumb is given in *Philosophical Investigations* §561, where Wittgenstein says that "the word 'is' is used with two different meanings (as copula and as **sign** of equality)" but that its meaning is not its use. That is to say, "is" has not one complex use (including both "Water is clear" and "Water is H_2O") and therefore one complex meaning, but two quite distinct meanings.

It is an accident that the same word has these two meanings. It is not an accident that people use the word "car" to refer to both Fords and Hondas. But what is accidental and what is **essential** to a **concept** depend on its users, on how they use the concept in question. This is not completely **arbitrary**, however. Depending on one's environment, one's physical needs and desires, one's emotions, one's sensory capacities, and so on, different concepts will be more natural or useful.

When a person says something, what she means depends not only on what is said but also on the context in which it is said. Importance, point, and meaning are given by the surroundings. Words, gestures, and expressions come alive, as it were, only within a **language-game**, a culture, or a **form of life**. If a picture, say, means something, then it means so *to somebody*. Its meaning is not an objective property of the picture in the way that its size and shape are. The same goes of any mental picture. Hence Wittgenstein's remark that "If God had looked into our minds, he would not have been able to see there whom we were speaking of" (***Philosophy of Psychology—A Fragment*** §284). Any internal image would need interpretation. If one interprets one's thought as being of **Hitler** and God sees it as Charlie Chaplin, who is right? Which of the two famous contemporaries of Wittgenstein's one really has in mind, he suggests, shows itself in the way one **behaves**, the things one does and says. It is in this that the use, the meaning, of a thought or mental picture lies. "The arrow points only in the application that a living creature makes of it" (PI §454).

This is why forms of life are so important to Wittgenstein. What matters to you depends on how you live (and *vice versa*), and this shapes your experience. So if a **lion** could speak, Wittgenstein says, we would not be able to understand it. We might realize that "roar" meant zebra, or that "roar roar" meant lame zebra, but we would not understand lion ethics, **politics**, **aesthetic** taste, **religion**, humor, and such like, if lions have these things. We could not honestly say, "I know what you mean" to a lion. Understanding another involves empathy, which requires the kind of similarity that we just do not have with lions, and that many people do not have with some other **human beings**.

See also GRAMMAR; INTENDING AND MEANING SOMETHING; METHOD OF PROJECTION.

MEANING-BODY. In ***Philosophical Investigations*** §559, Wittgenstein makes a reference to meaning-bodies, without explaining what he means. The expression comes in double parentheses at the end of the remark, which talks about thinking of a sentence as a mechanism and a word as having a particular function within this mechanism. The function becomes apparent only in "operating the **calculus**," which presumably means using the **language**. So a word has a **meaning** in the context of a sentence, but a sentence has meaning only in the context of a language. To a large extent this meaning depends on the use to which words and sentences are put, on human (and perhaps human-like) activity, in other words, not on something independent. A meaning-body would be a kind of thing with its own existence that was attached to a word. This is a metaphysical **picture** of meaning that Wittgenstein challenges.

When he discusses uses of words in a **secondary sense**, however, he says that such words are intended with their original, primary meaning despite being used in a very different context. In this case 'meaning' does seem to refer to something like a meaning-body and not to the use to which a word is put. If I say that I want to use the word 'blue' with its usual, color-related meaning to name a mood, for instance, then it would appear that I want to bring something like a meaning-body into relation with this mood. This kind of use of words is not the norm, but Wittgenstein does not insist that it is always nonsensical. In this limited sense, he might have had some use for the notion of a meaning-body.

MEMORY. Like **imagination**, memory presents us with mental **pictures**, either in the almost literal sense of things we feel that we can see (even though eyesight is irrelevant to this kind of **inner** seeing) or in the more metaphorical sense of something we can describe, something about which we have a view. Of course to remember something is to recall something that really happened, not to imagine something. If I am imagining things, then I am not remembering them, even if I think I am. A false memory is not really a memory at all, that is to say, not something that we would normally call a memory. These remarks on the **grammar** of the word 'memory' show that there is a sense in which memory is infallible, but also that what we think we remember might turn out to be false. So we are not guaranteed to avoid mistakes if we rely on what we think we remember.

This is important for questions of **language** and **meaning**, because it is often tempting to think of the meanings of words as being stored in the **mind** as memories that are triggered by the utterance of the word in question. Thus a child hears the word 'dog' when she sees a dog and makes a mental connection between the word and the animal. Then later when she wants to call this kind of animal to mind she uses the word 'dog' to do so. Words are memory-triggers and meanings are mental objects. **Augustine** offers something like this picture of how he learned language in his *Confessions*, and others do so too. Memory is certainly important in language: someone who forgets the meanings of words will struggle to understand and to be understood by others. But Wittgenstein encourages his readers not to think of meanings as objects in the mind. Nothing in my mind is the **criterion** of what 'red' means, for instance. For words to have correct and incorrect uses there must be standards, and these standards are not as subjective as mental pictures.

See also MEANING-BODY; PRIVATE LANGUAGE ARGUMENT.

METAPHOR. Wittgenstein makes great use of metaphors, especially in his later work. What he says about metaphors or similes is also important. In particular he distinguishes between a metaphorical use of words and what he calls the use of words in a **secondary sense**. When someone employs a metaphor, she could use a different metaphor instead or simply speak literally instead of metaphorically. It is this having an alternative that makes the difference between metaphorical and secondary uses of words, according to Wittgenstein. He insists that some important uses of language in **ethics** and **religion** are not metaphorical in this way, and since they cannot be paraphrased, they cannot be explained reductively (ethics as mere expression of emotive attitude, for instance) without distortion or inaccuracy. (The claim that ethical judgments are just expressions of emotion, then, could be a recommendation for a new conception of ethics, but would not be an accurate account of the current **meaning** of "ethical judgments.")

METAPHYSICS. Metaphysics can be defined roughly as the study of the ultimate nature of reality. In that sense it might sound like physics, or **science** in general, but traditionally metaphysicians have held that one can discover metaphysical **truths** purely by reasoning philosophically. Wittgenstein considered such **thinking** to be **confused**. A metaphysical question, according to him, is a question about **language** misconceived as a scientific question, a question about the nature of reality.

The ***Tractatus Logico-Philosophicus*** rejects metaphysical statements as **nonsense**, since they characteristically employ **formal concepts** (such as **fact** and **number**) as if they were real **concepts**. It is still possible to read Wittgenstein as suggesting that there are real truths to be known here, but that these must be shown rather than **said**. It is then possible to disagree with him and maintain that they can indeed be said after all. Hence the possibility of a metaphysical reading of the *Tractatus*. Certainly the book seems metaphysical at times, apparently presenting, for instance, a **theory** of **logical atomism**.

In the later ***Philosophical Investigations*** Wittgenstein defines his mission as antimetaphysical, being to retrieve words from metaphysical uses and return them to everyday ones. This has been taken by some to mean that there is something especially valuable about **ordinary language** in Wittgenstein's view. Others, such as **G. P. Baker**, have argued that 'everyday' in this context simply means 'non-metaphysical.' Many people interpret Wittgenstein as having metaphysical views of his own, despite these claims. For instance, *Philosophical Investigations* has been read as advocating a kind of linguistic **idealism** or **phenomenalism**. Such readings have not found general favor, however.

METER, STANDARD. In ***Philosophical Investigations*** §50 Wittgenstein says that the standard meter in Paris (a metal bar with two marks on it, the distance between which was once the defining paradigm of what counts as a meter) is neither a meter long nor not a meter long. This sounds strange, and the possibility that he is being ironical, or putting forward an idea that one is meant to reject or at least question, should never be dismissed out of hand in such cases. However, he seems to be making the point that a paradigm has a different role in a **language-game** than the things that it is used to measure. He gives the example also of a **color** sample. If one defined 'sepia' as whatever is the same color as *this*, then it would indeed seem to make no sense to ask whether *this* were sepia. "Everything is the same as itself" strikes many people as obviously true, a **tautology** or restatement of the law of **identity**, but to others it sounds like **nonsense**.

In the ***Tractatus Logico-Philosophicus*** Wittgenstein says that all tautologies lack sense (although he explicitly denies that they are nonsense in **proposition** 4.4611). Since they say nothing, that is they provide no information about **the world**, one cannot really assert them. There is nothing to assert, no content. If "This is sepia" were a tautology, an analytic statement, then this would show itself in the use made of the color sample, the role it plays in the system. It is not a **truth** that one could really say, since "This is sepia" said of the defining color sample would mean something like "If you were to hold this up against itself you would see that it is the same color as itself," but of course there is no such thing as comparing something with itself in this way. The same goes for the standard meter: it cannot be measured against itself, so it fails to fit the definition of a meter. The standard meter plays a role in **language** unlike any object that could be measured and found to be (or not to be) a meter long. Hence the standard meter (considered as a standard) neither is nor is not a meter long. On this issue then Wittgenstein's later view appears to be the same as the view expressed in the *Tractatus*.

METHOD OF PROJECTION. ***Tractatus Logico-Philosophicus*** 3.11 states that a **proposition**, the sensibly perceptible expression of a **thought** (such as a spoken or written sentence), is a projection of a possible situation. The method of projection, it continues, is to think of the sense of the proposition, or perhaps just to think the sense of the proposition (the original German is ambiguous). So, it might seem, one starts with a thought, a mental representation of some possible **state of affairs**. One then expresses this thought in words (sounds or writing). These words are then a projection of that possible state of affairs just as long as they are thought of as having that sense. Thinking is really doing all the work here, and communication between people who might have different thoughts seems impossible. All that they would have in common would be the perceptible **signs** of thought (i.e., words), but what these words meant would depend on incommunicable, ultimately inexpressible, thoughts. Thinking, or **psychology**—the study of thinking (or, rather, the study of the **mind** or **soul**)—would then be **essential** to **meaning**. Yet proposition 4.1121, following **Gottlob Frege's** opposition to **psychologism**, says that psychology is *not* especially important for **philosophy**. The concern of the philosopher is **logic**, not **science**. Proposition 5.5422 might also be relevant here, since it implies that a piece of **nonsense** (*ein Unsinn*) cannot be thought. So there are clearly problems for anyone who maintains that otherwise senseless combinations of words acquire sense through a mental process or act of meaning or thinking. A thought is not a thought, thinking is not thinking, unless it is logical, unless it has sense. Thus the concepts of thinking and logic seem to be **internally related**, as Wittgenstein presents them.

Perhaps this removes the problem of communication that seems to arise from the possibility of different people's thinking different senses in connection with the same sentence. A sentence is a **fact** and a fact has a certain definite **logical form**. Try to think any other with that sentence and one will inevitably fail. (One cannot say "the cat is on the mat" and mean "green is my favorite color" just by thinking of the latter sentence as one speaks the former. Or perhaps the speaker might mean that, but his sentence is not subject to his will—it has its own meaning whether he likes it or not.) Now thinking the sense of a proposition seems irrelevant to projecting a possible state of affairs by means of a perceptible sign. Yet proposition 3.11 seems to insist just the opposite.

Opinions vary on what to make of this. **Norman Malcolm** argues that 3.11 can and should be taken fairly straightforwardly, so that the method of projection is taken to be a mental act (thinking the sense of the proposition). This view is known as mentalism. **Peter Winch** and others argue instead that 3.11 is intended to explain what thinking the sense of a proposition is, namely that it is (means) the method of projection. Unfortunately what *this* means is not really explained in the *Tractatus*. Winch's point, though, is that Wittgenstein is saying that one **fact** means another (or a possible state of affairs) by sharing a common logical form or plan with it. Projecting just means translating (see propositions 4.014 and 4.0141) from one medium or mode to another, as when one 'derives' a symphony from a musical score, or from a recording on plastic of that symphony, or *vice versa*. An unexpressed thought must then exist in some medium (the brain, a **Cartesian soul**, or something else) but only the logical form of the thought concerns Wittgenstein, not its metaphysical substance. So a spoken sentence is a projection of a possible situation. It is so in virtue of expressing a thought, that is a semantic 'thing' with the same logical form as the situation in question. The sentence "The cat sat on the mat" means that the cat sat on the mat by having the same logical form as that fact (and any thought of it), not by being thought in the sense of having some mental act performed upon it. This is Winch's view.

Anscombe says (p. 69, note 1) that "Wittgenstein's use of 'projection' is a metaphorical extension of the mathematical use, which may be explained thus: 'The drawing of straight lines through every point of a given figure, so as to produce a new figure each point of which corresponds to a point of the original figure.'"

The mentalist thesis is supported, according to its proponents, by the following passage from a letter written by Wittgenstein to Russell (Wittgenstein, *Cambridge Letters*, p. 125):

> . . . I don't know *what* the constituents of a thought are but I know *that* it must have such constituents which correspond to the words of Language. Again the kind of relation of the constituents of thought and of the pictured fact is irrelevant. It would be a matter of psychology to find it out. . . .
>
> Does a Gedanke consist of words? No! But of psychical constituents that have the same sort of relation to reality as words. What those constituents are I don't know.

Against mentalists such as Hacker and Norman Malcolm, **Cora Diamond** has noted Wittgenstein's writing in this letter that the constituents of a thought (or *Gedanke*) "have the same sort of relation to reality as words." See Cora Diamond, "Peter Winch on the *Tractatus*, and the unity of Wittgenstein's philosophy," in *Wittgenstein: The Philosopher and His Works* edited by Alois Pichler and Simo Säätelä, pp. 141–171. On p. 148 she writes: "If the meaningfulness of sentences were mediated by intrinsically meaningful thoughts, as on Malcolm's view, the elements of those thoughts would not have the same relation to reality as do words. The letter would appear to rule out any view like Malcolm's."

Diamond notes also that Winch takes the very passage from the *Prototractatus* that Hacker cites to support his opposite interpretation of *Tractatus* 3.11. She rejects both Winch's view that the notion of a method of projection is not being explained in 3.11 and Hacker's view that thinking a sense is something one does in one's mind. Instead, she sees Wittgenstein's idea thus (pp. 155–156):

"we make pictures, using methods of depiction in space; these pictures, these representations, in that they are in logical space, are thoughts. In that they are thoughts, they think this or that situation; they think this or that sense. In that they are pictures in a space, the possibility of the representing picture in the space has internal to it the possibility of the represented situation in that space. The logical notion of depiction then explains (in *PT* 3.12 and 3.13) what Wittgenstein means by the application of the propositional sign: it is *used* as a picture, and thereby as a projection. The sort of projection involved in our use of propositions is thus tied to the notion of picturing, which itself is a basically projective notion: to use a perceptible sign as a picture is to use it as a projection of a possible situation."

The idea of a thought thinking, which sounds odd, and which Diamond treats Hacker as having neglected, comes from *Tractatus* 3.02. In the ***Philosophical Investigations*** Wittgenstein returned to this issue of meaning and its relation with logic or **grammar**. He points out (in §§139–142) that even a picture can be ambiguous or misinterpreted, so no picture (and perhaps no thought) can fix the meaning of a word. He also returns repeatedly to the idea, which he rejects, that meaning is something done with or in the mind. Rather, he suggests, the meaning of a word shows itself in its use in **language**. On Malcolm's view, this is a rejection of the *Tractatus* position. On Winch's, it is confirmation of it.

MILL, JOHN STUART (1806–1873). The greatest British philosopher of the 19th century, noted for his defense of **utilitarianism** and individual liberty. Like many other British philosophers, Mill was an **empiricist** and interpreted **mathematical** truths as very well supported **facts** about **the world**, neither **analytic** nor *a priori* as they are more often taken to be. Wittgenstein, like **Gottlob Frege**, opposed this view.

Mill was the godfather of **Bertrand Russell**. His best-known books are *On Liberty* (1859) and *Utilitarianism* (1863).

MIND. Unlike many philosophers who talk about the **philosophy** of mind, Wittgenstein tended to focus on the philosophy of **psychology**. The difference is basically that philosophy of mind focuses on the question "What is mind?" or "What is the mind?" whereas philosophy of psychology is more concerned with questions about particular mental states and processes such as **thoughts**, **beliefs**, emotions, and so on. It is more particular and diverse. This makes it hard to summarize what Wittgenstein said about these **concepts**, which perhaps fits his aversion to general **theories** or hypotheses in philosophy. It also means that it is very hard to say what, if anything, Wittgenstein took the mind to be. Some interpreters believe that he was a **behaviorist**, denying the reality of the **inner**. He certainly seems to have rejected **René Descartes's** conception of the mind or **soul** as a nonphysical object, and Wittgenstein is known to have influenced **Gilbert Ryle's** behaviorist critique of that theory. However, it might be more accurate to say that Wittgenstein had no theory at all about the mind. If he did, it is only expressed implicitly in what he says about such topics as **private language**, **rule-following**, and **pain**.

His observations about private language do not, as has been alleged, make Wittgenstein a behaviorist. He does not deny the existence of sensations or experiences. Pains, tickles, itches, etc. are all part of human life, of course. At ***Philosophical Investigations*** §293 Wittgenstein says that "if we construe the **grammar** of the expression of sensation on the model of 'object and name', the object drops out of consideration as irrelevant." This suggests not that pains and so on are irrelevant but that we should not construe the grammar of the expression of sensation on the model of 'object and name.' If we want to understand a concept such as pain, we should not think of a pain as a private object referred to somehow by the public word "pain." A pain is not "a something," just as love, democracy, and strength are not things, but it is no more "a nothing" than they are either (see *Philosophical Investigations* §304). Saying this is hardly satisfactory, but there is no simple answer to the question "What is pain?" Wittgenstein offers not an answer but a kind of philosophical **therapy** intended to clear away what can seem bafflingly obscure. The required clarity is (supposedly) achieved not by looking in at one's own pain but by looking outward at the use we make of the word 'pain.' This is not because there is nothing there when we talk about pain, nor because we are really talking about behavior rather than a sensation or feeling when we do so. A boy who complains of a toothache is not telling us about his behavior but about how he feels. To understand him and what he means we need to understand the point of his words, Wittgenstein thinks, not investigate something inside him that is accessible to him alone.

This puts Wittgenstein at odds with all the best-known theories in the philosophy of mind. He opposes the Cartesian idea that a pain (or a belief, **memory**, etc.) is something in the soul. He opposes the idea that a pain is something in the brain. He opposes the idea that a pain is a something defined by its functional role. And he opposes the eliminativist idea that we should abandon concepts such as 'pain' altogether. Instead of proposing any kind of theory about the mind or mental states, he suggests that we already understand them well enough and merely need to be reminded, or to remind ourselves, of what we already know. This is not to say that we know all that there is to be known about psychology. There might be much to learn about how to improve learning or memory, how to treat depression, and so on. It is more that if we find ourselves wondering what a mind or a memory is, then Wittgenstein thinks we are confused. We already know the meaning of 'mind' and of 'memory' perfectly well. These things only seem especially mysterious when we mistakenly take these words to be the names of objects.

Most contemporary philosophers find little of interest in Wittgenstein's work of deflationary reminding. Most would agree with him, however, in rejecting Descartes's idea that the mind is the soul.

MINING. *See* THE WITTGENSTEIN FAMILY.

MOORE, GEORGE EDWARD (1873–1958). One of the great early **analytic** philosophers. Moore is best known for a series of papers in which he attacks the **skepticism** and **idealism** that were prevalent in the British **philosophy** of the late 19th and early 20th centuries, and for the books *Principia Ethica* (1903) and *Ethics* (1912). Between 1925 and 1939, he was the professor of mental philosophy and **logic** at **Cambridge University**, which is how he came to know Wittgenstein. He also edited the journal *Mind* from 1921 to 1947.

Wittgenstein thought highly enough of Moore's work to read his books and attend his lectures, but he seems not to have agreed with much that Moore thought, and considered him both repetitious and overly concerned with trivial matters. Although they were friends, Moore advising Wittgenstein at various stages, for instance about the requirements for getting a degree at Cambridge, and visiting him in **Norway** as both a friend and a fellow philosopher, Wittgenstein does not seem to have admired him excessively. He once referred to Moore as being like a child, even if in a morally good way. On his part, Moore seems to have been slightly shy and a little afraid of Wittgenstein, who could be rude and temperamental.

Moore's most clear philosophical influence on Wittgenstein comes in ***On Certainty***, where Wittgenstein discusses at length examples used by Moore in his (Moore's) **arguments** against skepticism. Wittgenstein is obviously also against skepticism, and seems to think that Moore is on to something important, but also treats Moore as not fully appreciating the true nature or significance of his insight.

MULTIPLICITY. In ***Tractatus Logico-Philosophicus*** proposition 4.04 Wittgenstein asserts that a **proposition** must have the same logical or mathematical multiplicity as the state of things it presents. If the symbolism lacks the same multiplicity as that which it is to symbolize, then there will be states of things that it is unable to represent. If the multiplicity of the symbolism is too great, however, then it will be able to seemingly represent states that can never exist. This might lead to the production of confusing **nonsense**.

Allan Janik notes that **Heinrich Hertz** treats simplicity as relative rather than absolute. In particular, it is relative to the audience. "Hertz proceeds from the view that even within science it is necessary to construct different representations of the same data depending upon whom you want to talk to.

He offers us the analogy with presentations of grammar: pupils learning to master their mother tongue require an altogether different presentation of the rules of grammar than philologists do" (Janik p. 51). If simplicity is relative, perhaps multiplicity is too.

MUSIC. Wittgenstein came from a very musical family and loved music himself. Indeed, he once remarked that nobody was likely to understand him who did not understand what music had meant to him. Unfortunately, he did not elaborate. It has been suggested that there is a musical rhythm to the ***Philosophical Investigations***, but it seems unlikely that one would need to share Wittgenstein's taste in music in order to understand his **philosophy**. As with **architecture**, Wittgenstein regarded some music as being like **language** or like a gesture. His favorite composer was Ludwig van Beethoven and his least favorite was perhaps Gustav Mahler. The best source for Wittgenstein's views on music is ***Culture and Value***.

MYSTICISM. Wittgenstein has been labeled a mystic by some readers, especially because of things he says in the last 10 remarks of the ***Tractatus Logico-Philosophicus***. For instance, *Tractatus* proposition 6.44 says that "It is not *how* things are in the world that is mystical, but *that* it exists." A kind of spirituality hard to pin down to any organized, or simply recognized, **religion** seems to have pervaded his life. On the other hand, *Tractatus* 6.54 declares Wittgenstein's propositions to be nonsensical, and his later **lecture on ethics** characterized all attempts to speak ethics or religion as **nonsense**. Some have taken this as confirmation of the view that Wittgenstein believed in a class of important but ineffable **truths**. Others take more severely the **tautology** in the last line of the *Tractatus*, easily mistaken for an imperative: whereof we cannot speak, thereof we must be silent. This can be, and sometimes is, taken to imply that there is some mystery whereof we cannot speak, that we can perhaps show but not **say**. It can also be read as an empty (though seemingly profound) tautology. *Tractatus* 4.461 says that tautologies are senseless (*sinnlos*), but not nonsense. *Tractatus* 6.54 says that Wittgenstein's **propositions** are nonsensical (*unsinnig*). There are therefore three readings of *Tractatus* 7: it is sheer nonsense; it tells us nothing about **the world** (since it is a tautology) but is not therefore as nonsensical as 'bububu'; it is not in the part of the book that consists of nonsensical propositions and is in fact the culmination of Wittgenstein's work in the *Tractatus*, a final gesture toward the ineffable insight that he wants his readers to share. The second reading is probably the most common.

MYTHOLOGY. In his ***Remarks on Frazer's* Golden Bough** Wittgenstein says that "An entire mythology is stored within our **language**" (PO p. 133). He seems to mean that our language contains words such as 'ghost' and '**soul**,' which we still use, even if not always in a literal way. The currency of our language once had a very different value. It does not follow, and Wittgenstein does not say, that using such words implies **belief** in, say, ghosts, or that we should stop using these words. His point is more likely to be that we should recognize this connection with people who practice magic or perhaps have **religious** beliefs that we might consider to be primitive.

N

NAMES/NAMING. The ***Tractatus Logico-Philosophicus*** presents names as the elements of **propositions**. A proposition combines names into a **picture** of a **state of affairs**, a complex in which the **objects** for which the names stand are related to each other in a particular, determinate way. Names do not picture anything. They merely stand for, represent, or mean objects. They do this, however, only within propositions, which say something about the objects in question. So outside a proposition a name has no **meaning** (see *Tractatus* proposition 3.3). This might seem strange. If the meaning of a name is an object, then how can this meaning, as it were, cease to exist without a proposition? Does what exists depend on language? Wittgenstein's answer seems to be, No. The object named or meant by a name would still exist without any propositions referring to it. But there would be no *name* meaning it without such propositions. So no name would have that object as its meaning. A name's being a name depends not on its meaning but on its role or function in language. In Wittgenstein's notation, or **concept-script**, in the *Tractatus* this role is taken by variables such as x and y. In his later work, Wittgenstein tends to equate the meaning of any word, including names, with their use in language, so the distinction between meaning and use is, while not denied, emphasized much less than it is in the *Tractatus*.

NECESSITY. ***Tractatus Logico-Philosophicus*** proposition 6.37 says that the only kind of necessity that there is, is logical necessity. This is reminiscent of **David Hume's** point that we never observe one event (a cause) necessitating another (its effect), only repeatedly preceding or coinciding with it. Exactly how to interpret Hume's thinking on **causation** is controversial, but Wittgenstein might be taken as emphasizing the contingency of events in the empirical world. That is to say, it is possible to read Wittgenstein as making a claim about **metaphysics**, similar to the claim that Hume makes (on some readings of Hume). However, it is also possible to regard Wittgenstein's point as saying nothing at all about metaphysics but instead as being a point about **grammar** or the **meaning** of necessity (as he uses the word). It is, on this interpretation, a **tautology**.

In the context, though, Wittgenstein does seem to be making a connection with ideas about the laws of nature and **induction**. Whenever anything is identified as the explanation of some event or phenomenon, he seems to be saying, it is always possible to ask why that event made its effect inevitable (or necessary). For example, if a wooden house is burned down by a fire started by a carelessly discarded match, one can still ask why it is that fire has the power to burn wood. Whatever answer is given about the chemical properties of wood and fire, one can still ask why these properties are as they are, or why something with one set of properties produces a given result when interacting in a certain way with a thing with some other set of properties. One can keep going, that is to say, with the question "Why?" Any reference to a law of nature is really, Wittgenstein seems to imply, a way of saying "That is just how things are." The law of gravity, then, would be a kind of **description** of a regularity that scientists have observed. It does not **explain** anything. The same could be said of any other law of **science**. Stones do not *have* to fall to earth, or fire burn wood, even in ideal conditions, in any absolute sense. They simply do.

NEGATION. The **sign** for negation in **logic** is one of the **logical constants**. Wittgenstein says in the ***Tractatus Logico-Philosophicus*** that these do not represent anything. Thus words like 'not' do not represent or stand for anything. There is, one might say, no such thing as an absence for which they might stand (absence has no positive existence). But of course there is a difference between having money and having no money. Wittgenstein's point is that having no money is not, as the surface **grammar** of English might make one think, having some strange thing (namely "no money"). Rather it is its not being the case that one has money. So words or symbols used to indicate a negative say that a certain (positive) **state of affairs** is not the case. It might help to think of standard "no smoking" signs. They do not show people refraining from smoking but, typically, cigarettes crossed out. Similarly, the sentences "The man is smoking" and "The man is not smoking" refer to the same state of affairs (the man smoking) but say, respectively, that it holds and that it does not hold. It is a (necessary) feature of **propositions** that they can be negated. Thus **tautologies** or **logical truths** (whose negation cannot be) are not really propositions at all. See *Tractatus* 4.06–4.1.

NEWTON, ISAAC (1642–1727). A great mathematician and physicist. Newton is noted for his mechanical **theory** of physics, which dominated the subject into the late 20th century. Wittgenstein discusses this theory in propositions 6.341 and 6.342 of the ***Tractatus Logico-Philosophicus***. Newton's mechanics, he says there, tells us nothing about **the world**, and in this sense is like **logic**. Newtonian physics provides a means for describing whatever happens to be found in the world. It does not, for instance, *find* space to be three-dimensional but rather stipulates that it is so. What Newton provides then is a way to describe the world, a conceptual framework for scientific investigation. What says anything about the world is not this framework itself but how useful it is found to be. Can it capture all the facts? Can it do so elegantly or simply?

This Tractarian conception of Newtonian mechanics is reminiscent of what the later Wittgenstein says about the **arbitrariness of grammar**. If Newton offered a new **grammar**, though, a new conceptual framework and nothing more, then both **science** and logic might seem, on Wittgenstein's view, so autonomous of how the world actually is as to be completely **relative** to whatever society or age uses them. This is not what Wittgenstein says. *Tractatus* propositions 6.342, 6.3431, and 6.35 imply that logic is more general, more autonomous, than physics. Physics aims to describe how the world is, what the **facts** are. A **theory** such as Newton's does not say exactly what exists and where, and so on, but it is intended to be used in discovering and reporting such facts. Logic is one step further removed from the things themselves, having no contingent element whatsoever. Hence Newtonian physics can be, and has been, overthrown in favor of another, whereas there is no conceivable alternative to logic.

NIETZSCHE, FRIEDRICH (1844–1900). A philosopher and self-proclaimed Antichrist. Nietzsche rejected all previous **philosophy**, especially the work of **Plato**. Having intended to become a Lutheran minister, he lost his faith in **Christianity** and turned first to the philosophy of **Arthur Schopenhauer** and the **music** of Richard Wagner before developing his own vision of life. Instead of arguing for his ideas, or against the **theories** and ideas of others, however, he wrote in a more literary style (Wittgenstein considered him more a **poet** than a philosopher) and seems to have wanted to strike a chord with his readers and so prompt them to admit, or see, that he is right, rather than prove rationally or objectively that he is.

In this way Nietzsche is somewhat like **Søren Kierkegaard** or a psychoanalyst. He sometimes described his work as **psychology**, and without him it is arguable that **Sigmund Freud** would not have developed his theories. He tried to develop a new, more **aesthetic ethics** to replace the, to him distasteful, otherworldliness of Platonism and Christianity. His anti-Platonic, anti-**Cartesian** emphasis on the body and his critique of contemporary culture could be construed as somewhat Wittgensteinian.

Nietzsche's most important works are *The Gay Science* (1882), *Thus Spoke Zarathustra* (1883–1885), *Beyond Good and Evil* (1886), *On the Genealogy of Morality* (1887), *Twilight of the Idols* (August–September 1888), *The Antichrist* (September 1888), and *Ecce Homo* (October–November 1888).

NOMINALISM. A theory best understood as opposed to the kind of **realism** according to which types of things are real. The classic form of realism is **Platonism**, which holds that all spiders, for instance, share (or resemble or participate in) a common form or **essence** that might be called spiderness or the Form (or Idea) of Spider. This form is then held to be real, to exist as a kind of thing in its own right. For Plato this meant that Forms exist independently of physical things such as spiders, in a separate world of Forms. This kind of **metaphysics** is generally considered implausible today (as it quite possibly was by most people in Plato's day too).

There are other forms of realism closer to common sense, but nominalism denies them all. It says instead that general terms referring to types of thing are merely **names** that have been given, more or less **arbitrarily**, to things that people happen to group together for their purposes. Realists think that the way things are categorized can be right or wrong, true or false, whereas nominalists tend to think in terms merely of convenience or usefulness (like **pragmatists**). Wittgenstein's perceived anti-essentialism and anti-Platonism have led some people to think of him as a nominalist.

Philosophical Investigations §383 acknowledges that what Wittgenstein is doing looks like nominalism. However, he insists that this is not the case. Nominalists, he says, think of all words as names (of types of thing or action, and so on), which is precisely one of the main ideas that the *Investigations* sets out to criticize. The idea that words are names, Wittgenstein says, is not a description of their use but more like a draft on paper of such a description. It is the kind of **theory** about **meaning** that one might come up with if one did not take the trouble to look at (that is, really think about) how **language** is used. This is not a **negation** of nominalism of the kind that a Platonist might make, but a rejection of it as the wrong kind of thing altogether, which implies also a rejection of its mere negation.

NONSENSE. What Wittgenstein meant by 'nonsense' is one of the most controversial questions in contemporary Wittgenstein scholarship. The controversy concerns the German words *bedeutungslos* (meaningless), *Unsinn* (nonsense), *sinnlos* (senseless), and their cognates.

Tractatus Logico-Philosophicus proposition 6.54 says that Wittgenstein's **propositions** are nonsensical (*unsinnig*). If this means what it seems to at first sight, then the book surely does not put forward the **theories** that it appears to. Indeed, it would seem to say nothing at all. All the content of the book would apparently be withdrawn by this penultimate section of the book. This 'austere' interpretation is associated with **Cora Diamond**, **James Conant**, and the "new" or "American" school of Wittgenstein scholars.

The most forthright opponent of this school of thought is **P. M. S. Hacker**. Hacker favors the more orthodox view that Wittgenstein distinguished between the senseless and the meaningless. The term *sinnlos* is used in *Tractatus* propositions 4.461, 5.132, 5.1362, and 5.5351. There it is used to describe tautologies, contradictions, and related propositions (such as "*A* knows that *p*" where *p* is a **tautology**). Proposition 4.4611 says, though, that such propositions are not nonsense (*Unsinn*) since they are part of the symbolism we use. Tautologies, etc., say nothing about **the world**, as the number zero stands for nothing, but they still have **meaning** in another sense, just as 0 is importantly different from a random squiggle.

The term *bedeutungslos* (meaningless) occurs in 3.328, 4.442, 4.4661, and 5.47321. There it seems to refer to uselessness or redundancy, a property that could not be attributed to the very useful number zero or, arguably, statements of logical **truths**. So one can distinguish between the senseless (*sinnlos*), on one hand, and the nonsensical (*Unsinn*), on the other. Proposition 6.54 though does use the word *unsinnig* (nonsensical), suggesting that Wittgenstein's point was not merely that his propositions have the same technical status as tautologies. Indeed 6.54 could be taken to imply that the distinction between senselessness and nonsense (made in 4.4611) is itself nonsense.

The third, least fashionable, interpretation of Wittgenstein's use of these terms in the *Tractatus* is that even nonsense can express important truths of a **mystical** nature. These truths cannot be '**said**,' they are ineffable, but they can be shown. It is against this reading that Diamond and Conant first explicitly reacted.

No distinction between nonsense and mere senselessness appears in the ***Philosophical Investigations***, so the debate about nonsense is also a debate about **continuity** in Wittgenstein's work. *Philosophical Investigations* §282 does imply though that there are different kinds of nonsense. A nonsense poem is not nonsense in the same way as the sounds emitted by a child that cannot yet talk, Wittgenstein says there. Whether these differences are categorical or, on the contrary, impossible to characterize or log in any absolute or final way is another matter. There might not, in other words, be hard and fast differences that would allow for the categorization of a fixed number of distinct types of nonsense.

Philosophical Investigations §500 says that a sentence is called senseless when it is withdrawn from the **language**, not when its sense is senseless. This suggests that being senseless (*sinnlos*) really is the same thing as being nonsensical or meaningless (*unsinnig* or *bedeutungslos*). Senselessness simply is redundancy. Of course, though, this might not have been Wittgenstein's position when he wrote the *Tractatus*.

NORWAY. Wittgenstein first visited Norway for a vacation with his friend **David Pinsent** in 1913. He returned thinking that he ought to live there on his own. He spent a year in the village of Skjolden by the Sogne fjord working on **logic**. Then **World War I** intervened. During this time Wittgenstein had a cottage (often referred to as a hut) built for himself by the same fjord but away from the village. He returned to this cottage several times, but only for fairly short visits, not to live there.

NOTEBOOKS 1914–1916. These notebooks of Wittgenstein's were edited by **G. H. von Wright** and **G. E. M. Anscombe**. They show Wittgenstein working through the ideas that resulted in his ***Tractatus Logico-Philosophicus***. He also sets out quite clearly here some of his ideas about **ethics**, including thoughts on God, the **meaning** of life, and **suicide**. The *Notebooks* is thus an interesting and instructive book, but of course must be used with care for interpreting the *Tractatus*, since any remarks found only in the *Notebooks* might well have been left out because Wittgenstein changed his mind about them, as he appears to do a number of times within the *Notebooks* itself.

NOTES ON LOGIC. Wittgenstein's first philosophical work was a set of notes (taken by a secretary while Wittgenstein explained his ideas to **Bertrand Russell**) supplemented by a typescript that Wittgenstein dictated a few days later. This was in 1913, and it bears the title *Notes on Logic*. The *Notes* makes a series of comments about **philosophy** that could have been written at almost any time in Wittgenstein's life. Philosophy, it says, requires a distrust of **grammar** and does not deduce but **describes** (though not in such a way as to provide **pictures** of reality nor anything to confirm or disconfirm **scientific** investigations).

Otherwise, the main content of the *Notes* is an early version of Wittgenstein's **theory** of symbolism, the seed of the distinction between **saying and showing** that is made in the ***Tractatus Logico-Philosophicus***. What Russell tried to say in his **theory of types**, Wittgenstein believed, could not be said but must instead be shown by the symbolism used.

See also LOGIC.

NUMBERS. Wittgenstein's mature thinking on numbers might seem trivial or banal unless seen against some historical background. In particular he reacted against the work of **Bertrand Russell**. Russell reacted against **Gottlob Frege**, and Frege reacted against **John Stuart Mill**.

Mill argued that arithmetic is an empirical **science** based on observation. He defended this idea on the grounds that numbers are defined by reference to the fact that groups of things exist that strike the senses a certain way and that can be divided into lesser groups. For instance, three things together in a triangle create a certain impression, and those things can be moved so that they make the impressions associated with the numbers two and one. Frege's response is memorable: "What a mercy, then, that not everything in the world is nailed down; for if it were, we should not be able to bring off this separation, and 2 + 1 would not be 3!" (*The Foundations of Arithmetic* §7). Mill's view also raises the problem of how we could get the numbers 0, 1, and any number too large for us to take in at once in this way.

Mill treats number as a physical property of observed physical **objects**. But, Frege points out, if I observe a pack of cards, am I to say that what I observe is 1 (pack) or 52 (cards)? It is **arbitrary**—a matter of convention, not a matter of natural fact. Sense experience alone does not tell us how to conceptualize our experience or make judgments about it. It does not tell us whether we have 104 cards or 2 packs or 1 pile, nor whether these are cards or color patches or scraps of paper or pieces of trash or what.

Frege and Russell took a different approach. Following Frege, Russell defines the number two as the class of all couples (see *Introduction to Mathematical Philosophy* p. 18), the number three as the class of all trios, and so on. One problem with this kind of definition, though, is that it brings with it the notion of a class, which is potentially more trouble than it is worth. Russell's definition of number, he concedes, *looks* circular. Even if it is not, though, it will still be of very little value if it catches us up in paradox. And this is just what it can appear to do.

For anything at all (call it *x*) and any class at all (call it *y*) we can ask whether *x* belongs to *y*. A spoon, for instance, belongs to the class of spoons, but a barber does not, and a class belongs to the class of classes, but, again, a barber does not. A barber is neither a spoon nor a class. Some classes belong to themselves, such as the class of classes. But what about the class of classes that do not belong to themselves? If it belongs to itself, then it does not belong to itself. If it does not belong to itself, then it does. It looks as though we are stuck in a circle. Paradoxes in **logic** are no better than circles in definitions. The **theory of types** aims to rescue us from this problem, but it too has its problems.

Wittgenstein rejects the theory of types and the use of classes to define numbers. In ***Tractatus Logico-Philosophicus*** 6.031 he insists that the theory of classes is completely superfluous in **mathematics**. In 6.02 he defines numbers in terms of the number of applications of a symbolic procedure rather than the number of members of a class. One thing this does is to avoid a kind of contingency in Russell's theory. Russell says, "the class of all couples will *be* the number 2, according to our definition. At the expense of a little oddity, this definition secures definiteness and indubitableness" (*Introduction to Mathematical Philosophy*, Dover Publications, 1993, p. 18). But then the number 2 depends on the existence of a class of couples, i.e., on the existence of couples. And the number 1000 depends on the existence of 1000 things. And so on. But Russell admits that, "Logical propositions are such as can be known *a priori*, without study of the actual world," and it is not logically necessary that even one thing exists, he says, let alone 1000, or, even worse, infinity (*ibid*., p. 204). So Wittgenstein's new definition seems to be an improvement.

In the ***Philosophical Investigations*** he attempts nothing so technical. Instead he emphasizes the use of numerals. We can say that '3' stands for the number 3, for instance, but this does not tell us very much. We might **wonder** what the number 3 is, and the more we think about this the more likely we are to start to believe in some form of **Platonism** or simply to become confused. Wittgenstein's primary recommended way to dispel or avoid such confusion is to pay attention to how we use numerals such as '3.' It is not to refer to anything at all, let alone a supernatural entity (the mysterious, nonphysical number 3). Rather it is a **sign** we use when engaged in numbering, counting, subtraction, and so on. If I number a group of prisoners (so that one might be 5446, say) or count the eggs in my basket, then the sounds or written signs I make do not stand for anything. Or at least, if anyone wants to understand the meaning of these sounds or signs they would be ill advised to try to identify an object for which they supposedly stand.

O

OBJECT. At the very beginning of the ***Tractatus Logico-Philosophicus*** (propositions 1 to 2.01) Wittgenstein says that **the world** is everything that is the case, that what is the case is the existence of atomic **facts**, and that an atomic fact is a combination of objects. These objects are said to be simple, i.e., not compound. They are in that sense like atoms, impossible to analyze into more basic components. The form of an object is the possibility of its occurrence in atomic facts (2.0141), so what the real world has in common with all merely possible worlds is the objects. The elements of any picture or model of reality correspond to these objects. What they are is impossible to say, but they must exist, Wittgenstein says. The two main ideas about what they might be that Wittgenstein seems to have entertained (at least in his ***Notebooks***) are sense data, such as points in the visual field, and actual physical particles. This form of metaphysical **atomism** is clearly connected to the **picture theory** of **language**, which is attacked in Wittgenstein's later writings, notably the ***Philosophical Investigations***.

P. M. S. Hacker has suggested that Wittgenstein's notion of a simple object came from **Bertrand Russell's** idea of a *term* in *The Principles of Mathematics* (Cambridge University Press, 1903). Russell writes: "Whatever may be an object of thought, or may occur in any true or false proposition, or can be counted as *one*, I call a *term*. This, then, is the widest word in the philosophical vocabulary. I shall use as synonymous with it the words unit, individual, and entity. . . . A man, a moment, a number, a class, a relation, a chimaera, or anything else that can be mentioned, is sure to be a term; and to deny that such and such a thing is a term must always be false" (p. 43).

Hintikka identifies Wittgenstein's objects as "objects of my experience" (p. 14). He quotes **Frank Ramsey**: "Wittgenstein says it is **nonsense** to believe in anything not given in experience. . . . For to be mine, to be given in experience, is the formal [definitory] property to be a genuine entity." Hintikka calls these objects phenomenological entities but denies that they are mere phenomena. That is, they are what is given in immediate experience, but they are not only the contents of our consciousness. We have immediate experience of physical reality (which still remains to be defined), not only of the contents of our own minds.

According to McGuinness (pp. 72–73) objects are the form of the realms of **world**, **thought**, and **language**. So our 'acquaintance' with them "is not an experience or knowledge of something over against which we stand. Thus it is not properly experience or knowledge at all [see *Tractatus* 5.552]." Bearn adds that it is therefore misleading to call Wittgenstein a realist with respect to objects and equally misleading to call him an antirealist in respect of them. Objects are unchanging (see *Tractatus* 2.027) and whatever we can experience could always be otherwise (see *Tractatus* 5.643), so we cannot experience objects.

The ***Blue Book*** refers specifically to the *Tractatus* and the idea that a fact is a "complex of objects" (p. 31). The discussion there sounds like a discussion of **Plato's** idea of universals. Talk of facts as combinations of objects, Wittgenstein writes, springs from the following confusion: "We are misled by the substantives 'object of thought' and 'fact', and by the different meanings of the word 'exist'."

So Wittgenstein came to think of *Tractatus* 2.01 as a mistake. (And perhaps he already thought this way in the *Tractatus*, given what he writes at 6.54 about his propositions being nonsense.)

OGDEN, CHARLES KAY (1889–1957). A philosopher and friend of **Bertrand Russell** who helped get the ***Tractatus Logico-Philosophicus*** published in English by Kegan Paul. He also helped to translate it into English, with help from **Frank Ramsey** and Wittgenstein himself. Ogden was the author, with I. A. Richards, of *The Meaning of Meaning* (1923). In the late 1920s he developed what he called "Basic English," with a vocabulary of 850 words, intended as a medium of international communication to rival Esperanto.

ON CERTAINTY. A collection of notes made in the last year and a half of Wittgenstein's life, edited by **G. E. M. Anscombe** and **G. H. von Wright**. Most of the notes are responses to **G. E. Moore's** attempt to defend common sense and refute **skepticism**. Wittgenstein works through ideas by writing them down, making it hard to judge what his final thinking on any point is (or would have been had he lived longer). It has been suggested by some, notably Avrum Stroll and Danièle Moyal-Sharrock, that *On Certainty* represents an important new phase in Wittgenstein's thinking (the third after the ***Tractatus Logico-Philosophicus*** and ***Philosophical Investigations***).

Stroll argues that in this third phase Wittgenstein defends a form of epistemological **foundationalism** in which knowledge of the world is based on certain **hinge propositions** embedded in, or founded on, a **form of life**, which in turn rests on such things as the existence of the earth. Rudolf Haller and Gertrude Conway have offered similar readings. The standard view, however, is that Wittgenstein was an antifoundationalist, rejecting throughout his later writings the **Cartesian** idea that there is some ultimate justification to be found for any **beliefs** about **the world**.

ORDINARY LANGUAGE. Wittgenstein's later work is written in ordinary **language**, in the sense that it is nontechnical. It is generally taken to relate to technical issues, especially those raised in the ***Tractatus Logico-Philosophicus***, but it makes little use of specifically philosophical terms or symbols. Wittgenstein says that his aim is to return words from their metaphysical to their everyday use (***Philosophical Investigations*** §116). So he is concerned with the ordinary, that is to say, nonphilosophical, nonmetaphysical, use of words. What is metaphysical is open to attack, while what is ordinary is safe.

This has been taken by some to be an inherently **conservative** approach to **philosophy**, placing ordinary patterns of speech and even thought beyond philosophical reproach. Some, but not all, "ordinary language philosophers" have used ordinariness as a **criterion** of correctness. Wittgenstein never says that this is what he intends though. Indeed, he uses some very fanciful examples of strange tribes, expanding cheese, vanishing huts, and so on, suggesting that there is nothing un-Wittgensteinian about talking or thinking in unusual ways.

G. P. Baker has suggested that for Wittgenstein "ordinary" language is just any language that is not metaphysical. This interpretation of *Philosophical Investigations* §116 is controversial though, as is any view on what Wittgenstein meant by this remark and what he would have thought of the work of the various kinds of ordinary language philosophers, such as **Gilbert Ryle**, J. L. Austin, and **Norman Malcolm**, who followed him. Since Wittgenstein knew Ryle and Malcolm, and influenced them directly, one might suspect that he would have been sympathetic to their ideas, but it is impossible to know. Malcolm's interpretations of Wittgenstein are not, after all, regarded as being the last word by other scholars.

Indeed, ordinary language philosophers do not all agree with one another, so Wittgenstein could hardly be expected to agree with them all. In his book *Wittgenstein, Empiricism, and Language* (2000), John W. Cook has distinguished between three kinds of such philosophers: Standard (roughly those that believe that any philosophical conclusion that violates ordinary language is therefore wrong); Metaphysical (otherwise fairly traditional philosophers who claim that, despite appearances to the contrary, the true **meaning** of ordinary language matches their own favored theories—such as, allegedly,

St. Augustine, **Gottfried Leibniz**, and Bishop Berkeley); and Investigative (notably Cook himself and Frank Ebersole). Cook characterizes his and Ebersole's work as looking not only at the conclusions of philosophical **arguments** but also at the steps that lead up to them, and in paying careful attention to how the relevant words are actually used in everyday speech. As he sees it, it is not an approach that has been widely appreciated or followed.

Ordinary language philosophy in general has rather faded from the philosophical scene since its heyday in the Oxford of the 1950s. It has been attacked for being interested in merely semantic issues and for being unsystematic. In its place there has been a partial return to **metaphysics** and a conviction (inspired partly by the work of **W. v. O. Quine**) that **scientific** findings must be relevant to the philosophies of **mind** and **language**.

OSTENSIVE DEFINITION. Wittgenstein talks about ostensive definition (roughly, definition by pointing to something and saying, "*That* is what this means") in the ***Philosophical Investigations*** as part of his attack there on the **picture theory** and related ideas about **meaning**. He notes that one has to have some sense of what meaning and definition are in order to understand an ostensive definition, and that any ostensive definition can be misunderstood if one mistakes what is being pointed to (a red circle might be given as an example of either redness or circularity, for instance). There seems to be something wrong then with the popular idea that **language** is based on a process of pointing and **naming**.

Some readers of the ***Tractatus Logico-Philosophicus*** interpret it as implying that some such process must be fundamental to language (since the elements of **the world** are presented there as absolutely simple **objects** of which words are the names), but what Wittgenstein says there about the **context principle** suggests that this is a misinterpretation. Some readers of the *Investigations* take Wittgenstein to be attacking ostensive definition altogether, as if it could never work. Wittgenstein does not say this explicitly, though, and his discussion of the **standard meter** suggests that he thinks one can present a paradigmatic object as the definition of a term. Certainly, it appears that people point to examples (of **colors**, for instance) when explaining the meanings of words in real life. It does not seem charitable then to read Wittgenstein as saying that this can never be done. Rather, his point is surely that ostension cannot be the **foundation** of language, the means by which all words ultimately, or fundamentally, come to have meaning or to refer to things.

The idea of private ostensive definition inside one's own **mind** also comes under attack in the *Philosophical Investigations*, not so much because one might make a mistake in giving meaning to words such as '**pain**' or 'hope' but because the very idea of **inner** objects to be pointed at is questionable.

See also PRIVATE LANGUAGE ARGUMENT.

OTHER MINDS. The problem of other minds most obviously arises for those who subscribe to what **Gilbert Ryle** calls the official doctrine about the **mind**. This doctrine, derived from **René Descartes**, treats the mind as a nonphysical **object** that, nevertheless, somehow interacts with the body, presumably through the brain. Unlike the brain and the rest of the body, the mind on this account is taken to be undetectable by any of the five physical senses and knowable only to the person whose mind it is. Thus one can only know about other people's minds by observing their **behavior** and taking their word for what they are **thinking** or feeling. However, this knowledge seems really to be merely a kind of faith, since one cannot possibly tell the difference between a body that merely acts as if it houses a mind and one that really does. **Science** can detect the presence and activity of a brain, of course, but the mind is taken by Cartesians to be something else, something invisible to scientific inquiry. Hence the problem of how one can know whether minds other than one's own exist at all. If none exist, then a form of **solipsism** is true.

Philosophical Investigations §420 suggests that whether one thinks of others as having minds or not relates to **aspect-seeing**. That is, one can imagine people seeing, treating, and reacting to others as if they were mere automata, lacking, one might say, a **soul**. This is not how people ordinarily deal with others though, and it is nigh on impossible to adopt such an outlook voluntarily. Wittgenstein's point might be expressed by saying that one really does not *know* that other people have minds. Rather than expressing **skepticism**, though, these words should be taken to reject the idea that the issue is one of knowledge. It is only partly one of thinking at all. Seeing another **human being** as an embodied mind is hard to define or reduce to other more definite phenomena, but it includes thinking certain kinds of things about them, feeling certain things in connection with them (that their destruction would be terrible, say), and behaving in certain ways toward them. If one did not believe in other minds, one would be suffering, as most people would see it, from some sort of mental handicap or illness. No philosophical **argument** would be likely to effect a cure for such a defect.

OVERVIEW. ***Philosophical Investigations*** §122 says that one of the main sources of trouble in **philosophy**, of our failure to understand our own **language**, is the absence of an overview of the use of our words. If we had such a view, then we could see connections between uses. Since we do not have this kind of overview, we must instead seek out and invent intermediate cases to help us see the connections we otherwise overlook. Philosophical problems are characterized by a sense of being lost (see §123), and so the solution is to provide a kind of map or rather, since Wittgenstein apparently thinks it is not possible to produce such a map (an overview or surveyable representation of our language), a set of directions. Instead, the work of the Wittgensteinian philosopher is to produce reminders for a particular purpose (see §127). Thus in the preface to the *Investigations* Wittgenstein writes that what he provides therein is sketches of landscapes, and that this is related to the nature of the task he undertook in writing the book. The nature of philosophical investigation requires us to travel crisscross, on a series of long and meandering journeys.

P

PAIN. Wittgenstein's discussion of pain in the ***Philosophical Investigations*** is well known. He uses pain as an example of a sensation that one might think of as an **inner** object of which the word 'pain' would be the **name**. His implication that pain and other sensations are not **objects** of this kind has led to charges of **behaviorism**. In §304, however, Wittgenstein insists that he is rejecting only the **grammar** that "tries to force itself on us" when we think about pain. He denies that pain is "a nothing" but denies equally that it is a something. In other words, it is a sensation, not an object, and one will misunderstand sensations (or talk about sensations) if one thinks of them as objects, whether of a **queer**, **Cartesian** kind or a down-to-earth, neurological kind. The **criteria** for the correct use of words such as 'pain' might be largely behavioral, but pointing this out is not reducing pain to behavior.

PART II OF THE *PHILOSOPHICAL INVESTIGATIONS*. *See PHILOSOPHY OF PSYCHOLOGY—A FRAGMENT.*

PASCAL, FANIA. *See* RUSSIA.

PHENOMENOLOGICAL LANGUAGE. After his return to **philosophy**, at the beginning of his middle period, Wittgenstein seems to have wanted to develop a special **language** for talking about phenomena. This supports, but hardly proves true, the idea that there really is a **metaphysic** of **objects** in the ***Tractatus Logico-Philosophicus*** that is not meant to be dismissed as **nonsense**. Or perhaps Wittgenstein simply relapsed into what he would have thought of previously as nonsense after his time away from **Cambridge**. Another alternative is that he wanted to develop a phenomenological language precisely in order to show that it could not do what philosophers would want it to do. His interest appears to have been sincere and straightforward, however, and it implies that at least for this period he believed in, or experimented with, a form of phenomenalism or **idealism**. He worked on the project from February to October in 1929 before abandoning the attempt.

PHILLIPS, DEWI ZEPHANIAH (1934–2006). An influential Wittgensteinian philosopher of **religion**. Phillips has been thought of by some as a **fideist**, wrongly so according to him. He also wrote on **ethics** and the relation between **philosophy** and literature, as well as editing the leading Wittgenstein journal *Philosophical Investigations*. He was the professor of philosophy at the University of Wales, **Swansea**, and Danworth Professor of the Philosophy of Religion at Claremont Graduate School, California. His many books include *The Concept of Prayer* (1965), *Death and Immortality* (1970), *Faith after Foundationalism* (1988), *Interventions in Ethics* (1992), *Wittgenstein and Religion* (1993), and *Philosophy's Cool Place* (1999).

PHILOSOPHICAL GRAMMAR. Written in the years 1932–1934, just before the ***Blue Book*** was dictated, this work belongs to Wittgenstein's early middle period (or very early late period, if one recognizes only two periods in his career). It was edited by **Rush Rhees** and comes in two parts. The first deals with the **proposition** and its sense or **meaning**. The second concerns **logic** and **mathematics**. There is significant overlap between remarks in the *Philosophical Grammar* and those in ***Philosophical Remarks***, ***Philosophical Investigations***, and ***Zettel***. There is also much material that is unique to this work, especially in Part II.

PHILOSOPHICAL INVESTIGATIONS. Generally regarded as Wittgenstein's most important work. It was written in the years 1929–1949 and was almost, but not quite, finished at the time of his death in 1951. The original editors, **G. E. M. Anscombe**, **Rush Rhees**, and **G. H. von Wright**, believed that if Wittgenstein had lived, he would have removed a lot of the material from the last 30 or so pages of the main portion of the book (which they labeled Part I) and replaced it with material from what they called Part II (now called ***Philosophy of Psychology—A Fragment***) and elsewhere. Likely sources of such material have been published as ***Remarks on the Philosophy of Psychology*** and ***Last Writings on the Philosophy of Psychology***.

Wittgenstein had hoped that the book would be published along with the ***Tractatus Logico-Philosophicus***, and much of it is clearly a response to ideas found (although not necessarily endorsed) in that earlier work. The remarks that make up the book concern **mind**, **rules**, **logic**, **language**, and the nature of **philosophy**. It is here that he introduces the important concepts of **language-games** and **forms of life**.

The most recent edition of the book is the fourth, published in 2009. This includes the German text along with an English translation by Anscombe, **P. M. S. Hacker**, and Joachim Schulte. It is edited by Hacker and Schulte.

PHILOSOPHICAL OCCASIONS. Edited by James C. Klagge and Alfred Nordmann, this collection of writings spans Wittgenstein's entire philosophical career from 1912 (a review of P. Coffey's *The Science of Logic*) to 1951 (a letter to **G. H. von Wright**). The book contains the text of Wittgenstein's **lecture on ethics**, notes on **causation** and **free will**, the ***Remarks on Frazer's*** **Golden Bough**, remarks on **philosophy** from the **Big Typescript**, and other notes and letters.

PHILOSOPHICAL PSYCHOLOGY. Wittgenstein wrote at length about the **philosophy** of **psychology**, as well as making various remarks about individual psychologists such as **Sigmund Freud** and **Wolfgang Köhler**, but he can also be regarded as engaging in philosophical work that is intended to take the place of psychology rather than simply analyzing or discussing it. Köhler suggested that psychology was a young **science** with much progress still to make, but Wittgenstein thought that psychology never could be a science in the way that physics, for instance, is. The brain can be studied scientifically, of course, as can, perhaps, **behavior**. The scientific study of behavior is likely to be complicated by the fact that behavior might change in response to being observed, though, either directly because of factors such as self-consciousness or indirectly because findings in the behavioral sciences could lead to new behaviors. For instance, if businesses find ways to increase profits as a result of the findings of behavioral economists or social psychologists, then informed consumers might learn to behave differently so as to save money. Even inanimate objects can be affected by observation, but the problem seems especially great (though not necessarily unsolvable) in the social sciences.

This, though, was not Wittgenstein's worry about psychology. Rather, it was its attempt to study the **inner** on the model of sciences that study publicly observable phenomena. Whether one agrees that there is conceptual confusion in such a project or not, in fact psychology has largely moved away from introspective methods, which were found to be unproductive, and toward the study of brains (along with other internal organs and systems) and behavior.

PHILOSOPHICAL REMARKS. A transitional work, edited posthumously from Wittgenstein's writings by **Rush Rhees**. It contains some of the first indications of the kind of ideas that appeared in the ***Philosophical Investigations*** and the ***Remarks on the Foundations of Mathematics***. The text is that of a typescript that Wittgenstein gave to **Bertrand Russell** in May 1930 entitled *Philosophische Bemerkungen* (Philosophical Remarks). The manuscripts from which Wittgenstein took these remarks were written between 2 February 1929 and 24 April 1930.

PHILOSOPHY. Western philosophy arose in Greece and seems not to have been distinguished at the time from what would now be called **science**. (Eastern philosophy, for instance **Buddhism**, is more a cross between what Western philosophy later became and **religion**.) The first philosophers happily mixed religion and **poetry** too with the new subject. This began to change with **Socrates**, who was much more interested in questions of **ethics** than anything of a scientific nature. Since Socrates and his student **Plato**, Western philosophy has been, roughly speaking, the attempt to use reason or **logic** to discover **truths** about **metaphysics** and ethics (including such related subjects as **politics**, religion, and **aesthetics**). Since **Aristotle**, philosophers have treated logic itself as a subject for inquiry. There has also been, especially since the time of **René Descartes**, a significant interest in epistemology (with emphasis on combating **skepticism**). This tradition has come under a series of attacks, starting in the 19th century with figures such as **Søren Kierkegaard** and **Friedrich Nietzsche**. Wittgenstein too rejects the traditional idea of what philosophy is, should, or can be.

Unlike some of his other ideas, Wittgenstein's conception of philosophy seems to have changed little over his life. In the ***Tractatus Logico-Philosophicus*** he says in proposition 4.111 that "philosophy is not one of the natural sciences," and in 4.112 that "Philosophy aims at the logical clarification of thoughts." Philosophy as Wittgenstein claims to practice it is not descriptive but elucidatory. It might use **description** of certain uses of **language** as a method, but its goal is not to describe language, nor to police its use. Rather, its aim is to clear up muddle and **confusion**. It follows that philosophers should not concern themselves so much with what is actual, keeping up with the latest science, say. That would be appropriate if the object of philosophy were truth, but Wittgenstein's objective is not so much truth as clarity. This is not because the truth does not matter or can never be known, but because truth is not the only thing that matters, and perhaps also because philosophy is ill-suited to discover truths about the world. Science, broadly conceived, is the way to find out about the world. The philosopher's proper concern is not what is the case but what is possible, or rather, with what is conceivable. This depends on the available **concepts** and the ways they fit together as seen in language. What is conceivable and what is not, what makes sense and what does not, depends on the **rules** of language, of **grammar**.

In 1931 (see ***Culture and Value***, p. 18e) Wittgenstein described his task thus:

> Language sets everyone the same traps; it is an immense network of easily accessible wrong turnings. And so we watch one man after another walking down the same paths and we know in advance where he will branch

> off, where walk straight on without noticing the side turning, etc. etc. What I have to do then is erect signposts at all the junctions where there are wrong turnings so as to help people past the danger points.

As Wittgenstein sees it, such signposts are all that philosophy can offer and there is no certainty that they will be noticed or followed correctly. And we should remember that a signpost belongs in the context of a particular problem area. It might be no help at all elsewhere, and should not be treated as dogma. So philosophy offers no truths, no theories, nothing exciting, but mainly reminders of what we all know. This is not a glamorous role, but it is difficult and important. It requires an almost infinite capacity for taking pains (which is one definition of genius) and could have enormous implications for anyone who is drawn to philosophical contemplation or who is misled by bad philosophical theories. This applies not only to professional philosophers but to any people who stray into philosophical confusion, perhaps not even realizing that their problems are philosophical rather than, say, scientific.

In ***Philosophical Investigations*** §90 Wittgenstein says: "Our investigation is therefore a grammatical one. And this inquiry sheds light on our problem by clearing misunderstandings away." Apart from the **continuity** in his thought (concerning ends if not means) implied by these quotations from the early *Tractatus* and the late *Investigations*, two points should be noted. The first is the emphasis that Wittgenstein puts on language. It was largely his and **Gottlob Frege's** work that started the so-called linguistic turn in 20th century philosophy. Secondly, since Wittgenstein tended to regard philosophical thinking as symptomatic of confusion, he did not so much disagree with one **theory** or set of theories (which might imply that he agreed with their opposites) as reject entire debates, such as those between **realists and antirealists**.

It is worth saying a little more about the importance of language to philosophy. The similarities between the sentences "I'll keep it in mind" and "I'll keep it in this box," for instance, (along with many others) can lead one to think of the **mind** as a thing something like a box with contents of its own. The nature of this box and its mental contents can then seem very mysterious. Wittgenstein suggests that one way, at least, to deal with such mysteries is to recall the different things one says about minds, **memories**, **thoughts**, and so on, in a variety of contexts.

What one says, or what people in general say, can change. Ways of life and uses of language change, so **meanings** change, but not utterly and instantaneously. Things shift and evolve, but rarely if ever so drastically that one loses all grip on meaning. So there is no timeless **essence** of at least some and perhaps all concepts, but people still **understand** one another well enough most of the time.

When **nonsense** is spoken or written, or when something just seems fishy, one can sniff it out. The road out of confusion can be a long and difficult one, hence the need for constant attention to detail and particular examples rather than generalizations, which tend to be vague and therefore potentially misleading. The slower the route, the surer the safety at the end of it. Wittgenstein said that in philosophy the winner is the one who finishes last. But one cannot escape language or the confusions to which it gives rise except by dying. In the meantime, Wittgenstein offers four main methods to avoid philosophical confusion, as summed up by **Norman Malcolm**: describing circumstances in which a seemingly problematic expression might actually be used in everyday life, comparing the actual use of words with imaginary **language-games**, imagining fictitious natural history, and explaining psychologically the temptation to use a certain expression inappropriately.

According to Wittgenstein there can, however, be no progress in philosophy in the way that there is in science. Similar, or even the very same, problems are always likely to recur. This suggests that what is needed is not so much solutions to philosophical problems as a method, or methods, for dealing with them. This is what Wittgenstein claims to provide, or to demonstrate, in the *Philosophical Investigations*. Most Wittgensteinians believe that he also does solve some real problems along the way, proving that various theories (such as the idea that there could be a **private language**) are nonsensical.

There is often talk of a middle Wittgenstein and, recently, of a "third" Wittgenstein. It is certainly true that the author of the *Investigations* would not have accepted everything that the author of the ***Blue Book*** wrote. Nor should we rule out the possibility that ***On Certainty*** contains new developments in his thought. It is worth bearing in mind, however, that every active intellect is likely to change, if only in small ways, almost constantly, so the attempt to count Wittgensteins is always in danger of futility. Moreover, the only philosophical works that Wittgenstein came close to finishing were the *Tractatus* and the *Investigations*. His other 'works' are the products of editors (using Wittgenstein's notes as raw material), or unfinished, or abandoned. If the notes published as *On Certainty* differ from the *Investigations* in significant ways, it is possible that Wittgenstein would have corrected them had he lived longer.

PHILOSOPHY OF PSYCHOLOGY—A FRAGMENT. Formerly known as Part II of the ***Philosophical Investigations***. This material consists of 372 remarks on the philosophy of psychology, mostly written between May 1946 and May 1949. **G. E. M. Anscombe** and **Rush Rhees** believed that Wittgenstein would have worked these remarks into the *Investigations* if he had lived long enough to do so, perhaps replacing some of the last 30 pages of the book with this and other new material. It is possible that Wittgenstein told them that this was his intention. Unfortunately, there is no written evidence that this is what he meant to do. Consequently, the status of these remarks has been somewhat downgraded in the fourth edition of the *Investigations*, from making up the second part of Wittgenstein's most finished, mature work to being in effect a separate unfinished work that happens to be published with the *Investigations*. Among other things, these remarks are the main source for Wittgenstein's views on the primary and secondary **meanings** of words, or **secondary sense**.

PHYSIOGNOMY. ***Philosophical Investigations*** §568 says that **meaning** is a physiognomy. 'Physiognomy' means face, especially as indicative of character, or else the study of character by means of observation of physical features, especially those of the face. So Wittgenstein's claim (if that is what it is—the remark is in double parentheses, so perhaps it is just a note, an expression of an idea that Wittgenstein does not necessarily endorse) is a strange one. In ***Philosophy of Psychology—A Fragment*** (§38) Wittgenstein says that "one would like to say" (but perhaps should not?) that every word has an abiding single character or face, even though it can also have a different character in different contexts. He also says, though, that a face in a painting looks at us. So one should probably not take him too literally here. Faces in paintings *seem* to look at us and perhaps this is one reason why people have such paintings, but they do not really look at us. Similarly, Wittgenstein seems to be saying, words seem to have a certain character that remains in them even when they are used in different ways, with different characters, in various contexts. The word 'green' can suggest health (when linked with salad) or sickness (when linked with facial color), naïveté or envy, and so on. The very sight or sound of the word can make one think of just these things, so that the physical properties of the symbol 'green' can seem perfectly to match its meaning. Perhaps this is why meaning can seem to be a matter of feeling, something very subjective, even though the role a symbol plays in a public **language** cannot be individual in this way.

The idea that words have a character that persists through different uses and is their real meaning seems both **Platonic/essentialist** and foolishly subjective or even romantic. However, it is worth bearing in mind that Wittgenstein himself expected people's appearances to match their characters (whether he regarded this expectation as reasonable or not is not known) and that he identifies those who do not see words as having this kind of character as aspect-blind (and thus rather alien). Those who see no character in a person's face might be said not to believe in **other minds**, while those with no sense that words have characters would seem to be incapable of appreciating **poetry** and **secondary sense**. They might also be incapable of grasping a **rule** in any way that was not an interpretation. So, strange as it might seem, the idea of physiognomy is very important to Wittgenstein.

Indeed, rather than rejecting the idea of physiognomy, Wittgenstein tells us (in *Investigations* §235) that he is showing the physiognomy of, in this case, what we ordinarily call following a rule. He shows, that is, both what we call 'following a rule' (the face) and how we see it (the character behind the face). In fact what he has just described before he makes this remark is feeling astonished that we all **agree** about what the next step is when we follow a rule. This is *not* part of everyday life. We do not ordinarily feel such astonishment. In other words, by describing a *different* character than the one we ordinarily perceive or experience, Wittgenstein takes himself to have shown something of the character that rule-following *is* experienced as having. He also seems to have shown that this character is in a way inessential to the meaning of 'rule-following' (it might still be what is called rule-following even if people experienced it in this other way).

One might argue that philosophical **theories** about following rules that suggest that people ought to feel astonished when they agree (that treat the ability to follow rules as a real mystery) are thus shown to be doubly wrong. They are intuitively wrong because they feel wrong, they misrepresent the felt character of following rules. More importantly, they are wrong because they imply that this character is essential to rule-following when in fact it is not. The **criteria** of rule-following, the way one identifies instances of rule-following, are compatible with rule-following seeming inevitable (and so unsurprising), astonishing, or neither. Attempts to analyze the concept of rule-following that imply that one such kind of feeling would be more apt than another are in effect metaphysical, dismissing some intelligible possibilities about what rule-following might be and insisting that only one of these possibilities counts (should count) as *real* rule-following, rather than purely logical or conceptual. Wittgenstein does not say that **metaphysics** is wrong, but he detects **confusion** in purported conceptual inquiries that lead to debatable hypotheses.

This interpretation would not be universally accepted, however. Perhaps one cannot, in fact, imagine what is ordinarily called rule-following among people who are genuinely amazed and delighted at their good fortune when they find that they all agree on what constitutes, say, adding two. In this case the character behind the face *is* important. Certainly Wittgenstein raises questions about what one can imagine. There are limits, but he does not try to define or dictate where these are.

On such matters controversy is hard to avoid. On the one hand, Wittgenstein says that we do not know what feelings others have when they hear or use the words we do, and yet we still communicate with them using those words. So these feelings appear to be irrelevant to meaning. On the other, he says that when a musical piece is played with a particular feeling, the feeling is not something additional to or separable from the **music**. In the same way, perhaps, the meaning of a person's words might depend on the feeling with which they are said, and this feeling would seem thus to be intrinsic to what is said. So feelings appear to be inextricable from meaning. Perhaps one should say that with meaning (using words) and following rules, as long as everyone goes on the same way then there is no problem. In this case there is (apparently limited) room for various feelings or associations. However, if these feelings intrude into or affect one's performance or behavior, for instance if every time people agree or seem to **understand** one another they stop and thank God for this miracle, then one might say that what is happening is no longer speaking the same language or following the same rules. The limits of concepts such as 'same' and 'language' do not seem to be very definite. Certainly Wittgenstein offers no explicit map of their borders.

PICTURE THEORY. One of the most important ideas in the ***Tractatus Logico-Philosophicus*** is that sentences or **propositions** are **pictures** of **states of affairs** in **the world**. When the picture matches a real state of affairs, the sentence is true, otherwise the sentence is false. Each element of a sentence corresponds to some element of the world (an **object**). The question of **truth** depends solely on whether these elements are in fact arranged in the same order as the sentence represents them as being. This **theory** offers an **explanation** of how **language** can connect with reality. It also offers an explanation as to how one can meaningfully talk and think about things (combinations of elements) that do not exist, a question that had troubled **Bertrand Russell** and Alexius Meinong.

It follows from the picture theory that any possible state of affairs can be described in a proposition, but propositions that do not represent possible states of affairs in the world are senseless. Anything normative, supernatural, or (one might say) metaphysical must therefore have no sense. The same goes for statements about the world as a whole and **logic**, which is not an empirical **science** as Wittgenstein conceives of it. **Logical positivists** have been keen to use this as ammunition in their rejection of all talk about **ethics**, **religion**, and **metaphysics**.

Unfortunately, this theory seems to lead to serious problems since by its own lights the *Tractatus*'s use of words such as 'object,' 'reality,' and 'world' is illegitimate. These **concepts** are purely **formal** or *a priori*. A statement such as "There are objects in the world" does not picture a state of affairs. Rather it is, as it were, presupposed by the notion of a state of affairs. The picture theory therefore denies sense to just the kind of statements of which the *Tractatus* is composed, to the framework supporting the picture theory itself.

Presumably this is why proposition 6.54 of the *Tractatus* describes Wittgenstein's own propositions as **nonsense**. However, most scholars distinguish, following Wittgenstein's choice of words before (but not in) 6.54, between sentences that lack sense (in German *sinnlos*) and those that are sheer nonsense (*Unsinn*). Whether this distinction is important to keep or itself something that 6.54 tells us to discard is a matter of some dispute. The picture theory of language is attacked (some would say again) in the opening passages of the ***Philosophical Investigations***.

PICTURES. In ***Tractatus Logico-Philosophicus*** propositions 2.1–2.225, Wittgenstein presents **propositions** as pictures of possible **states of affairs**. The elements of such a picture stand for or represent **objects** and the picture shows how these objects are (claimed to be) combined or related. In the ***Philosophical Investigations*** propositions are treated as less fundamental or **essential** to **language**, and the relation between propositions and **the world** is treated as both more diverse and more dynamic than the earlier **picture theory** suggests.

When Wittgenstein talks about pictures in the later work, he means something more like mind-sets from whose grip the philosophically inclined are to free themselves (see *Philosophical Investigations* §115 for instance). This is not to say that all such pictures are necessarily bad, but Wittgenstein is alert to the possibility of being captured by one and thereby blinkered. Indeed, he suggests that the *Tractatus* shows what such captivity can be like, referring explicitly to a remark about the general form of propositions (4.5) as an example of mistaking **grammar** for **metaphysics** (thinking "that one is tracing the outline of the thing's nature . . . [when] one is merely tracing round the frame through which we look at it" [§114]).

PINSENT, DAVID HUME (1891–1918). One of Wittgenstein's closest friends. They met at **Bertrand Russell's** house in **Cambridge**. Pinsent shared Wittgenstein's taste in **music**, and the two went on vacations to Iceland and **Norway** together. The ***Tractatus Logico-Philosophicus*** was dedicated to Pinsent, who was a military test pilot and died in an accident during **World War I**. Wittgenstein called him, "my first and my only friend" (see Monk p. 154). Pinsent's diaries from 1912–1914 have been edited by **G. H. von Wright** and published by Basil Blackwell under the title *A Portrait of Wittgenstein as a Young Man* (1990).

PLATO (c. 428–c. 348 BCE). One of the greatest philosophers in Western history. Plato studied with **Socrates** and taught **Aristotle**. His ideas are known to us through a collection of dialogues, most of which feature a character called Socrates who is mostly a mouthpiece for Plato's own ideas. These ideas include a kind of dualism similar to **René Descartes's** and the theory of Forms, a version of which has come to be known simply as Platonism. Generally considered too counterintuitive to be plausible, Platonism is the idea that there exists a realm of ideal types beyond the physical. Thus in

ethics, for instance, a Platonist would regard goodness as a kind of object, only not a physical one, an object whose **essence** was (non-relative) goodness in itself. In **mathematics** Platonists are those who believe that such things as numbers and geometric shapes have a real, nonphysical existence and that mathematics is the activity of discovering the properties of, and relations between, these objects. For almost every one of our **concepts**, Plato argued, there exists an unchanging, pure archetype in another world, a world to which the **souls** of the virtuous dead go when they leave this world. These archetypes (better known as Forms or Ideas) include **Truth**, Beauty, and Goodness. Plato can thus be thought of as the ultimate **realist** and antirelativist. Famously, **Friedrich Nietzsche** referred to **Christianity** as Platonism for the masses, and **A. N. Whitehead** described the history of Western **philosophy** as a series of footnotes to Plato. His best-known work is the *Republic*.

POETRY. In poetry, Wittgenstein suggests in ***Philosophical Investigations*** §531, words are used in something like a **secondary sense**. That is to say, they cannot be paraphrased without loss, a loss of **meaning**. The same is true of **music**. One phrase cannot be substituted for another. In ***Culture and Value*** (p. 24e, 1933–1934), he writes that **philosophy** should be written only as poetry, and that this shows that he is unable to do exactly what he would like to be able to do. It is hard to know what to make of this. Certainly it suggests that Wittgenstein would like to be very precise in his choice of words, as poets must be, since no other words will have quite the meaning that they require. It might also make one expect to find a similarity between Wittgenstein's work and that of **Martin Heidegger**, but there are few obvious similarities between them. Perhaps what Wittgenstein means is that ideally it would be possible to write philosophy as poetry (as, arguably, Heidegger and **Friedrich Nietzsche** tried to do), but that in fact this was impossible, just as Wittgenstein would have liked to dedicate his works to the glory of God but felt that this was no longer possible. His work does have a literary quality, but it is more dialectical, less didactic, than poetry tends to be. The ***Tractatus Logico-Philosophicus***, though, is usually read as didactic and has been characterized as poetic.

See also LITERATURE.

POLITICS. Wittgenstein wrote little about politics, and his own political beliefs are hard to pin down. He certainly did not do political philosophy in the usual sense of the term, but it is possible that his work was intended to have significance for the culture at large, and thus indirectly for politics in a broad sense. Wittgenstein's sympathies were more with the left than with the right, and he even considered moving to the Soviet Union. However, a visit there put him off the idea, partly because he was not offered the kind of work that he wanted to do, but also because he disliked the bureaucracy there.

See also CONSERVATISM; MARXISM; RUSSIA; SCIENCE AND SCIENTISM.

POPPER, KARL (1902–1994). A philosopher and sometime rival of Wittgenstein. Born in **Vienna**, Popper became a British citizen in 1945. He shared the interests of the **Vienna Circle** but disagreed with the theory of **verification**, preferring instead his own theory that genuinely scientific hypotheses must be falsifiable, that is, open to possible refutation. He also rejected the positivists' idea that all nonscience is **nonsense**. He did, however, attack anything that he saw as pseudoscience, notably **Marxism** and **Freudian** psychoanalysis. In addition to his **philosophy** of **science**, he is best known for his defense of freedom and attack on philosophers that he took to be dangers to it, such as **Plato**, **G. W. F. Hegel**, and Karl Marx.

Popper took part in a famous debate with Wittgenstein in 1946 at the Moral Science Club in **Cambridge**. Popper believed that Wittgenstein regarded philosophy as being all a matter of pseudo-problems and **confusion**, whereas, in Popper's view, philosophical problems are very important and require real solutions. The debate was unproductive and heated, but reports vary as to exactly what happened. At one point Wittgenstein picked up a poker and is alleged to have pointed it menacingly at Popper before storming out of the meeting.

PRAGMATISM. The **meaning** of pragmatism has been disputed even by such paradigmatic pragmatists as **William James** and C. S. Pierce. It is perhaps best understood, however, as a **theory** about **truth** according to which true statements are those that work or are useful. This reminds some people of Wittgenstein's comments about meaning and use. It also has a strong **utilitarian** flavor to it, which would be unlikely to appeal to Wittgenstein. His distaste for the pragmatist John Dewey is expressed in the only slightly ambiguous remark recorded by **O. K. Bouwsma** in his *Wittgenstein: Conversations 1949–1951*: "Dewey—was Dewey still living? Yes. Ought not to be" (pp. 28–29). (This is ambiguous because Wittgenstein could merely have meant that Dewey belonged to an earlier time, but this interpretation seems doubtful.)

In ***On Certainty*** §422, Wittgenstein comments that he is trying to say something that sounds like pragmatism and that in this attempt he is thus thwarted by a sort of *Weltanschauung*. In other words, he knows that what he is saying is likely to be misunderstood as a version of pragmatism, because that is the kind of thing people expect to hear or read about. But of course pragmatism is a **theory**, in contrast to which Wittgenstein said that he offered **descriptions** of uses of **language**, observations that everyone will accept (see ***Philosophical Investigations*** §599). His aim was to bring words back from their philosophical or **metaphysical** (or epistemological?) use to their everyday use (see *Investigations* §116 and *On Certainty* §347). Wittgenstein emphasizes the importance of practice or **behavior** but does not, it seems, mean to propose any pragmatic theory of knowledge or **certainty**. Whether he succeeds in this is a controversial matter. The most famous contemporary philosopher in the pragmatist tradition is **Richard Rorty**, who also takes inspiration from Wittgenstein's work.

PRIVACY. A mental state, such as a **pain** or a **memory**, can be thought to be private in the sense that it belongs inescapably to the person who has it and in the sense that only this person can know of it directly. The **picture** here is of the **mind** as a kind of internal theatre on whose screen or stage mental states appear, perceived only and unavoidably by the **inner** eye of the **Cartesian** ego or self. Wittgenstein tried to loosen the grip of this picture in our thinking about **psychology**.

There are several problems with the picture, however attractive or even useful we might find it. For one thing, there is not literally a theatre inside us, nor anything that has been identified as the neurological equivalent of a theatre (unless it is the whole brain). For another, in this picture mental states are treated as **objects** of a peculiar kind (they are not physical, for instance, and they are private in the two senses mentioned above). But it is difficult to make sense of such objects, since they lack the properties of the kind of objects that physics (and chemistry) deals with as well as the properties that common sense might expect objects to have (such as size, shape, weight, location, and so on). Not least among the problems that arise when we think of mental states as objects (and calling them "mental states" might encourage such thinking, and therefore be part of the problem) are those to do with privacy.

If a pain in my foot is a funny kind of object, why could it not conceivably move from my foot to yours? We might think of it as being like a fish that can only survive in a certain, watery environment. But pains don't thrash and die when we remove them from our bodies. There is no such thing as moving a pain out of someone's body, except as an odd way of saying that a pain has been ended or killed, perhaps by means of an anesthetic or painkiller. How do we know there is no such thing? Not because of a history of experimentation, but because it makes no sense to talk of such a thing. It is a matter of **grammar**. However much the word 'pain' or '**belief**' or 'memory' might function like the name of a kind of object, it also does *not* function in this way to an important extent. Once we are reminded of this, we are less likely to be confused about what a strange kind of object these mental things are.

Instead, we might accept that they are not really objects at all, or not objects in the usual sense of the word, or only objects in an extended, and potentially confusing, sense of the word. It does not really matter very much what we say, as long as the point is seen.

Secondly, Wittgenstein attacks the idea that only I can know whether I am in pain, or remember the Alamo, or believe in elves. His method here is the same one of grammatical investigation and reminders, but his conclusion is different. It is not so much that only I can know what I believe or feel. Rather, in an important sense, I alone *cannot* know these things. Typically, after all, what is known is first found out, and can be forgotten later or gotten wrong. It is hard to make sense, though, of talk about finding out that one is in pain, or forgetting one's political beliefs, or making a mistake about one's own thoughts. Such talk is not always, necessarily **nonsense**. It is possible to imagine circumstances in which it might make sense, but these will not be normal circumstances. If you ask me what I am thinking of, I might misspeak or lie, but I can hardly misidentify the object of my thoughts in the same way that I might misidentify a physical object that I see at some distance. One way I might misidentify what I am thinking about is through the workings of the subconscious mind, which might cause even me, the person having the thoughts, not to recognize their, for example, embarrassing sexual nature. But this is quite different from mistaking a wolf for a large dog. If I think I am looking at a large dog, I might be mistaken: it might be a wolf. If I think I am thinking about a large dog, then I cannot be mistaken in the same way. (Although, at the risk of overcomplicating matters, I can be mistaken in another way if I am thinking about Homer, whom I believe to be a large dog, and Homer is actually a wolf.) We think about things under a description, and we cannot be straightforwardly mistaken about the description under which we are thinking of something. More simply, at least in normal circumstances, I have pains. There is no *process* of discovering that I have them. Nor can I mistake a belief for a pain, even though there are times when it might be hard to decide how best to characterize some feeling that I have. Is it a pain or a tickle? Or an itch? Is this pain or mere discomfort? One can make a mistake in cases like these, or decide in retrospect that one has gotten it wrong. Such a mistake belongs to a different kind, though, than mistakes about physical objects. I can fail to see a golf ball that is right under my nose. I cannot fail to feel a pain that is right there in my consciousness. I can mistake the golf ball for a piece of chalk if all I see is something white in the grass. I cannot mistake a pain for some other type of mental state as a result of imperfectly perceiving it (because an imperfectly perceived pain is not much of a pain, while an imperfectly perceived golf ball is still just as much a golf ball as any other). And I can perceive a sensation perfectly well and still not be sure whether to call it a pain or a tickle. The problem lies in knowing which words to apply, not in perceiving the sensation.

On the other hand, it is perfectly possible, even in normal circumstances, for other people to find out what I remember, believe, think, or feel. It is possible for them to forget or make mistakes about these things too. I simply feel (or have) my pains, remember (or have) my memories, think my thoughts, believe my beliefs, and so on. I do not (in normal circumstances, speaking normally) know that I feel them, know that I remember them, and so on. But you can. You can know (learn, forget, mistakenly believe) that I am in pain. You can know that, and what, I remember. You can know what I think. And so on. Hence these mental states really are not private with regard to knowledge, i.e., epistemically private, at all.

See also PRIVATE LANGUAGE ARGUMENT.

PRIVATE LANGUAGE ARGUMENT. One of the most important of Wittgenstein's contributions to **philosophy** is generally taken to be his private **language** argument, which appears in the ***Philosophical Investigations***. The **argument** is important because it seems, if sound, to disprove the very possibility of a language in principle incomprehensible to anyone but the person whose language it is. (The language is meant to be private in this sense because its vocabulary is defined by sensations to which only that person has any access.) And that matters because such a language is arguably presupposed, even if only implicitly, by most philosophers who deal with the **mind** and how it has knowledge, from **René Descartes** to the present day. For instance, **John Locke** held that people talk to each other by translating a personal mental language into a public language, such as English, which is then retranslated in the interlocutor's mind into her personal mental vocabulary. **Bertrand Russell** explicitly raised the idea of a private language in his lectures on **logical atomism**. The private language argument is then an attack on a way of **thinking** about the mind that has survived for hundreds of years and which, many Wittgensteinians would say, persists today in less obvious forms. Exactly where in Wittgenstein's work the argument appears is a matter of some disagreement, though, as is the question of precisely what the argument is or whether there really is any such argument at all.

The mainstream view is that the argument appears in the *Philosophical Investigations*, somewhere between §243 and §315, and more precisely between §256 and §271. Here Wittgenstein begins consideration of a language "which only I myself can understand," the language that describes my **inner** experiences (see §256). In §258 Wittgenstein asks the reader to imagine someone who has a certain sensation that cannot be defined but that he dubs 'S.' Whenever he has the sensation, he writes 'S' in his diary. Wittgenstein appears to show that 'S' has no **meaning**. Nobody else can ever tell the man that he has made a mistake in his use of 'S.' Nor can he recall the original sensation in order to check that a current sensation that seems similar really is the same. Even if he could, it is not clear what similarities he ought to look for, in which respects any similarity would be relevant. Nor can he revert to his former **self** in order to know what he would have counted as relevant when he performed the original dubbing. In short, there seem to be no possible **criteria** or standards for the correct use of 'S.' And a 'word' without rules for its correct use seems not to qualify as part of any language. So 'S' in fact has no meaning. There cannot be a language of such words designating inner objects of private experience, nor can any language include such words. Words for sensations and other **psychological** phenomena must not, since they are meaningful, get their meaning by private inner association with (or **ostensive definition** by means of) mental **objects**.

Some critics have taken Wittgenstein to be denying the existence of what one might think of as mental objects, such as **pains**, for instance. He denies that he is a **behaviorist** though and says, perhaps not very helpfully, that a pain is neither a nothing nor a something (see §304). This does seem to deny at least that pains (and other mental or inner states) are the *kind* of object that **Cartesian** and **empiricist** philosophers have generally taken them to be. It does not, of course, deny the phenomenon of pain. What Wittgenstein explicitly rejects is a certain **grammar** or way of talking (and thinking) about pain and other sensations.

Another way in which he mounts this attack is with his example of the **beetle in the box**. In this case we are asked to imagine that everyone has a box with something in it called a "beetle." No one can see anyone else's beetle, and the only way for anyone to know what a beetle is is to look inside his or her own box. Whatever is in it is a beetle, by definition. So "beetle" means "contents of one's box," whatever this might be, including nothing at all or a constantly changing something. Or rather, it is to the contents that the word "beetle" refers, but the use of the word "beetle" might be quite different from the use made of "the contents of one's box." The terms "flyover states" and "the heartland" might refer to the same geographic region, but their meanings are different in the sense that the use, the point, of each is different. In the case of "beetle," however, there is no such relevant common referent. Only the use can matter to the word, therefore, and this use is common to all speakers of the language.

The words of a "private" language, one whose words' meanings were the boxed-in contents of each speaker's head, would have no real meaning at all. This is because the meaning in question of each word is supposed to be whatever is in the person's mind or head when she says (or writes, or thinks) 'beetle' or 'S.' Not that the meaning is: *whatever is in my head when I say 'S.'* That is perfectly intelligible. Rather, the meaning is supposed to be the actual thing, whatever it might happen to be, and this could be anything or nothing. A language whose words mean anything or nothing is no language at all.

Saul Kripke has influentially argued that the question of private language is really settled before §256 by the preceding discussion of **rule-following**. According to Kripke's interpretation of Wittgenstein, all rules require public, shared standards of correctness, and so of course there could never be private rules of the kind required for a private language. All language is necessarily public, as many Wittgensteinians agree. Kripke's critics insist that Wittgenstein did not mean that whatever the public, or its prevailing part, says is right must therefore really be right. Others have taken Wittgenstein to be just such a **relativist**, indeed a self-refuting one, since most people would not accept such a **theory**.

Still others see a contradiction between Wittgenstein's claims to be merely **describing** uses of language on the one hand and trying to prove that a private language is impossible on the other. Those of this ilk who are sympathetic to Wittgenstein claim that summaries of his ideas that present anything like a valid deductive argument against the possibility of a private language must be distortions of his actual meaning. What that meaning is would pretty much have to be found by reading Wittgenstein's own words in full. There one would see, on this interpretation, Wittgenstein showing that various combinations of words (such as "private language") that one is tempted to try to use when doing philosophy in fact do not mean what one wants them to mean and that such meaning as they do have will never satisfy one's **metaphysical** impulses. In other words, rather than showing that there could never be a private language (as if it were perfectly clear what that would be), Wittgenstein shows that philosophers have failed to give the words "private language" any meaning. They could do so, but then, such Wittgensteinians would expect, that meaning would not be what had been wanted (being as ordinary as all meaning is, not the profound kind of foundation of all thought, meaning, and knowledge that philosophers in the Cartesian tradition typically seem to want from a private language).

Most Wittgensteinians, it should be stressed, do take the private language argument to be an argument, and a good one. Indeed, it is often regarded as the best (or only good) thing in Wittgenstein's later philosophy by those who look to philosophy for theses and arguments in their support.

A question that remains is why any of this should be thought to matter. It is not as if generations of philosophers have insisted that there is or could be such a thing as a private language. It is common, though, to think that words mean things, so that the meaning of a word is some thing, and philosophers have wondered what thing is referred to by words such as *pain*, ***memory***, and *I*. The Cartesian view is that such words refer to objects that can be identified by an observing mind independent of other people and any bodily behavior. Wittgenstein's aim in these remarks, therefore, appears to be to expose a kind of incoherence at the heart of the Cartesian tradition.

See also PRIVACY.

PROPOSITIONAL ATTITUDES. A phrase coined by **Bertrand Russell** for attitudes toward **propositions**, such as **belief** (that some proposition is **true**), judgment (that some proposition is true), and **thinking** (that some proposition is true). Russell treated such attitudes as relating a proposition to an **object** of some kind (the subject or person who does the believing, etc.). Wittgenstein's criticism of this **analysis** or **theory** of sentences was a serious blow to Russell's confidence in his ability as a philosopher of **logic**.

The criticism is given very briefly in the ***Tractatus Logico-Philosophicus*** propositions 5.542 to 5.5422. It is said there to show that there is no such thing as the **soul** as understood by contemporary, superficial **psychology**. Wittgenstein's view seems to be that one cannot judge or believe or think a piece of **nonsense**. One can believe that Obama is a good president or that Obama is not a good president, but one cannot believe that cockadoodledoo. This is a matter of logic, not psychology, as Wittgenstein sees it. To think (that) a proposition *p* (is true) is somehow (it does not matter how, except to a psychologist) to represent, express, or **picture** *p*, just as saying "*p*" is. So "*A* thinks *p*" means something like "*Something* represents/expresses/pictures/says *p*." This something could as well be a sentence as anything else, such as a person. So, as Wittgenstein puts it in proposition 5.542, "*A* thinks *p*" has the same form as "'*p*' says *p*."

PROPOSITIONS. According to the ***Tractatus Logico-Philosophicus*** a proposition is a **picture** or model of reality or part of **the world**. It shows us how things are if it is **true**, and it asserts that things are this way. True or false, it represents a possible **state of affairs**, a position or set of coordinates in **logical space**. It thereby implies or depends on the rest of logical space (see *Tractatus* 3.42). Propositions that do not picture reality can be neither true nor false. Thus they are not really propositions at all. So propositions cannot **say** anything about **logic**, because logic lacks the contingency of reality. No truth of logic is even possibly false (and logical falsehoods, i.e., **contradictions**, are not possibly true). While propositions do show the logical form of reality, they cannot report on it. The general form of a proposition is: This is how things are (see 4.5).

Tractatus 3.1 says that a **thought** is expressed perceptibly in a proposition (*Satz*). So a proposition or sentence can be understood as the perceptible expression of a thought. A completely analyzed proposition is one broken down into its elements, which are **names** of **objects**. Names cannot be further **analyzed**. Their **meanings** are the objects for which they stand. But they do not stand for anything outside the **context** of a proposition. In this sense the true elements of a proposition are themselves propositions, those that cannot be further analyzed into still more **elementary propositions**. A proposition, such as "It might rain" could, perhaps, be analyzed into "Either it will rain or it will not rain." To know when one has reached the final analysis, one would need to know when one has gotten down to the level of the simplest objects. Since Wittgenstein notoriously fails to give any examples of what these might be, it is hard to know when to stop.

Most of the time when Wittgenstein talks about a proposition he uses the word '*Satz*,' which would more usually be translated as 'sentence.' Some scholars prefer this translation, at least partly because propositions can seem to have a mysterious, almost **Platonic**, kind of existence. The original translation of the *Tractatus Logico-Philosophicus*, however, was approved by Wittgenstein himself and uses the word 'proposition.'

PSYCHOLOGISM. In the **philosophy** of **logic**, the **theory** that logic is a branch of **psychology**. Thus advocates of psychologism might claim that logic is contingent on the workings of the human brain or the practices of a given culture. Psychologism is associated with **empiricism**, especially that of **John Stuart Mill**. It was vigorously opposed by **Gottlob Frege**, who maintained that the laws of logic are objective and independent of the human **mind**. They cannot be reduced to anything empirical or psychological. Wittgenstein seems to have agreed with Frege on this throughout his career, and to have opposed any similar attempt to reduce, for instance, **aesthetics**, **ethics**, or **religion** to psychology. Given that the laws of logic are normative, dictating how one ought to reason, a reduction of logic to psychology would seem to involve a reduction of the normative to the positive, of 'ought' to 'is.' Since **David Hume** implied that one cannot derive an 'is' from an 'ought' such moves have seemed illegitimate to most philosophers.

PSYCHOLOGY. Wittgenstein took a great interest in psychology, despite saying in the ***Tractatus Logico-Philosophicus*** that psychology was no more relevant to **philosophy** than is any other **science** (see proposition 4.1121). Perhaps his interest was the result of a conviction that the **soul** or **mind** could not be studied scientifically. Psychologists have certainly differed about what their subject really is and how it should be studied. If Wittgenstein is right that such things as **pains** are not really (best thought of as) things or **objects** at all, then this might explain some of the methodological difficulties of psychologists. Another possible explanation is that, historically, psychology has grown out of philosophy (**David Hume**, **John Stuart Mill**, and **Friedrich Nietzsche** are important figures in the history of psychology), and so psychology might share some of the problems that Wittgenstein perceived in philosophy.

In addition to a general interest in such phenomena as pain, sight, reading, and **thinking**, Wittgenstein had significant ideas about some particular psychologists and their theories. Notes taken by **Rush Rhees** after conversations with Wittgenstein about **Sigmund Freud** have proved to be of great interest, with Wittgenstein both criticizing Freud and, elsewhere, calling himself a Freudian. What to make of this is unclear. Wittgenstein seems to have thought that Freud had very interesting, attractive ideas, but that he was muddled about the nature of these ideas. There is no real scientific basis to Freud's thinking, though he mistakenly believed that there was.

The other psychologist that most interested Wittgenstein was **William James**. Many passages in the ***Philosophical Investigations*** and ***Zettel*** can easily be read as commentaries on things James says in his *The Principles of Psychology*. There is a useful list of these parallel passages in Appendix 2 of *A Wittgenstein Workbook* by Christopher Coope, **Peter Geach**, Timothy Potts, and Roger White (1970). His study of psychology also influenced Wittgenstein's thinking about **aspect-seeing**.

See also PHILOSOPHICAL PSYCHOLOGY; PRIVACY.

Q

QUEERNESS. Wittgenstein did not deny that **the world** might be a queer place or contain queer things, but he did seem to regard a feeling of queerness as a **sign** that something was wrong in one's thinking. When a **psychological** process, say, strikes one as queer, mysterious, or occult, this is the time to apply a **grammatical** investigation to try to bring the relevant words back to their ordinary use. So at least the later Wittgenstein seems to have thought. The queerness in question is a philosophical puzzlement or **confusion**, not a **religious** sense of mystery or awe. Telling the difference might be hard, but perhaps it is just that the former can be dispelled by philosophical investigation while the latter cannot.

QUIETISM. A form of **mysticism** requiring annihilation of the **will**. This sounds like the kind of religion that might have appealed to Wittgenstein, but when philosophers talk about quietism in connection with him, they generally just mean being quiet. Thus Wittgenstein's idea that philosophers should not advance theses is referred to as a form of quietism, as is his apparent view that about **ethics** there is really nothing to be said. All attempts to "talk ethics," he says in his **lecture on ethics**, inevitably result in **nonsense**.

QUINE, WILLARD VAN ORMAN (1908–2000). An American philosopher, one of the most important since **World War II**. Quine was influenced especially by **Bertrand Russell** and **Rudolf Carnap**, and can be thought of as one of the philosophical heirs of **David Hume**. Although much of his work was on mathematical **logic** and set theory, he is best known for his rejection of the distinction between the **analytic** and the synthetic. Quine denied that there was any absolute distinction between analytic knowledge (about **concepts**) and synthetic knowledge (about things in the **world**). That bachelors are unmarried might seem to be an analytic truth, indeed one knowable *a priori*, but it is true only in virtue of the meanings of the words 'bachelor' and 'unmarried.' These meanings are knowable only *a posteriori*, by experience, since they depend on human usage. So the truth of "Bachelors are unmarried" depends on facts about the world, just as do the truths discovered by **science**.

If this is right, then the kind of radical distinction seen in Wittgenstein's work between **philosophy** and science would seem to break down or simply be in error. If all knowledge is in some way about the world and to be discovered either **mathematically** or **empirically**, then the idea of analytic philosophy (that philosophers should analyze concepts while scientists investigate the world) rests on an untenable distinction. One of the main reasons why Wittgenstein's work has fallen out of favor is that so many philosophers, especially in the **United States**, agree with Quine on this issue.

How different Quine really is from Wittgenstein, though, is itself a somewhat controversial question. **Richard Rorty**, for instance, was influenced by both Quine and Wittgenstein, and, given his emphasis on the idea of **family resemblance**, one might expect Wittgenstein to sympathize with any denial of an essential difference between science and philosophy. He might, on the other hand, insist that these are two different **language-games** or that they have different **grammars**.

One possibly important difference between Quine and Wittgenstein is that the former takes a more empirical approach to philosophy, theorizing in the third person about how various things are known. Wittgenstein, on the other hand, wrote his later philosophical work in something more akin to dialogue form, engaging the reader as an equal authority on the concepts and grammar in question. A possible inference is that, in Wittgenstein's view, **meanings** are not known in the way that empirical facts are known, because they are not independent of language-users in the way that empirical facts are. There is room for creativity in following linguistic rules, and language-users (such as Wittgenstein and his interlocutors) have authority concerning which uses of language are acceptable or correct. From the more objective, one might say anthropological, perspective of Quine the analytic-synthetic distinction might break down, but from the point of view of the language-user *qua* language-user, it might not. If this is right, then the distinction depends on the perspective of the philosopher, and which perspective one thinks ought to be adopted will depend on whether one conceives of philosophy along scientific lines, as Quine does, or as something quite different, as Wittgenstein seems to.

R

RAMSEY, FRANK PLUMPTON (1903–1930). A **Cambridge** mathematician, philosopher, and economist. Ramsey came to know Wittgenstein as a result of his interest in the ***Tractatus Logico-Philosophicus***, which he translated into English (a translation later modified by **C. K. Ogden** and Wittgenstein) and of which he wrote the review for the journal *Mind*. Ramsey's main work was in **logic**, and he made an important early contribution to the **theory** of subjective probability. His book *The Foundations of Mathematics and Other Logical Essays* (1931) collects the best work that he published during his short life. He died after an operation at **Guy's Hospital** in London. In the preface to the ***Philosophical Investigations*** (p. viii), Wittgenstein writes that it was criticism from Ramsey that helped him to realize that there were "grave mistakes" in the *Tractatus*.

REALISM AND ANTIREALISM. Roughly speaking, realism is the **theory** that **the world** exists independently of **human beings** and their **concepts**, and that, even so, it is possible for human beings to gain objective knowledge of **truths** about this world. Antirealism denies some or all of this, for instance insisting that all knowledge is based on subjective experience, or that some form of **idealism** is true. (Two important contemporary antirealists influenced by Wittgenstein are **Michael Dummett** and **Crispin Wright**.) The debate between realists and antirealists involves questions of both **metaphysics** and epistemology, and allows room for a great variety of views. It has become one of the main focuses of disagreement in contemporary **philosophy**.

Wittgenstein's place in this debate is an interesting one. His emphasis on **language** and human **behavior** makes him a prime candidate for antirealism in many people's eyes. He has even been accused of linguistic idealism, the idea that language is the ultimate reality. The laws of physics, say, would by this theory just be laws of language, the rules of the **language-game** of physics. Antirealist **skepticism** of this kind has proved quite popular in the philosophy of **science** and in theology, as well as more generally in metaphysics and **ethics**. Wittgenstein's writings on **mathematics** and **mathematical proof** especially lend themselves to an antirealist interpretation.

On the other hand, there is a school of Wittgensteinian realism, which is less well known. Wittgenstein's views on **religion**, for instance, are often compared with those of Simone Weil, who was a **Platonist** of sorts. Sabina Lovibond argues for a kind of Wittgensteinian realism in ethics in her *Realism and Imagination in Ethics* (1983), and the influence of Wittgenstein is clear in Raimond Gaita's *Good and Evil: An Absolute Conception* (1991). However, one should not go too far with the idea of Wittgensteinian realism. Lovibond, for instance, equates objectivity with intersubjectivity (universal agreement), so her realism is of a controversial kind.

Both realism and antirealism, though, are **theories**, or schools of theories, and Wittgenstein explicitly rejects the advocacy of theories in philosophy. This does not prove that he practiced what he preached, but it might give one pause. It is also worth noting that supporters of Wittgenstein often claim that he was neither a realist nor an antirealist, at least with regard to metaphysics. There is something straightforwardly un-Wittgensteinian about the realist's belief that language or thought can be compared with reality and found to "agree" with it. The antirealist says that one could not get outside thought or language (or **form of life** or language-games) to compare the two. But, some would claim, Wittgenstein was concerned not with what one can or cannot do, but with what makes sense. If metaphysical realism is incoherent then so is its opposite. The nonsensical utterance "laubgefraub" is not to be contradicted by saying, "No, it is not the case that laubgefraub," or "Laubgefraub is a logical impossibility." If realism is truly incoherent, as Wittgenstein might say, then so is antirealism.

RELATIVISM. The term 'relativism' is used to refer to a host of different ideas. The basic idea is that there is a plurality of **truths**, or sets of truths. Relativism in **ethics**, or moral relativism, is then the idea that there are multiple moral "truths," none of which can really be 'absolute' regardless of what its adherents might claim. Since this statement itself seems to imply an absolute standpoint outside the various, merely "relative," truths, it is often taken to be a self-refuting doctrine worthy of attention only because it is a popular error. Some philosophers, though, believe that there is more to the idea than this trivial falsehood or **nonsense**.

Wittgenstein's later work is often thought to imply some form of relativism, since truth, as he sees it, might seem to be relative to a **language-game** or **form of life**. Wittgenstein never says that he believes this, but that in itself proves little. Whether he had beliefs that imply relativism depends on whether he had any **theories** at all, and then on what these are. In other words, it depends on how one interprets his remarks about language-games and forms of life (and perhaps also **rule-following**). None of these remarks seem obviously to support relativism, so the opinion that Wittgenstein was a relativist is a minority one, although his work is notoriously open to a variety of readings.

RELIGION. Wittgenstein opposed interpretations of religion that emphasize doctrine or **philosophical** arguments intended to prove God's existence, but was greatly drawn to religious rituals and symbols, and considered becoming a priest. There has been much speculation about his relation to **Christianity** (and, less obviously, to **Buddhism**). His emphasis on **behavior** and ritual in religion has led to accusations of **fideism**. One example of this emphasis is that he likened the ritual of religion to a great gesture, as when one kisses a photograph. This is not based on the false **belief** that the person in the photograph will feel the kiss or return it, nor is it based on any other belief. Neither is the kiss just a substitute for a particular phrase, such as "I love you." Like the kiss, religious activity does express an attitude, but it is not *just* the expression of an attitude in the sense that several other forms of expression might do just as well. There might be no substitute that would do, as when one uses words in what Wittgenstein calls a **secondary sense**. The same might be said of the whole **language-game** (or games) of religion, but this is a controversial point.

If religious utterances, such as "God exists," are treated as gestures of a certain kind, then this seems not to be treating them as literal statements. Many religious believers, including some Wittgensteinian ones, would object strongly to this. There is room, though, for a good deal of sophisticated disagreement about what it means to take a statement literally. For instance, Charles Taylor's view, roughly, is that the real is whatever will not go away. If we cannot reduce talk about God to anything else, or replace it, or prove it false, then perhaps God is as real as anything else. The conclusion to draw might be that some elements of religion are expressive and some are not. This idea has a plausibly Wittgensteinian anti-essentialism about it and would seem to fit the fact that Wittgenstein was fond of **William James**'s *The Varieties of Religious Belief*.

The main source of information about Wittgenstein's thoughts on religion is secondhand reports of things he said in lectures or conversation, and scattered remarks in notebooks. See, especially, his lectures on religious belief (in LC), ***Culture and Value***, and the so-called **Koder diaries** in ***Ludwig Wittgenstein: Public and Private Occasions***.

REMARKS ON COLOUR**.** A short book of 63 pages made up of 350 remarks taken from notes written at the same time as those that constitute ***On Certainty*** (the last 18 months of Wittgenstein's life). They were edited by **G.**

E. M. Anscombe. Various **facts** about **color**, such as that transparent red can be clear in a way that transparent white cannot be, seem **metaphysical** and yet are really more **logical** or grammatical, as Wittgenstein sees it. This appears to be the reason for his interest in color, although it is also possible that this interest is a holdover from his **theory** of **objects** in the ***Tractatus Logico-Philosophicus***, his later attempt to develop a **phenomenological language**, or his interest in **Johann Wolfgang von Goethe**. It is quite possible that all these issues were related in his mind.

One reason why color is interesting is that the experience of it, or of any particular patch of color, seems to be immediate and (therefore) indubitable. Thus claims such as, "I seem to see some red," or "*This*, whether a hallucination or not, is what I call blue," can seem to offer the kind of **certainty** that philosophers in the tradition of **René Descartes** have sought in order to provide a **foundation** for all other knowledge. In this way color is like **mathematics**. Not only do claims about color experiences or about elementary arithmetic appear to be indubitable, they also seem to **say** much more about the world than the Wittgensteinian idea that they are 'merely' grammatical appears to allow. One is tempted to say that it is not just because of the (apparently entirely contingent) **rules** of **language** that the same object cannot be both red and green all over. It *really* cannot. This kind of temptation interested Wittgenstein. The idea that the rules of **grammar** are **arbitrary** was an important topic for him. Resistance to the idea that certain truths are grammatical perhaps motivates some of the opposition to Wittgenstein's work. It could also be held to show just how badly understood Wittgenstein's conception of grammar is, and how deeply grammar lies in **thinking**. Wittgenstein's critics say that he was simply wrong, that some or all of what he considers grammatical **truths** are in fact metaphysical, or just physical, or even false. What matters to Wittgenstein is not so much getting right the identification of particular truths as grammatical but rather the distinction in general between empirical or contingent truths on the one hand and grammatical or logical ones on the other. If something cannot *conceivably* be red and green, then this is a truth about *concepts*, according to Wittgenstein. And concepts belong to grammar, just as words belong to sentences according to the **context principle**, which Wittgenstein learned from **Gottlob Frege**.

***REMARKS ON FRAZER'S* GOLDEN BOUGH.** *See* FRAZER, JAMES GEORGE (1854–1941).

REMARKS ON THE FOUNDATIONS OF MATHEMATICS. Published posthumously in 1956, edited by **G. H. von Wright**, **Rush Rhees**, and **G. E. M. Anscombe**, these remarks were written mostly between September 1937 and April 1944. The book is divided into seven parts given in chronological order. Part I is a complete reproduction of a typescript that had served as the basis for an early version of the ***Philosophical Investigations***. Wittgenstein then reworked the remarks, and it is the reworked order that is published in the *Remarks*. Parts II, III, IV, V, and VII are selected from various manuscripts. Part VI consists of almost all of manuscript 164, which Wittgenstein wrote sometime between 1941 and 1944. Its main subject is **rule-following**. Other topics addressed in the book are attempts by **Bertrand Russell** and **David Hilbert** to find some sort of **foundation** for **mathematics**, the nature of proof, **necessity** in mathematics, and mathematical discoveries. Wittgenstein also discusses the work of **Kurt Gödel**, **Georg Cantor**, and Richard Dedekind.

See also MATHEMATICAL PROOF.

REMARKS ON THE PHILOSOPHY OF PSYCHOLOGY. These remarks, published posthumously, were written after Wittgenstein had finished what is now the main text of the ***Philosophical Investigations***. They deal with **psychological** concepts such as **thinking**, **believing**, **understanding**, **pain**, and so on. Volume I was edited by **G. E. M. Anscombe** and **G. H. von Wright**. It consists of all the remarks from typescript 229, which were dictated by Wittgenstein to a typist in the fall of 1947. These remarks came from manuscripts 130–134, which he wrote between 10 May 1946 and 11 October 1947. Volume II was edited by von Wright and Heikki Nyman. It consists of all the remarks from typescript 232, covering manuscripts 135–137, which date from 19 November 1947 to 25 August 1948. Wittgenstein dictated the typescript around September or October 1948.

Philosophy of Psychology—A Fragment (formerly known as Part II of the *Investigations*) consists of the remarks found in MS 144, which Wittgenstein compiled from various sources, mostly notes he wrote after October 1948. He also drew on other earlier sources, such as those contained in the *Remarks on the Philosophy of Psychology*. Other remarks from MSS 130–138 that Wittgenstein had typed and then cut up into slips are published as ***Zettel*** (Slips of Paper). So most of the ideas found in these two volumes of *Remarks* will be familiar to readers of the *Investigations* and *Zettel*. Nevertheless, with 1,137 remarks in Volume I and 737 in Volume II, these books are a useful resource for anyone interested in the development of Wittgenstein's later **philosophy**.

RESPINGER, MARGUERITE (1904–2000). A Swiss woman with whom Wittgenstein had a relationship between 1926 and 1932 (although their last correspondence was in 1948, when Wittgenstein wrote to thank her for a gift that she had sent him). Given his **sexuality**, one might expect this to have been a mere friendship, but Wittgenstein's feelings were clearly stronger than that. He fell in love with her and wanted to marry her, although apparently on condition that their relationship be childless. Her feelings for him were complicated. They kissed, and at one point she wanted to marry him (see PPO p. 143, entry dated 11 January 1932), but she ended up marrying Talla Sjögren (1902–1945) instead in 1933. He was the brother of **Arvid Sjögren** and friend of Wittgenstein's nephew Thomas Stonborough. She was perhaps put off by Wittgenstein's desire to have no children, or by his difficult personality and demanding ethics. The end of her relationship with him coincided with the beginning of her relationship with Talla Sjögren, and the thought that she might become engaged to him tormented Wittgenstein.

RHEES, RUSH (1905–1989). A close friend of Wittgenstein's and one of his best students. Rhees later taught **philosophy** at the University College of **Swansea**, in Wales, where he was influential in creating the so-called Swansea school of Wittgensteinian philosophy that includes such people as **Peter Winch**, **D. Z. Phillips**, and David Cockburn. Even after he had officially retired, Rhees continued to hold a seminar with graduate students and studied Wittgenstein's works until his death. He is the author of *Without Answers* (1969) and *Discussions of Wittgenstein* (1996). Some of his papers, dealing with **ethics** and **religion** as well as issues more central in Wittgenstein's work, have been edited and published by D. Z. Phillips.

RILKE, RAINER MARIA (1875–1926). A poet, also admired by **Martin Heidegger**. Rilke was one of the beneficiaries of Wittgenstein's gift to Austrian artists, receiving 20,000 crowns. Although it was **Ludwig von Ficker** who suggested Rilke, Wittgenstein welcomed the suggestion, admiring Rilke's work despite his general antipathy for modern **poetry**. He called Rilke a noble human being and described himself as devoted to him. Rilke's later work was not to Wittgenstein's taste, however.

RORTY, RICHARD MCKAY (1931–2007). A controversial philosopher who turned against **analytic** philosophy and has since been widely studied by academics specializing in other disciplines within the humanities. Rorty is often thought of as a kind of continental philosopher (roughly nonanalytic philosophers in the same tradition as **Søren Kierkegaard**, **Friedrich Nietzsche**, and **Martin Heidegger**), but he presented himself as a **pragmatist** and as bringing to this American philosophical tradition lessons learned from Wittgenstein and Heidegger. Whether he was truly a pragmatist (or, indeed, a philosopher) is controversial, but such labels were not his concern. What he rejected was **Platonism**. What he meant to promote was social solidarity and liberal values. His critics claim that what he in fact promoted is **relativism**.

The most obvious similarities between Rorty and Wittgenstein are their opposition to the philosophical tradition and their interest in the use of words (in connection with **meaning**). The most obvious differences are Rorty's quasi-**utilitarianism**, his rejection of the concept of **truth** (which he regarded as too close to Platonism and, indeed, theism for comfort), and his rejection of the notion of **nonsense** in favor of a focus simply on usefulness.

Rorty ended his career as a professor in the Department of Comparative Literature at Stanford University, having previously taught at the University of Virginia and at Princeton. He was the author of numerous books and papers, including *Philosophy and the Mirror of Nature* (1979), *Contingency, Irony, and Solidarity* (1989), and three volumes of *Philosophical Papers* (1991–1998).

RULE-FOLLOWING. One of the most important subjects addressed in ***Philosophical Investigations*** is what it means to follow a rule. **Gottfried Leibniz** pointed out that rules are open to a variety of interpretations, and that each interpretation can itself be regarded as a rule, which is in turn open to various interpretations. In the 20th century **Saul Kripke** famously resurrected this problem in his attempt to respond to Wittgenstein's work on the subject. Kripke's great clarity has helped make his interpretation very influential and also makes it a good place to begin to **understand** what Wittgenstein wrote about it.

Rules, laws, and instructions are obviously important. All kinds of problems would arise if they had no clear **meaning**, if people could not tell how to follow them, or whether someone had followed them or not. This would clearly be a problem in law courts, but perhaps more fundamentally people might not understand each other at all, all communication might break down, if people could not reliably follow the rules of **language**, namely **grammar**. Yet it can seem hard to comprehend how there can be a real standard of right and wrong, of genuinely following a rule and failing to follow it, if every rule is always open to multiple, perhaps even infinite, interpretations. A rule given as a **joke** should be ignored. A rule given sarcastically might really mean the opposite of its literal meaning. Less obviously, any number of exceptions to the rule could be expected or implied. Rules of thumb are like this, and it is not always clear which rules are of this kind and which are not.

Even less obviously, the literal meaning itself of a rule is in a sense impossible to specify. A rule is abstract in a way that applications of the rule are not. There could be infinitely many circumstances in which a rule might be applied, and the rule itself will not say what is to be done in each case (at least not explicitly). Even if a rule is as simple as "No matter what, do *x*," there can still be questions about what counts as doing *x*. If a woman paints her barn red and a man paints his too, has he done "the same thing?" Yes, if one means "painted one's barn red." No, if one means "painted *her* barn red" or "painted one's barn one's favorite color." So what it means to do the same thing or to follow a rule can be problematic. Indeed, Kripke suggests that there is no fact of the matter with regard to what someone means by a rule such as addition (or by a word such as 'plus'). That is to say, there is no identifiable connection between what one now means by 'plus' and one's future **behavior**. Nothing about a person now guarantees that she will follow one pattern in her future use of 'plus' rather than another. So in relation to current use, or the current interpretation of a rule, what standard could there be by which to judge future uses as correct or incorrect (as doing the same thing or something different)? The solution that Kripke suggests is that it is the community that determines what counts as following a rule, what counts as the same thing. Whatever the community says is right, is right. Thus there is a standard. Furthermore, it is public, so there cannot be a **private language**.

This solves one problem but raises another, namely whether the community can possibly be wrong if this account is true. It could be, but only by the standards of some other, perhaps larger, community. Thus a form of **relativism** arises. Indeed, a kind of relativism that would seem to make disagreement with the community literally meaningless. Another problem is that one very often seems to know whether or not someone has followed a rule without checking with the community. Is **certainty** of this kind really just a kind of confidence about what the community at large would say about the person's action? This seems unlikely.

Kripke's work raises the question of the relation between language and forms or ways of life. For instance, could just one person have a language of her own? If Kripke is right, then it seems not. Indeed, to imagine an individual solitary from birth is scarcely to imagine a **form of life** at all, but more like just imagining a life-form. Moreover, language involves rules establishing certain linguistic practices. Rules of grammar express the fact that it is our practice to say this (e.g., "half past twelve") and not that (e.g., "half to one"). Agreement is essential to such practices. Could a solitary individual, then, engage in any practice, including linguistic ones? With whom could he or she agree? However, not everyone agrees with Kripke, and this is a controversial issue in the interpretation of Wittgenstein. **Gordon Baker** and **P. M. S. Hacker** hold that such a solitary man *could* speak his own language, follow his own rules, and so on, agreeing, over time, with himself in his judgments and behavior. Others reject this interpretation.

Norman Malcolm has argued that rules are only ever followed, given, and enforced against a background of instruction and acceptance. An individual who was solitary from birth would not have such a background, and hence would not follow rules. He or she might behave in a regular way, but would not thereby be guided by, or really *follow*, any rules. Mere regularity of behavior does not constitute following rules, whether they be rules of grammar or any other kind. A car that never starts in cold weather does not follow the rule "Don't start when it's cold," nor does a songbird follow a rule in singing the same song every day. Whether a solitary-from-birth individual would ever do anything that we would properly call following a rule is at least highly doubtful. How could he or she give himself or herself a rule to follow without language? And how could he or she get a language? Inventing one would involve inventing meaning, as **Rush Rhees** has argued, and this sounds incoherent. (The most famous debate about this was between Rhees and A. J. Ayer. Unfortunately for Wittgenstein, Ayer is generally considered to have won.) Alternatively, perhaps the Crusoe-like figure just does behave, sound, etc., exactly like a native speaker of, say, English. But this is to imagine either a freakish automaton, not a human being, or else a miracle. In the case of a miracle, Wittgenstein says, it is significant that we imagine not just the pseudo-Crusoe but also God. In the case of the automatic speaker, we might adopt what Daniel Dennett calls an "intentional stance" toward him, calling what he does "speaking English," but he is obviously not doing what the rest of us English-speakers—who learned the language, rather than being born speaking it, and who influence and are influenced by others in our use of the language—do.

In trying to reach a conclusion about this issue, it is important to note that in *Philosophical Investigations* §201 Wittgenstein says that there is a way of grasping a rule that is not a matter of interpreting it in any way at all. It is more a kind of noncognitive reaction to the rule or to the behavior that expresses the rule (the things others say, the things one perhaps tells oneself, the signs placed along roads, and so on). When someone points, one is expected to look in the direction of her finger (rather than, say, at the finger itself). The act of pointing could be interpreted in numerous ways, but this is how people (most of them, anyway) tend to 'interpret' or, better, react to it. In a similar kind of way, those who share the same form of life tend to behave in (what is recognized as or considered) the same way when given various rules to follow, including very complicated **mathematical** ones, for instance. So rule-following does not come down to interpretation (it is, instead, more a matter of reaction). So the problem of how there can be a correct interpretation does not necessarily arise in the first place. So Kripke's attempt to solve this (nonexistent) problem arguably misses the point. This, at any rate, is what *Philosophical Investigations* §201 seems to imply and what most Wittgenstein scholars agree on. Still, Kripke's work has struck many philosophers as right and has encouraged **antirealism** in contemporary **philosophy**.

See also PHYSIOGNOMY.

RUSSELL, BERTRAND ARTHUR WILLIAM (1872–1970). One of the greatest philosophers of the 20th century. Wittgenstein studied with Russell at **Cambridge**, where he first visited him in October 1911. Indeed, although Wittgenstein attended some of **G. E. Moore's** lectures and **W. E. Johnson** tried to teach him some **logic**, Russell was by far his main teacher when it came to **philosophy**. He was also a good friend to Wittgenstein, although their philosophical disagreements and very different outlooks on life strained their relationship.

Russell's interests were extremely broad and his mind very active. He reconsidered issues and developed new solutions to problems so often that it is difficult to say precisely what Russell thought without specifying the year in which he adhered to that particular view. As far as the ***Tractatus Logico-Philosophicus*** goes, Russell's most important works were *The Principles of Mathematics* (1903), *Principia Mathematica* (co-written with **Alfred North Whitehead**, 1910–1913), and *Theory of Knowledge* (written in 1913). Some of the ideas contained in these works also show up in the more accessible *Introduction to Mathematical Philosophy* (1919) and *The Problems of Philosophy* (1912).

In his book *Mind and Matter*, p. 143, Russell wrote that the "savage superstitions of cannibals" were enshrined in ordinary language, a remark that recalls Wittgenstein's **thinking** on **mythology**. The use, instead, of a more mathematical **language** to show the true **logical form** of propositions he called "philosophical logic." This can be regarded as the subject of Wittgenstein's *Tractatus*, to which Russell wrote an introduction that helped Wittgenstein get the book published. He did not like the introduction, though, thinking that Russell had misunderstood his work.

One of Russell's most important ideas for Wittgenstein is the **theory of types**. This was developed in order to avoid paradoxes that arise when talking about classes, and classes are involved in Russell's attempt to define **numbers**. Following **Gottlob Frege**, Russell defines the number two as the class of all couples (see *Introduction to Mathematical Philosophy*, Dover Publications, 1993, p. 18), the number three as the class of all trios, and so on. This definition brings with it the notion of a class, and this causes problems. Some classes belong to themselves, such as the class of classes, while others do not, such as the class of pencils. The class of pencils is not a pencil. The class of classes that do not belong to themselves is the really difficult one. Any attempt to work out whether or not it belongs to itself leads to paradox. The theory of types was Russell's attempt to get out of this problem.

The theory divides what we might think of as objects into different types, only one of which consists of real objects. Classes of objects are a different type of thing, because classes do not count as real objects. Classes of classes are a different type again. (Because classes of classes are not really classes perhaps?) It is not difficult to imagine objections to the theory, but it is an attempt to deal with a real problem. The "ramified" version of the theory introduces more distinctions: properties of properties, and so on. This covers more ground and invites still more objections. Russell himself was not satisfied with the theory, but believed that some version of it was simply necessary.

A related idea is the axiom of infinity, which postulates the existence of an infinite collection or set. If the number two is the class of all couples, then there must be at least one couple. Otherwise we could not talk meaningfully about two. Reference to infinity is certainly useful in **mathematics**. If it is to be meaningful, on Russell's view, it seems that we must believe in a class of infinitely many things, even though we cannot know whether such a thing exists. It is quite possible, according to Russell, that a complete analysis of **the world** would show that all there is can be divided into a *finite* number of logically indivisible, unanalyzable things. These would be the basic units of reality ("**logical atoms**"), and knowledge of them would have to come from direct acquaintance.

Unlike Frege, Russell was very much an empiricist. We are acquainted with, i.e., directly aware of, sense data in sensory perception and in introspection, he believed. The objects with which we are acquainted include particulars and universals. Particulars include existents and complexes "such as this-before-that, this-above-that, the-yellowness-of-this" (*Mysticism and Logic and Other Essays*, Penguin Books, 1953, p. 201). Existents include such things as the 'this' and 'that' referred to here. Universals include "all objects of which no particular is a constituent." They are general ideas, such as beardedness, diversity, and so on. We are not acquainted with physical objects or other people's minds, but we can believe in them on the basis of objects with which we are acquainted. For instance, we may well believe that sense data with which we are acquainted are caused by physical objects that are beyond our immediate experience. If all I smell are smells, all I see are sights, all I hear are sounds, and so on, then I do not directly sense three-dimensional solid objects. But I can still believe in the existence of such objects, as I might believe that the sounds, smells, and so on (the sense data) that I experience are caused by three-dimensional objects around me. I can then refer to these objects by **name** even though I am not directly acquainted with them. According to Russell, any object, physical or otherwise, can be named, a name being "a simple symbol, directly designating an individual which is its meaning, and having meaning in its own right, independently of the meanings of all other words" (*Introduction to Mathematical Philosophy*, p. 174).

However, not every apparent name is *really* a name. Some are disguised descriptions. For instance, if I want to, I can call a particular point in my visual field Ishmael. I could also call my dog Ishmael. But I might also use the apparent name "Ishmael" as shorthand for "the narrator of *Moby Dick*," which is a description (if it were a name, this would imply that it referred to a subsistent entity, according to Russell). So it is not always obvious what is a name and what is a description. "The King of France" looks like a name, but, since there is no such person anymore, Russell analyzes these words as a disguised description. Thus "The King of France is bald" turns out to be false, not meaningless, despite its lack of reference to any real person. What the sentence is really doing, according to Russell, is claiming that there is a person who matches the description: a) is King of France, b) is bald. Wittgenstein seems to have been impressed by this theory of descriptions.

As well as being a philosopher and mathematician, Russell was committed to a variety of liberal moral and political causes. He was imprisoned because of his pacifism in **World War I**, and was later a leading figure in the Campaign for Nuclear Disarmament. For a time he was the head of a progressive school. He was an outspoken proponent of sexual freedom, and an outspoken critic of **Christianity**.

His most important books other than those mentioned above are *Analysis of Mind* (1921) and *History of Western Philosophy* (1945). In 1950 he was awarded the Nobel Prize for Literature.

RUSSIA. In 1934 Wittgenstein had the idea to live in Russia and work as a manual laborer there with **Francis Skinner**. In preparation for the trip, Fania Pascal taught Wittgenstein and Skinner Russian in 1935. She was one of the friends to whom Wittgenstein made his well-known **confession** of sins (such as having allowed people to believe that he was less ethnically **Jewish** than was the case).

Wittgenstein's political sympathies were vaguely left-wing (he shared the left's concerns about growing unemployment and fascism), but he was certainly not a **Marxist**. His attraction to life in the Soviet Union seems to have had more to do with his taste for the works of **Leo Tolstoy** and **Fyodor Dostoevsky**. He traveled to Leningrad (now St. Petersburg again) and Moscow in September 1935. Whereas Wittgenstein wanted to work on a collective farm, the government of the Soviet Union wanted him only as a **philosophy** professor. He did not return after this visit.

It is possible that this is only because he could not do there the work that he wanted to, but he spoke very little about his reasons for abandoning his Russian plan. The low unemployment rate impressed him and the totalitarianism did not seem to bother him, but he indicated that life was such that petty dishonesty was necessary just to survive in the Soviet Union. The reason he said so little about his impressions of the country was, he said, that he did not want his name to be used in anti-Soviet propaganda. The inference to be drawn is that he would have had little good to say about Stalin's regime.

RYLE, GILBERT (1900–1976). An Oxford philosopher who was greatly influenced by Wittgenstein. Ryle was the Waynflete Professor of Metaphysical Philosophy, Fellow of Magdalen College, Oxford, from 1945 to 1968, and the editor of the journal *Mind* from 1948 to 1971. He is best known for his anti-**Cartesian** book *The Concept of Mind* (1949). This is generally regarded as the classic expression of logical **behaviorism**, although Ryle himself denied being a behaviorist. Presumably, by this he meant that his behaviorism was strictly of the logical, and not the **metaphysical**, kind, but there are passages in *The Concept of Mind* that suggest otherwise. He also wrote *Dilemmas* (1954), *Plato's Progress* (1966), and two volumes of *Collected Papers* (1971).

S

SAYING AND SHOWING. ***Tractatus Logico-Philosophicus*** **proposition** 4.1212 says that what can be shown cannot be said, marking the distinction between saying and showing as absolute. **Bertrand Russell's** axiom of infinity is given by *Tractatus* proposition 5.535 as an example of an attempted solution to problems that itself only creates more problems, because it is an attempt to say what should instead be shown by having infinitely many **names** with different **meanings**. What **solipsism** means is shown (and is quite correct) but cannot be said, according to 5.62. Again, 6.36 claims that "There are laws of nature" cannot be said but must instead show itself.

It is hard to know quite what to make of all this. Wittgenstein seems to be quite serious and to be making a real distinction, but when he first says something and then claims that this cannot be said, one scratches one's head. "There are laws of nature" does not look like **nonsense** or a failed attempt to say something that is in some sense **true** but beyond what can be expressed in propositional form. This kind of objection is often made by quoting **Frank Ramsey**, who said that what cannot be said cannot be said, and it cannot be whistled either.

Contemporary Wittgensteinians as diverse as **P. M. S. Hacker** and **Cora Diamond** would agree with this, and so perhaps Wittgenstein himself would have too. That which cannot be said is not much of a that at all, it seems. There are three views on this: the saying/showing distinction is important (i.e., there really are 'truths' of **ethics**, **logic**, or **metaphysics** that can only be shown or made manifest, and that cannot be articulated straightforwardly); the saying/showing distinction is a mistake; the saying/showing distinction is just the kind of nonsense that the *Tractatus* itself says ultimately that one should throw away or overcome. Of course, if one did throw the philosophical distinction away, the ordinary idea that 'saying' and 'showing' have different meanings would still remain.

SCHLICK, FRIEDRICH ALBERT MORITZ (1882–1936). A German philosopher who moved to **Vienna** in 1922 to become the Professor of the Philosophy of the Inductive Sciences. There a group of like-minded philosophers formed around him, becoming known as the **Vienna Circle**. He shared their devotion to the clarity of **logic** and the rigor of **science**, but he also took an interest in **ethics**, analyzing judgments of **value** as desires and hence as **facts** about human **psychology**. His career was cut short when he was murdered by a mentally ill student. His publications include *Allgemeine Erkenntnislehre* (1918, published as *General Theory of Knowledge*, 1974) and *Fragen der Ethik* (1930, published as *Problems of Ethics*, 1930).

SCHOOL REFORM MOVEMENT. When Wittgenstein trained to become an elementary school teacher, his training was carried out in accordance with the principles of the School Reform Movement, a new attempt to prepare children for life as citizens in a democracy. One principle of the movement was that learning should not be a matter of memorization and repetition, but that instead children should be led to solve problems for themselves. This involved a lot of hands-on, practical work, for instance, with skeletons, looking at the night sky, and so on. Interestingly, Wittgenstein's later philosophy is characterized by a move away from the 'dictatorial' style of the ***Tractatus Logico-Philosophicus*** to a more reader-involving (one might say interactive) approach in the ***Philosophical Investigations***. It should be noted, however, that readings of the *Tractatus* by **Cora Diamond** and **James Conant** present it as being much less straightforward in style and intent than has traditionally been thought. And, of course, any similarity between the method of the *Philosophical Investigations* and the principles of the School Reform Movement might just be coincidence.

SCHOPENHAUER, ARTHUR (1788–1860). A pessimistic German philosopher influenced by **Immanuel Kant** and interested in Asian philosophies such as **Buddhism**. From Schopenhauer (perhaps) Wittgenstein got his interest in **solipsism** and in the ethical nature of the relation between the **will** and **the world**. Like Schopenhauer, Wittgenstein's **ethics** were fundamentally anti-egoistic and his first **metaphysical** beliefs were Schopenhauerian, given up only when he discovered the works of **Gottlob Frege**. He later criticized Schopenhauer for being shallow.

Wittgenstein read Schopenhauer's *The World as Will and Representation* as a teenager and accepted much of it as true. **Peter Geach**, the husband of **G. E. M. Anscombe**, has reported that Wittgenstein himself stated in conversation that when he was young he believed Schopenhauer to have been fundamentally right, although he was unable to make sense of the idea of the "objectification of the Will." What this means we will see below.

Schopenhauer presents his views as a kind of synthesis of the best of Western and Eastern ideas, both ancient and modern, about the ultimate nature of reality and how one ought to live. The world, he says, is representation or idea. When I talk about things around me, for instance, I mean things I am aware of, but all that I am really ever aware of is a) things as they are presented to me by my senses, and b) other ideas or phenomena in my **mind**. So what I mean by "the world" is really contents, or potential contents, of my mind. The world is a kind of appearance of which I am conscious, an appearance in my consciousness. In this sense the world is little more real than a dream. Its ending when I die will really be no great loss (although, of course, it will *seem so* to me as the subject whose object is this world). This is the world as representation.

On the other hand, Schopenhauer argues (following **Immanuel Kant**), the very idea of representation or appearance (or phenomena) implies the idea of something that is represented, something that exists in itself, not just in the mind. Kant argued that we cannot have knowledge of any such thing, as this would require, impossibly, knowledge without the mind, but Schopenhauer does not quite see it this way. After all, one of the phenomena or appearances in this world is me. Surely I can know what I am. Technically, Schopenhauer admits, I cannot, but he does think that one has something *like* knowledge here, some kind of insight. Intuitively I know what I am, and what I am is will. Hands are the will to touch, hold, and grasp made flesh; eyes the will to look and see; tongues the will to taste; and so on. Put together, the **human being**, like all animals, is the will to live. Our primary drives are reproduction and survival.

One problem here is how I can know what anyone else is underneath or behind the appearances. There is a certain plausibility to the idea that I should know what I am even if, strictly speaking, such knowledge is impossible (because the knowing subject can only ever know objects as they appear to it, i.e., appearances, not the subject itself *as* a subject). But why should I know what you are, except as you appear to me? Schopenhauer's answer is that the alternative is crazy. If reality in itself is my will, then I am something like God. It is madness to think that I am significantly different from anyone else, or anything else, in the world. So if I am will, the only sane thing to believe is that everyone and everything else is too. And not *my* will, but simply will. The ultimate nature of reality is the will to live, a blind and fundamentally pointless striving to reproduce and survive that manifests itself in the various kinds of things we see around us in the world: human beings, oak trees, clouds, flies, dogs, and so on. This, what appears in these forms, is the world as will.

Schopenhauer believed that Kant had proved time, space, and causality to be features, not of reality in itself or the world as will, but of phenomena only. Our minds cannot experience the world except as made up of causally interactive objects in time and space so these are, inevitably, features of the world as representation, the world as it appears to us. But that is all they are. The will, as thing in itself, is not in space or time, and it neither causes nor is caused by anything else. Nor is the phenomenal world, the world as representation, itself caused, or in time, or in space. Asking where the world is, or at what time it began, or what caused it, makes no sense. True reality, including, so to speak, the real me and you, is eternal, i.e., not in time. Not being separated by time or space, the real you *is* the real me. Behind the veil of phenomena, all is one.

It follows, as Schopenhauer sees it, that egoism is an enormous mistake. Those who care only about themselves care only about something that is hardly real at all. They are also bound to be disappointed, because the self that they love so much is doomed to die. The altruist, however, in caring about all people equally, evaluates her own importance accurately. And if I love not *my* life but *life itself* then death will be nothing much to fear, as life will always go on. Attachment to worldly goods and one's own life is false and morally bad, while stoical (or Buddhist) detachment and altruism are correct and morally good.

As well as compassion, Schopenhauer values **art**, because it has the power to detach us from our worldly concerns and somehow communicate to us things "under the aspect of eternity." A still life, for instance, shows us fruit or flowers without reference to questions of ownership, time, or place. And **music** seems almost to occupy a different realm altogether.

Wittgenstein believed much, perhaps even most, of this, at least for a while. He denied that he ever believed that the world is will, but he did initially accept the idea of the world as representation. He also seems to have shared much of Schopenhauer's ethical outlook. For instance, he did not have to fight in **World War I** (he had a hernia) but volunteered to do so anyway, asking to be posted to the front in order to test his fear of death. If he feared death (on Schopenhauer's view), then he had a wrong view of the world. He gave away his fortune, some to artists and the rest to other members of his family. Throughout his life he took art very seriously (especially music) and lived abstemiously. All this is in line with Schopenhauer's ethics.

There is little sign of Schopenhauer's influence in Wittgenstein's later philosophical work, but it certainly shows up in the ***Tractatus Logico-Philosophicus***. For instance, Schopenhauer's claim that "The world is my idea" (from *The World as Will and Idea*) is echoed in such remarks as "The world is *my* world" (from proposition 5.62). What Wittgenstein means here, where he also says that what the solipsist means is quite correct but cannot be said, is obscure and controversial. Some have taken him to mean that solipsism is true but for some reason cannot be expressed. H. O. Mounce, in his valuable *Wittgenstein's Tractatus: An Introduction*, says that this interpretation is surely wrong. Mounce's view is that Wittgenstein holds solipsism itself to be a **confusion**, but one that sometimes arises when one tries to express the fact that "I have a point of view on the world which is without neighbours" (Mounce p. 91). Whether this itself makes sense is also open to debate though. Wittgenstein was not a solipsist, but he remained interested in solipsism and related problems of **skepticism** throughout his life. Given that much of his later work was a response to his own early work, and that this work was in considerable part a response to Schopenhauer (though also, and probably more so, to **Gottlob Frege** and **Bertrand Russell**), it can be said that Schopenhauer's work influenced Wittgenstein throughout his life.

SCIENCE AND SCIENTISM. Wittgenstein distinguished between **philosophy**, which aims at clarity, and science, which aims at discovering new truths. The progressive spirit of science, indeed of contemporary civilization generally (at least, according to Wittgenstein, in Europe and North America), is not one he shared. For him, clarity had **value** in itself. This value seems to be lost to those who see progress as the only goal, and thus science as the only method for dealing with any problem whatsoever. Not only are there other values than the kind of **truth** that science discovers, but such knowledge might itself have no value at all, Wittgenstein thought. He half hoped that science and the technology that it produces might destroy themselves through some sort of disaster like **atomic** war. The alternative, he seems to have believed, was that they would destroy humanity, condensing **the world** into one unit, and a peaceless one at that. Thus science and scientism (the worshipful attitude toward science that sees all questions as fundamentally scientific in nature) are key features of what Wittgenstein referred to as "the darkness of this time" (see p. viii of the preface to the ***Philosophical Investigations***).

On this he is similar to **Martin Heidegger** (who hoped, at least briefly, that National Socialism would provide an alternative, better future). Wittgenstein was more likely to look to Soviet communism than Nazism, but seems to have been dissatisfied with all the political options available. His philosophical work can thus be seen to have an almost political dimension (or to be an alternative to **politics**). To strive for clarity is to show that this too can be one's goal, in addition to, or instead of, scientific knowledge. Within this clarificatory work he tried also to show that such important subjects as **art** and **religion** cannot be understood wholly in scientific terms, that here at least science is demonstrably (though still controversially) not the answer.

See also POLITICS; RUSSIA.

SECONDARY SENSE. Wittgenstein's best-known discussion of secondary sense concerns his claim in ***Philosophy of Psychology—A Fragment*** §§274–278 that Wednesday is fat and Tuesday is thin (or at least that this is what he would say if he had to apply each adjective to either noun). He says after this that a word can only have a secondary sense if it also has a different primary sense. So he is not saying that Wednesday is *literally* fat, whatever that might mean, but, he adds, neither is he saying that Wednesday is **metaphorically** fat. The very word "fat" is the only one that will do to express his **meaning**, even though he does not mean what he would if he called a person fat. The issue here is tied up with Wittgenstein's ideas about **physiognomy** and **aspect-seeing**.

Cora Diamond has also argued that there is an important connection between secondary sense and the use of words in **ethics** and **religion**. The precision without literalness of secondary sense is the kind of use of language often found in **poetry** (see ***Philosophical Investigations*** §531). In his **lecture on ethics** Wittgenstein gives several examples of experiences he has had, and that he expects other people to have had too, which he associates with the ethical (by which he means a certain kind of value having to do with the meaning of life). One of these is the experience of feeling absolutely safe. The idea here is that one feels safe *no matter what happens*. This, though, seems to be **nonsense**. One can hardly be safe if one is being injured or killed, and no one is ever immune to death. Although there is more to his **argument** than this, Wittgenstein concludes that when we talk ethics, we inevitably talk nonsense. If I say that I feel absolutely safe (or safe in the hands of God, Wittgenstein adds), then I am both speaking in a way that is characteristic of ethical (and religious) talk and speaking nonsense.

The point might be easier to accept with a different example. **Socrates** famously said that it is better to suffer evil than to do evil. We might agree. The idea might even seem banal. But in an obvious sense it is good to be a winner and bad to be a loser, even if the winning is done unethically. The sense in which it is *good* to be an ethical loser is really quite obscure, however quickly we might claim to believe that this is good (assuming that the only alternative is to be an unethical winner). Wittgenstein's suggestion in the lecture is that it is nonsense to say that it is better to be a murder victim than a murderer, other things being equal. Words have meaning in virtue of referring to **the world**, and in no worldly sense is it better to lose what you prize than to get what you want. Hence ethical talk is nonsense, albeit an interesting kind of nonsense, one that Wittgenstein says he respects and takes seriously.

Clearly such "nonsense" is different from random combinations of syllables. Someone who says sincerely that we are in God's hands is not making random sounds. She really means God and really means hands, even though God is a nonphysical being and so does not literally have hands. In other words, the literal, primary meaning of 'hands' is wanted here, even though it does not apply. This is why Wittgenstein calls such uses secondary in his later work (after the lecture on ethics, for instance). They are neither primary uses of words, or uses of words in their primary sense, or with their primary meaning, nor straightforward nonsense.

Nor are they metaphorical. It is not *as if* it were better to be a victim of crime than to be a criminal. Typically ethical people believe that it *really is* better to be the victim in the case of a crime like robbery, even if the relative benefits are impossible to specify. (If they can be specified, for instance by referring to the likelihood that the robber will be caught and punished, then the concern is no longer ethical but merely prudential.) And the person who says we are in God's hands does not mean that it is as if a giant friendly ghost were protecting us with mighty invisible hands. She means that we *actually are* in God's hands. No other words will do. Even though, to repeat, even believers acknowledge that God does not have (literal) hands.

Three final points are worth noting about this. Firstly, Wittgenstein does not say that what he calls secondary sense in the later work is what he called nonsense in the lecture on ethics. He does describe them in similar ways, distinguishing them from both literal statements and metaphors, but he goes no further than this. Secondly, his later examples of Wednesday's being fat and so on bring out the distinct possibility that one person's secondary sense will be another person's nonsense. One can therefore agree with Wittgenstein and still reject talk about the hands of God as nonsense. Thirdly, the main place where Wittgenstein writes about secondary sense is no longer thought of as Part II of the *Philosophical Investigations* (and therefore part of his major mature work) but as *Philosophy of Psychology—A Fragment* (and therefore less reliable and less significant). Scholarly interpretation should not be guided too much by editorial decisions about labeling, of course, but this probably does reflect the majority view of the importance and value of the concept of secondary sense.

SELF. Rather like **Immanuel Kant** and **Arthur Schopenhauer**, in the ***Tractatus Logico-Philosophicus*** Wittgenstein denies that the self, conceived as the subject of experience (the subjective self), exists as a phenomenon or thing in **the world**. The subject *qua* subject is never experienced or found in the world by anyone. It cannot be described, so it cannot be pictured, so it cannot be **thought** of at all (according to the **picture theory** of **meaning**). For Kant and Schopenhauer this gives it a unique status and makes it a candidate for the role of immortal **soul** or **ethical** self, if such a thing exists (which, according to Kant, we can never know but must believe if we are to be ethical). For Wittgenstein, though, it gives it no status at all. What cannot be thought cannot be thought. The alternative is to read him as genuinely holding that **solipsism** is true, but the kind of **mystical truth** that lies beyond words. This reading is doubtful.

See also THE FIRST-PERSON SINGULAR.

SENTENCES. *See* PROPOSITIONS.

SEXUALITY. Wittgenstein is often thought to have been gay, and he did have at least one male lover, but he also loved at least one woman, and he appears generally not to have been a very sexual person. His sex life has been the subject of some gossip, but is probably best regarded as irrelevant to his work. He had a relationship with a Swiss woman named **Marguerite Respinger** that lasted several years, and he seriously considered marrying her. This is somewhat surprising since Wittgenstein's friends seem not to have cared for her on the whole. She was not as intellectual as Wittgenstein, and she was apparently somewhat **anti-Semitic**. Given Wittgenstein's general asceticism it is possible that at least some of his "lovers" are better thought of as **disciples**.

See also BARTLEY, WILLIAM WARREN (1934–1990); CONFESSION.

SHEFFER STROKE. A form of logical notation invented by Henry Sheffer, and written as ·|·, meaning 'neither/nor.' Thus '*p*|*q*' means 'neither *p* nor *q*.' Wittgenstein introduces this notation to the ***Tractatus Logico-Philosophicus*** in proposition 5.1311. It can be used to replace other **logical constants** and thus clarify the relations between **propositions** in a **concept-script**. For instance, instead of ~*p* ('not *p*') one can write *p*|*p* and instead of *p* v *q* ('*p* or *q*') one can write *p*|*q*·|·*p*|*q* ('neither [neither *p* nor *q*] nor [neither *p* nor *q*]'—in other words, at least one of *p* and *q* is true). In one way this is not a simplification at all, of course, but clarity can be gained by expressing all propositions in the same way. All (possible) complex propositions, according to Wittgenstein, can be generated by applying the Sheffer stroke to **elementary propositions**. It is the only logical constant one really needs, and hence it shows the common form of all **language**.

SHOW/SHOWING. *See* SAYING AND SHOWING.

SIGN/SYMBOL. ***Tractatus Logico-Philosophicus*** 3.31 identifies every part of a **proposition** that characterizes its sense as an expression, and then seemingly identifies an expression in this sense as a symbol. Proposition 3.32 then adds that a sign is what is sensibly perceptible of a symbol. In other words, signs are what can be perceived, but symbols are what have sense or **meaning**. The signs 'green' and '5' are mere appearances, things we can perceive with the senses, and so *are* the same as long as they *look* the same. Symbols are not like this. If I say of John Green, who is seasick, that "Green is green," then two different symbols are involved, even though the same sign ('green') is used twice. Similarly, in "555" the same sign occurs three times, but three different symbols are involved (one meaning five, one meaning fifty, and one meaning five hundred).

Tractatus 3.324 identifies this potentially confusing use of the same sign for different symbols as a cause of fundamental confusions throughout philosophy. In *Logical Atomism* (a work based partly on Wittgenstein's ideas) **Bertrand Russell** says that it is "a disgrace to the human race" (p. 172) that we use the same word 'is' to express both identity (as in "Clark Kent is Superman") and the relation of subject and predicate (as in "Superman is tall"). Wittgenstein makes a similar point about 'is' in *Tractatus* 3.323, adding that it can also indicate existence. Both Russell and Wittgenstein suggest the same remedy: a **concept-script** in which the same sign is not used for different symbols, one that obeys logical **grammar** or what Wittgenstein calls **logical syntax**.

In ***Philosophical Investigations*** §558 and §561 Wittgenstein returns to the word 'is' and its multiple uses. If the meaning of a word is its use in the language (see *Investigations* §43) then we might say that the word 'is' has just one, complicated meaning. This is not what Wittgenstein says, however. In the sentence "Clark Kent is Superman" we could put an equals sign in place of 'is', but we cannot do this (without violating the rules of grammar) in the sentence "Superman is tall." This shows that the grammatical rules governing the first kind of 'is' are not those governing the second. Hence they have different meanings. (This shows something about what Wittgenstein means by 'use' in *Investigations* §43.)

In §§561–570 Wittgenstein takes this theme up again. He does not want to say that the different uses of 'is' constitute one single, albeit perhaps two-part, use or meaning. The question then arises how to justify saying what he wants to say. The justification has to do with what is **essential** and what is inessential or accidental. And this has to do with the point of the notation or **language-game**. Both our interests and the character, the **physiognomy**, of the linguistic activity in question are relevant here. Would our purposes be advanced or hindered if we used different words or signs for these different uses of 'is'? Would our language-games be changed in essential ways? Would they take on a different character? It seems clear enough that Wittgenstein thinks the answer is No, that it would make no difference if we used different words in these cases. Unlike the author of the *Tractatus* (and very unlike Russell, who perhaps caught some of his moral fervor from the young Wittgenstein), the later Wittgenstein does not suggest a change in our language. Far from insisting that we end the "disgraceful" use of one sign 'is' for three different symbols (identity, copula, and existence), in the *Investigations* Wittgenstein makes no recommendation at all. He leaves it open whether such a change would be an improvement, a problem, or neither. Instead he clarifies what is at stake, which has to do with our interests. He does not tell us either what these are or what they ought to be.

SILENCE. The ***Tractatus Logico-Philosophicus*** famously ends with the claim that what we cannot speak about we must pass over in silence. Ostrow (p. 133) sees an ethical obligation here, since failure to remain silent would indicate a refusal to accept reality or the course of one's own experience. A different view might be discerned in the **lecture on ethics** where Wittgenstein says that attempts to speak **ethics** result in **nonsense**, yet he respects the tendency to produce it. He does not, that is, say that there is an obligation to remain silent. If his saying that talk about ethics is nonsensical implies an obligation to be silent, then this is a duty whose violation he appears to be prepared to admire.

Eli Friedlander (see pp. 149–150) has shown that Wittgenstein's views on silence were not simple, at least later in his life. We must not, he seems to have thought, be silent about important matters (e.g., God) just because chatterboxes talk a lot of nonsense about such things. But it still seems important to him not to be one of these chatterboxes. He gave his word to a friend of his (**Maurice Drury**) that he would not refuse to talk to him about God or **religion**. It does not follow that he would have no objection to a philosopher publishing works for a general (i.e., wide, impersonal) audience on such subjects.

Arthur Schopenhauer, in *On the Fourfold Root of the Principle of Sufficient Reason* (trans. E. F. J. Payne, Open Court, 1974, p. 154), writes: "Indeed, there are some [ideas] which never find words, and alas these are the best."

Black (p. 378) quotes Silesius: "Schweig, Allerliebster, schweig: kannst du nur gänzlich schweigen,/So wird dir Gott mehr Gut's, als du begehrst, erzeigen." This is translated thus: "Silence, Beloved, be still; if you be wholly quiet,/God will show you more good than you know how to desire" in Angelus Silesius, *The Cherubinic Wanderer*, translated by Maria Shrady, Paulist Press, Mahwah NJ, 1986, p. xi.

See also QUIETISM.

SJÖGREN, ARVID. *See* DISCIPLES.

SKEPTICISM. A perennial concern of philosophers, especially since **René Descartes** tried and, most philosophers now think, failed to disprove it. Descartes's goal was to take skepticism as far as it could go, setting aside every **belief** of his that could possibly be false, and then to rebuild knowledge from a secure, indubitable **foundation**. He succeeded in making almost every belief seem open to doubt but not in convincing the philosophical community that much if any of this doubt could be dispelled by rational **argument**. Epistemology, that is philosophical questions and **theories** about knowledge, then became central to modern **philosophy**.

It is this tradition that Wittgenstein found himself in, and against which he reacted. The ***Tractatus Logico-Philosophicus*** seems quite dismissive of the kind of universal skepticism (skepticism about everything at once) that is inherited from Descartes. *Tractatus* proposition 6.51 declares skepticism to be **nonsensical** when it raises doubts in answer to which nothing can be said. When nothing can be said, no answer could, even in principle, be given. And when this is the case, when no answer could possibly be given, what looks like a question is really nothing of the sort. It is meaningless. How much skepticism is really of this kind is not clear, however.

A seemingly different and much more explicitly worked out response to skepticism is contained in ***On Certainty***. There Wittgenstein draws a distinction between empirical **propositions**, which are open to both doubt and confirmation, and other so-called **hinge propositions**, that have a different role in **language**. The basic idea is that one cannot doubt everything at once. The use of the words "I doubt everything" presupposes that the **meaning** of these words is not doubted, for instance. However, it is no easy matter to say exactly what the nature or status of "hinge propositions" is. Put into words ("This sentence has meaning," say) they look just like empirical propositions, and Wittgenstein even says that a proposition might go from being part of the riverbed of certainty to being a proposition open to doubt. The distinction he has drawn between hinge propositions and empirical propositions is, or can be, blurred. Nevertheless, he treats it as being of the utmost importance in countering the errors of both philosophical skeptics and those, such as **G. E. Moore**, who would dismiss their doubts too casually, without going to the root of skeptical arguments.

SKINNER, FRANCIS (1911–1941). Perhaps Wittgenstein's dearest ever friend and **disciple**. Skinner was a student of **mathematics** at **Cambridge** (from 1930–1933), which was where he met Wittgenstein, in the autumn of 1932. He was extremely intelligent, shy, good-looking, and gentle. The two became very close, planning at one stage to live together in **Russia**. Under Wittgenstein's influence Skinner abandoned the academic career for which he seemed destined. Having been rejected on medical grounds by the International Brigade, for whom he volunteered to fight in the Spanish Civil War, he instead worked as a mechanic. He died of polio.

SOCRATES (470–399 BC). Arguably the first philosopher ever. Certainly he was among the first great Western philosophers, and others who preceded him are generally classed together merely as pre-Socratics. He wrote no **philosophy** but questioned people in public places, trying to tease out of them definitions that would capture the **essence** of this or that **concept**, such as justice, courage, knowledge, and so on. His views have survived mostly through the works of **Plato**, who wrote a series of Socratic dialogues, some of which are considered to be fairly reliable guides to his teacher's thoughts and method. In these dialogues Socrates's interlocutors are typically made to look foolish, as he shows how little they understand of the concepts with which their expertise is mostly closely associated (he interviews generals about courage, a self-righteous man about piety, and so on). Wittgenstein was puzzled by these dialogues, which seemed to him pointless unless their aim was precisely to show that we know nothing. His own philosophical work is often, at least in his later period, concerned with showing precisely that, *pace* Socrates, there need be no essence that a **definition** of a word could capture. This shows the degree of his opposition to the philosophical tradition.

SOLIPSISM. The idea that oneself alone exists. This means not that one is the only **human being**, or **mind**, that exists, but that all that exists can only be either oneself (conceived of as a mind or subject of experience) or else part of oneself (the contents of one's mind). If the most certain **truth** of all is taken to be **René Descartes's** *cogito ergo sum* (I think, therefore I am), then it can be difficult to see how anyone could be sure that solipsism is not true. In ***Tractatus Logico-Philosophicus*** proposition 5.62, Wittgenstein even says that what the solipsist **means** is quite correct (only it cannot be **said**). In 5.61, though, which 5.62 says is the key to **understanding** how much truth there is in solipsism, he identifies what one cannot say with what one cannot **think**. And if solipsism is then unthinkable, as these two remarks imply, then the amount of truth in it seems to be zero. The claim that what the solipsist means is quite correct would then need to be read ironically. This is not how it is generally taken, however. Interpretations of Wittgenstein's remarks on this subject range from accepting that he was a solipsist, through the idea that he was some sort of solipsist (just not one of a straightforward, or indeed fully articulable, kind), to the idea that he was a mocking antisolipsist.

See also SCHOPENHAUER, ARTHUR (1788–1860).

SOUL. ***Tractatus Logico-Philosophicus*** proposition 5.5421 says that there is no such thing as the soul as conceived by the "superficial **psychology**" of today. This is presented as being shown by 5.542, which says that sentences such as '*A* judges that *p*' correlate **facts**, not a fact with an **object**. And this is supposed to be simply "clear" even though such philosophers as **Bertrand Russell** and **G. E. Moore** (named in 5.541) have not seen it. Apparently the reader is expected to be more perceptive than two of the greatest philosophers of the 20th century. About the only other help the reader is given is

proposition 5.5422, which says that an explanation of the form of '*A* judges that *p*' and other such sentences must show that *p* is something that can be judged to be true, that it is not **nonsense**.

All **beliefs**, **thoughts**, judgments, and so on are **intentional**, they have a kind of content or object, namely that which they are of or about. One cannot believe *p* if it is nonsense, because then *p* would not really be a proposition at all, in a sense it would not exist. If one believes something, then one must **mean** it, not in the sense of being sincere but in the sense that what one does will not constitute believing if the 'belief' in question is nonexistent, the sentence or thought 'expressing' it mere nonsense. It must be shown, Wittgenstein says, that it is impossible to judge, think, or believe nonsense. This impossibility must be logical impossibility since impossibility is necessary falseness and the only **necessity** that Wittgenstein recognizes in the *Tractatus* is logical necessity. So *A*, the believer or judger, must stand in a logical relation to *p*. Since *p* is complex (being a picture of a **state of affairs**, not the name of a simple object), whatever thinks, says, judges, or believes *p* must be similarly complex. Therefore '*A*' cannot be the name of any simple or unitary object. It cannot refer to *the* subject of experience, like a **Leibnizian** monad. If *A* believes *p*, then there must be some part or feature of *A* that has the same logical structure or form as *p*. So whatever believes, thinks, etc., cannot be a simple object, such as the soul as conceived by the psychologists that Wittgenstein is criticizing.

Proposition 5.641 of the *Tractatus* says that **philosophy** *can* talk about the **self**, in a sense related to **solipsism**, but that this is not the soul whose existence he has earlier denied.

With regard to immortality, there can be no guarantee of the immortality of the soul, if any such thing exists, Wittgenstein says in proposition 6.4312. Within space and time, or just time, one is dealing with phenomena or contingencies. So there can never be a guarantee (or **necessity**) that something will last for any specific length of time, including all time. More to the point, it is not more life but better that one needs, so such immortality is beside the point as Wittgenstein sees it. Life cannot be given meaning by being extended in time, adding more of the same. It must be changed more radically if it is to go from being meaningless to being meaningful. And **value** (whatever might determine what is better or more meaningful) lies outside this contingent **world**. Clearly Wittgenstein is not denying that the soul exists, nor that it is immortal. What he says is that the soul *as it is conceived by some people* does not exist.

In the ***Philosophical Investigations*** §422, he writes that the belief that people have souls gives us a certain **picture**, but its sense, that is its application, is distant from us or hard to see. This reference to a picture and its sense is reminiscent of his remarks about **physiognomy**. Indeed, in §530 he refers to the character of a word, which one, as it were, sees in its face, as its 'soul' (the inverted commas are his). This soul matters, for instance in **poetry**, but there could be a people, there could be a **language**, to which it was irrelevant. They might happily substitute one word for another, as normal people sometimes do. For them there could be no **secondary sense**, and so perhaps no **art**, **ethics**, or **religion** as Wittgenstein thinks of these things. Perhaps this explains his distaste for Esperanto, the artificial international **language** (see ***Culture and Value*** p. 52).

The picture of the soul comes up again in section iv of ***Philosophy of Psychology—A Fragment*** (previously known as Part II of the *Investigations*). Wittgenstein contrasts the idea of someone's being an automaton with the idea of her having a soul. Neither makes sense as an opinion or belief, he says. Rather it is a question of attitude. Presumably this might change if evidence came to light that someone really was an automaton. Once wires start to protrude from someone's face, then it makes sense to have beliefs about whether or not she is really a human being. Even then perhaps we might have an attitude toward her as to another soul or fellow being. But in the absence of any reason to regard someone as anything but human, it makes no sense to do so.

Words and paintings can equally present a picture of the **human being** as "having a soul." What this means though depends on how one uses the picture, on what one does with it. This is very complex, since it is a question of how one lives with other people, including one's thoughts, feelings, actions, and reactions. The best picture of the human soul, he says, is the human body. So **René Descartes's** picture is rejected here, as elsewhere in Wittgenstein's work. Apparently a three-dimensional object (the body) can be a picture as well as sentences and paintings. Its **meaning**, presumably, will be its role in people's lives. And, of course, in the case of the human body this is large, rich, and complex.

SPENGLER, OSWALD (1880–1936). The author of *Decline of the West* (1918), a book that influenced Wittgenstein's **thinking**, and pessimism, about culture. Spengler attempted to **understand** history by looking for analogies between different epochs, much as **Johann Wolfgang von Goethe** had tried to understand nature by looking at different forms of plant. The emphasis here is on looking at (not so much for) similarities and seeing these as expressions or manifestations of something inside them. Goethe was explicitly trying to avoid the kind of mechanistic view found in other **science** since **Isaac Newton**. There are echoes of the Goethe-Spengler approach in Wittgenstein's later methodology in **philosophy**.

SRAFFA, PIERO (1898–1983). An economist who left his native Italy because of his opposition to Benito Mussolini. Sraffa was introduced to Wittgenstein by **John Maynard Keynes**, and the two became friends who met regularly for discussions. The preface of the ***Philosophical Investigations*** attributes "the most fruitful ideas" of the book to Sraffa's criticism (see *Investigations* p. 4). Wittgenstein said that Sraffa gave him an 'anthropological' way of looking at philosophical problems. The *Philosophical Investigations* emphasizes the importance of the role uses of **language** play in life, making ideas such as **form of life** much more important than they appear to have been in the ***Tractatus Logico-Philosophicus***.

The best-known story of Sraffa and Wittgenstein has Wittgenstein telling his friend that every **proposition** must have a **grammar**. To this Sraffa responds with an insulting gesture used in Italy (brushing his chin with his fingers) and asks what the grammar of that is. The story comes from Wittgenstein himself, who told it to both **Norman Malcolm** and **G. H. von Wright**. One well-known version of this story has been acknowledged by Malcolm, Sraffa, and von Wright to be false. It concerns Wittgenstein's idea that all propositions must have the same **logical form** as what they depict. In this version, Sraffa makes the gesture and asks, "What is the logical form of *that*?" This was supposed to have shown that the **picture theory** of **meaning** is not right. The fact that Sraffa was actually talking about grammar, not logical form, makes this failed criticism of the *Tractatus* irrelevant.

STATES OF AFFAIRS. Wittgenstein's remarks on states of affairs, in propositions 2 to 2.0141 in the ***Tractatus Logico-Philosophicus***, are offered as **elucidations** of his remarks about **facts**. A fact, he says, is a state of affairs, a combination of **objects** in some particular way. These objects could have been combined differently, so their arrangement is contingent. However, nothing in **logic** is contingent, so all the possibilities for an object, all the states of affairs of which it could be a component, must be, as it were, written into the object itself. New possibilities for an object cannot somehow emerge later or from elsewhere.

The German term that Wittgenstein used is *Sachverhalt*, and not everyone agrees that it is best translated as "state of affairs." Max Black prefers 'atomic fact,' which is how **C. K. Ogden** translates it too. A *Sachverhalt* is "the objective counterpart of an *unanalysable* contingent truth (see, for instance, 4.2211)" (Black, pp. 39–40). However, Black notes, Wittgenstein uses *Sachverhalt* in seemingly inconsistent ways. Most of the time he uses it to mean an actual combination of objects, but he also sometimes uses it to mean a combination that does not exist (e.g., at 2.06 and 4.3). Erik Stenius (p. 31) says that "a *Sachverhalt* is something that could *possibly* be the case," but 2.0124 talks of possible *Sachverhalte*, which would be odd in that case. (This objection is Black's.) Black argues (pp. 41–45) quite convincingly that *Sach-*

verhalte should be understood as facts rather than possibilities, at least most of the time. One problem for this idea, however, is that proposition 4.2211 talks about the possibility of each fact consisting of infinitely many states of affairs, which suggests that facts and states of affairs are not the same thing.

According to Pasquale Frascolla: "states of affairs and facts differ in two ways: first, a state of affairs is merely a possible combination of objects, whereas a minimal fact is an actual combination; second, when a fact is spoken of, it is not necessary that it be thought of as *one* obtaining state of affairs: several obtaining states of affairs can constitute a fact" (p. 84). Frascolla notes, though, that Wittgenstein's distinction between facts and states of affairs is weakened by his introduction of the term "negative fact" (at 2.06), since now facts are not necessarily actual.

SUICIDE. In his ***Notebooks*** Wittgenstein described suicide as "so to speak, the elementary sin," although he also wondered on the same page whether "even suicide" is "in itself neither good nor evil" (p. 91). He does seem to think that if anything is evil, then it is suicide, since, presumably, suicide is a complete rejection of life or **the world**. There could be a link between such an **ethic** and **solipsism**. At least two, and possibly three, of Wittgenstein's brothers committed suicide, and he reported having had such a tendency himself. Some people have linked this depression with an **inner** turmoil about his **homosexuality**. There is little evidence of such turmoil, though, and some reason to think that male members of the **Wittgenstein family** were perhaps genetically predisposed to suicidal depression.

SUPERSTITION. Wittgenstein talks about superstition in several places in connection with **religion** and **science**. The difference between religious faith and superstition, he says in ***Culture and Value*** (p. 72e, from 1948), is that the former is a kind of trusting while the latter stems from fear and is a form of false science. ***Tractatus Logico-Philosophicus*** proposition 5.1361 calls superstition what one might think of as the scientific **belief** in the **causal nexus**. Such a belief is false according to Wittgenstein, with echoes of **David Hume**, because no event makes another **necessary**. Everything outside **logic** is contingent. So belief in a nexus of **causation**, understood as a chain of nonlogical necessities, is multiply absurd. Such belief might be neither fearful nor scientific, but it is false. Generally Wittgenstein means something like **metaphysics** when he talks about superstition, something that is like religion, science, and **philosophy** but not quite any of them in a respectable (or well **thought** out) way.

What is or is not a superstition, though, might ultimately depend on a **value** judgment. In *Culture and Value* (p. 83, from 1949) Wittgenstein writes that a **picture** firmly rooted in us can be compared to a superstition, but that a picture at the root of all our thinking ought not to be treated as (or called?) a superstition. The reason for this is that something is always rooted in us in this way, something always underlies our thinking or way of seeing **the world**. What is unavoidable, presumably Wittgenstein means, should not be disparaged with a term as pejorative as 'superstition.'

Wittgenstein's contrast between religion (good) and superstition (bad) is often cited as a point in his defense against charges of **fideism**. Such evaluative terms, though, would seem not to belong in any purely conceptual or **grammatical** investigation. ***Philosophical Investigations*** §599, after all, says that philosophy done properly should **say** only what is admitted by everyone. Not everyone is likely to agree that any particular belief is superstitious (such as, most obviously, those who hold the belief in question). This suggestion, of course, is controversial and would be rejected by many who want to insist that Wittgenstein was not a fideist.

SWANSEA. A city in south Wales where **Rush Rhees** taught. Having visited him there, Wittgenstein decided that it would be a good place to work on his book (the ***Philosophical Investigations***). He lived there, in lodgings at Langland Bay, from March 1944 to October 1945. The company of Rhees, the Welsh coastline, and the people of Swansea seem to have been the main attractions for Wittgenstein, and he returned only grudgingly to **Cambridge**. Rhees's philosophical influence helped to make the University College of Swansea a center for Wittgenstein studies, and a school of thought known as "the Swansea school" emerged. Prominent members of this school include Rhees, **D. Z. Phillips**, and **Peter Winch**.

T

TAGORE, RABINDRANATH (1861–1941). An Indian **poet** who was a great advocate of Bengali **language** and culture. In 1913 he won the Nobel Prize for Literature for his *Gitanjali: Song Offerings*. Around this time he achieved great popularity in Germany and Austria, and, to a lesser extent, in the rest of Europe too. Wittgenstein first read his play *The King of the Dark Chamber* in 1921. It became one of his favorite books, and he even 'translated' it for himself (along with Yorick Smythies), not from the original Bengali but from Tagore's poetic English translation into Wittgenstein's preferred, more down-to-earth, English. The play is about a King who, like God, is never seen and whose existence is doubted by some. Others resent what they see as the cruelty of his actions. In the course of the play the Queen, Sudarshana, overcomes her initial proud resentment to become devoted and humble. She does this not as a result of any reasoning or the acquisition of new information but by defeating her own inner rebelliousness. Wittgenstein seems to have believed that this is how **religious** belief should be.

TAUTOLOGY. ***Tractatus Logico-Philosophicus*** proposition 4.46 defines as tautological **propositions** that are true for all **truth**-possibilities of their **elementary propositions**. In other words, a proposition that cannot but be true, that is true no matter what, is a tautology. In 4.461 he gives the example: "Either it is raining or it is not raining." The proposition "It is raining" is probably not an elementary proposition in Wittgenstein's sense, but this does not matter in order to understand his point about tautologies. Whether "It is raining" is true or false, and whether "It is not raining" is true or false, the proposition "Either it is raining or it is not raining" is still true. Thus it is a tautology. Because of this true-no-matter-what feature of tautologies, they can tell us nothing about **the world** and thus "lack sense" (4.461). They **say** nothing. *Tractatus Logico-Philosophicus* 6.1 says that all the propositions of **logic** are tautologies. This, says 6.12, shows the formal or logical properties of **language** and the world. These properties, belonging to the class of things that can be shown, cannot be said or directly articulated. The "propositions" of logic thus say nothing, and there is nothing one can say about their content.

THEORY. General explanations of the kind offered by theories did not tend to interest Wittgenstein, and his later work at least is often characterized as being antitheory. There are two important caveats to note about this, however. The first is that Wittgenstein's personal antipathy toward theories should not be mistaken for a philosophical (i.e., reasoned or, indeed, theoretical) rejection of all theories whatsoever, as if physics and economics, for instance, were somehow undermined by Wittgenstein's **philosophy** simply because they involve theories. The second is that most commentators on Wittgenstein insist that there *are* theories of **language**, **meaning**, **truth**, and so on to be found throughout Wittgenstein's philosophical work. Whether this is true depends partly on what one means by 'theory.' His later work is certainly not obviously focused on developing or arguing for specific theories, and seems to be more concerned with offering descriptions and clarification of **grammar**, or **therapy** of some kind.

THEORY OF TYPES. A theory developed by **Bertrand Russell** in response to a fundamental problem he discovered in **Gottlob Frege's** attempt to provide a logical **foundation** for arithmetic. Frege's definition of **number** involves the concept of classes. Classes are defined as the extensions of **concepts**, that is as the **objects** to which the concepts correspond. It was axiomatic for Frege that there is at least one object that corresponds to each meaningful concept. Russell raised the question: What about classes themselves? Specifically, what about the class of classes that are members of themselves? The class of boxes does not belong to itself because it is a class, not a box. The class of classes, though, does belong to itself. Now, consider the class of classes that do not belong to themselves. Is this class a member of itself? If it is, then it is a class that does not belong to itself, so it is not. If it is not, then it is a class that does not belong to itself, so it is. Either way we have a contradiction. So Frege's system of **logic** is badly flawed.

Russell tried to get around this problem by introducing a hierarchy of types. In *The Principles of Mathematics* (1903) he proposed his first, simple version of the theory, and in "Mathematical Logic as Based on the Theory of Types" (1908) he proposed the "ramified" version. The basic idea of the theory of types is that classes are not objects. This makes for a simpler ontology (theory of what there is), and means that it is **nonsense** to talk about a class being a member of a class in the way that an object (a spoon or a barber, say) can be a member of a class. In the simple theory, there are types of objects (real objects, classes of objects, classes of classes, and so on). In the ramified theory there are also types of properties (properties, properties of properties, etc., e.g., shyness is nice or red is a property of objects). Sets, he stipulated, must consist only of things of the same type. Classes belong to a different type, according to Russell's hierarchy, than classes of classes. Thus the theory of types rules out the question of the class of classes that do not belong to themselves belonging to itself. Without the question, the problem disappears. The problem now is, what reason is there to accept this theory or hierarchy except as a convenient way to brush the original problem under the carpet?

Wittgenstein became fascinated by this problem while he was in **Manchester** and worked on it for years, resulting in his ***Notes on Logic***. There is still disagreement about the correct solution to the problem that Russell first identified and then tried to solve with his theory of types.

Russell himself was not completely happy with it: "Now the theory of types emphatically does not belong to the finished and certain part of our subject: much of this theory is still inchoate, confused, and obscure. But the need of *some* doctrine of types is less doubtful than the precise form the doctrine should take" (*Introduction to Mathematical Philosophy*, Dover Publications, 1993, p. 135).

Classes are logical fictions, and if they are treated as being real objects, whose names have real signification, then the sentences in which they are treated this way will be devoid of meaning. "The supposition that a class is, or that it is not, a member of itself is meaningless in just this way" (*ibid.*, p. 137).

F. P. Ramsey ("Predicative Functions and the Axiom of Reducibility" in his *The Foundations of Mathematics*), following Wittgenstein, objects to this theory. Propositional functions are symbols, while individuals are objects. So talk of functions of functions is not like talk of functions of individuals.

> For the range of values of a function of individuals is definitely fixed by the range of individuals, an objective totality which there is no [getting?] away from. But the range of **arguments** to a function of functions is a range of symbols, all symbols which become propositions by inserting in them the name of an individual. And this range of symbols, actual or possible, is not objectively fixed, but depends on our methods of constructing them and requires more precise definition.

Mounce (p. 56) puts Wittgenstein's objection to Russell's theory of types this way:

> One cannot in a correct symbolism construct a proposition which refers to itself without making it evident that the contained proposition has a different function from the proposition which contains it. But then it will be evident that one cannot construct a proposition which refers to itself. For,

> given such a misguided attempt, it will be evident that what one has is not one proposition, referring to itself, but *different* propositions. In short, a *theory* of types is entirely unnecessary.

White (p. 9) says that Wittgenstein explained his objection to Russell more clearly in *Philosophical Remarks*, p. 55:

> Grammatical conventions cannot be justified by describing what is represented. Any such description already presupposes the grammatical rules. That is to say, if anything is to count as nonsense in the grammar that is to be justified, then it cannot at the same time pass for sense in the grammar of the propositions that justify it (etc.).

THERAPY. The idea that Wittgenstein's **philosophy** is intended as a kind of therapy has become surprisingly popular given that in the ***Tractatus Logico-Philosophicus*** he does not mention the idea at all, and in the ***Philosophical Investigations*** he mentions it only once. There, in a note to §133, he writes that philosophy has methods, not one single method, and that these methods are like different therapies. He also compared his approach to philosophy to **Sigmund Freud's** method of psychoanalysis, although he strongly rejected the idea that his philosophy simply is a form of such **analysis**.

Proposition 6.54 of the *Tractatus* talks about helping the reader to see the **world** in the right way by providing **elucidations** that enable him or her to overcome the propositions that make up the book. This sounds like a kind of therapy, although there is much disagreement about what to make of this passage. Wittgenstein's various remarks about battling **confusion** also suggest a kind of therapeutic purpose to his work.

THOUGHT/THINKING. ***Tractatus Logico-Philosophicus*** proposition 3 **says** that a thought is a logical **picture** of a **fact**. Thus all thought is logical and anything that can be thought can *be*, is possible. Anything logically impossible would, on this interpretation, be literally unthinkable. An 'illogical thought' would not be a thought at all, it would have no **meaning**.

Tractatus proposition 4 says that a thought is a significant **proposition**, that is, a picture or model of reality. Exactly what this means might not be clear, since it is not immediately clear just what a logical picture of reality (or indeed a proposition) might be. A logical picture is not a visible picture, that is to say, the expressions "logical picture" and "visible picture" are not synonymous. The **essential** features of a logical picture are presumably logical rather than physical (or spiritual). Clearly Wittgenstein does not have in mind the idea that a thought is part of the brain or the **soul** or anything like that. He does not *deny* that it is something of this sort, but his claim is not that it *is* any particular thing of this kind. For Wittgenstein, claims of that kind belong to **psychology**, not to **philosophy**.

Propositions are generally taken to be something like the common feature of sentences in different languages that all mean the same thing. The same proposition (or meaning, or thought) is expressed by these different sentences (e.g., "It is raining," "Il pleut," and "Es regnet"). The ontological status of propositions or thoughts has puzzled some philosophers. However, since he is not doing psychology, Wittgenstein's interest is in **logic**, not ontology. It does not matter to him what a thought is so much as what the role of thoughts is in making sense. The word "role" here is meant in a purely functional or logical sense, not an efficient or productive one. Making sense is *having* meaning, not creating it. (This interpretation is controversial, though. Some scholars believe that meaning, for Wittgenstein in the *Tractatus*, depends on a psychological act of thinking.)

This radical anti-Cartesianism or antimetaphysics (depending on whether one reads Wittgenstein as offering an alternative **metaphysics** or an alternative *to* metaphysics) continues in Wittgenstein's later work, where he takes up the puzzle about the seemingly phantom process that is called thinking. Wittgenstein does not explicitly say what he thinks thinking is, nor what it is not, but his efforts seem aimed at moving the reader away from any **Cartesian** picture of thinking as an **inner** process (a process, that is, within some medium) and toward the ways people actually use words such as 'thinking' in connection with, usually, publicly observable **behavior**.

See also METHOD OF PROJECTION.

TOLSTOY, LEV NIKOLAYEVICH (LEO) (1828–1910). A great **Russian** novelist, much admired by Wittgenstein for his short stories and his writings on **religion**. Wittgenstein shared some of his anti-institutional spirituality and agrarian romanticism, as well as his tendency to depression and even **suicide** (a temptation that both resisted). During **World War I** Wittgenstein became known as "the man with the gospels" because he always carried a copy of Tolstoy's *The Gospel in Brief* with him. He had bought the book simply because it had been the only one for sale in a shop he had found, but became devoted to Tolstoy's selfless spirituality.

Although Tolstoy is best known for *War and Peace* and *Anna Karenina* Wittgenstein preferred *Hadji Murad*, which he read in the summer of 1912. This was apparently Tolstoy's own favorite of all his stories. It is much shorter than his more famous novels, and is closely based on a true story so there is little room for the kind of preaching (or trying to **say** what should be shown) to which Wittgenstein objected. The central character is a kind of tragic hero, acting nobly in the face of certain death. The story itself is presented as a **memory** prompted by the narrator's vain attempt to pluck a flower that is too tough to be plucked without crushing it. In its natural environment it looks beautiful, but elsewhere it looks simply out of place. Similarly, Hadji Murad is killed for no good reason, caught up in a war he did not create. His integrity is impressive, but no good (in a **utilitarian** sense) comes of it. Many comparisons between a man's life and that of a flower in a plowed field suggest themselves, but Tolstoy simply tells the story without sentimentality or sermonizing.

TRACTATUS LOGICO-PHILOSOPHICUS. Originally called *Logisch-Philosophische Abhandlung* (Logico-Philosophical Treatise), this was the only **philosophy** book published under Wittgenstein's name in his lifetime. It was originally published, with some difficulty, in the German journal *Annalen der Naturphilosophie*. The Latin title (which means the same as the German) was suggested by **G. E. Moore** and accepted by Wittgenstein as less than ideal but preferable to **Bertrand Russell's** suggested "Philosophical Logic," which Wittgenstein thought made no sense. In the process of trying to find someone to publish the work, Wittgenstein told **Ludwig von Ficker** that the point of the *Tractatus* was ethical.

Three translations of the *Tractatus* are currently available in print. Daniel Kolak's translation (McGraw-Hill, 1997) is designed to provide a lyrical and poetic English version of the book, which might make the reading experience more pleasant and in some ways closer to what Wittgenstein wanted, but it does not help those who care about understanding the precise meaning of each sentence. Far more popular with scholars are the translations by **C. K. Ogden** (available in various editions) and by D. F. Pears and B. F. McGuinness (Routledge & Kegan Paul, 1974). The obvious choice is Ogden's translation, since Wittgenstein himself helped with the project. However, that translation is neither completely accurate nor completely in accordance with Wittgenstein's suggestions (although he did approve the whole). Hence the popularity of Pears's and McGuinness's version of the text, which is also more readable than Ogden's. Unfortunately, this translation is arguably too readable, sacrificing accuracy and fidelity to Wittgenstein's explicit instructions for the sake of easier comprehension. This version of the book has also been accused of over-translation and leading the reader to interpret the text in one way when the original German is at least equally open to another interpretation. Ideally, one might look at two or three of these translations, gaining an initial understanding from the work of Pears and McGuinness (or Kolak) and then checking this understanding for accuracy by looking at Ogden's rendering of the text.

In the preface to the book Wittgenstein says that its **value** consists in two things: "that thoughts are expressed in it" and "that it shows how little is achieved when these problems are solved." The problems he refers to are the problems of philosophy defined, one may suppose, by the work of **Gottlob Frege** and Russell, and perhaps also **Arthur Schopenhauer**. At the end of the book (proposition 6.54) Wittgenstein says: "My **propositions** serve as

elucidations in the following way: anyone who understands me eventually recognizes them as nonsensical." What to make of the *Tractatus*, its author, and the propositions it contains is no easy matter.

The book consists of numbered propositions in seven sets. Proposition 1.2 belongs to the first set, and is a comment on proposition 1. Proposition 1.21 is about proposition 1.2, and so on. The seventh set contains only one proposition, the famous "What we cannot speak about we must pass over in **silence**."

Despite what Wittgenstein said to Ficker, very few of these propositions are about **ethics**. Wittgenstein's general aim seems to be to show up as **nonsense** the things that philosophers (himself included) are tempted to say. Philosophical **theories**, he suggests, are attempts to answer questions that are not really questions at all (they are nonsense), or to solve problems that are not really problems. How much of the *Tractatus* is itself nonsense is a matter of some controversy. Some, notably **P. M. S. Hacker**, defend the orthodox idea that the *Tractatus* contains important insights regarding **logic**, say, as Hacker sees it, or the ineffability of ethics in the view of others. **Cora Diamond** and **James Conant**, on the other hand, have argued that Wittgenstein is quite serious when he says that his propositions are *nonsense* and that one should throw them away (completely, they might add).

At several points in the *Tractatus* (e.g., 1, 4.01, 4.121, 4.5, and 5.4711) Wittgenstein seems to be saying that the essence of the world and of life is: This is how things are. One is tempted to add "–deal with it." That seems to fit what Diamond has called his "accept and endure" ethics, but he says that the propositions of the *Tractatus* are *meaningless*, not profound insights, ethical or otherwise. What are we to make of this?

Many commentators ignore or dismiss what Wittgenstein said about his work and its aims, and instead look for regular philosophical theories in his work. This, after all, seems more profitable than writing off the whole work as nonsense, and many of its sentences appear not only to make sense but to be true, even importantly so. Wittgenstein says in proposition 4.003:

> Most of the propositions and questions of philosophers arise from our failure to understand the logic of our language. (They belong to the same class as the question whether the good is more or less identical than the beautiful.) And it is not surprising that the deepest problems are in fact *not* problems at all.

Philosophers, then, have the task of presenting the logic of our language clearly. This will not solve important problems, but it will show that some things that we take to be important problems are really not problems at all. The gain is not wisdom but an absence of confusion. This is not a rejection of philosophy or logic. Wittgenstein took philosophical puzzlement very seriously indeed, but he thought that it needed *dissolving* by analysis rather than *solving* by the production of theories or the providing of answers to questions that, he believed, are not genuine questions. The *Tractatus* presents itself as a key for untying a series of knots both profound and highly technical.

The most obvious evidence in favor of the orthodox reading of the *Tractatus* is that so much of it seems not only to make sense but to be both true and important to many very competent philosophers. Russell, for instance, was attracted to **logical atomism**; the **picture theory** of **meaning** has seemed right to many people; and the distinction between **saying and showing** has many Wittgensteinian adherents today. Against this reading are such things as proposition 6.54 (quoted in part above) and Wittgenstein's later judgment of the *Tractatus* as "fishy" rather than false or nonsensical, perhaps suggesting that it was not meant straightforwardly (see PPO p. 396). An entry in one of his diaries refers to some of the *Tractatus* as "good and genuine," which implies an absence of irony, but also to "kitsch" that fills in "the gaps," with Wittgenstein reporting that he cannot tell how much of the book is like this (see PPO p. 39, written in 1930). Some Wittgensteinians will take this as evidence that the views put forward in the *Tractatus* are not Wittgenstein's own but a combination of Russell's, Frege's, Schopenhauer's, and plausible guff that Wittgenstein threw in to lead the reader to see that *all* the theses proposed in the book need to be discarded. This interpretation is bolstered by another ambiguous remark (see PPO p. 387) that can be read as saying that the *Tractatus* was intended as a road map showing the way out of a wood. Those who prize the trees through which this road passes (such as, arguably, Hacker and most other commentators on Wittgenstein's work) would then be missing the point. What is wrong with the *Tractatus*, Wittgenstein seems to be saying, is that it is written as if there is only one way out, when in fact there are others too. These, some would say, are explored in the later ***Philosophical Investigations***. The debate about how ironic Wittgenstein was being in the *Tractatus*, about whether he is saying what he seems to be saying (and about what that is), is ongoing between the "old" and "new" Wittgensteinians, as is the debate about the degree of **continuity** between the *Tractatus* and the later work.

TRATTENBACH. In 1920, when Wittgenstein became an elementary school teacher, he worked first in what he described to **Bertrand Russell** as, "a tiny village . . . in the mountains, about four hours' journey south of **Vienna**" (see Monk p. 193). The village was Trattenbach. He was energetic but very strict as a teacher and did not get on well with his fellow teachers, nor the villagers, with whom he had very little in common. He left the village in 1921.

See also HAIDBAUER CASE; SCHOOL REFORM MOVEMENT.

TRUTH. ***Philosophical Investigations*** §544 says that the concepts **meaning** and truth sometimes merge. The truth of a **proposition** might be its meaning. If meaning is use, then can truth be too? Very roughly, Wittgenstein seems to be suggesting that truth is something like the correct use of a proposition, use according to whatever **rules** apply. This sounds like **relativism**, making truth relative to whomever it is that makes the rules. The rules that govern the use of words such as 'true' and 'false,' though, do not generally refer to any group of authoritative people. It is the **facts** that are authoritative.

This fact about the **grammar** of 'truth' is emphasized by the correspondence **theory** of truth, which holds (in a way reminiscent of Wittgenstein's **picture theory** of meaning) that truth is correspondence with reality. ***Tractatus Logico-Philosophicus*** 2.222 says that the truth or falsity of a **picture** consists in the agreement or disagreement of its sense with reality, which certainly looks like a version of the correspondence theory of truth. However, sometimes one might rightly say that something were true if it cohered with other well-established, or at least undoubted, truths. This is how coherence theories define all truth. The other main theory of truth is **pragmatism**, roughly the idea that truth is whatever works. Wittgenstein once said in a lecture that "it is nonsense to try to find *a* theory of truth, because we can see that in everyday life we use the word quite clearly and definitely in these different senses" (WLC p. 76). The implication is that each of these theories is partially true, but that the grammar of truth is too varied to be captured by any one of them completely without distortion.

See also TRUTH-FUNCTION; TRUTH-TABLE.

TRUTH-FUNCTION. Complex **propositions**, according to the ***Tractatus Logico-Philosophicus***, are truth-functions of **elementary propositions**. That is to say, their truth or falsity (truth-value) depends on the truth-value of their constituent elementary propositions. The exact nature of this dependence can be shown by means of a **truth-table**.

In his book *Assembling Reminders: Studies in the Genesis of Wittgenstein's Concept of Philosophy* (p. 61), Allan Janik writes that:

> If one simply reads the seven propositions that constitute the main ideas of the *Tractatus* consecutively one quickly comes to the realization that the book's center is in fact propositions 5 and 6. Proposition 5 tells us that all meaningful sentences are truth-**functions**; whereas 6 tells us that double negation is the general form of all truth-functions. The force of this assertion is that all of the propositions of logic are of equal logical significance.

Proposition 6 defines the general form of truth-functions symbolically, identifying it with the general form of propositions. Denis McManus's *The Enchantment of Words: Wittgenstein's Tractatus Logico-Philosophicus* (p. 140) renders the idea here as: "Every proposition is an elementary proposition or a (possibly very complex) complex proposition." He sees it as problematic because no **argument** is really given in its favor and because it seems to bring metaphysical commitments with it. If there is a general form of propositions, then there is, he suggests, a general form of the world (see 2.04). Wittgenstein's claim is in effect that "all logical incompatibility is a matter of contradiction" (p. 153), but this is only a possibility, not something that Wittgenstein has proved must be the case. For instance, if a spot is red, it cannot also be blue. But is "This spot is red" a contradiction of "This spot is blue"? Or could it be a kind of empirical knowledge that a spot cannot be both red and blue? Wittgenstein assumes that the meanings of the logical constants that connect elementary propositions into complex propositions are topic-neutral, the same in all contexts. He later abandoned this assumption. (See, e.g., PG 269 and RPP I 38.) At the time it probably seemed bland and inoffensive. He later saw that it brought unwanted problems and commitments.

TRUTH-TABLE. If one has a **proposition** of the form "If *p* then *q*," for instance, then one can draw up a table with columns for *p*, *q*, and the proposition itself, and rows for each possible combination of either T (for true) or F (for false) in each column. In this case, the column for the proposition as a whole will get a T every time, except when there is a T in the *p* column and an F in the *q* column. Logical **functions** (along the lines of "if . . . then," "and," and so on) can be defined using such tables, making their precise **meaning** explicit and removing the kind of ambiguity that attends natural **language** expressions. For example, "or" can mean "either/or but not both" (the exclusive sense) or "and/or" (the inclusive sense). So "or" just by itself is ambiguous. A logical function defined using truth-tables would have no such ambiguity. As a definition, a truth-table could be substituted for any other symbol used for the function in question. This could help to show that **logical constants** do not stand for anything, a fact that Wittgenstein emphasized as fundamental in proposition 4.0312 of the ***Tractatus Logico-Philosophicus***.

Wittgenstein uses truth-tables in *Tractatus* proposition 4.31, and it is widely believed (although sometimes disputed) that he invented them. The earliest truth-table that has been discovered was created by Charles Peirce in 1893 (see Irving H. Anellis "Peirce's Truth-functional Analysis and the Origin of the Truth Table" in *History and Philosophy of Logic*, Volume 33, Issue 1, 2012), but this is in an unpublished manuscript. **Bertrand Russell** may have helped Wittgenstein develop truth-tables, but it was in Wittgenstein's work that they were first published.

TURING, ALAN (1912–1954). A pioneer in computer science and artificial intelligence. Turing was one of Wittgenstein's students. He is best known today for having invented both the Turing machine and the Turing test. Computers as they are generally known today are very similar to Turing machines (theoretical devices with infinite memory that respond to binary commands). The main difference is that real computers have limited memory. The Turing test is regarded by some people as the measure of intelligence, so that any machine that passes it will count as being intelligent. The test requires that people communicating with the machine via teletype not be able to tell whether it is indeed a machine or a human being. No machine has yet passed the test, but there is debate among philosophers about whether passing the test would really prove that a machine was intelligent, rather than merely able to simulate the behavior of intelligent beings. Turing's most important philosophical work is a paper called "Computing Machinery and Intelligence," which was published in the journal *Mind* in 1950.

U

UNDERSTANDING. Understanding can be thought of as one side of a coin that has **meaning** on the other. If the meaning of a word is its use in the **language**, then, understanding the word would seem to be knowing how it is used in the language. It could be either knowing that it is so used or actually being able to use it oneself, or both of these things.

Then again, if the meaning of a word is its use in the language then one should look at how the word "understanding" is used in the language. This requires **imagination** more than **anthropological** fieldwork, since (one may assume) philosophers are competent, and thus authoritative, speakers of the language they use. They (i.e., *we*) know, in some sense determine, the **rules** that govern the correct use of "understand" and its cognates. This is the kind of method that Wittgenstein uses in his later **philosophy**, imagining various situations in which one would (and would not) use a particular word whose meaning is troubling us or causing **confusion**.

UNITED STATES. Wittgenstein traveled to the United States near the end of his life to visit **Norman Malcolm** at Cornell. There he also met **O. K. Bouwsma**, who recorded his conversations with Wittgenstein. Wittgenstein hoped that the new world would be able to produce a different culture than the one he saw as declining or even dead in Europe, but he was not optimistic. Most of the time he talked of North American and European culture in the same breath, seemingly thinking that neither represented the way forward. For a while he had some hopes for **Russia**, because of what he described as the energy there, but he seems to have been disillusioned by a visit there and was never a believer in **Marxism**.

USE THEORY OF MEANING. *See* MEANING.

UTILITARIANISM. A **theory** in **ethics** that has ancient roots but that was developed and defended in modern times by the English philosophers Jeremy Bentham and **John Stuart Mill**. The key ideas of utilitarians are that the ultimate goal in life is happiness or pleasure (and the avoidance of **pain**) and that right acts are those that produce the most happiness and/or the least pain. The idea that happiness or pleasure is the only ultimate good is called hedonism and was denounced by **Friedrich Nietzsche** as something that only Englishmen believed (others, he implied, **value** something like purpose more). The idea that acts should be judged solely by their results has been given the name consequentialism by **G. E. M. Anscombe**, and denounced by her for holding and encouraging the **belief** that the end justifies the means and, indeed, can justify almost any means whatsoever if the circumstances are apt.

Bentham believed in a hedonic calculus (a quasi-mathematical formula) that could be used to add up the probable amount of pleasure each action would produce and thereby judge in any set of circumstances what is the right thing to do. Mill rejected this version of utilitarianism on the grounds that it failed to distinguish between types of pleasure. The "happiness" of **Socrates**, he argued, is superior to that of a fool, *even if the fool is more content or satisfied.* According to **O. K. Bouwsma**, Wittgenstein rejected Bentham's simple form of utilitarianism as too crude, and Mill's sophisticated version as a failed attempt to paper over the cracks of Bentham's absurd doctrine (see Bouwsma p. 60, 14 September 1950).

V

VALUE. ***Tractatus Logico-Philosophicus*** proposition 6.4 states that all **propositions** are equal in value. All propositions merely state what is the case (or what is, in fact, not the case if they are false). They state **facts**, but facts and values are radically distinct. At least many philosophers since **David Hume** have thought that they are distinct, and the *Tractatus* seems clearly to be of this opinion. Proposition 6.41 expands on this idea. All that is the case is contingent or accidental. Values, one infers, are not of this kind. What is evil (murder, say) is not something that could have been good, the way that dry land could have been under the sea. There is a **necessity** about value, and whatever creates this necessity must lie outside **the world**. It cannot be, as it were, a contingent necessity. So value is not part of the world but instead can only lie "outside" it. It is thus beyond **language** if language is only meaningful insofar as it pictures **states of affairs** within the world. This can be taken as an expression of a **mystical** ethics or as a repudiation of the **picture theory**. Wittgenstein repeated a similar view in his later **lecture on ethics**, but he wrote little about **ethics** or value after this. A good sense of Wittgenstein's personal values can be gained from Ray Monk's biography, from **O. K. Bouwsma's** record of his conversations with Wittgenstein, from Wittgenstein's own writings in ***Culture and Value***, and from the "private" material in ***Ludwig Wittgenstein: Public and Private Occasions***, especially the **Koder diaries**.

VERIFICATION PRINCIPLE. One of the core ideas of the **Vienna Circle** of **logical positivists**. The principle was inspired by remarks made by Wittgenstein in the course of his conversations with the Vienna Circle. It states that every empirical **proposition** must be verifiable in order to be meaningful. That is to say, it must be possible at least in principle to determine whether the proposition is **true**. A claim that an undetectable being is in the room, for instance, would be not false but meaningless since, being undetectable, the being's existence could not possibly be verified. As an alternative, **Karl Popper** argued that falsifiability is the real test.

Wittgenstein clearly believed in something like verificationism, at least for a while, but denied that he ever meant it as a dogma or **theory** of **meaning**. Asking how one would verify an assertion was simply, he said, one good way to ascertain its meaning. In his later work he avoided remarks that even sounded like the verification principle.

VIENNA. Wittgenstein grew up in Vienna at a time when that city was perhaps at its most fertile culturally, in a house that was one of the centers of this cultural life. This was the Vienna of **Karl Kraus**, **Adolf Loos**, Arnold Schönberg, **Fritz Mauthner**, Robert Musil, and **Oskar Kokoschka**. The wealthy **Wittgenstein family** patronized some of these figures and took an interest in all the **arts**, especially **music**. This rich cultural background clearly influenced Wittgenstein's thinking about culture and **language**, although exactly how is hard to say with both precision and confidence.

VIENNA CIRCLE. A group of **logical positivists**. The members of the Circle were greatly impressed by what they found in the ***Tractatus Logico-Philosophicus***, especially the idea that **logic** and **mathematics** are **analytic**, the **verification principle**, and the idea that **philosophy** is an activity aimed at clarification, not the discovery of **facts**. Wittgenstein, though, said that it was what is *not* in the *Tractatus* that matters most. So, although he did meet with the Circle to discuss philosophy (and to read **poetry** to them, which they might not have appreciated), Wittgenstein does not really seem to have shared its ideology. Members of the Circle include **Rudolf Carnap**, **Moritz Schlick**, and **Friedrich Waismann**. Perhaps the best introduction to their ideas is A. J. Ayer's *Language, Truth, and Logic* (1936).

VISUAL ROOM. ***Philosophical Investigations*** §§398–400 introduce and discuss the concept of a 'visual room,' something like the field of vision conceived, like images in the **imagination**, as being something in the **mind**. When one imagines things, one might think of these **objects** in the imagination as private or **inner** objects, of a nonphysical sort presumably, that one *possesses*. The space of imagination, the visual room, and all its contents belong to me, one might say. Wittgenstein says that if one wants to talk about the visual room on the model of a real room, as it is tempting to do, then one should remember that a real room can be described with no reference to an *owner* and, indeed, might not have an owner at all. One is not *in* one's visual room, and to speak of one's being *outside* it is to treat it as if it were a room in the same space that a **human being** occupies. Yet the whole point of its being something specially private or internal to the mind was to deny this idea. Only an imaginary being, perhaps one can say, could be the owner of the visual room, the room of imagination. So it is not *one's own* visual room.

This is reminiscent of the remarks Wittgenstein makes about the **metaphysical** subject or **self** in propositions 5.631–5.6331 of the ***Tractatus Logico-Philosophicus***.

W

WAISMANN, FRIEDRICH (1896–1959). A member of the **Vienna Circle** with whom Wittgenstein worked closely. The two planned at one stage to work together on a book entitled ***Logik, Sprache, Philosophie*** (Logic, Language, Philosophy). In preparation for this project, Wittgenstein dictated a set of theses to Waismann (repeating and elucidating ideas found in the ***Tractatus Logico-Philosophicus***), but he quickly became dissatisfied with this formulation of his ideas and abandoned the book.

In **mathematics** Waismann argued for **conventionalism**, arguing that mathematics is based on chosen, human conventions and not on independent necessary **truths**. He also believed that conventions in **language** can shape perception of reality. Unlike other **logical positivists**, he argued that few statements are strictly subject to the **verification principle** because most empirical **concepts** have an "open texture." This means that, though not vague, they have the *possibility* of vagueness inherent in them, because one cannot foresee all of the possible circumstances in which they might be used. Hence, he argues, one cannot know all the circumstances in which a statement using such concepts will be true (or false). Waismann taught at the universities of **Cambridge** and Oxford. His most important philosophical works are *An Introduction to Mathematical Thinking* (1936), *The Principles of Linguistic Philosophy* (1965), and *How I See Philosophy* (1968), a collection of papers.

WEININGER, OTTO (1880–1903). The controversial author of *Sex and Character* and *On Last Things*. In 1903 Weininger first published *Sex and Character* and then shot himself in the house where Ludwig van Beethoven had died. He was 23 years old. His dramatic **suicide** and August Strindberg's description of his book as "awe-inspiring" gained huge attention for Weininger's work. The book offers a dim view of the modern age and is riddled with misogyny and **anti-Semitism**, although the emphasis is on women and **Jews** as **psychological** types rather than biologically defined ones. Weininger himself was gay and Jewish, and both the book and his suicide appear to have been motivated by self-loathing. The only life worth living, Weininger claims, is the spiritual life (that is nonsexual, non-womanly as he sees it). It is the life of genius. Wittgenstein read the book as a teenager and the subtitle of Ray Monk's biography, *Ludwig Wittgenstein: The Duty of Genius*, is a reference to it.

Wittgenstein's self-confessed admiration for such a figure is puzzling, but three things about it are important to note. The first is that Wittgenstein did not claim to agree with Weininger. On the contrary, he said that it is not possible to agree with him, but that if one were to place a negation **sign** before the whole of *Sex and Character*, then one would have expressed an important truth. In other words, at least roughly speaking, Weininger is *completely* wrong, but about great things. The second point to note is that it seems to have been *On Last Things* that Wittgenstein preferred. It is possible that he recommended *Sex and Character* to others simply because this was the only one of Weininger's works to have been translated into English. Thirdly, it is worth bearing in mind Joachim Schulte's view that Weininger's writing is full of ironical play because of which it is "hard to understand why Weininger is generally taken to be nothing but a solemn, zealous and bigoted stickler for nasty and stupid principles" (*Wittgenstein Reads Weininger*, edited by David G. Stern and Béla Szabados, Cambridge University Press, 2004, p. 122). Nevertheless, this *is* how Weininger is generally taken, and that should be remembered too.

WHITEHEAD, ALFRED NORTH (1861–1947). A British mathematician who became a philosopher and taught first at **Cambridge**, then at Imperial College, London, and finally at Harvard. He wrote *Principia Mathematica* (three volumes, 1910–1913) with **Bertrand Russell**, who was a student of his. The book aims to show that **mathematics** can largely be derived from **logic**. His other best-known works are *The Concept of Nature* (1920) and *Process and Reality* (1929). In 1945 he was awarded the Order of Merit.

See also LOGICISM.

WILL. ***Tractatus Logico-Philosophicus*** proposition 6.423 says that one cannot speak about the will as the subject of the ethical, what **Immanuel Kant** might call the noumenal **self** (the self-in-itself, as it is independent of any perception or knowledge of it). Kant distinguished between noumena (things-in-themselves, which are unknowable to the subjects of experience) and phenomena (things as they are to the subject, as mediated by the comprehending faculties of the **mind**). He identified all phenomenal beings as subject to **causation** and therefore not free, hence not morally responsible for what they do. But he noted that people are not only objects of experience (phenomena) but also subjects. Subjects can be known as objects, but the subject *qua* subject cannot be the object of knowledge. It seems then that there is an aspect of being that is unknowable. *Qua* noumena perhaps people are free. Indeed, he argues, if one is to keep faith in **ethics**, then one must believe that people are free and souls immortal, so that justice can be meted out after **death**. **Arthur Schopenhauer** identified this "moral self" with the will and agreed that it was immortal. Thus between them Kant and Schopenhauer say a lot about what is supposedly beyond the human mind. Kant maintains that one cannot know these things (since they concern noumena) but must instead have faith. Schopenhauer seems to think that one really can know them.

Both the **verification principle** and the **picture theory** of **meaning** suggest that what is not only unknown but unknowable cannot meaningfully be talked about. And what can be talked about, the will as a phenomenon, *Tractatus* proposition 6.423 continues, is of interest only to **psychology**. The sense of 'will' that is interesting to philosophers, in other words, is beyond the realm of things about which one can **say** anything intelligible.

WINCH, PETER GUY (1926–1997). A well-known Wittgensteinian philosopher of the **Swansea** school. Winch taught for many years at the University of Illinois and is best known for his short book *The Idea of a Social Science and its Relation to Philosophy* (1958). In this he argues that the study of human **behavior** is the study of **rule-following** and hence perhaps not best thought of as **science**. Winch argues that **human beings** cannot be well understood except in terms of their own self-**understanding**, which will include reference to the rules they follow and the **concepts** they employ. If social science is to be something distinct from biology or physics, then it must treat human behavior as intentional, not **causally** determined. His critics accuse Winch of **relativism**. Other important publications of his include *Ethics and Action* (1972), *Trying to Make Sense* (1987), and *Simone Weil* (1989).

WISDOM. There are several remarks about wisdom in ***Culture and Value***. There Wittgenstein describes wisdom, at least as seen by **Christianity**, as passionless, gray, and cold. He contrasts wisdom with faith, **religion**, and life, which are, he says, full of **color**. Wisdom consists of sound doctrines, but these cannot take hold of one's life in the way that passion does, and indeed they can hide the **truth**, in the way that cold ashes hide glowing embers. One can perhaps see here (the reason for) Wittgenstein's antipathy to **theory**.

WISDOM, ARTHUR JOHN TERENCE DIBBEN (1904–1993). A **Cambridge** philosopher who held the chair in **philosophy** (as had Wittgenstein) from 1952 to 1968 and then moved to Oregon, where he taught from 1968 to

1972. Wisdom was one of the most important of the so-called **ordinary language** philosophers influenced by Wittgenstein. Distinctively, though, he regarded **nonsense** of the philosophical variety as at least potentially illuminating and not to be dismissed out of hand. Philosophical **theories**, he argued, might be perceptive as well as **confused**. His major works are *Problems of Mind and Matter* (1934), *Other Minds* (1952), *Philosophy and Psychoanalysis* (1953), and *Paradox and Discovery* (1965). His cousin J. O. Wisdom (who, confusingly, is also known by the first name John) is also a well-known philosopher.

THE WITTGENSTEIN FAMILY. Wittgenstein's paternal great-grandfather was originally named Moses Meier. When, in 1808, Napoleon decreed that all **Jews** take a surname, he adopted the name of his employer, a German aristocrat. This is how Wittgenstein came to share a last name with a princely family despite being unrelated to it by blood. His paternal grandparents were Fanny (née Figdor, 1814–1890) and Hermann Christian Wittgenstein (1802–1878). Hermann made his living by buying and selling farms and dealing in wool. He and Fanny had 10 children. The sixth of these, Karl (1847–1913), married Leopoldine ("Poldi") Kalmus. These were Ludwig's parents.

Karl Wittgenstein was a rich industrialist and patron of the **arts**. He made his fortune in the steel industry through a combination of technical knowledge, rationalization, and hard work. Leopoldine was a skilled pianist and brought the composer Joseph Labor to the Wittgenstein house. She and Karl had eight children, of which Ludwig was the youngest.

Wittgenstein's sisters were Hermine (known as Mining, 1874–1949), Margarete (known as Gretl), and Helene (known as Lenka). Margarete married Jerome Stonborough and had two sons, Thomas and John. Helene married Max Salzer and had two children, Felix and Clara. Clara Salzer went on to marry Arvid Sjögren, who had been one of Ludwig's **disciples**.

Wittgenstein's brothers were Hans, Kurt, Rudolf, and Paul. Hans was a brilliant **musician** who left **Vienna** for the **United States** when pressed by his father to give up art for a career in business. He died in 1902, it is believed by drowning in Chesapeake Bay, apparently having thrown himself into the water. Similarly Kurt (known as Konrad, 1878–1918) was a cellist and shot himself in November 1918 with defeat and capture seeming inevitable, the troops under his command refusing to fight. Rudolf (known as Rudi, 1881–1904) also committed suicide by taking cyanide in a bar in Berlin where he had moved to pursue a career in the theatre. Paul (1887–1961) was a concert pianist even after he lost his right arm in **World War I**. He had made his debut in Vienna just a year before this loss. Richard Strauss, Benjamin Britten, Sergei Prokofiev, and Maurice Ravel composed for him. He became a citizen of the United States in 1947, having settled in New York in

1940. Unlike Ludwig and his other brothers, Paul married and had children: daughters named Joan and Elizabeth, and a son named Paul, who was given the middle name Ludwig.

WOMEN. Wittgenstein's relations with women are something of a mystery. His **sexuality** was somewhat ambiguous (he was probably either gay or bisexual) and accusations that he was a sexist have been challenged. He seems not to have liked academic women generally, has been quoted as saying that "Men are foul, but women are viler," and once said to **Elizabeth Anscombe**, "Thank God we've got rid of the women!" when some women had left a lecture he was giving. He also referred to Anscombe as an "honorary man," and refused to teach **Alice Ambrose** after she published an article discussing his ideas. This treatment of Ambrose does not appear to have had anything to do with her gender (R. B. Braithwaite, a man, suffered a similar fate), but anyone who witnessed his behavior toward her might have inferred that he had something against women generally.

That this was not the case is suggested by the fact that women such as Anscombe were among his favorite students. One of the two students he chose to take the dictation that became the ***Brown Book*** in 1934–1935 was Ambrose (the other was **Francis Skinner**). In the previous academic year, when he dictated the ***Blue Book***, his five favorite students included two women: Margaret Masterman and Ambrose (the others were Skinner, H. S. M. Coxeter, and Louis Goodstein). His lectures were particularly popular with women, but many of them did not stay the course. This might explain his remark to Anscombe expressing relief that "the women" (though obviously not she) had left. He did not like having students who were not sufficiently serious attend his classes. Whether he thought that women were typically less serious than men is hard to tell, but there is some evidence that he did.

WONDER. Wittgenstein uses the experience of wonder at the existence of **the world** as his prime example in the **lecture on ethics**, an example, that is, of the kind of thing that he wants to express when he talks about absolute value or ethical value. Such talk, he says, misuses **language**, because one cannot imagine or conceive of its not being the case that the world exists. I can intelligibly wonder at an elephant's being this size rather than that, either so big or so small, but I cannot wonder at its being an elephant. "This elephant is an elephant" is a **tautology**, not a wondrous **fact**. The same goes, at least according to Wittgenstein, for "The world exists." (In the earlier ***Tractatus Logico-Philosophicus*** he had written that not how the world is but that it is, is the **mystical**.)

In 1930 he wrote that "Man has to awaken to wonder" (see ***Culture and Value***, p. 5), and that **science** is a way of sending him to sleep. His idea seems to have been, though, that science done in a certain spirit is likely to send people to sleep, to reduce their sense of surprise, fear, or wonder at the phenomena of the natural world. No amount of scientific knowledge forces us to stop being awestruck by the night sky or a sunrise, any more than scientific knowledge of some disease would stop us being afraid of it. So Wittgenstein was not making a criticism of all science in this remark. Nor was he demanding that people wake to wonder. Rather that wonder at natural phenomena, including the phenomena of human life, is not a given but is something that only exists if it happens to emerge. There is no reason to assume that primitive people must have marveled at birth, death, or storms, Wittgenstein argues, because they surely witnessed such events all the time. Marveling is a kind of achievement, and it is an achievement that can be undone.

WOOD-SELLERS (EXAMPLE OF). In the ***Remarks on the Foundations of Mathematics*** Part I §§143–152, Wittgenstein describes people who buy and sell wood in strange ways. At first he imagines them charging by the volume of a pile of logs, regardless of weight, number of logs, and so on. This seems conceivable as, he points out, is a group of people who simply give wood away. But then he goes on, less believably, to consider people who sell wood according to the area of the base of the pile, regardless of how high the pile of logs is.

There is disagreement about the point of these examples. Perhaps the reader is meant to see that calculations of volume and area belong to a **form of life** and are not intelligible as such when one does not understand the form of life in question. The passage in §152 talks about insanity. Perhaps Wittgenstein is here expressing a kind of **relativism** about what constitutes rational behavior. The exercises in **imagination** that the reader is asked to engage in clearly are meant to relate to the problem of **rule-following**, but any ideas about how they do this are bound to be controversial.

THE WORLD. The ***Tractatus Logico-Philosophicus*** begins with a statement about **the world**, saying that it is all that is the case, a collection of **facts**, not of things. This is apparently a statement of **metaphysics**, but it might be seen to push the reader away from ontology (the study of what is, or of being) toward **logic**. In this sense logic would be something like the study of structural possibilities or possibilities of structure, of how things can be and are related to one another in **states of affairs**. The logical structure of any given state of affairs, Wittgenstein says, is necessarily held in common by any **proposition** describing that state of affairs or asserting that it is the case. So the limits of **language** are the limits of the world. This could be taken as a form of linguistic **idealism** or as a redefinition of "the world" as a linguistic version of **Immanuel Kant's** phenomenal world. A linguistic version of Kant might be just as much an idealist as he was, but it can be argued that Wittgenstein was in fact proposing no such **theory**, since *Tractatus* proposition 6.54 describes Wittgenstein's propositions as **nonsense**. What to make of this claim though is highly controversial.

WORLD WAR I. Wittgenstein volunteered for the Austrian army in the First World War and was decorated for his bravery. He sought out particularly dangerous, though not **suicidal**, positions, apparently in an effort to test his fearlessness. A death wish and a desire to do his duty to the utmost are also possible motives. He was known by his fellow soldiers for his devotion to **Leo Tolstoy's** version of the Gospels. Near the end of the war he was captured and worked on the ***Tractatus Logico-Philosophicus*** in a prisoner-of-war camp in Italy.

WORLD WAR II. Wittgenstein was in England during the Second World War and of course would not have fought for **Adolf Hitler's** Germany (he was a left-wing sympathizer and counted as **Jewish** by Nazi standards). He did various kinds of medical work, as a hospital porter and helping with research at **Guy's Hospital**, as well as working on the ***Philosophical Investigations*** during the war.

See also POLITICS.

WRIGHT, CRISPIN (1942–). A British philosopher interested in both Wittgenstein and **Gottlob Frege**. Wright's views are similar to **Saul Kripke's** (on **rule-following**) and **Michael Dummett's** (on **realism and antirealism**). On following a rule, Wright argues that the correct next step is the one in accordance with the rule followers' best judgment of what they previously intended or **meant** by the rule in question. Thus human judgment is essential, so rules do not have a mysterious, **Platonic** existence independent of **human beings**, but also there is an objective standard of correctness, since not just any judgment or **belief** will count as people's best judgment. Critics contend that what does so count is impossible to specify without circularity. Wright is the author of many books, including *Realism, Meaning and Truth* (1993) and *Rails to Infinity* (2001). He teaches at the University of St. Andrews and New York University.

WRIGHT, GEORG HENRIK VON (1916–2003). A noted Finnish philosopher and student of Wittgenstein's. Von Wright first studied in Helsinki with Eino Kaila, a philosopher and **psychologist** who had been an associate member of the **Vienna Circle**. In 1939 he went to **Cambridge University**. There he studied with **G. E. Moore** but also, when he found out about them, started to attend Wittgenstein's seminars. He married Baroness Maria Elisabeth von Troil in 1941. In 1948, with Wittgenstein's blessing, von Wright succeeded him as the professor of philosophy at Cambridge. At the time he was only 32 years old. Three years later he returned to Finland, where he taught at the University of Helsinki. He was also a visiting professor at Cornell University from 1965 to 1977.

Von Wright was one of Wittgenstein's three literary executors (the others being, originally, **Rush Rhees** and **G. E. M. Anscombe**). It was von Wright who wrote the official list of manuscripts and typescripts that Wittgenstein had left. All three worked to ensure that first the best of this material and then all of it was made public.

Von Wright's own philosophical work is mostly on philosophical **logic**, **ethics**, and the **philosophy** of action. He wrote many books, in Swedish, German, and Finnish. In 1951 he published *A Treatise on Induction and Probability* and *An Essay in Modal Logic*. With an article entitled "Deontic Logic," which was published in the journal *Mind*, von Wright developed this work on logic into the realm of ethics and thus established a new branch of study. Deontic logic introduces symbols to represent moral permissibility and obligatoriness, similar to those used in modal logic to represent possibility and **necessity**. More directly ethical work appeared in his books *Varieties of Goodness* and *Norm and Action*, which were both published in 1963. His main work on the philosophy of action is contained in *Explanation and Understanding* (1971) and *Freedom and Determination* (1980). In these books he argues against a positivistic view of human **behavior**, insisting that reference to mere **causation** cannot explain human action, since **human beings** act intentionally, in accordance with reasons, which are not reducible to causes.

He was also a public intellectual in Finland and Scandinavia generally, writing on various social and cultural issues. These writings covered authors such as **Oswald Spengler**, **Fyodor Dostoevsky**, and **Leo Tolstoy** as well as what he saw as the harmful effects of **science and scientism**. In 1961 he became a member of the prestigious Academy of Finland. A volume devoted to him in the Library of Living Philosophers series was published in 1989.

Z

ZETTEL. A book made up from remarks written by Wittgenstein and then cut from the pages on which they were originally typed and kept in a box-file (the title means "Slips of Paper"). These remarks date mostly from the years 1945–1948 and deal with similar topics to those addressed in the ***Philosophical Investigations***, which was written around the same time. The earliest remark comes from 1929, the latest (as far as it is possible to tell) from August 1948. It seems that Wittgenstein kept these remarks together because he considered them particularly important. If he had lived longer, at least some of them might have become part of the *Philosophical Investigations*, which was not quite finished when he died. It is thus considered an important source for **understanding** Wittgenstein's mature **thinking**.

Bibliography

CONTENTS

INTRODUCTION

Wittgenstein wrote a great deal but published very little during his lifetime. Since then almost everything philosophical that he wrote has been published in some form, and much of it has been translated into English. There is also an enormous secondary literature. In 1990 Guido Frongia and Brian McGuinness published a 438-page bibliographical guide to Wittgenstein, and of course much has been published on him since then. What follows is therefore inevitably incomplete, but it is hoped that it will be useful nonetheless.

The most important books by Wittgenstein are generally agreed to be his *Tractatus Logico-Philosophicus* and *Philosophical Investigations*. Wittgenstein wanted the latter to be published alongside the former, and his later work is probably best understood in comparison with his earlier work. The *Tractatus* and other early work will be easiest understood by those somewhat familiar with the work of Bertrand Russell, Gottlob Frege, and Arthur Schopenhauer. To understand these philosophers it will help to know Immanuel Kant, and to understand him it helps to know the work of such philosophers as David Hume and Gottfried Leibniz. And so on back through the history of Western philosophy. Indeed Wittgenstein often refers to philosophy in general, seemingly meaning the entire Western tradition from Plato onward, so those coming to Wittgenstein's work from outside philosophy will have their work cut out in making sense of what he says.

This is a problem for philosophers too, the *Tractatus* being dense and technical while the *Investigations* is much easier to read but often hard to understand in the sense of seeing its point. For this reason secondary literature is especially valuable for the student of Wittgenstein's work, but there is considerable disagreement about how to interpret it, and readers should beware of having their understanding prejudiced by relying too heavily on just one commentator. Wittgenstein did not want to spare his readers the work of thinking for themselves, and there is no real orthodoxy to rely on in interpreting what he meant.

Having said that, it is possible to give some guidance with regard to the main figures in Wittgenstein scholarship. Wittgenstein himself appointed G. E. M. Anscombe, Rush Rhees, and G. H. von Wright as his literary executors, so presumably he had some regard for their appreciation of his work. None of them, though, wrote a general, introductory book on Wittgenstein's philosophy as a whole. Anscombe's book on the *Tractatus* is highly regarded, but hardly easy reading. The beginner would be better off turning to works by the second generation of Wittgenstein scholars.

Rhees taught at the University College of Swansea, in Wales, and effectively founded what has become known as the Swansea school of Wittgensteinianism. This school includes Peter Winch, who taught for many years at the University of Illinois, and others such as H. O. Mounce, Ilham Dilman, and D. Z. Phillips. Mounce's introduction to the *Tractatus* is the most readable, and one of the best, on the subject. Phillips edited the leading journal for Wittgensteinian philosophers (*Philosophical Investigations*) and published numerous books of his own, especially on Wittgenstein and religion.

Cora Diamond, who studied with Anscombe, was also briefly at Swansea. She is now primarily associated with the so-called new Wittgensteinians (who of course think of their interpretation as right rather than new), along with James Conant. Diamond and Conant are best known for their unorthodox reading of the *Tractatus*, according to which the differences between the early and the late Wittgensteins, though real, are not nearly as great as has generally been supposed. The label "new" was applied (in the anthology *The New Wittgenstein*) to a whole group of philosophers, though, including such big names as Stanley Cavell and John McDowell. If a label must be given to this group, "American" might be better than "new," given the location of most of the philosophers in question.

Far closer to something like orthodoxy are some of the Wittgensteinians based in England. These include Anthony Kenny and Ray Monk (author of an excellent biography of Wittgenstein). Hans-Johann Glock (who wrote the very useful *Wittgenstein Dictionary* for Blackwell) could also be included in this group, although he now teaches at the University of Zurich. Foremost among these scholars is P. M. S. Hacker, who has produced, with Gordon Baker, a detailed commentary on the *Investigations*, and who continues to publish important works at an amazing rate since his split with Baker. Hacker has also written one of the best-known general books on Wittgenstein's philosophy (*Insight and Illusion*), and contributed a powerful counterblast at the end of *The New Wittgenstein*. Wittgenstein's friend and student Norman Malcolm would best fit in this group too.

Georg von Wright has made Scandinavia also a fertile place for Wittgenstein studies. Preeminent today are the Finnish philosophers Jaako Hintikka (who teaches at Boston University) and Lars Hertzberg (professor emeritus at Åbo Akademi University in Finland).

It should be stressed that these groups are rather artificial constructions and of limited use. It should not be thought that Kenny agrees with Hacker on everything, for instance. Nor is geography as reliable a guide as labels such as "American Wittgensteinians" and "Swansea Wittgensteinians" suggest. By no means do all American Wittgenstein scholars agree with Diamond and Conant, and not all English Wittgenstein scholars are orthodox. Oxford University's Stephen Mulhall is a new and important voice in the conversation about Wittgenstein, and his "new Wittgensteinian" former student Rupert Read is now at the heart of the School of Philosophy at the University of East Anglia. In short, any simplified guide to Wittgensteinians by location is likely to be misleading.

What matters is the work. The beginner should perhaps read Mounce on the *Tractatus* and Hacker's *Insight and Illusion* first, in conjunction with, or perhaps after, reading the *Tractatus* and the *Investigations*, but bear in mind that their views are by no means universally held. A good next step would be to read *The New Wittgenstein*. Also helpful are *Wittgenstein's Vienna* by Allan Janik and Stephen Toulmin, which gives an account of the cultural background to Wittgenstein's life and work; *Wittgenstein's Philosophical Investigations* by William H. Brenner, a clear introduction to Wittgenstein's later work, much praised by Cora Diamond; and *Wittgenstein: An Introduction* by Joachim Schulte, covering the whole of Wittgenstein's work and called "the best available introduction to Wittgenstein's philosophy" by the noted scholar Newton Garver. The most painless introduction to Wittgenstein without dumbing down would probably be to read Malcolm's short and sweet memoir, then Brenner and Schulte. Edward Kanterian's account of the relation between Wittgenstein's life and thought in his *Ludwig Wittgenstein* is worth mentioning here too.

There is also an ever-growing supply of overviews and other work on the internet. The best of this work can be found via such sites as "Wittgenstein News" (http://wittgenstein-news.org/), the website of the British Wittgenstein Society (http://www.editor.net/BWS/), and "The Ludwig Wittgenstein Page" (www.helsinki.fi/~tuschano/lw/). The first of these websites is provided by the Wittgenstein Archives at the University of Bergen, Norway. My translation of the *Tractatus*, which includes a commentary and guide to the secondary literature, is available online at http://tractatusblog.blogspot.com/. There are several active Wittgenstein-related blogs, too, including Lars Hertzberg's "Language is things we do" (http://languageisthingswedo.blogspot.com/) and Kelly Dean Jolley's "Quantum Est In Rebus Inane" (http://kellydeanjolley.com/).

Other universities and libraries with notable Wittgenstein collections include the Wittgenstein Archive in Cambridge, England, the Wren Library of Trinity College (also in Cambridge), the Bodleian Library in Oxford, and the Austrian National Library in Vienna. The archive in Cambridge has the world's largest collection of photographs and letters relating to Wittgenstein's life. The Wren Library has most of his original manuscripts. The Bodleian has two, and the Austrian National Library has all the rest. The Bergen Electronic Edition of Wittgenstein's *Nachlass* is available on CD-ROM from Oxford University Press.

New scholarly work on, or inspired by, Wittgenstein can be found most obviously in the journals *Philosophical Investigations* (published by Blackwell in Oxford, England), the *Nordic Wittgenstein Review* (published by De Gruyter in Berlin, Germany, and available in Open Access form online at http://www.nordicwittgensteinreview.com), and *Wittgenstein-Studien* (published by Peter Lang in Frankfurt, Germany). These journals are dedicated specifically to Wittgenstein-related work. Other journals that also publish relevant work include *The Philosophical Quarterly*, *The European Journal of Philosophy*, *Philosophy*, and *The British Journal of Aesthetics*.

WITTGENSTEIN TEXTS IN GERMAN

Bemerkungen über die Farben. Frankfurt: Suhrkamp, 1984.

Bemerkungen zu den Grundlagen der Mathematik. Frankfurt: Suhrkamp, 1974.

Bemerkungen zur Philosophie der Psychologie. Frankfurt: Suhrkamp, 1984.

Eine Philosophische Betrachtung. Ed. Rush Rhees. *Schriften* 5. Frankfurt: Suhrkamp, 1970. 117–237.

Geheime Tagebücher. Ed. W. Baum. Vienna: Turia & Kant, 1991.

Letzte Schriften zur Philosophie der Psychologie. Frankfurt: Suhrkamp, 1984.

Logisch-Philosophische Abhandlung. Kritische Edition. Ed. Brian McGuinness and Joachim Schulte. Frankfurt: Suhrkamp, 1989.

Ludwig Wittgenstein und der Wiener Kreis. Frankfurt: Suhrkamp, 1984.

Philosophische Bemerkungen. Frankfurt: Suhrkamp, 1984.

Philosophische Grammatik. Frankfurt: Suhrkamp, 1984.

Philosophische Untersuchungen: Kritisch-Genetische Edition. Frankfurt: Suhrkamp, 2001.

Tagebücher 1914–16. Frankfurt: Suhrkamp, 1984.

Über Gewißheit. Frankfurt: Suhrkamp, 1984.

Vermischte Bemerkungen. Frankfurt: Suhrkamp, 1984.

Wörterbuch für Volksschulen. Vienna: Hölder-Pichler-Tempsky, 1926.

WITTGENSTEIN TEXTS IN ENGLISH (INCLUDING GERMAN-ENGLISH PARALLEL TEXTS)

The Big Typescript: TS 213. Trans. C. G. Luckhardt and Maximilian A. E. Aue. Malden, MA: Wiley-Blackwell, 2005.

The Blue and Brown Books. Oxford: Basil Blackwell, 1958.

Culture and Value: A Selection from the Posthumous Remains. Trans. Peter Winch. Ed. G. H. von Wright in collaboration with Heikki Nyman. Oxford: Basil Blackwell, 1998.

Last Writings on the Philosophy of Psychology Volume I: Preliminary Studies for Part II of Philosophical Investigations. Trans. C. G. Luckhardt and Maximilian A. E. Aue. Ed. G. H. von Wright and Heikki Nyman. Oxford: Blackwell, 1982.

Last Writings on the Philosophy of Psychology Volume II: The Inner and the Outer 1949–1951. Trans. C. G. Luckhardt and Maximilian A. E. Aue. Ed. G. H. von Wright and Heikki Nyman. Oxford: Blackwell, 1992.

Lectures and Conversations on Aesthetics, Psychology and Religious Belief. Compiled from notes taken by Yorick Smythies, Rush Rhees, and James Taylor. Ed. Cyril Barrett. Oxford: Basil Blackwell, 1966.

Ludwig Wittgenstein and the Vienna Circle. Notes recorded by Friedrich Waismann. Ed. B. F. McGuinness. Oxford: Blackwell, 1979.

Ludwig Wittgenstein: Public and Private Occasions. Ed. James C. Klagge and Alfred Nordmann. Lanham, MD: Rowman & Littlefield, 2003.

Notebooks 1914–1916. 2nd ed. Trans. G. E. M. Anscombe. Ed. G.H. von Wright and Anscombe. Oxford: Blackwell, 1979.

On Certainty. Trans. D. Paul and G. E. M. Anscombe. Ed. Anscombe and G. H. von Wright. Oxford: Blackwell, 1969.

Philosophical Grammar. Trans. Anthony Kenny. Ed. Rush Rhees. Oxford: Blackwell, 1974.

Philosophical Investigations. Philosophical Investigations. The German text, with an English translation by G. E. M. Anscombe, P. M. S. Hacker, and Joachim Schulte. Revised 4th edition by P. M. S. Hacker and Joachim Schulte. Oxford: Wiley-Blackwell, 2009.

Philosophical Occasions 1912–1951. Contains reprints of: "Review of P. Coffey, *The Science of Logic*," "Some Remarks on Logical Form," "A Lecture on Ethics," and various notes for and from Wittgenstein's lectures. Ed. James Klagge and Alfred Nordmann. IN: Hackett, 1993.

Philosophical Remarks. Trans. R. Hargreaves and R. White. Ed. Rush Rhees. Oxford: Blackwell, 1975.

Proto-Tractatus. Trans. D. F. Pears and B. F. McGuinness, with an introduction by G. H. von Wright. Ed. McGuinness, T. Nyberg, and von Wright. London: Routledge & Kegan Paul, 1971.

Remarks on Colour. 2nd ed. Trans. Linda L. McAlister and Margarete Schättle. Ed. G. E. M. Anscombe. Oxford: Blackwell, 1980.

Remarks on the Foundations of Mathematics. 2nd ed. Trans. G. E. M. Anscombe. Ed. G. H. von Wright, Rush Rhees, and Anscombe. Oxford: Blackwell, 1978.

Remarks on the Philosophy of Psychology, Volume I. Trans. G. E. M. Anscombe. Ed. Anscombe and G. H. von Wright. Oxford: Blackwell, 1980.

Remarks on the Philosophy of Psychology, Volume II. Trans. C. G. Luckhardt and M. A. E. Aue. Ed. G. H. von Wright and H. Nyman. Oxford: Blackwell, 1980.

Tractatus Logico-Philosophicus. Trans. D. F. Pears and B. F. McGuinness. London: Routledge & Kegan Paul, 1961.

The Voices of Wittgenstein: The Vienna Circle. Ludwig Wittgenstein and Friedrich Waismann. Ed. Gordon Baker. Abingdon, UK, and New York: Routledge, 2013.

Wittgenstein's Lectures, Cambridge 1930–1932. From the notes of J. King and Desmond Lee. Ed. Lee. Oxford: Blackwell, 1980.

Wittgenstein's Lectures, Cambridge 1932–1935. From the notes of Alice Ambrose and Margaret MacDonald. Ed. Ambrose. Oxford: Blackwell, 1979.

Wittgenstein's Lectures on the Foundations of Mathematics, Cambridge 1939. From the notes of R. G. Bosanquet, Norman Malcolm, Rush Rhees, and Yorick Smythies. Ed. Cora Diamond. Chicago: University of Chicago Press, 1975.

Wittgenstein's Lectures on Philosophical Psychology 1946–47. Notes by Peter Geach, K. J. Shah, and A. C. Jackson. Ed. Geach. Hassocks: Harvester Press, 1988.

Zettel. 2nd ed. Trans. G. E. M. Anscombe. Ed. Anscombe and G. H. von Wright. Oxford: Basil Blackwell, 1967.

CORRESPONDENCE

Briefe. Ed. B. F. McGuinness and G. H. von Wright. Frankfurt: Suhrkamp, 1980.

Briefe an Ludwig von Ficker. Ed. G. H. von Wright and W. Methlagl. Salzburg: Müller, 1969.

Letters from Ludwig Wittgenstein, with a Memoir by Paul Engelmann. Trans. L. Furtmüller. Ed. B. F. McGuinness. Oxford: Blackwell, 1967.

Letters to C. K. Ogden. Ed. G. H. von Wright. Oxford: Blackwell, 1973.

Letters to Russell, Keynes and Moore. Ed. G. H. von Wright. Oxford: Blackwell, 1974.

BIBLIOGRAPHICAL AIDS

Biggs, Michael A. R., and Alois Pichler. *Wittgenstein: Two Source Catalogues and a Bibliography: Catalogues of the Published Texts and of the Published Diagrams, Each Related to Its Sources*. Bergen, Norway: Wittgensteinarkivet ved Universitetet i Bergen, 1993.

Biletzki, Anat. *(Over)Interpreting Wittgenstein.* Dordrecht, Netherlands: Kluwer Academic Publishers, 2003.

Frongia, Guido, and Brian McGuinness. *Wittgenstein: A Bibliographical Guide*. Cambridge, MA: Blackwell, 1990.

Gabel, Gernot Uwe. *Ludwig Wittgenstein: A Comprehensive Bibliography of International Theses and Dissertations, 1933–1985.* Cologne: 1988.

Lapointe, François. *Ludwig Wittgenstein: A Comprehensive Bibliography*. Westport, CT: Greenwood Press, 1980.

Philipp, Peter. *Bibliographie zur Wittgenstein-Literatur*. Bergen: Working Papers from the Wittgenstein Archives at the University of Bergen 13, 1996.

Shanker, V. A., and S. G. Shanker. *A Wittgenstein Bibliography*. Wolfeboro, NH: Croom Helm, 1986.

Stagaman, David J., James Kraft, and Kristin Sutton. *Wittgenstein & Religion: A Bibliography of Articles, Books, and Theses in the Twentieth Century That Relate the Philosophy of Ludwig Wittgenstein to the Study of Religion and Theology*. Quezon City, Philippines: Office of Research and Publications Ateneo de Manila University, 2001.

INTRODUCTORY WORKS

Addis, Mark. Wittgenstein: A Guide for the Perplexed. London: Continuum, 2006.

Ahmed, Arif. *Wittgenstein's Philosophical Investigations: A Critical Guide*. Cambridge: Cambridge University Press, 2010.

Ayer, A. J. *Wittgenstein*. New York: Random House, 1985.

Brenner, William H. *Wittgenstein's Philosophical Investigations*. Albany: State University of New York Press, 1999.

Child, William. *Wittgenstein*. New York: Routledge, 2011.

Coope, Christopher, Peter Geach, Timothy Potts, and Roger White (eds.). *A Wittgenstein Workbook*. Berkeley and Los Angeles: University of California Press, 1970.

Fogelin, Robert J. *Wittgenstein*. 2nd ed. New York: Routledge, 1987.

Grayling, A. C. *Wittgenstein: A Very Short Introduction*. Oxford: Oxford University Press, 2001.

Hacker, P. M. S. Insight and Illusion: Themes in the Philosophy of Wittgenstein. Bristol, UK: Thoemmes Press, 1997.

———. *Wittgenstein: On Human Nature*. London: Phoenix, 1997.

Hallett, Garth. *A Companion to Wittgenstein's "Philosophical Investigations."* Ithaca, NY: Cornell University Press, 1977.

Hamilton, Andy. *Routledge Philosophy Guidebook to Wittgenstein and On Certainty*. New York: Routledge, 2014.

Hanfling, Oswald. *Wittgenstein's Later Philosophy*. Albany: State University of New York Press, 1989.

Heaton, John, Judy Groves, and Richard Appignanesi. *Introducing Wittgenstein*. Cambridge: Icon Books, 1999.

Janik, Allan, and Stephen Edelston Toulmin. *Wittgenstein's Vienna*. New York: Simon and Schuster, 1973.

Jolley, Kelly Dean. *Wittgenstein: Key Concepts*. Durham: Acumen, 2010.

Kenny, Anthony John Patrick. *Wittgenstein*. Cambridge, MA: Harvard University Press, 1973.

Kuusela, Oskari, and Marie McGinn, eds. *The Oxford Handbook of Wittgenstein*. Oxford: Oxford University Press, 2011.

McGinn, Marie. *Elucidating the Tractatus: Wittgenstein's Early Philosophy of Logic and Language*. Oxford: Oxford University Press, 2006.

———. *The Routledge Philosophy Guidebook to Wittgenstein and the Philosophical Investigations*. London: Routledge, 1997.

McManus, Denis. *The Enchantment of Words: Wittgenstein's Tractatus Logico-Philosophicus*. New York: Oxford University Press, 2006.

Monk, Ray. *How to Read Wittgenstein*. New York: Norton, 2005.

Morris, Michael. *Routledge Philosophy Guidebook to Wittgenstein and the Tractatus Logico-Philosophicus*. New York: Routledge, 2008.

Mounce, H. O. *Wittgenstein's Tractatus: An Introduction*. Chicago: University of Chicago Press, 1981.

Nordmann, Alfred. *Wittgenstein's Tractatus: An Introduction*. Cambridge: Cambridge University Press, 2005.

Pears, David Francis. *Ludwig Wittgenstein*. New York: Viking Press, 1970.

Peterman, James F. *Philosophy as Therapy: An Interpretation and Defense of Wittgenstein's Later Philosophical Project*. Albany: State University of New York Press, 1992.

Peursen, Cornelis Anthonie van. *Ludwig Wittgenstein: An Introduction to His Philosophy*. London: Faber, 1969.

Pitcher, George. *The Philosophy of Wittgenstein*. Englewood Cliffs, NJ: Prentice-Hall, 1964.

Pole, David. *The Later Philosophy of Wittgenstein; A Short Introduction, with an Epilogue on John Wisdom*. London, University of London: Athlone Press, 1963.

Ross, John J. *Reading Wittgenstein's Philosophical Investigations: A Beginner's Guide*. Lanham, MD: Lexington Books, 2009.

Schroeder, Severin. *Wittgenstein: The Way out of the Fly-Bottle*. Malden, MA: Polity Press, 2006.

Schulte, Joachim. *Wittgenstein: An Introduction*. Albany: State University of New York Press, 1992.

Sheehan, Sean. *Wittgenstein*. London: Hodder & Stoughton Educational, 2001.

Sluga, Hans D. *Wittgenstein*. Malden, MA: Wiley-Blackwell, 2011.

Stern, David G. *Wittgenstein's Philosophical Investigations: An Introduction*. New York: Cambridge University Press, 2004.

Strathern, Paul. *Wittgenstein in 90 Minutes*. Chicago: I. R. Dee, 1996.

Tejedor, Chon. *Starting with Wittgenstein*. New York: Continuum, 2011.

White, Roger M. *Wittgenstein's Tractatus Logico-Philosophicus: Reader's Guide*. New York: Continuum, 2006.

BIOGRAPHIES AND BACKGROUND MATERIAL

Åmås, Knut Olav, and Rolf Larsen. *Det Stille Alvoret: Ludwig Wittgenstein I Norge 1913–1950*. Oslo: Norske samlaget, 1994.

Bartley, William Warren. *Wittgenstein*. London: Cresset, 1986.

Baum, Wilhelm. *Ludwig Wittgenstein*. Berlin: Colloquium Verlag, 1985.

Bouwsma, O. K. *Wittgenstein: Conversations 1949–1951*. Indianapolis: Hackett, 1986.

Chauviré, Christiane. *Ludwig Wittgenstein*. Paris: Seuil, 1989.

Flowers, F. A., ed. *Portraits of Wittgenstein*. Bristol: Thoemmes Press, 1999.

Fredriksson, Gunnar. *Wittgenstein*. Stockholm: Bonnier, 1993.

Grasshoff, Gerd. *Wittgenstein's World of Mechanics: Including Transcripts of Lectures by Wittgenstein's Teacher Joseph Petzoldt and Related Texts on Mechanics*. Vienna: Springer, 2006.

Janik, Allan, and Hans Veigl. *Wittgenstein in Vienna: A Biographical Excursion through the City and Its History*. Vienna: Springer Verlag, 1999.

Kanterian, Edward. *Ludwig Wittgenstein*. London: Reaktion Books, 2007.

Klagge, James Carl, ed. *Wittgenstein: Biography and Philosophy*. Cambridge: Cambridge University Press, 2001.

———. *Wittgenstein in Exile*. Cambridge, MA: MIT Press, 2011.

Landini, Gregory. *Wittgenstein's Apprenticeship with Russell*. Cambridge: Cambridge University Press, 2007.

Leitner, Bernhard, and Hermine Wittgenstein. *The Architecture of Ludwig Wittgenstein: A Documentation, with Excerpts from the Family Recollections by Hermine*. New York: London Academy Editions, 1995.

Malcolm, Norman, and G. H. von Wright. *Ludwig Wittgenstein: A Memoir*. Oxford: Oxford University Press, 1984.

McGuinness, Brian. *Wittgenstein, a Life: Young Ludwig, 1889–1921*. Berkeley: University of California Press, 1988.

Monk, Ray. *Ludwig Wittgenstein: The Duty of Genius*. New York: Free Press Maxwell Macmillan International, 1990.

Oxaal, Ivar. *On The Trail to Wittgenstein's Hut: The Historical Background of the Tractatus Logico-Philosophicus*. New Brunswick, NJ: Transaction Publishers, 2011.

Pinsent, David Hume. *A Portrait of Wittgenstein as a Young Man: From the Diary of David Hume Pinsent 1912–1914*. Ed. G. H. von Wright. Oxford: Blackwell, 1990.

Rhees, Rush. *Ludwig Wittgenstein, Personal Recollections*. Totowa, NJ: Rowman & Littlefield, 1981.

Somavilla, Ilse, ed. *Begegnungen Mit Wittgenstein: Ludwig Hänsels Tagebücher 1918–1919 und 1921–1922*. Innsbruck: Haymon Verlag, 2012.

Sterrett, Susan G. *Wittgenstein Flies a Kite: A Story of Models of Wings and Models of the World*. New York: Pi Press, 2006.

Wall, Richard. *Wittgenstein in Ireland*. London: Reaktion, 2000.

Wittgenstein, Hermine, and Rush Rhees. *Recollections of Wittgenstein*. Oxford: Oxford University Press, 1984.

WITTGENSTEIN AND AESTHETICS

Abrams, M. H., and Michael Fischer. *Doing Things with Texts: Essays in Criticism and Critical Theory*. New York: W. W. Norton, 1989.

Allen, Richard, and Malcolm Turvey, eds. *Wittgenstein, Theory and the Arts*. London: Routledge, 2001.

Appelqvist, Hanne. *Wittgenstein and the Conditions of Musical Communication*. Helsinki: Hakapaino Oy, 2008.

Arbo, Alessandro, Michel Du, and Sabine Plaud, eds. *Wittgenstein & Aesthetics: Perspectives & Debates*. Frankfurt am Main: Ontos Verlag, 2012.

Bering, Kunibert. *Die Rolle der Kunst in der Philosophie Ludwig Wittgensteins, Impulse für die Kunstgeschichte?* Essen: Die Blaue Eule, 1986.

Bossart, Yves. *Ästhetik nach Wittgenstein: Eine Systematische Rekonstruktion*. Berlin: De Gruyter, 2013.

Bru, Sascha, Wolfgang Huemer, and Daniel Steuer, eds. *Wittgenstein Reading*. Boston, MA: De Gruyter, 2013.

Eldridge, Richard Thomas. *Literature, Life, and Modernity*. New York: Columbia University Press, 2008.

Eldridge, Richard Thomas, and Bernard Rhie, eds. *Stanley Cavell and Literary Studies: Consequences of Skepticism*. New York: Continuum, 2011.

Gibson, John, and Wolfgang Huemer. *The Literary Wittgenstein*. New York: Routledge, 2004.

Gmür, Felix. *Ästhetik bei Wittgenstein: Über Sagen und Zeigen*. Freiburg: K. Alber, 2000.

Hagberg, Garry. *Art as Language: Wittgenstein, Meaning, and Aesthetic Theory*. Ithaca, NY: Cornell University Press, 1995.

Haller, Rudolf, ed. *Aesthetics*. Vienna: Hölder-Pichler-Tempsky, 1984.

Högel, Klaus-Peter. *Ludwig Wittgenstein, Architekt*. Vienna: Institut für Baukunst und Bauaufnahmen, Technische Universität Wien, 1993.

Johannessen, Kjell S., and Tore Nordenstam, eds. *Wittgenstein: Aesthetics and Transcendental Philosophy: Proceedings of a Symposium at Bergen (Norway) 1980*. Vienna: Hölder-Pichler-Tempsky, 1981.

Kaspar, Rudolf F. *Wittgensteins Ästhetik: Eine Studie*. Vienna: Europaverlag, 1992.

Klebes, Martin. *Wittgenstein's Novels*. New York: Routledge, 2006.

Lamarque, Peter. "Wittgenstein, Literature, and the Idea of a Practice." *British Journal of Aesthetics* 50, no. 4 (2010): 375–388.

Last, Nana. *Wittgenstein's House: Language, Space, & Architecture*. New York: Fordham University Press, 2008.

Le Rider, Jacques, and Gérard Raulet, eds. *Verabschiedung der (Post-)Moderne?: Eine Interdisziplinäre Debatte*. Tübingen: Narr, 1987.

Lee, Edward N., and Maurice Mandelbaum, eds. *Phenomenology and Existentialism*. Baltimore, MD: Johns Hopkins Press, 1967.

Lewis, Peter. *Wittgenstein, Aesthetics, and Philosophy*. Burlington, VT: Ashgate, 2003.

Lütterfelds, Wilhelm and Stefan Majetschak, eds. *"Ethik und Ästhetik sind Eins": Beiträge zu Wittgensteins Ästhetik und Kunstphilosophie*. New York: Peter Lang, 2007.

Miller, J. Hillis. *Speech Acts in Literature*. Stanford, CA: Stanford University Press, 2001.

Mulhall, Stephen. *The Self and Its Shadows: A Book of Essays on Individuality as Negation in Philosophy and the Arts*. Oxford: Oxford University Press, 2013.

Paden, Roger. *Mysticism and Architecture: Wittgenstein and the Meanings of the Palais Stonborough*. Lanham, MD: Lexington, 2007.

Poisson, Céline, ed. *Penser, Dessiner, Construire: Wittgenstein et l'Architecture*. Paris: Éditions de l'Éclat, 2007.

Read, Rupert J., and Jerry Goodenough, eds. *Film As Philosophy: Essays in Cinema after Wittgenstein and Cavell*. New York: Palgrave Macmillan, 2005.

Schalkwyk, David. *Literature and the Touch of the Real*. Newark: University of Delaware Press, 2004.

Schwarte, Ludger. *Die Regeln der Intuition: Kunstphilosophie nach Adorno, Heidegger und Wittgenstein*. Munich: W. Fink, 2000.

Scruton, Roger. "A Bit of Help from Wittgenstein." *British Journal of Aesthetics* 51, no. 3 (2011): 309–320.

Shaffer, E. S. *The Third Culture: Literature and Science*. Berlin: Walter de Gruyter, 1998.

Smith, Paul, and Carolyn Wilde, eds. *A Companion to Art Theory*. Oxford: Blackwell, 2002.

Steiner, Robert. *Toward a Grammar of Abstraction: Modernity, Wittgenstein, and the Paintings of Jackson Pollock*. University Park: Pennsylvania State University Press, 1992.

Thommes, Armin. *Ludwig Wittgenstein über Wahrheit und Kunst*. Frankfurt: Peter Lang, 1995.

Wiesing, Lambert. *Stil Statt Wahrheit: Kurt Schwitters und Ludwig Wittgenstein über Ästhetische Lebensformen*. Munich: W. Fink, 1991.

Ziarek, Ewa Plonowska. *The Rhetoric of Failure: Deconstruction of Skepticism, Reinvention of Modernism*. Albany: State University of New York Press, 1995.

WITTGENSTEIN AND EPISTEMOLOGY

Coliva, Annalisa. *Moore and Wittgenstein: Scepticism, Certainty, and Common Sense*. New York: Palgrave Macmillan, 2010.

McManus, Denis, ed. *Wittgenstein and Scepticism*. New York: Routledge, 2013.

Moyal-Sharrock, Danièle, ed. *The Third Wittgenstein: The Post-Investigations Works*. Burlington, VT: Ashgate, 2004.

———. *Understanding Wittgenstein's On Certainty*. New York: Palgrave Macmillan, 2004.

WITTGENSTEIN AND ETHICS

Audi, Paul. *Supériorité de L'éthique de Schopenhauer à Wittgenstein*. Paris: Presses Universitaires de France, 1999.

Ayer, A. J. *Freedom and Morality and Other Essays*. Oxford: Clarendon Press, 1984.

Barnes, James William. *Wittgenstein and Ethics*. Newcastle upon Tyne: University of Newcastle upon Tyne, 1989.

Brenner, William H. "Chesterton, Wittgenstein and the Foundations of Ethics." *Philosophical Investigations* 14, no. 4 (1991): 311–23.

Cahill, Kevin. *The Fate of Wonder: Wittgenstein's Critique of Metaphysics and Modernity*. New York: Columbia University Press, 2011.

Cavalier, Robert J. *Ludwig Wittgenstein's Tractatus Logico-Philosophicus: A Transcendental Critique of Ethics*. Washington, DC: University Press of America, 1980.

Crary, Alice, ed. *Wittgenstein and the Moral Life: Essays in Honor of Cora Diamond*. Cambridge, MA: MIT Press, 2007.

Daly, Cahal B. *Moral Philosophy in Britain: From Bradley to Wittgenstein*. Blackrock, Ireland: Four Courts Press, 1996.

Donatelli, Piergiorgio. *Wittgenstein e L'etica*. Rome: Laterza, 1998.

Edwards, James C. *Ethics without Philosophy: Wittgenstein and the Moral Life*. Tampa: University Presses of Florida, 1982.

Elliott, Carl. *A Philosophical Disease: Bioethics, Culture, and Identity*. New York: Routledge, 1999.

———. *Slow Cures and Bad Philosophers: Essays on Wittgenstein, Medicine, and Bioethics*. Durham, NC: Duke University Press, 2001.

Ermann, M. David, Mary B. Williams, and Michele S. Shauf, eds. *Computers, Ethics, and Society*. 2nd ed. Oxford: Oxford University Press, 1997.

Fonteneau, Françoise. *L'éthique du Silence: Wittgenstein et Lacan*. Paris: Seuil, 1999.

Forsberg, Niklas, Mikel Burley, and Nora Hamalainen, eds. *Language, Ethics and Animal Life: Wittgenstein and Beyond*. New York: Bloomsbury, 2012.

Gaita, Raimond, ed. *Value and Understanding: Essays for Peter Winch*. London: Routledge, 1990.

Gillett, Grant. "Virtue and Truth in Clinical Science." *The Journal of Medicine and Philosophy* 20, no. 3 (1995): 285–298.

Gleeson, Andrew, ed. *Philosophical Papers. Special Issue: Ethics in the Light of Wittgenstein* 31, no. 3 (2002).

Grieco, Agnese. *Die Ethische Übung: Ethik und Sprachkritik bei Wittgenstein und Sokrates*. Berlin: Lukas Verlag, 1996.

Günther, Klaus. *The Sense of Appropriateness: Application Discourses in Morality and Law*. Albany: State University of New York Press, 1993.

Gustafsson, Ylva, Camilla Kronqvist, and Hannes Nykanen, eds. *Ethics and the Philosophy of Culture: Wittgensteinian Approaches*. Newcastle upon Tyne: Cambridge Scholars Publishing, 2013.

Iczkovits, Yaniv. *Wittgenstein's Ethical Thought*. New York: Palgrave Macmillan, 2012.

Johnston, Paul. *The Contradictions of Modern Moral Philosophy: Ethics after Wittgenstein*. London: Routledge, 1999.

———. *Wittgenstein and Moral Philosophy*. London: Routledge, 1989.

Kallenberg, Brad J. *Ethics as Grammar: Changing the Postmodern Subject*. Notre Dame, IN: University of Notre Dame Press, 2001.

Litwack, Eric B. *Wittgenstein and Value: The Quest for Meaning*. New York: Continuum, 2009.

Lovibond, Sabina. *Realism and Imagination in Ethics*. Minneapolis: University of Minnesota Press, 1983.

Lüttenfelds, Wilhelm. *Globales Ethos: Wittgensteins Sprachspiele Interkultureller Moral und Religion*. Würzburg: Königshausen & Neumann, 2000.

Marini, Sergio. *Etica e Religione nel "Primo Wittgenstein."* Milan: Vita e pensiero; Università Cattolica del Sacro Cuore, 1989.

Matthews, Gareth B. *The Augustinian Tradition*. Berkeley: University of California Press, 1999.

McDonald, Henry. *The Normative Basis of Culture: A Philosophical Inquiry*. Baton Rouge: Louisiana State University Press, 1986.

Miner, Robert C. "What Does Obligation Add to Virtue-Descriptions? Some Uses of Anscombe's Law/Game Analogy." *Christian Bioethics* 14, no. 2 (2008): 165–174.

Morscher, Edgar, and Rudolf Stranzinger, eds. *Ethics: Foundations, Problems, and Applications: Proceedings of the Fifth International Wittgenstein Symposium, 25th to 31st August 1980, Kirchberg Am Wechsel (Austria)*. Vienna: Hölder-Pichler-Tempsky, 1981.

O'Connor, Peg. *Morality and Our Complicated Form of Life: Feminist Wittgensteinian Metaethics*. University Park: Pennsylvania State University Press, 2008.

———. *Oppression and Responsibility: A Wittgensteinian Approach to Social Practices and Moral Theory*. University Park: Pennsylvania State University Press, 2002.

Pandey, K. C. *Ludwig Wittgenstein, Ethics and Religion*. Jaipur: Rawat Publications, 2008.

Perissinotto, Luigi, and Vicente Sanfelix, eds. *Doubt, Ethics and Religion: Wittgenstein and the Counter-Enlightenment*. New Brunswick, NJ: Ontos, 2010.

Phillips, D. Z. *Interventions in Ethics*. Albany: State University of New York Press, 1992.

———. *Philosophy's Cool Place*. Ithaca, NY: Cornell University Press, 1999.

Phillips, D. Z., and H. O. Mounce. *Moral Practices*. New York: Schocken Books, 1970.

Reguera, Isidoro. *El Feliz Absurdo de la Ética: (El Wittgenstein Místico)*. Madrid: Tecnos, 1994.

Sádaba, Javier. *La Filosofía Moral Analítica de Wittgenstein a Tugendhat*. Madrid: Mondadori, 1989.

Smith, R. Scott. *Virtue Ethics and Moral Knowledge: Philosophy of Language after MacIntyre and Hauerwas*. Aldershot, UK: Ashgate, 2003.

Stokhof, M. J. B. *World and Life as One: Ethics and Ontology in Wittgenstein's Early Thought*. Stanford, CA: Stanford University Press, 2002.

Themudo, Marina Ramos. *Etica e Sentido: Ensaio de Reinterpretação do Tractatus Logico-Philosophicus de Ludwig Wittgenstein*. Coimbra, Portugal: Livraria Almedina, 1989.

Tilghman, Benjamin R. *Wittgenstein, Ethics, and Aesthetics: The View from Eternity*. Albany: State University of New York Press, 1991.

Tranøy, Knut Erik. *The Moral Import of Science: Essays on Normative Theory, Scientific Activity and Wittgenstein*. Søreidgrend, Norway: Sigma Forlag, 1988.

Williams, Bernard Arthur Owen. *Moral Luck: Philosophical Papers, 1973–1980*. Cambridge: Cambridge University Press, 1981.

Wisnewski, Jeremy. *Wittgenstein and Ethical Inquiry: A Defense of Ethics as Clarification*. New York: Continuum, 2007.

Zhok, Andrea. *L'etica del Metodo: Saggio su Ludwig Wittgenstein*. Milan: Mimesis, 2001.

WITTGENSTEIN AND LANGUAGE

Aaltola, Juhani. *Merkitys Opettamisen Ja Oppimisen Näkökulmasta: Wittgensteinin Myöhäisfilosofian Ja Pragmatismin Valossa*. Jyväskylä: Jyväskylän yliopisto, 1989.

Altieri, Charles. *Act & Quality: A Theory of Literary Meaning and Humanistic Understanding*. Amherst: University of Massachusetts Press, 1981.

Ambrose, Alice, and Morris Lazerowitz. *Ludwig Wittgenstein, Philosophy and Language*. Bristol: Thoemmes Press, 1996.

Ammereller, Erich, and Eugen Fisher, eds. *Wittgenstein at Work: Method in the Philosophical Investigations*. New York: Routledge, 2004.

Arrington, Robert L., and Hans-Johann Glock, eds. *Wittgenstein and Quine*. London: Routledge, 1996.

———. *Wittgenstein's Philosophical Investigations: Text and Context*. London: Routledge, 1991.

Badiou, Alain. *Wittgenstein's Antiphilosophy*. Trans. Bruno Bosteels. Brooklyn, NY: Verso, 2011.

Baghramian, Maria. *Modern Philosophy of Language*. London: J. M. Dent, 1998.

Baker, Gordon P. *Wittgenstein's Method: Neglected Aspects: Essays on Wittgenstein*. Ed. Katherine J. Morris. Malden, MA: Blackwell, 2004.

———, and P. M. S. Hacker. *An Analytical Commentary on the Philosophical Investigations*. Oxford: Blackwell, 1988–2000.

———. *Scepticism, Rules and Language*. Oxford: Blackwell, 1984.

Beaney, Michael. *The Analytic Turn: Analysis in Early Analytic Philosophy and Phenomenology*. New York: Routledge Taylor & Francis Group, 2007.

Beermann, Wilhelm. *Die Radikalisierung der Sprachspiel-Philosophie: Wittgensteins These in "Über Gewissheit" Und Ihre Aktuelle Bedeutung*. Würzburg: Königshausen & Neumann, 1999.

Benarab, Gertrud. *Die Operativ-Pragmatische Basis der Sprachphilosophie Ludwig Wittgensteins: Eine Studie zur Kontinuität der Sprachphilosophie Ludwig Wittgensteins*. Hamburg: [s.n.], 1974.

Biggs, Michael A. R. *Editing Wittgenstein's "Notes on Logic."* Bergen: Wittgensteinarkivet ved Universitetet i Bergen, 1996.

Biletzki, Anat, and Anat Matar. *The Story of Analytic Philosophy: Plot and Heroes*. London: New York, 1998.

Binkley, Timothy. *Wittgenstein's Language*. The Hague: Nijhoff, 1973.

Birnbacher, Dieter. *Die Logik der Kriterien: Analysen Zur Spätphilosophie Wittgensteins*. Hamburg: F. Meiner, 1974.

Black, Max. Companion to Wittgenstein's Tractatus. Ithaca, NY: Cornell University Press, 1964.

Blackburn, Simon. "Symposium: Realism and Truth. Wittgenstein, Wright, Rorty, Minimalism." *Mind* 107, no. 425 (1998): 157–181.

Blair, D. C. *Wittgenstein, Language, and Information: Back to the Rough Ground!* Dordrecht: Springer, 2006.

Block, Irving, ed. *Perspectives on the Philosophy of Wittgenstein*. Cambridge, MA: MIT Press, 1981.

Bogen, James. *Wittgenstein's Philosophy of Language: Some Aspects of Its Development*. New York: Humanities Press, 1972.

Boghossian, Paul A. "The Rule-Following Considerations." *Mind* 98, no. 392 (1989): 507–549.

Bonino, Guido. *The Arrow and the Point: Russell and Wittgenstein's Tractatus*. Frankfurt: Ontos, 2008.

Botwinick, Aryeh. *Wittgenstein and Historical Understanding*. Washington, DC: University Press of America, 1981.

Brockhaus, Richard R. *Pulling up the Ladder: The Metaphysical Roots of Wittgenstein's Tractatus Logico-Philosophicus*. La Salle, IL: Open Court, 1991.

Brosch, Annette. *Die Logik des Tractatus: Eine Logisch-Semantische Untersuchung Dessen, "Was Der Fall" Sein Kann*. Frankfurt: Peter Lang, 1995.

Brown, Cecil H. *Wittgensteinian Linguistics*. The Hague: Mouton, 1974.

Brown, Stuart C. *Language and Reality: Philosophical Investigations 1–137*. Milton Keynes: Open University Press, 1976.

Caleo, Marcello. *Il Tractatus Logico-Philosophicus di L. Wittgenstein: Decifrato*. Salerno: Elea Press, 1996.

Cambi, Fabrizio. *La Recezione della Filosofia del Linguaggio di L. Wittgenstein nell'opera di Ingeborg Bachmann*. Pisa: Giardini, 1979.

Canfield, John V., ed. *The Philosophy of Wittgenstein*. New York: Garland, 1986.

———. *Wittgenstein, Language and World*. Amherst: University of Massachusetts Press, 1981.

Canfield, John V., and Stuart Shanker, eds. *Wittgenstein's Intentions*. New York: Garland, 1993.

Carey, Rosalind. *Russell and Wittgenstein on the Nature of Judgement*. London: Continuum, 2007.

Carruthers, Peter. *The Metaphysics of the Tractatus*. Cambridge: Cambridge University Press, 1990.

———. *Tractarian Semantics: Finding Sense in Wittgenstein's Tractatus*. Oxford: Blackwell, 1989.

Cavell, Stanley. *The Claim of Reason: Wittgenstein, Skepticism, Morality, and Tragedy*. Oxford: Clarendon Press, 1979.

———. *Must We Mean What We Say? A Book of Essays*. New York: Scribner, 1969.

Cerezo, María. *Lenguaje y Lógica en el Tractatus de Wittgenstein: Crítica Interna y Problemas de Interpretación*. Pamplona: Ediciones Universidad de Navarra, 1998.

Cody, Arthur B. *Thinking in Language*. Torino: Edizioni di Filosofia, 1967.

Conant, James. "Wittgenstein on Meaning and Use." *Philosophical Investigations* 21 (1998): 222–251.

Cook, John W. *The Undiscovered Wittgenstein: The Twentieth Century's Most Misunderstood Philosopher*. Amherst, NY: Humanity Books, 2004.

———. *Wittgenstein, Empiricism, and Language*. New York: Oxford University Press, 2000.

Copi, Irving M., and Robert W. Beard, eds. *Essays on Wittgenstein's Tractatus*. New York: Macmillan, 1966.

Costa, Claudio F. *Wittgensteins Beitrag zu einer Sprachphilosophischen Semantik*. Konstanz: Hartung-Gorre Verlag, 1990.

Crary, Alice Marguerite, and Rupert J. Read, eds. *The New Wittgenstein*. London: Routledge, 2000.

Dauber, Kenneth, and Walter Jost, eds. *Ordinary Language Criticism: Literary Thinking after Cavell after Wittgenstein*. Evanston, IL: Northwestern University Press, 2003.

Day, William, and Víctor J. Krebs, eds. *Seeing Wittgenstein Anew*. Cambridge: Cambridge University Press, 2010.

De Mauro, Tullio. *Ludwig Wittgenstein. His Place in the Development of Semantics*. Dordrecht: D. Reidel, 1967.

De Pellegrin, Enzo, ed. *Interactive Wittgenstein: Essays in Memory Of Georg Henrik Von Wright*. Dordrecht: Springer, 2011.

Deloch, Heinke. *Verstehen Fremder Kulturen: Die Relevanz des Spätwerks Ludwig Wittgensteins für die Sozialwissenschaften*. Frankfurt: IKO-Verlag für Interkulturelle Kommunikation, 1997.

Dienstag, J. F. "Wittgenstein among the Savages: Language, Action and Political Theory." *Polity* 30, no. 4 (1998): 579–605.

Dietrich, Rolf-Albert. *Sprache und Wirklichkeit in Wittgensteins Tractatus*. Tübingen: M. Niemeyer, 1973.

Dilman, Ilham. *Language and Reality: Modern Perspectives on Wittgenstein*. Leuven: Peeters, 1998.

———. *Studies in Language and Reason*. Totowa, NJ: Barnes & Noble Books, 1981.

———. *Wittgenstein's Copernican Revolution: The Question of Linguistic Idealism*. New York: Palgrave, 2002.

Donnell, Franklin H., ed. *Aspects of Contemporary American Philosophy*. Würzburg: Physica-Verlag, 1965.

Droescher, Hans-Michael. *Grundlagenstudien zur Linguistik: Wissenschaftstheoret. Untersuchungen D. Sprachphilosoph. Konzeptionen Humboldts, Chomskys U. Wittgensteins*. Heidelberg: Groos, 1980.

Dromm, Keith. *Wittgenstein on Rules and Nature*. London: Continuum, 2008.

Dunlop, Charles E. M. *Philosophical Essays on Dreaming*. Ithaca, NY: Cornell University Press, 1977.

Edelman, John T., ed. *Sense and Reality: Essays out of Swansea*. Frankfurt: Ontos, 2009.

Egidi, Rosaria. *Wittgenstein: Mind and Language*. Dordrecht: Kluwer, 1995.

Engel, S. Morris. *Wittgenstein's Doctrine of the Tyranny of Language: An Historical and Critical Examination of His Blue Book*. The Hague: Martinus Nijhoff, 1975.

Engelmann, Mauro Luiz. *Wittgenstein's Philosophical Development: Phenomenology, Grammar, Method, and the Anthropological View*. New York: Palgrave Macmillan, 2013.

Erickson, Stephen A. *Language and Being: An Analytic Phenomenology*. New Haven, CT: Yale University Press, 1985.

Ertz, Timo-Peter. *Regel und Witz: Wittgensteinsche Perspektiven auf Mathematik, Sprache und Moral*. New York: W. De Gruyter, 2008.

Fahrenwald, Claudia. *Aporien der Sprache: Ludwig Wittgenstein und die Literatur der Moderne*. Vienna: Passagen, 2000.

Faustino, Sílvia. *Wittgenstein: O Eu e Sua Gramática*. São Paulo: Editora Atica, 1995.

Fekete, John. *The Structural Allegory: Reconstructive Encounters with the New French Thought*. Minneapolis: University of Minnesota Press, 1984.

Finch, Henry Le Roy. *Wittgenstein—the Later Philosophy: An Exposition of the Philosophical Investigations*. Atlantic Highlands, NJ: Humanities Press, 1977.

Findlay, J. N. *Language, Mind, and Value; Philosophical Essays*. London: Allen & Unwin, 1963.

Fischer, Eugen. *Philosophical Delusion and Its Therapy: Outline of a Philosophical Revolution*. New York: Routledge, 2011.

Fischer, Hans Rudi. *Sprache und Lebensform: Wittgenstein über Freud und die Geisteskrankheit*. Frankfurt: Athenäum, 1987.

Fleming, Richard. *First Word Philosophy: Wittgenstein-Austin-Cavell, Writings on Ordinary Language Philosophy*. Lewisburg: Bucknell University Press, 2004.

Fogelin, Robert J. *Taking Wittgenstein at His Word: A Textual Study*. Princeton, NJ: Princeton University Press, 2009.

Frascolla, Pasquale. *Understanding Wittgenstein's Tractatus*. New York: Routledge, 2007.

French, Peter A., Theodore Edward Uehling, and Howard K. Wettstein, eds. *The Wittgenstein Legacy*. Notre Dame, IN: University of Notre Dame Press, 1992.

Fretlöh, Sigrid. *Relativismus Versus Universalismus: Zur Kontroverse über Verstehen und Übersetzen in der Angelsächsischen Sprachphilosophie: Winch, Wittgenstein, Quine*. Aachen: Alano/Rader Publikationen, 1989.

Friedlander, Eli. *Signs of Sense: Reading Wittgenstein's Tractatus*. Cambridge, MA: Harvard University Press, 2001.

Gass, William H. *Finding a Form: Essays*. Ithaca, NY: Cornell University Press, 1996.

Gefwert, Christoffer. *Wittgenstein on Thought, Language, and Philosophy: From Theory to Therapy*. Aldershot, UK: Ashgate, 2000.

Geier, Manfred. *Das Sprachspiel der Philosophen: Von Parmenides bis Wittgenstein*. Reinbek bei Hamburg: Rowohlt, 1989.

Gellner, Ernest. *Language and Solitude: Wittgenstein, Malinowski, and the Habsburg Dilemma*. Cambridge: Cambridge University Press, 1998.

———. *Words and Things: An Examination of, and an Attack on, Linguistic Philosophy*. Rev ed. London: Routledge & Kegan Paul, 1979.

Gier, Nicholas F. *Wittgenstein and Phenomenology: A Comparative Study of the Later Wittgenstein, Husserl, Heidegger, and Merleau-Ponty*. Albany: State University of New York Press, 1981.

Glauner, Friedrich. *Sprache und Weltbezug: Adorno, Heidegger, Wittgenstein*. Freiburg: Verlag K. Alber, 1997.

Glendinning, Simon. *On Being with Others: Heidegger, Derrida, Wittgenstein*. London: Routledge, 1998.

Glock, Hans-Johann, and John Hyman, eds. *Wittgenstein and Analytic Philosophy: Essays for P. M. S. Hacker*. Oxford: Oxford University Press, 2009.

Goddard, Leonard, and Brenda Judge. *The Metaphysics of Wittgenstein's Tractatus*. Melbourne: Australasian Association of Philosophy, 1982.

Goodman, Russell B. *Wittgenstein and William James*. Cambridge: Cambridge University Press, 2002.

Gorlée, Dinda L. *Wittgenstein in Translation: Exploring Semiotic Signatures*. Boston: De Gruyter Mouton, 2012.

Green, Karen. *Dummett: Philosophy of Language*. Cambridge: Polity Press, 2001.

Grene, Marjorie Glicksman. *Philosophy in and out of Europe*. Berkeley: University of California Press, 1976.

Griffin, James. *Wittgenstein's Logical Atomism*. Seattle: University of Washington Press, 1969.

Griffiths, A. Phillips, ed. *Wittgenstein Centenary Essays*. Cambridge: Cambridge University Press, 1991.

Guetti, James L. *Wittgenstein and the Grammar of Literary Experience*. Athens: University of Georgia Press, 1993.

Gustafsson, Martin, and Lars Hertzberg, eds. *The Practice of Language*. Dordrecht: Kluwer, 2002.

Hacker, P. M. S. *Wittgenstein: Comparisons and Context*. Oxford: Oxford University Press, 2013.

———. *Wittgenstein: Connections and Controversies*. Oxford: Clarendon Press, 2001.

Halais, Emmanuel. *Wittgenstein et l'Énigme de l'Existence: La Forme et l'Expression*. Paris: Presses Universitaires de France, 2007.

Haller, Rudolf, and Wolfgang Grassl, eds. *Language, Logic and Philosophy: Proceedings of the Fourth International Wittgenstein Symposium, 28th August to 2nd September 1979, Kirchberg Am Wechsel (Austria)*. Vienna: Hölder-Pichler-Tempsky, 1980.

Hallett, Garth. *Darkness and Light: The Analysis of Doctrinal Statements*. New York: Paulist Press, 1975.

———. *Essentialism: A Wittgensteinian Critique*. Albany: State University of New York Press, 1991.

———. *Linguistic Philosophy: The Central Story*. Albany: State University of New York Press, 2008.

Hanfling, Oswald. *Philosophy of Language: Meaning and Use in Wittgenstein's Blue and Brown Books*. New rev. ed. Milton Keynes: Open University Press, 1980.

———. *Wittgenstein and the Human Form of Life*. London: New York, 2002.

———. *Wittgenstein's Later Philosophy*. Albany: State University of New York Press, 1989.

Hardwick, Charles S. *Language Learning in Wittgenstein's Later Philosophy*. The Hague: Mouton, 1971.

Harré, Rom, and Roy Harris, eds. *Linguistics and Philosophy: The Controversial Interface*. Oxford: Pergamon Press, 1993.

Harris, Roy. *Language, Saussure and Wittgenstein: How to Play Games with Words*. London: Routledge, 1988.

Hartshorne, Charles. *Creative Synthesis and Philosophic Method*. La Salle, IL: Open Court, 1970.

Harward, Donald W. *Wittgenstein's Saying and Showing Themes*. Bonn: Bouvier, 1976.

Hawkins, Denis John Bernard. *Wittgenstein and the Cult of Language*. London: Blackfriars, 1957.

Heal, Jane. *Fact and Meaning: Quine and Wittgenstein on Philosophy of Language*. Oxford: Blackwell, 1989.

Henry, Paul, and Arild Utaker. *Wittgenstein and Contemporary Theories of Language*. Bergen, Norway: University of Bergen, 1992.

Herbert, Manfred. *Rechtstheorie als Sprachkritik: Zum Einfluss Wittgensteins auf die Rechtstheorie*. Baden-Baden: Nomos, 1995.

High, Dallas M. *Language, Persons, and Belief; Studies in Wittgenstein's Philosophical Investigations and Religious Uses of Language*. New York: Oxford University Press, 1967.

Hintikka, Jaakko. *Ludwig Wittgenstein: Half-Truths and One-and-a-Half-Truths*. Dordrecht: Kluwer, 1996.

Hodges, Michael P. *Transcendence and Wittgenstein's Tractatus*. Philadelphia: Temple University Press, 1990.

Hogan, Patrick Colm. *Philosophical Approaches to the Study of Literature*. Gainesville: University Press of Florida, 2000.

Horwich, Paul. *Wittgenstein's Metaphilosophy*. Oxford: Oxford University Press, 2012.

Hota, Sabita Rani. *Philosophy in Linguistic Perspectives: (Study in the Philosophy of Wittgenstein, Ryle and Austin)*. Meerut, India: Anu Books, 2002.

Hubík, Stanislav. *Jazyk a Metafyzika: Kritika Wittgensteinovy Filozofie*. Praha: Academia, 1983.

Hunnings, Gordon. *The World and Language in Wittgenstein's Philosophy*. Albany: State University of New York Press, 1988.

Hunter, J. F. M. *Understanding Wittgenstein: Studies of Philosophical Investigations*. Edinburgh: Edinburgh University Press, 1985.

———. *Wittgenstein on Words as Instruments: Lessons in Philosophical Psychology*. Savage, MD: Barnes & Noble Books, 1990.

Hutto, Daniel D. *Wittgenstein and the End of Philosophy: Neither Theory nor Therapy*. New York: Palgrave Macmillan, 2003.

Hymers, Michael. *Wittgenstein and the Practice of Philosophy*. Buffalo, NY: Broadview Press, 2010.

Isava, Luis Miguel. *Wittgenstein, Kraus, and Valéry: A Paradigm for Poetic Rhyme and Reason*. New York: P. Lang, 2002.

Johnson, David Martel, and Christina E. Erneling, eds. *The Future of the Cognitive Revolution*. New York: Oxford University Press, 1997.

Jolley, Kelly Dean. *The Concept "Horse" Paradox and Wittgensteinian Conceptual Investigations: A Prolegomenon to Philosophical Investigations*. Burlington, VT: Ashgate, 2007.

Jost, Walter. *Rhetorical Investigations: Studies in Ordinary Language Criticism*. Charlottesville: University of Virginia Press, 2004.

Kahane, Guy, and Edward Kanterian, eds. *Wittgenstein and His Interpreters: Essays in Memory of Gordon Baker*. Oxford: Blackwell, 2007.

Kannisto, Heikki. *Thoughts and Their Subject: A Study of Wittgenstein's Tractatus*. Helsinki: Philosophical Society of Finland Distributed by Akateeminen Kirjakauppa, 1986.

Kenny, Anthony John Patrick, and Brian McGuinness, eds. *Wittgenstein and His Times*. Chicago: University of Chicago Press, 1982.

Kienzler, Wolfgang. *Ludwig Wittgensteins "Philosophische Untersuchungen."* Darmstadt: Wissenschaftliche Buchgesellschaft, 2007.

Kishik, David. *Wittgenstein's Form of Life*. New York: Continuum, 2008.

Klemke, E. D., ed. *Essays on Wittgenstein*. Urbana: University of Illinois Press, 1971.

Klemm, David E., and Günter Zöller. *Figuring the Self: Subject, Absolute, and Others in Classical German Philosophy*. Albany: State University of New York Press, 1997.

Knott, H. A. *Wittgenstein, Concept Possession and Philosophy: A Dialogue*. New York: Palgrave Macmillan, 2007.

Kölbel, Max, and Bernhard Weiss, eds. *Wittgenstein's Lasting Significance*. New York: Routledge, 2004.

Kripke, Saul A. *Wittgenstein on Rules and Private Language: An Elementary Exposition*. Cambridge, MA: Harvard University Press, 1982.

Kuhrt, David. *Wittgenstein the Tartar*. Palo Alto, CA: Academica Press, 2013.

Kusch, Martin. *A Sceptical Guide to Meaning and Rules: Defending Kripke's Wittgenstein*. Ithaca, NY: McGill-Queen's University Press, 2006.

Kuusela, Oskari. *The Struggle against Dogmatism: Wittgenstein and the Concept of Philosophy*. Cambridge, MA: Harvard University Press, 2008.

Lamb, David. *Language and Perception in Hegel and Wittgenstein*. New York: St. Martin's Press, 1980.

Landscheid, Ulf. *Wittgenstein, Theorien und Tatsachen: Wittgensteins Sprachanalytische Methode und die Lösung der Leib-Seele-Probleme*. Freiburg: Alber, 2000.

Lang, Martin. *Wittgensteins Philosophische Grammatik: Entstehung und Perspektiven der Strategie eines radikalen Aufklärers*. The Hague: Martinus Nijhoff, 2013.

Lange, Ernst Michael. *Ludwig Wittgenstein: Logisch-Philosophische Abhandlung: Ein Einführender Kommentar in den "Tractatus."* Paderborn: F. Schöningh, 1996.

———. *Ludwig Wittgenstein, "Philosophische Untersuchungen": Eine Kommentierende Einleitung*. Paderborn: Schöningh, 1998.

Laugier, Sandra. *Why We Need Ordinary Language Philosophy*. Trans. Daniela Ginsburg. Chicago: University of Chicago Press, 2013.

Lazerowitz, Morris. *The Language of Philosophy: Freud and Wittgenstein*. Dordrecht: Kluwer, 1977.

Leinfellner, Werner, Eric Kraemer, and Jeffrey Schank, eds. *Sprache und Ontologie: Akten des Sechsten Internationalen Wittgenstein Symposiums, 23. Bis 30. August 1981, Kirchberg Am Wechsel (Österreich)*. Vienna: Hölder-Pichler-Tempsky, 1982.

Lemaire, Eric, and Padilla Gálvez, Jesús, eds. *Wittgenstein: Issues and Debates*. New Brunswick, NJ: Transaction Books, 2010.

Lemoine, Roy Emanuel. *The Anagogic Theory of Wittgenstein's 'Tractatus.'* The Hague: Mouton, 1975.

Lindskog, Dale. *Diagnosis and Dissolution: From Augustine's Picture to Wittgenstein's Picture Theory*. New York: Peter Lang, 2007.

Luntley, Michael. *Wittgenstein: Meaning and Judgement*. Oxford: Blackwell, 2003.

Lütterfelds, Wilhelm. *Erinnerung an Wittgenstein: "Kein Sehen in die Vergangenheit"?* New York: Peter Lang, 2004.

Mackie, J. L. *Contemporary Linguistic Philosophy; Its Strength and Its Weakness*. Dunedin, New Zealand: University of Otago, 1956.

Malcolm, Norman. *Wittgenstein: The Relation of Language to Instinctive Behaviour: J. R. Jones Memorial Lecture Delivered at the College on May 12, 1981*. Swansea: University College of Swansea, 1981.

Marconi, Diego. *Il Mito del Linguaggio Scientifico. Studio Su Wittgenstein*. Milano: U. Mursia, 1971.

Marques, António, and Nuno Venturinha, eds. *Knowledge, Language and Mind: Wittgenstein's Thought in Progress*. Boston: De Gruyter, 2012.

Marques, Edgar da Rocha. *Wittgenstein und die Möglichkeit eines Kategorialen Diskurses*. Konstanz: Hartung-Gorre, 1995.

Martinich, Aloysius. *The Philosophy of Language*. 2nd ed. New York: Oxford University Press, 1990.

Maslow, Alexander. *A Study in Wittgenstein's Tractatus*. Bristol: Thoemmes Press, 1997.

McCarthy, Timothy, and Sean C. Stidd, eds. *Wittgenstein in America*. Oxford: Clarendon Press, 2001.

McDonald, Henry. "Nietzsche, Wittgenstein, and the Tragic Henry James." *Texas Studies in Literature and Language* 34, no. 3 (1992): 403–449.

McDonough, Richard M. *The Argument of the Tractatus: Its Relevance to Contemporary Theories of Logic, Language, Mind, and Philosophical Truth*. Albany: State University of New York Press, 1986.

McFarlane, Adrian Anthony. *A Grammar of Fear and Evil: A Husserlian-Wittgensteinian Hermeneutic*. New York: P. Lang, 1996.

Miller, Alexander, and Crispin Wright. *Rule-Following and Meaning*. Chesham: Acumen, 2002.

Morris, Wesley. *Friday's Footprint: Structuralism and the Articulated Text*. Columbus: Ohio State University Press, 1979.

Mounce, H. O. *Metaphysics and the End of Philosophy*. New York: Continuum, 2007.

Mulhall, Stephen. *On Being in the World: Wittgenstein and Heidegger on Seeing Aspects*. London: Routledge, 1990.

———. *Philosophical Myths of the Fall*. Princeton, NJ: Princeton University Press, 2005.

———. *The Conversation of Humanity*. Charlottesville: University of Virginia Press, 2007.

———. *Wittgenstein's Private Language: Grammar, Nonsense and Imagination in Philosophical Investigations, §§ 243–315*. Oxford: Oxford University Press, 2006.

Mundle, C. W. K. *A Critique of Linguistic Philosophy with Second Thoughts: An Epilogue after Ten Years*. 2nd rev. ed. London: Glover & Blair, 1979.

Munz, Volker A. *Satz und Sinn: Bemerkungen zur Sprachphilosophie Wittgensteins*. New York: Rodopi, 2005.

Nayak, Bijaya Krushna. *Wittgenstein: Language, Meaning and Value*. Meerut, India: Anu Books, 2002.

Needham, Rodney. *Belief, Language, and Experience*. Chicago: University of Chicago Press, 1972.

Neumann, Walter. *Responsum Dico: Wittgensteins Tractatus Logico-Philosophicus: Eine Kritische Untersuchung*. Würzburg: Königshausen & Neumann, 1990.

Neumer, Katalin. *Traditionen Wittgensteins*. New York: Peter Lang, 2004.

Newman, Andrew, ed. *The Correspondence Theory of Truth: An Essay on the Metaphysics of Predication*. Cambridge: Cambridge University Press, 2002.

Nieli, Russell. *Wittgenstein: From Mysticism to Ordinary Language: A Study of Viennese Positivism and the Thought of Ludwig Wittgenstein*. Albany: State University of New York Press, 1987.

Nielsen, Keld Stehr. *The Evolution of the Private Language Argument*. Burlington, VT: Ashgate, 2008.

Niiniluoto, Ilkka, and Risto Vilkko, eds. *Philosophical Essays in Memoriam Georg Henrik Von Wright*. Helsinki: Philosophical Society of Finland, 2005.

Nilsson, Arne. *Das Spiel der Sprache: Wittgenstein, Lacan und Novalis zur Semantisierung von Wirklichkeit und Subjektivität in der Bewegung des Dialogs*. Regensburg: S. Roderer, 1997.

Nyíri, János Kristóf. *Tradition and Individuality: Essays*. Dordrecht: Kluwer, 1992.

Ohler, Matthias. *Sprache und ihre Begründung: Wittgenstein Contra Searle*. Cologne: Janus Presse, 1988.

Ostrow, Matthew B. *Wittgenstein's Tractatus: A Dialectical Interpretation*. Cambridge: Cambridge University Press, 2002.

Padilla Gálvez, Jesús and Margit Gaffal, eds. *Forms of Life and Language Games*. Frankfurt: Ontos-Verlag, 2011.

Palmieri, Fulvio. *Wittgenstein e la Grammatica*. Milan: Jaca book, 1997.

Pampapathy Rao, A. *Understanding Principia and Tractatus: Russell and Wittgenstein Revisited*. San Francisco: International Scholars Publications, 1998.

Parajón, Carlos. *Ideas y Metáforas: Ensayos Filosóficos Sobre el Lenguaje*. Buenos Aires: Biblos, 1985.

Pears, David. *Paradox and Platitude in Wittgenstein's Philosophy*. Oxford: Clarendon Press, 2006.

Perloff, Marjorie. *Wittgenstein's Ladder: Poetic Language and the Strangeness of the Ordinary*. Chicago: University of Chicago Press, 1996.

Peters, Michael, Nicholas C. Burbules, and Paul Smeyers. *Showing and Doing: Wittgenstein as a Pedagogical Philosopher*. Boulder, CO: Paradigm Publishers, 2008.

Peterson, Donald. *Wittgenstein's Early Philosophy: Three Sides of the Mirror*. Toronto: Buffalo, 1990.

Phillips, D. Z., and Peter Winch, eds. *Wittgenstein: Attention to Particulars: Essays in Honour of Rush Rhees*. London: Macmillan, 1989.

Piana, Giovanni. *Interpretazione del Tractatus di Wittgenstein*. Milan: Guerini e associati, 1994.

Pichler, Alois. *Wittgensteins Philosophische Untersuchungen: Vom Buch Zum Album*. New York, NY: Rodopi, 2004.

———. *Wittgensteins Philosophische Untersuchungen: Zur Textgenese von PU [Paragraphen] 1–4*. Bergen: Wittgensteinarkivet ved Universitetet i Bergen, 1997.

Pichler, Alois, and Simo Säätelä, eds. *Wittgenstein: The Philosopher and His Works*. Piscataway, NJ: Transaction Books, 2006.

Pihlström, Sami. *Wittgenstein and the Method of Philosophy*. Helsinki: Societas Philosophica Fennica, 2006.

Pinto, António Vaz. *Introdução ao Tractatus Logico-Philosophicus de Ludwig Wittgenstein*. Braga: Publicações da Faculdade de Filosofia, 1982.

Potter, Michael D. *Wittgenstein's Notes on Logic*. Oxford: Oxford University Press, 2009.

Pradhan, R. C. *Language and Experience: An Interpretation of the Later Philosophy of Wittgenstein*. Meerut, India: Anu Prakashan, 1981.

Prado, C. G. *A House Divided: Comparing Analytic and Continental Philosophy*. Amherst, NY: Humanity Books, 2003.

Price, Jeffrey Thomas. *Language and Being in Wittgenstein's Philosophical Investigations*. The Hague: Mouton, 1973.

Proops, Ian. *Logic and Language in Wittgenstein's Tractatus*. New York: Garland, 2000.

Putnam, Hilary. *Pragmatism: An Open Question*. Oxford: Blackwell, 1995.

Raatzsch, Richard. *Eigentlich Seltsames: Wittgensteins Philosophische Untersuchungen*. Paderborn: F. Schöningh, 2003.

Read, Rupert J. *A Wittgensteinian Way With Paradoxes*. Lanham, MD: Lexington Books, 2013.

———. *Applying Wittgenstein*. Ed. Laura L. Cook. New York: Continuum, 2007.

———. *Wittgenstein among the Sciences: Wittgensteinian Investigations into the "Scientific Method."* Ed. Simon Summers. Burlington, VT: Ashgate, 2011.

Reck, Erich H., ed. *From Frege to Wittgenstein: Perspectives on Early Analytic Philosophy*. Oxford: Oxford University Press, 2002.

Reeder, Harry P. *Language and Experience: Descriptions of Living Language in Husserl and Wittgenstein*. Washington, DC: Center for Advanced Research in Phenomenology & University Press of America, 1984.

Reguera, Isidoro. *La Miseria De La Razón: (El Primer Wittgenstein)*. Madrid: Taurus, 1980.

Rhees, Rush. *Without Answers*. New York: Schocken Books, 1969.

———, and D. Z. Phillips. *Wittgenstein and the Possibility of Discourse*. Cambridge: Cambridge University Press, 1998.

Richardson, John T. E. *The Grammar of Justification: An Interpretation of Wittgenstein's Philosophy of Language*. New York: St. Martin's Press, 1976.

Richter, Duncan. *Wittgenstein at His Word*. New York: Continuum, 2004.

Ritter, Ulrike. *Language as Chiffre: Wittgenstein's Theory of Symbols*. Frankfurt: Peter Lang, 2001.

Rosen, Stanley. *The Elusiveness of the Ordinary: Studies in the Possibility of Philosophy*. New Haven, CT: Yale University Press, 2002.

Roser, Andreas. *Die Privatsprache der Privatsprachenkritik bei Ludwig Wittgenstein*. Frankfurt: Peter Lang, 1991.

Rundle, Bede. *Wittgenstein and Contemporary Philosophy of Language*. Oxford: Blackwell, 1990.

Salinas Moya, Ana. *El Problema del Lenguaje en la Obra de Wittgenstein*. Cordoba: Publicaciones del Monte de Piedad y Caja de Ahorros de Córdoba, 1990.

Savickey, Beth. *Wittgenstein's Art of Investigation*. London: Routledge, 1999.

Savigny, Eike von. *Ludwig Wittgenstein, Philosophische Untersuchungen*. Berlin: Akademie Verlag, 1998.

Schärtl, Thomas. *Jenseits von Innen und Aussen: Ludwig Wittgensteins Beitrag zu einer Nichtdualistischen Philosophie des Geistes*. Münster: Lit, 2000.

Scheer, Brigitte, and Günter Wohlfart. *Dimensionen der Sprache in der Philosophie des Deutschen Idealismus*. Würzburg: Königshausen & Neumann, 1982.

Scheier, Claus-Artur. *Wittgensteins Kristall: Ein Satzkommentar zur "Logisch-Philosophischen Abhandlung."* Freiburg: Verlag K. Alber, 1991.

Schmidt, Siegfried J. *Sprache und Denken als Sprachphilosophisches Problem von Locke bis Wittgenstein*. The Hague: Martinus Nijhoff, 1969.

Schmitz, Barbara. *Wittgenstein über Sprache und Empfindung: Eine Historische und Systematische Darstellung*. Paderborn: Mentis, 2002.

Schneider, Hans Julius. Wittgenstein's Later Theory of Meaning*: Imagination and Calculation*. Malden, MA: Wiley-Blackwell, 2013.

Schneider, Hans Julius, and Matthias Kross. *Mit Sprache Spielen: Die Ordnungen und das Offene nach Wittgenstein*. Berlin: Akademie, 1999.

Schroeder, Severin. *Das Privatsprachen-Argument: Wittgenstein über Empfindung & Ausdruck*. Paderborn: F. Schöningh, 1998.

Sedmak, Clemens. *Kalkül und Kultur: Studien zu Genesis und Geltung von Wittgensteins Sprachspielmodell*. Amsterdam: Rodopi, 1996.

Sefler, George F. *Language and the World; A Methodological Synthesis within the Writings of Martin Heidegger and Ludwig Wittgenstein*. New York: Humanities Press, 1974.

Sengupta, Kalyan Kumar. *Language and Philosophy*. Bombay: New York Allied Publishers, 1969.

Shang, Zhiying. *Xun Zhao Jia Yuan: Duo Wei Shi Ye Zhong Di Weitegensitan Yu Yan Zhe Xue*. Beijing: Ren min chu ban she, 1992.

Shibles, Warren A. *Wittgenstein: Language & Philosophy*. Dubuque, IA: Kendall/Hunt, 1969.

Sigwart, Christoph. *Die Impersonalien: Eine Logische Untersuchung*. Passau: DLWG-Verlag, 1996.

Sini, Carlo. *Scrivere il Silenzio: Wittgenstein e il Problema del Linguaggio*. Milan: Egea, 1994.

Soulez, Antonia, François Schmitz, and Jan Sebestik. *Grammaire, Sujet et Signification*. Paris: Harmattan, 1994.

Specht, E. K. *Die Sprachphilosophischen und Ontologischen Grundlagen im Spätwerk Ludwig Wittgensteins*. Cologne: Kölner Universitäts-Verlag, 1963.

Standish, Paul. *Beyond the Self: Wittgenstein, Heidegger, and the Limits of Language*. Aldershot, UK: Avebury, 1992.

Stegmüller, Wolfgang. *Kripkes Deutung der Spätphilosophie Wittgensteins: Kommentarversuch über einen Versuchten Kommentar*. Stuttgart: A. Kröner, 1986.

Stein, Christian A. *Regeln und Übereinstimmung: Zu einer Kontroverse in der Neueren Wittgenstein-Forschung*. Pfaffenweiler: Centaurus-Verlags-gesellschaft, 1994.

Stenius, Erik. *Wittgenstein's Tractatus: A Critical Exposition of Its Main Lines of Thought*. Ithaca, NY: Cornell University Press, 1964.

Stetter, Christian. *Sprachkritik und Transformationsgrammatik: Zur Bedeutung der Philosophie Wittgensteins für die Sprachwissenschaftliche Theoriebildung*. Düsseldorf: Pädagogischer Verlag Schwann, 1974.

Stocker, Barry. *Post-Analytic Tractatus*. Burlington, VT: Ashgate, 2002.

Stroud, Barry. *Meaning, Understanding, and Practice: Philosophical Essays*. Oxford: Oxford University Press, 2000.

Suits, Bernard. *The Grasshopper: Games, Life and Utopia*. Peterborough, ON: Broadview Press, 2005.

Sullivan, Peter M. and Michael D. Potter, eds. *Wittgenstein's Tractatus: History and Interpretation*. Oxford: Oxford University Press, 2013.

Taylor, Charles. *Philosophical Arguments*. Cambridge, MA: Harvard University Press, 1995.

Taylor, Paul W. *Normative Discourse*. Westport, CT: Greenwood Press, 1973.

Teuwsen, Rudolf. *Familienähnlichkeit und Analogie: Zur Semantik Genereller Termini bei Wittgenstein und Thomas Von Aquin*. Freiburg im Breisgau: K. Alber, 1988.

Thornton, Tim. *Wittgenstein on Language and Thought: The Philosophy of Content*. Edinburgh: Edinburgh University Press, 1998.

Travis, Charles. *The Uses of Sense: Wittgenstein's Philosophy of Language*. Oxford: Clarendon, 2001.

———. *Thought's Footing: A Theme in Wittgenstein's Philosophical Investigations*. Oxford: Clarendon Press, 2006.

Valent, Italo. *La Forma del Linguaggio: Studio sul Tractatus Logico-Philosophicus*. Padua: Francisci Editore, 1983.

Vander Veer, Garrett L. *Philosophical Skepticism and Ordinary-Language Analysis*. Lawrence: Regents Press of Kansas, 1978.

Venturinha, Nuno, ed. *The Textual Genesis of Wittgenstein's Philosophical Investigations*. New York: Routledge, 2013.

———. *Wittgenstein after His Nachlass*. New York: Palgrave Macmillan, 2010.

Vermeiren, Koen. *Willem Frederik Hermans en Ludwig Wittgenstein: Een Taalspelen-Analyse van het Prozawerk van Willem Frederik Hermans, Uitgaande van de Levensvorm van het Sadistische en Chaotische Universum*. Utrecht: Hes, 1986.

Villanueva, Enrique. *El Argumento del Lenguaje Privado: Introduccion, Seleccion de Textos y Bibliografia*. Mexico: UNAM Instituto de Investigaciones Filosoficas, 1979.

Volk, Ulrich. *Das Problem eines Semantischen Skeptizismus: Saul Kripkes Wittgenstein-Interpretation*. Rheinfelden: Schäuble, 1988.

Vossenkuhl, Wilhelm. *Ludwig Wittgenstein, Tractatus Logico-Philosophicus*. Berlin: Akademie Verlag, 2001.

———. *Solipsismus und Sprachkritik: Beiträge zu Wittgenstein*. Berlin: Parerga, 2009.

Wabel, Thomas. *Sprache als Grenze in Luthers Theologischer Hermeneutik und Wittgensteins Sprachphilosophie*. Berlin: Walter de Gruyter, 1998.

Wallgren, Thomas. *Transformative Philosophy: Socrates, Wittgenstein, and the Democratic Spirit of Philosophy*. Lanham, MD: Lexington Books, 2006.

Wefald, Eric. *Truth and Knowledge: On Some Themes in Tractarian and Russellian Philosophy of Language*. Lanham, MD: University Press of America, 1996.

Werhane, Patricia Hogue. *Skepticism, Rules, and Private Languages*. Atlantic Highlands, NJ: Humanities Press, 1992.

Wettstein, Howard K. *The Magic Prism: An Essay in the Philosophy of Language*. New York: Oxford University Press, 2004.

White, Morton Gabriel, ed. *The Age of Analysis; Twentieth Century Philosophers*. Boston: Houghton Mifflin, 1955.

Whiting, Daniel. *The Later Wittgenstein on Language*. New York: Palgrave Macmillan, 2010.

Wiggershaus, Rolf. *Sprachanalyse und Soziologie: Die Sozialwissenschaftliche Relevanz von Wittgensteins Sprachphilosophie*. Frankfurt: Suhrkamp, 1975.

Wilhelmi, Juan. *Språk Och Mänsklig Förståelse: En Kritisk Undersökning Av Några Samhällsfilosofiska Tolkningar Av Den Senare Wittgenstein*. Nora: Nya doxa, 1995.

Williams, Meredith. *Blind Obedience: Paradox and Learning in the Later Wittgenstein*. New York: Routledge, 2010.

———. *Wittgenstein's Philosophical Investigations: Critical Essays*. Lanham, MD: Rowman & Littlefield Publishers, 2007.

Wilson, Brendan. *Wittgenstein's Philosophical Investigations: A Guide*. Edinburgh: Edinburgh University Press, 1998.

Winch, Peter. *Studies in the Philosophy of Wittgenstein*. New York: Humanities Press, 1969.

Worthington, B. A. *Selfconsciousness and Selfreference: An Interpretation of Wittgenstein's Tractatus*. Aldershot, UK: Avebury, 1988.

Wright, Crispin, and Alexander Miller. *Rule-Following and Meaning*. Montreal: McGill-Queen's University Press, 2002.

Wright, Crispin. "Critical Notice of Wittgenstein on Meaning by Colin McGinn." *Mind* 98, no. 390 (1989): 289–305.

Zalabardo, José L., ed. *Wittgenstein's Early Philosophy*. Oxford: Oxford University Press, 2012.

Zemach, Eddy M. *The Reality of Meaning & the Meaning of "Reality."* Hanover, NH: Published by University Press of New England [for] Brown University Press, 1992.

Zilhão, António. *Linguagem da Filosofia e Filosofia da Linguagem: Estudos Sobre Wittgenstein*. Lisbon: Edições Colibri, 1993.

Zimmermann, Jörg. *Wittgensteins Sprachphilosophische Hermeneutik*. Frankfurt: Klostermann, 1975.

WITTGENSTEIN AND MATHEMATICS

Frascolla, Pasquale. *Wittgenstein's Philosophy of Mathematics*. New York: Routledge, 2013.

Friederich, Simon. "Motivating Wittgenstein's Perspective on Mathematical Sentences as Norms." *Philosophia Mathematica* 19, no. 1 (2011): 1–19.

Mühlhölzer, Felix. *Braucht die Mathematik eine Grundlegung?: Ein Kommentar des Teils III von Wittgensteins Bemerkungen über die Grundlagen der Mathematik*. Frankfurt, M.: Klostermann, 2010.

WITTGENSTEIN AND MIND

Addis, Mark. *Wittgenstein: Making Sense of Other Minds*. Aldershot, UK: Ashgate, 1999.

Anscombe, G. E. M. *The Collected Philosophical Papers of G. E. M. Anscombe*. Minneapolis: University of Minnesota Press, 1981.

Bakhurst, David, and Christine Sypnowich, eds. *The Social Self*. London: Sage, 1995.

Bax, Chantal. *Subjectivity after Wittgenstein: The Post-Cartesian Subject and the Death of Man*. New York: Continuum, 2011.

Bouveresse, Jacques. *Wittgenstein Reads Freud: The Myth of the Unconscious*. Trans. Carol Cosman. Princeton, NJ: Princeton University Press , 2013.

Budd, Malcolm. *Wittgenstein's Philosophy of Psychology*. New York: Routledge, 2013.

Chisholm, Roderick M., ed. *Philosophie des Geistes, Philosophie der Psychologie: Akten Des 9. Internationalen Wittgenstein Symposiums: 19. bis 26. August 1984, Kirchberg Am Wechsel (Österreich)*. Vienna: Hölder-Pichler-Tempsky, 1985.

Cornish, Kimberley. *The Jew of Linz: Wittgenstein, Hitler and Their Secret Battle for the Mind*. London: Century, 1998.

Coulter, Jeff. *Rethinking Cognitive Theory*. New York: St. Martin's Press, 1983.

———. *The Social Construction of Mind: Studies in Ethnomethodology and Linguistic Philosophy*. Totowa, NJ: Rowman & Littlefield, 1979.

Diamond, Cora. *The Realistic Spirit: Wittgenstein, Philosophy, and the Mind*. Cambridge, MA: MIT Press, 1995.

Ellis, Jonathan, and Daniel Guevara, eds. *Wittgenstein and the Philosophy of Mind*. New York: Oxford University Press, 2012.

French, Peter A., Theodore Edward Uehling, and Howard K. Wettstein, eds. *Studies in Metaphysics*. Minneapolis: University of Minnesota Press, 1979.

Good, Justin. *Wittgenstein and the Theory of Perception*. New York: Continuum, 2006.

Gustafson, Donald F., and Bangs L. Tapscott, eds. *Body, Mind, and Method: Essays in Honor of Virgil C. Aldrich*. Dordrecht: D. Reidel, 1979.

Hacker, P. M. S. *Wittgenstein: On Human Nature*. London: Phoenix, 1997.

———. "Is There Anything It Is Like to Be a Bat?" *Philosophy* 77 (2002): 157–174.

Hagberg, Garry. *Describing Ourselves: Wittgenstein and Autobiographical Consciousness*. Oxford: Clarendon Press, 2008.

Haldane, John. *Mind, Metaphysics, and Value in the Thomistic and Analytical Traditions*. Notre Dame, IN: University of Notre Dame Press, 2002.

Harré, Rom, and Michael A. Tissaw. *Wittgenstein and Psychology: A Practical Guide*. Burlington, VT: Ashgate, 2005.

Hartshorne, Charles. *Insights and Oversights of Great Thinkers: An Evaluation of Western Philosophy*. Albany: State University of New York Press, 1983.

Heaton, John M. *The Talking Cure: Wittgenstein's Therapeutic Method for Psychotherapy*. New York: Palgrave Macmillan, 2010.

Hookway, Christopher, and Donald Peterson, eds. *Philosophy and Cognitive Science*. Cambridge: Cambridge University Press, 1993.

Hyman, John. *Investigating Psychology: Sciences of the Mind after Wittgenstein*. London: Routledge, 1991.

Kerr, Fergus. *Work on Oneself: Wittgenstein's Philosophical Psychology*. Arlington, VA: Institute for the Psychological Sciences Press, 2008.

Kimball, Roger. *Lives of the Mind: The Use and Abuse of Intelligence from Hegel to Wodehouse*. Chicago: Ivan R. Dee, 2002.

Lakoff, George. *Women, Fire, and Dangerous Things: What Categories Reveal about the Mind*. Chicago: University of Chicago Press, 1987.

Livingston, Paul M. *Philosophical History and the Problem of Consciousness*. Cambridge: Cambridge University Press, 2004.

Locke, Don. *Myself and Others: A Study in Our Knowledge of Minds*. Oxford: Clarendon Press, 1968.

Malcolm, Norman. *Problems of Mind: Descartes to Wittgenstein*. London: Allen and Unwin, 1972.

———. *Thought and Knowledge: Essays*. Ithaca, NY: Cornell University Press, 1977.

McDowell, John Henry. *Mind, Value, and Reality*. Cambridge, MA: Harvard University Press, 1998.

Moyal-Sharrock, Danièle. *Perspicuous Presentations: Essays on Wittgenstein's Philosophy of Psychology*. New York: Palgrave Macmillan, 2007.

Nagel, Thomas. *Other Minds: Critical Essays, 1969–1994*. New York: Oxford University Press, 1995.

Newman, James Roy. *Science and Sensibility*. Garden City, NY: Doubleday, 1963.

Overgaard, Søren. *Wittgenstein and Other Minds: Rethinking Subjectivity and Intersubjectivity with Wittgenstein, Levinas, and Husserl*. New York: Routledge, 2007.

Read, Rupert. "On Approaching Schizophrenia through Wittgenstein." *Philosophical Psychology* 14 (2001): 449–475.

Rosenbaum, S. P., ed. *English Literature and British Philosophy; A Collection of Essays*. Chicago: University of Chicago Press, 1971.

Rudd, Anthony. *Expressing the World: Skepticism, Wittgenstein, and Heidegger*. Chicago: Open Court, 2003.

Rust, Alois. *Wittgensteins Philosophie der Psychologie*. Frankfurt: V. Klostermann, 1996.

Ryan, John Kenneth, ed. *Twentieth-Century Thinkers: Studies in the Work of Seventeen Modern Philosophers*. Staten Island, NY: Alba House, 1965.

Sass, Louis Arnorsson. *The Paradoxes of Delusion: Wittgenstein, Schreber, and the Schizophrenic Mind*. Ithaca, NY: Cornell University Press, 1994.

Schroeder, Severin, ed. *Wittgenstein and Contemporary Philosophy of Mind*. Houndmills, UK: Palgrave, 2001.

Shanker, S. G., and David Kilfoyle, eds. *Ludwig Wittgenstein*. London: Routledge, 2001.

Sluga, Hans D., and David G. Stern, eds. *The Cambridge Companion to Wittgenstein*. Cambridge: Cambridge University Press, 1996.

Stern, David G. *Wittgenstein on Mind and Language*. Oxford: Oxford University Press, 1995.

Stock, Guy. *Appearance versus Reality: New Essays on Bradley's Metaphysics*. Oxford: Clarendon Press, 1998.

Suter, Ronald. *Interpreting Wittgenstein: A Cloud of Philosophy, a Drop of Grammar*. Philadelphia: Temple University Press, 1989.

Tanney, Julia. *Rules, Reason, and Self-Knowledge*. Cambridge, MA: Harvard University Press, 2012.

Vesey, Godfrey Norman Agmondisham. *Impressions of Empiricism*. New York: St. Martin's Press, 1976.

Vohra, Ashok. *Wittgenstein's Philosophy of Mind*. La Salle, IL: Open Court, 1986.

Williams, Meredith. *Wittgenstein, Mind, and Meaning: Toward a Social Conception of Mind*. London: Routledge, 1999.

Wollheim, Richard, ed. *Freud: A Collection of Critical Essays*. Garden City, NY: Anchor Books, 1974.

WITTGENSTEIN AND OTHER THINKERS

Aenishänslin, Markus. *Le Tractatus de Wittgenstein et L'Ethique de Spinoza: Étude de Comparaison Structurale*. Basel: Birkhäuser Verlag, 1993.

Baker, Gordon P. *Wittgenstein, Frege, and the Vienna Circle*. Oxford: Blackwell, 1988.

Baltas, Aristeides. *Peeling Potatoes or Grinding Lenses: Spinoza and Young Wittgenstein Converse on Immanence and Its Logic*. Pittsburgh, PA: University of Pittsburgh Press, 2012.

Bearn, Gordon C. F. *Waking to Wonder: Wittgenstein's Existential Investigations*. Albany: State University of New York Press, 1997.

Braver, Lee. *Groundless Grounds: A Study of Wittgenstein and Heidegger*. Cambridge, MA: MIT Press, 2012.

Carl, Wolfgang. *Sinn und Bedeutung: Studien zu Frege und Wittgenstein*. Königstein: Hain, 1982.

Cavell, Stanley. *In Quest of the Ordinary: Lines of Skepticism and Romanticism*. Chicago: University of Chicago Press, 1988.

———. *Philosophical Passages: Wittgenstein, Emerson, Austin, Derrida*. Oxford: Blackwell, 1995.

———. *This New Yet Unapproachable America: Lectures after Emerson after Wittgenstein*. Albuquerque, NM: Living Batch Press, 1989.

Conant, James. *Three Philosophers: Kierkegaard, Nietzsche and James: A Thesis*. Dissertation (Ph.D.), Harvard University, 1991.

Dejnozka, Jan. *The Ontology of the Analytic Tradition and Its Origins: Realism and Identity in Frege, Russell, Wittgenstein, and Quine*. Lanham, MD: Littlefield Adams Books, 1996.

Edwards, James C. *The Authority of Language: Heidegger, Wittgenstein, and the Threat of Philosophical Nihilism*. Tampa: University of South Florida Press, 1990.

Egan, David, Stephen Reynolds, and Aaron Wendland, eds. *Wittgenstein and Heidegger*. New York: Routledge, 2013.

Garver, Newton, and Seung-Chong Lee. *Derrida & Wittgenstein*. Philadelphia: Temple University Press, 1994.

Glendinning, Simon, ed. *Arguing with Derrida*. Oxford: Blackwell, 2001.

———. *On Being with Others: Heidegger, Derrida, Wittgenstein*. London: Routledge, 1998.

Hodges, Michael P., and John Lachs. *Thinking in the Ruins: Wittgenstein and Santayana on Contingency*. Nashville, TN: Vanderbilt University Press, 2000.

Horn, Patrick Rogers. *Gadamer and Wittgenstein on the Unity of Language: Reality and Discourse without Metaphysics*. Burlington, VT: Ashgate, 2005.

Jones, W. Gareth. *Tolstoi and Britain*. Oxford: Berg, 1995.

Lange, Ernst Michael. *Wittgenstein und Schopenhauer: Logisch-Philosophische Abhandlung und Kritik des Solipsismus*. Cuxhaven: Junghans, 1989.

Lawn, Chris. *Wittgenstein and Gadamer: Towards a Post-Analytic Philosophy of Language*. New York: Continuum, 2004.

Leinfellner, Elisabeth, ed. *Wittgenstein and His Impact on Contemporary Thought: Proceedings of the Second International Wittgenstein Symposium, 29th August to 4th September 1977, Kirchberg/Wechsel (Austria)*. Vienna: Hölder-Pichler-Tempsky, 1980.

Matuštík, Martin Joseph, and Merold Westphal, eds. *Kierkegaard in Post/Modernity*. Bloomington: Indiana University Press, 1995.

Micheletti, Mario. *Lo Schopenhauerismo di Wittgenstein*. Bologna: Zanichelli, 1967.

Mulligan, Kevin. *Wittgenstein et la Philosophie Austro-Allemande*. Paris: Librairie Philosophique J. Vrin, 2012.

Munz, Peter. *Beyond Wittgenstein's Poker: New Light on Popper and Wittgenstein*. Burlington, VT: Ashgate, 2004.

Nyíri, János Kristóf, and Tamás Demeter, eds. *Essays on Wittgenstein and Austrian Philosophy: In Honour of J. C. Nyiri*. Amsterdam: Rodopi, 2004.

Perissinotto,Luigi, and Begoña Ramón Cámara,eds. *Wittgenstein and Plato: Connections, Comparisons and Contrasts*. New York: Palgrave Macmillan, 2013.

Plant, Bob. *Wittgenstein and Levinas: Ethical and Religious Thought*. New York: Routledge, 2005.

Putnam, Hilary. *Jewish Philosophy as a Guide to Life: Rosenzweig, Buber, Lévinas, Wittgenstein*. Bloomington: Indiana University Press, 2008.

Romdenh-Romluc, Komarine, ed. *Wittgenstein and Merleau-Ponty*. New York: Routledge, 2013.

Schönbaumsfeld, Genia. *A Confusion of the Spheres: Kierkegaard and Wittgenstein on Philosophy and Religion*. Oxford: Oxford University Press, 2007.

Shen, Aimin. *The Limits of Language: A Comparative Study of Kant, Wittgenstein, and Lao Tzu*. Lewiston, NY: Edwin Mellen Press, 2011.

Staten, Henry. *Wittgenstein and Derrida*. Lincoln: University of Nebraska Press, 1984.

Stenholm, Stig. *The Quest for Reality: Bohr and Wittgenstein, Two Complementary Views*. Oxford: Oxford University Press, 2011.

Stern, David G., and Béla Szabados, eds. *Wittgenstein Reads Weininger*. Cambridge: Cambridge University Press, 2004.

Thompson, Caleb. *Wittgenstein's Confessions: A Study of the Influence of Augustine's and Tolstoy's Confessions on the Philosophy of Wittgenstein*. Dissertation (Ph.D.), University of Virginia, 1994.

Weiner, David Avraham. *Genius and Talent: Schopenhauer's Influence on Wittgenstein's Early Philosophy*. Rutherford, NJ: Fairleigh Dickinson University Press, 1992.

Zijlstra, Onno. *Language, Image, and Silence: Kierkegaard and Wittgenstein on Ethics and Aethetics*. New York: Peter Lang, 2006.

WITTGENSTEIN AND POLITICS

Allen, Barry. *Truth in Philosophy*. Cambridge, MA: Harvard University Press, 1995.

Boyers, Robert, and George Steiner, eds. *Homosexuality: Sacrilege, Vision, Politics*. Saratoga Springs, NY: Skidmore College, 1983.

DeAngelis, William James. *Ludwig Wittgenstein—A Cultural Point of View: Philosophy in the Darkness of This Time*. Burlington, VT: Ashgate, 2007.

Heyes, Cressida J. *The Grammar of Politics: Wittgenstein and Political Philosophy*. Ithaca, NY: Cornell University Press, 2003.

Holt, Robin. *Wittgenstein, Politics and Human Rights*. London: New York, 1997.

Janik, Allan. *Style, Politics, and the Future of Philosophy*. Dordrecht: Kluwer, 1989.

Kitching, G. N., and Nigel Pleasants, eds. *Marx and Wittgenstein: Knowledge, Morality and Politics*. London: Routledge, 2002.

Laitinen, Arto, Nicholas H. Smith, and Charles Taylor. *Perspectives on the Philosophy of Charles Taylor*. Helsinki: Societas Philosophica Fennica, 2002.

Lessnoff, Michael H. *Ernest Gellner and Modernity*. Cardiff: University of Wales Press, 2002.

Levin, David Michael. *Sites of Vision: The Discursive Construction of Sight in the History of Philosophy*. Cambridge, MA: MIT Press, 1997.

Livingston, Paul M. *The Politics of Logic: Badiou, Wittgenstein, and the Consequences of Formalism*. New York: Routledge, 2012.
Lyotard, Jean François. *Tombeau de L'intellectuel: Et Autres Papiers*. Paris: Editions Galilée, 1984.
Norris, Andrew John. *The Claim to Community: Essays on Stanley Cavell and Political Philosophy*. Stanford, CA: Stanford University Press, 2006.
Patterson, Dennis M. *Law and Truth*. New York: Oxford University Press, 1996.
———. *Wittgenstein and Law*. Burlington, VT: Ashgate, 2004.
———, ed. *Wittgenstein and Legal Theory*. Boulder, CO: Westview Press, 1992.
Peters, Michael, Mark Olssen, and Colin Lankshear, eds. *Futures of Critical Theory: Dreams of Difference*. Lanham, MD: Rowman & Littlefield, 2003.
Redner, Harry. *Malign Masters: Gentile, Heidegger, Lukács, Wittgenstein: Philosophy and Politics in the Twentieth Century*. New York: St. Martin's Press, 1997.
Robinson, Christopher C. *Wittgenstein and Political Theory: The View from Somewhere*. Edinburgh: Edinburgh University Press, 2009.
Szabados, Béla. *Ludwig Wittgenstein on Race, Gender, and Cultural Identity: Philosophy as a Personal Endeavour*. Lewiston: Edwin Mellen Press, 2010.
Weinberger, Ota, Peter Koller, and Alfred Schramm, eds. *Law, Politics, Society: Reports of the 12th International Wittgenstein Symposium, 7th to 14th August 1987, Kirchberg Am Wechsel, Austria*. Vienna: Hölder-Pichler-Tempsky, 1988.
Wilson, Sean. *The Flexible Constitution*. Lanham, MD: Lexington Books, 2013.
Winfield, Richard Dien. *Freedom and Modernity*. Albany: State University of New York Press, 1991.

WITTGENSTEIN AND RELIGION

Addis, Mark, and Robert L. Arrington, eds. *Wittgenstein and Philosophy of Religion*. London: Routledge, 2000.
Amesbury, Richard. "Has Wittgenstein Been Misunderstood by Wittgensteinian Philosophers of Religion?" *Philosophical Investigations* 26 (2003): 44–72.
Arnswald, Ulrich. *In Search of Meaning: Ludwig Wittgenstein on Ethics, Mysticism, and Religion*. Karlsruhe: Universitätsverlag Karlsruhe, 2009.

Arnswald, Ulrich, and Anja Weiberg. *Der Denker als Seiltänzer: Ludwig Wittgenstein über Religion, Mystik und Ethik*. Düsseldorf: Parerga, 2001.

Atkinson, James. *The Mystical in Wittgenstein's Early Writings*. New York: Routledge, 2009.

Barrett, Cyril. *Wittgenstein on Ethics and Religious Belief*. Oxford: Blackwell, 1990.

Bell, Richard H., ed. *The Grammar of the Heart: New Essays in Moral Philosophy & Theology*. San Francisco: Harper & Row, 1988.

Bolle, Kees W. *The Enticement of Religion*. Notre Dame, IN: University of Notre Dame Press, 2002.

Burley, Mikel. *Contemplating Religious Forms of Life: Wittgenstein and D. Z. Phillips*. New York: Continuum, 2012.

Canfield, John V., ed. *Aesthetics, Ethics and Religion*. New York: Garland, 1986.

Cell, Edward. *Language, Existence & God: Interpretations of Moore, Russell, Ayer, Wittgenstein, Wisdom, Oxford Philosophy and Tillich*. Nashville, TN: Abingdon Press, 1971.

Chaturvedi, Vibha. *Wittgenstein's Fideism: Belief, Reason, and Practice*. New Delhi: Om Publications, 2002.

Clack, Beverley, and Brian R. Clack. *The Philosophy of Religion: A Critical Introduction*. Cambridge: Polity Press, 1998.

Clack, Brian R. *An Introduction to Wittgenstein's Philosophy of Religion*. Edinburgh: Edinburgh University Press, 1999.

———. *Wittgenstein, Frazer, and Religion*. New York: St. Martin's Press, 1999.

Creegan, Charles L. *Wittgenstein and Kierkegaard: Religion, Individuality, and Philosophical Method*. London: Routledge, 1989.

Downey, John K. *Beginning at the Beginning: Wittgenstein and Theological Conversation*. Lanham, MD: University Press of America, 1987.

Drury, M. O'C. *The Danger of Words and Writings on Wittgenstein*. Bristol, UK: Thoemmes Press, 2003.

Elliott, Carl. *Slow Cures and Bad Philosophers: Essays on Wittgenstein, Medicine, and Bioethics*. Durham, NC: Duke University Press, 2001.

Ferreira, M. Jamie. "The Point Outside the World: Kierkegaard and Wittgenstein on Nonsense, Paradox and Religion." *Religious Studies* 30, no. 1 (1994): 29–44.

Fronda, Earl Stanley B. *Wittgenstein's (Misunderstood) Religious Thought*. Boston: Brill, 2010.

Glebe Møller, Jens. *Wittgenstein Og Religionen*. Copenhagen: Gad, 1969.

Gombocz, Wolfgang Leopold, ed. *Philosophy of Religion*. Vienna: Hölder-Pichler-Tempsky, 1984.

Harré, Rom. "Wittgenstein: Science and Religion." *Philosophy* 76 (2001): 211–237.

High, Dallas M., ed . *New Essays on Religious Language*. New York: Oxford University Press, 1969.

Hoshikawa, Keiji. *Witogenshutain to Shukyo Tetsugaku: Gengo, Shukyo, Komittomento*. Tokyo: Yorudan-Sha, 1989.

Hudson, W. D. *Wittgenstein and Religious Belief*. New York: St. Martin's Press, 1975.

Jareño Alarcón, Joaquín. *Religión y Relativismo en Wittgenstein*. Barcelona: Ariel, 2001.

Kampits, Peter, Anja Weiberg, and Khristo Kholiolchev, eds. *Ethik und Religion im Werk Ludwig Wittgensteins*. Vienna: Verein "Freunde des Hauses Wittgenstein," 1999.

Kaufmann, Walter Arnold. *Critique of Religion and Philosophy*. Princeton, NJ: Princeton University Press, 1978.

Keightley, Alan. *Into Every Life a Little Zen Must Fall: A Christian Philosopher Looks to Alan Watts and the East*. London: Wisdom Publications, 1986.

Kerr, Fergus. *Theology after Wittgenstein*. 2nd ed. London: SPCK, 1997.

Koritensky, Andreas. *Wittgensteins Phänomenologie der Religion: Zur Rehabilitation Religiöser Ausdrucksformen im Zeitalter der Wissenschaftlichen Weltanschauung*. Stuttgart: Kohlhammer, 2002.

Kurtén, Tage. *Grunder för en Kontextuell Teologi: Ett Wittgensteinskt Sätt Att Närma Sig Teologin i Diskussion Med Anders Jeffner*. Åbo: Åbo akademi Distribution Tidningsbokhandeln, 1987.

Labron, Tim. *Science and Religion in Wittgenstein's Fly Bottle*. New York: Continuum, 2014.

———. *Wittgenstein and Theology*. London: T & T Clark, 2009.

———. *Wittgenstein's Religious Point of View*. New York: Continuum, 2006.

Lazenby, J. Mark. *The Early Wittgenstein on Religion*. London: Continuum, 2006.

Lurie, Yuval. *Wittgenstein on the Human Spirit*. New York: Rodopi, 2012.

Magee, Bryan, and A. J. Ayer, eds. *Modern British Philosophy*. New York: St. Martin's Press, 1971.

Magnanini, Dina. *Il Pensiero Religioso di Ludwig Wittgenstein*. Rome: La Goliardica, 1981.

Malcolm, Norman, and Peter Winch. *Wittgenstein: A Religious Point of View?* Ithaca, NY: Cornell University Press, 1994.

McCutcheon, Felicity. *Religion within the Limits of Language Alone: Wittgenstein on Philosophy and Religion*. Aldershot, UK: Ashgate, 2001.

Munz, Regine. *Religion als Beispiel: Sprache und Methode bei Ludwig Wittgenstein in Theologischer Perspektive*. Düsseldorf: Parerga Verlag, 1997.

Murdoch, Iris. *Metaphysics as a Guide to Morals*. New York: Allen Lane Penguin Press, 1993.

Nicholson, M. W. "Abusing Wittgenstein: The Misuse of the Concept of Language Games in Contemporary Theology." *Journal of the Evangelical Theological Society* 39, no. 4 (1996): 617–629.

Niedballa, Thomas. *Christliches Sprachspiel und Religiöse Erfahrung: Wittgenstein und die Theologie*. Münster: Lit, 1993.

Nielsen, Kai. *An Introduction to the Philosophy of Religion*. New York: St. Martin's Press, 1983.

Nielsen, Kai, and Phillips, D. Z. *Wittgensteinian Fideism?* London: SCM Press, 2005.

Phillips, D. Z. *Belief, Change, and Forms of Life*. Atlantic Highlands, NJ: Humanities Press International, 1986.

———. *The Concept of Prayer*. New York: Schocken Books, 1966.

———. *Death and Immortality*. New York: St. Martin's Press, 1970.

———. *Faith after Foundationalism: Plantinga-Rorty-Lindbeck-Berger: Critiques and Alternatives*. Boulder, CO: Westview Press, 1995.

———. *Faith and Philosophical Enquiry*. New York: Schocken Books, 1971.

———. *From Fantasy to Faith: The Philosophy of Religion and Twentieth-Century Literature*. Basingstoke, UK: Macmillan, 1991.

———. *Recovering Religious Concepts: Closing Epistemic Divides*. New York: St. Martin's Press, 2000.

———. *Religion and the Hermeneutics of Contemplation*. Cambridge: Cambridge University Press, 2001.

———. *Religion and Hume's Legacy*. New York: St. Martin's Press Scholarly and Reference Division, 1999.

———. *Religion without Explanation*. Oxford: Blackwell, 1976.

———. *Religion without Transcendence?* New York: St. Martin's Press, 1997.

———. *Through a Darkening Glass: Philosophy, Literature, and Cultural Change*. Notre Dame, IN: University of Notre Dame Press, 1982.

———. *Wittgenstein and Religion*. New York: St. Martin's Press, 1993.

———, ed. *Religion and Understanding*. New York: Macmillan, 1967.

———, ed. *Can Religion Be Explained Away?* New York: St. Martin's Press, 1996.

Phillips, D. Z., and Mario Von der Ruhr, eds. *Rush Rhees on Religion and Philosophy*. Cambridge: Cambridge University Press, 1997.

Phillips, D. Z., and Timothy Tessin, eds. *Philosophy of Religion in the 21st Century*. New York: Palgrave, 2001.

Ramal, Randy. *Metaphysics, Analysis, and the Grammar of God: Process and Analytic Voices in Dialogue*. Tübingen: Mohr Siebeck, 2010.

Rhees, Rush, *Religion and Wittgenstein's Legacy*. Eds. D. Z. Phillips and Mario von der Ruhr. Burlington, VT: Ashgate, 2005.

Rhees, Rush. "On Religion: Notes on Four Conversations with Wittgenstein." *Faith and Philosophy: Journal of the Society of Christian Philosophers* 18 Part 4 (2001): 409–415.

Richter, Duncan. "Missing the Entire Point: Wittgenstein and Religion." *Religious Studies* 37 (2001): 161–175.

Rouner, Leroy S. *Loneliness*. Notre Dame, IN: University of Notre Dame Press, 1998.

———. *On Community*. Notre Dame, IN: University of Notre Dame Press, 1991.

Salmann, Elmar, and Aniceto Molinaro, eds. *Filosofia e Mistica: Itinerari di un Progetto di Ricerca*. Rome: Pontificio Ateneo S. Anselmo, 1997.

Sanders, Andy F. *D. Z. Phillips' Contemplative Philosophy of Religion: Questions and Responses*. Burlington, VT: Ashgate, 2007.

Schoedinger, Andrew B. *Our Philosophical Heritage*. 3rd ed. Dubuque, IA: Kendall/Hunt Publishing, 2000.

Sherry, Patrick. *Religion, Truth, and Language-Games*. New York: Barnes & Noble Books, 1977.

Shields, Philip R. *Logic and Sin in the Writings of Ludwig Wittgenstein*. Chicago: University of Chicago Press, 1993.

Sontag, Frederick. *Wittgenstein and the Mystical: Philosophy as an Ascetic Practice*. Atlanta, GA: Scholars Press, 1995.

Stout, Jeffrey, and Robert MacSwain, eds. *Grammar and Grace: Reformulations of Aquinas and Wittgenstein*. London: SCM, 2003.

Strandberg, Hugo. *The Possibility of Discussion: Relativism, Truth, and Criticism of Religious Beliefs*. Burlington, VT: Ashgate, 2006.

Studhalter, Kurt. *Ethik, Religion und Lebensform bei Ludwig Wittgenstein*. Innsbruck: Österr. Kommissionsbuchh. in Komm., 1973.

Tessin, Timothy, and Mario Von der Ruhr, eds. *Philosophy and the Grammar of Religious Belief*. New York: St. Martin's Press, 1995.

Thomas, Emyr Vaughan. *Wittgensteinian Values: Philosophy, Religious Belief and Descriptivist Methodology*. Aldershot, UK: Ashgate, 2001.

Työrinoja, Reijo. *Uskon Kielioppi: Uskonnollisten Väitteiden Ja Käsitteiden Luonne Ludwig Wittgensteinin Myöhäisfilosofian Valossa*. Helsinki: Suomalainen Teologinen Kirjallisuusseura, 1984.

Vardy, Peter. *What Is Truth?* Sydney: University of New South Wales Press, 1999.

Weger, Karl-Heinz. *Religionskritik von der Aufklärung bis zur Gegenwart: Autoren-Lexikon von Adorno bis Wittgenstein*. Freiburg: Herder, 1983.

Weiberg, Anja. *"Und die Begründung Hat ein Ende": Die Bedeutung von Religion und Ethik für den Philosophen Ludwig Wittgenstein und das Verständnis Seiner Werke*. Vienna: WUV-Univ.-Verlag, 1998.

Whittaker, John H., ed. *The Possibilities of Sense*. New York: Palgrave, 2002.

Xirau, Ramón. *Cuatro Filósofos y lo Sagrado: Teilhard de Chardin, Heidegger, Wittgenstein, Simone Weil.* México, D.F.: Editorial Joaquín Mortiz, 1986.

Young, William. *Wittgenstein and Christianity.* Vienna: Hölder-Picher-Temsky, 1984.

About the Author

Duncan Richter (B.A. University of Oxford; M.Phil. University College of Swansea; Ph.D. University of Virginia) is a professor of philosophy at the Virginia Military Institute, where he has taught since 1995. He is the author of *Ethics after Anscombe* (2000), *Wittgenstein at His Word* (2004), *Why Be Good?* (2008), and *Anscombe's Moral Philosophy* (2011). His work on Wittgenstein has appeared in such scholarly journals as *Erkenntnis*, *Philosophical Papers*, *Philosophical Topics*, *Religious Studies*, and *The Southern Journal of Philosophy*. He is the author also of the entries on Wittgenstein and Wittgenstein's student G. E. M. Anscombe in the Internet Encyclopedia of Philosophy. In 2008 he received a lifetime Outstanding Faculty Award from the State Council of Higher Education for Virginia on the basis of his teaching, scholarship, and service. He is a member of the North American Wittgenstein Society, past president of the Virginia Philosophical Association, and author of the Wittgenstein-related blog "Language Goes on Holiday" (http://languagegoesonholiday.blogspot.com).

Lightning Source UK Ltd.
Milton Keynes UK
UKHW041403110821
388685UK00001B/24

9 781442 233089